This book is due on the date indicated below and is subject to an overdue fine as posted at the circulation desk.

EXCEPTION: Date due will be earlier if this item is RECALLED.

JAN 1 2 2004

PROVIDING PROTECTION FOR PLANT GENETIC RESOURCES

PATENTS, *SUI GENERIS* SYSTEMS, AND BIOPARTNERSHIPS

Patricia Lucia Cantuária Marin

New York • The Hague • London

Published by Kluwer Law International
P.O. Box 85889
2508 CN The Hague, The Netherlands

Sold and distributed in the USA and Canada by
Kluwer Law International
Order Department
101 Philip Drive
Norwell, MA 02061, USA

Sold and distributed in all other countries by
Kluwer Law International
Distribution Centre
P.O. Box 322
3300 AH Dordrecht, The Netherlands

ISBN 90-411-8875-4

© 2002 Kluwer Law International
New York, The Hague, London

http://www.kluwerlaw.com

10 9 8 7 6 5 4 3 2 1

A C.I.P. record for this book is available from the Library of Congress

All rights reserved

No part of this book may be reproduced, stored in a retrieval system, or transmitted in any form or by any means, electronic, mechanical, photocopying, microfilming, recording, or otherwise, without written permission from the Publisher

Printed in the United States of America

ACKNOWLEDGEMENTS

I thank God for giving me health and inspiration through out the elaboration of this book.

Special thanks to my family:
my parents for their constant and valuable support, stimulus and advice;
my brothers for their solidarity, affection and friendship;
my grandmother for all her phone calls and visits;
my husband for his love, patience and wisdom.

Thank you very much to Michael Bowman for correcting all my drafts and for his creative thoughts which he will find reflected throughout this book.

I am extremely grateful to all the people around the world who sent me information and answered my questions.

Thank you to all my friends in Brazil and in other countries for all our happy moments and for their encouragement.

I warm-heartedly thank CAPES for funding my studies which was the first step that made the elaboration of this book possible.

I dedicate this book to all the people who believe that countries can live in harmony among themselves and with Nature.

PREFACE

Under the Trade-Related Aspects of Intellectual Property Rights, all Parties of World Trade Organisation must allow patents on micro-organisms and provide protection of plant varieties either by patents, by an effective *sui generis* system or a combination of both. This book will show that the patent option should be discarded and States should adopt alternative forms of protection under their liberty to create their own *sui generis* system. *Sui generis* systems to protect plant varieties and biopartnerships are instruments countries have at their disposal to comply to the objectives of the Biological Diversity Convention, their duties under the Trade-Related Aspects of Intellectual Property Rights, and their particular environmental, social, economic and developmental objectives.

This book shall analyse *sui generis* proposals that have been made, examining their positive aspects, their weaknesses and offering innovative solutions to make them more effective. Furthermore, the author proposes fair, ethical and equitable biopartnerships as a complement to the laws that protect both biotechnological and traditional knowledge and innovations. As reality moves faster than the law, biopartnerships offer a solution to reach consensus between stakeholders and a balance of interests, rights and duties. However, is necessary to adopt a law to regulate the minimum aspects of biopartnerships, as well as a code of conduct in order to avoid abuses and domination of the strongest part. On the other hand, they should not be over-regulated and a flexibility of negotiation should be kept so that biopartnerships can respect the particular characteristics and aims of each country and every stakeholder.

The author proposes biopartnerships and a *sui generis* system to protect traditional knowledge and innovations as a means of Brazil achieving sustainable development and harmonising it with the country's economic and technological aspirations. Such solutions respect Brazil's social, ethnical, economic and environmental reality.

CONTENTS

ABBREVIATIONS _____ *xiii*

CHAPTER ONE _____ *1*

INTRODUCTION _____ *1*

CHAPTER TWO _____ *4*

PATENT REGULATIONS TO PROTECT PLANT GENETIC RESOURCES AND PLANT VARIETIES _____ *4*

   1 - GENERAL INTRODUCTION _____ 4

   2 - PLANT VARIETY AND PLANT GENETIC RESOURCE PROTECTION IN THE UNITED STATES _____ 5

   3 - PLANT VARIETY AND PLANT GENETIC RESOURCE PROTECTION IN EUROPE _____ 11

   4 - THE INTERNATIONAL INTELLECTUAL PROPERTY SYSTEM ___ 15
      4.1 - Paris Convention for the Protection of Industrial Property ____ 15
      4.2 - Patent Co-operation Treaty _____ 17
      4.3 - Agreement on Trade-Related Aspects of Intellectual Property Rights ____ 18
         4.3.1 - Introduction _____ 18
         4.3.2 - Patentable Subject Matter _____ 19
         4.3.3 - Rights and the Patent Holder _____ 23
         4.3.4 - Burden of Proof _____ 24
         4.3.5 - TRIPs Implementation _____ 25
         4.3.6 - Conclusion _____ 26

   5 - GENERAL CONCLUSION _____ 28

CHAPTER THREE _____ *29*

BREEDERS' RIGHTS UNDER THE UPOV _____ *29*

   1 - GENERAL INTRODUCTION _____ 29

   2 - UPOV 1978 _____ 30
      2.1 - Introduction _____ 30
      2.2. - Conditions Required for Protection _____ 30
      2.3 - Scope of Protection _____ 31
      2.4 - Double Protection _____ 33
      2.5 - Duration of Protection _____ 34
      2.6 – Conclusion _____ 34

   3 - UPOV Act of 1991 _____ 34
      3.1 - Introduction _____ 34
      3.2 - Conditions for the Grant of the PBRs _____ 34
      3.3 - Scope of Protection _____ 35
      3.4 - Double Protection _____ 37
      3.5 - Duration of Protection _____ 37
      3.6 – Conclusion _____ 38

   4 - DIFFERENCES AND SIMILARITIES BETWEEN PBRS AND PATENT RIGHTS _____ 38

   5 - PLANT PIRACY IN AUSTRALIA _____ 40

6 - GENERAL CONCLUSION	42
CHAPTER FOUR	**44**
FAO GLOBAL SYSTEM FOR THE CONSERVATION AND UTILISATION OF PLANT GENETIC RESOURCES FOR FOOD AND AGRICULTURE	**44**
1 - GENERAL INTRODUCTION	44
2 - THE INTERNATIONAL UNDERTAKING	46
2.1- Introduction	46
2.2- Definition of and Access to PGRs	46
2.3- Annexes to the International Undertaking	48
2.3.1- FAO Resolution 4/89	49
2.3.2- FAO Resolution 5/89	51
2.3.3- FAO Resolution 3/91	53
2.4 – Revision of International Undertaking	57
2.5 – International Code of Conduct for Plant Germplasm Collecting and Transfer	58
2.6 - Conclusion	60
3 - EXAMPLES OF CASES INVOLVING FARMERS AND BIOTECHNOLOGY COMPANIES	61
3.1- Introduction	61
3.2- Neem Tree	62
3.3 – "Terminator Technology"	63
3.4 - Conclusion	64
4 - GENERAL CONCLUSION	65
CHAPTER FIVE	**68**
ALTERNATIVE SUI GENERIS SYSTEMS TO PROTECT PLANTS, PLANT VARIETIES AND ASSOCIATED TRADITIONAL KNOWLEDGE	**68**
1 - GENERAL INTRODUCTION	68
2 - *SUI GENERIS* SYSTEM ON THE INTERNATIONAL LEVEL	68
2.1 - Introduction	68
2.2 - *Sui Generis* Systems Based on Intellectual Property Rights other than Patents	69
2.2.1 - Trademarks	69
2.2.2 - Geographic Indications	71
2.2.3 - Trade Secrets	72
2.3 - UNESCO/WIPO Model Provisions for National Laws on Protection of Expressions of Folklore Against Illicit Exploitation and other Prejudicial Actions	74
2.4 - Organisation of African Unity Draft Model Legislation on Community Rights on Access to Biological Resources	77
2.5 - Conclusion	79
3 - *SUI GENERIS* SYSTEM ON THE NATIONAL LEVEL	80
3.1 - Introduction	80
3.2 - *Sui Generis* System Combining Patents And Plant Breeders' Rights	80
3.3 - Thammasat Resolution	81
3.4 – Discoverer's Rights	82
3.5 - Convention of Farmers and Breeders	85
3.6 - Conclusion	88
4 - GENERAL CONCLUSION	89
CHAPTER SIX	**92**

IMPLEMENTATION OF THE CONVENTION ON BIOLOGICAL DIVERSITY: BALANCING THE INTERESTS OF THE SCIENTIFIC AND TRADITIONAL COMMUNITIES _____ 92

1 - GENERAL INTRODUCTION _____ 92

2 - OBJECTIVES OF THE CDB _____ 93
2.1 - Introduction _____ 93
2.2 - CONSERVATION OF BIODIVERSITY _____ 94
2.3 - Sustainable Use of The Components of Biological Diversity _____ 98
2.4 - Equitable Share of Benefits Derived from the Utilisation of its Components _____ 101
2.5 - Conclusion _____ 106

3 – MECHANISMS AVAILABLE FOR STATES TO NEGOTIATE THE EQUITABLE SHARE OF BENEFITS DERIVED FROM THE USE OF THEIR BIODIVERSITY _____ 106
3.1 - Introduction _____ 106
3.2 - Prior Informed Consent _____ 107
3.3 - Mutually Agreed Contracts _____ 108
3.4 - Conclusion _____ 109

4 - COMPREHENSIVE NATIONAL BIODIVERSITY LEGISLATION-COSTA RICA _____ 110
4.1 - Definition of Biodiversity _____ 110
4.2 - Objectives _____ 111
4.3 - Access To Genetic Resources _____ 112
4.4 - Conclusion _____ 112

5 - GENERAL CONCLUSION _____ 113

CHAPTER SEVEN _____ *115*

BIOPARTNERSHIPS _____ *115*

1 - GENERAL INTRODUCTION _____ 115

2 - GLOBAL INEQUITY _____ 116

3 - BIOPARTNERSHIPS _____ 117
3.1 - Introduction _____ 117
3.2 - Biopartnership Contracts _____ 119

4 - BIOPARTNERSHIP CASE-STUDIES _____ 120
4.1 - Introduction _____ 120
4.2 - Merck-INBio Agreement _____ 121
4.3 - Sustainable Development Treaties between the Netherlands and Costa Rica, Bhutan and Benin _____ 123
4.4 - The Bioresources Development and Conservation Program _____ 126
4.5 - ICBG Biopartnership Project in Suriname _____ 129
4.6 - The Genetic Resources Recognition Fund of the University of California, Davis _____ 131
4.7 - Conclusion _____ 133

5 - GENERAL CONCLUSION _____ 134

CHAPTER EIGHT _____ *137*

THE EFFECTS OF INTERNATIONAL REGIMES IN BRAZIL _____ *137*

1 - GENERAL INTRODUCTION _____ 137

2 - SOCIAL EQUALITY, ENVIRONMENTAL AND INTELLECTUAL PROPERTY PROTECTION IN THE BRAZILIAN CONSTITUTION _____ 137

3 - PATENT LAW _____ 140
3.1 - Introduction _____ 140

3.2 - General Principles	141
3.3 - Patentable Subject Matter	141
3.4 - "Prior User" Concept	143
3.5 - Term of Protection	144
3.6 - Conclusion	144

4 - PLANT VARIETY PROTECTION LAW 145

5 - BIOSAFETY REGULATIONS 149
- 5.1 - Introduction 149
- 5.2 - Biosafety Law 149
- 5.3 - Transgenic Soya Case 150
- 5.4 - Labelling Genetically Modified Foods 152
- 5.5 - Conclusion 154

6 - PROPOSED LEGISLATION TO REGULATE ACCESS TO BRAZIL'S GENETIC RESOURCES AND DERIVED PRODUCTS 155
- 6.1 - Introduction 155
- 6.2 - Objectives of Bill 306/95 156
- 6.3 - Scope of Bill 306/95 158
- 6.4 - Who Can Access Brazil's Genetic Resources 158
- 6.5 - Access Contracts 159
  - 6.5.1 - Responsible Organ for Access Proceedings 160
  - 6.5.2 - Pre-established Requirements of the Access Contracts 161
- 6.6 - Conclusion 164

7 - GENERAL CONCLUSION 165

CHAPTER NINE *167*

BRAZILIAN BIOPARTNERSHIPS *167*

1 – GENERAL INTRODUCTION 167

2 - ACCESS TO PLANT GENETIC RESOURCES OF PLANTS OF TRADITIONAL SPIRITUAL VALUE: CASE-STUDY THE AYAHUASCA PLANTS 167
- 2.1 - Introduction 167
- 2.2 - Access Bills and Access to the Sacred Plants Mariri and Chacrona 168
- 2.3 - Conclusion 175

3 - POEMA: PROGRAM POVERTY AND ENVIRONMENT IN AMAZONIA 175
- 3.1 - Sanitation and Nutrition 175

3.2 - Agriculture in Layers, Commercialisation of Forest Products and BIOPartnerships 176
- 3.3 - Conclusion 179

4 - BUILDING THE SCENERY OF TRADITIONAL KNOWLEDGE 179
- 4.1 - Introduction 179
- 4.2 - The Scenery System 180
- 4.3 - Conclusion 183

5 - GENERAL CONCLUSION 184

CHAPTER TEN *185*

FINAL CONCLUSION *185*

BIBLIOGRAPHY *190*

INDEX *203*

ABREVIATIONS

APBRO	Australia Plant Breeders' Rights Office
ASEAN	Association of South-East Asian Nations
BDCP	Bioresources Development and Conservation Programme
BGVS	Bedrijf Geneesmiddelen Voorziening Suriname
BIOAMAZONIA	Brazilian Association for the Sustainable Use of the Biodiversity of Amazonia
BIOTHAI	Thai Network on Community Rights and Biodiversity (Thailand)
BMS	Bristol-Myers Squibb Pharmaceutical Research Institute
CBD	Convention on Biological Diversity
CGIAR	Consultative Group on International Agricultural Research
CGRFA	Commission on Genetic Resources for Food and Agriculture
CI	Conservation International
CIEL	Centre for International Environmental Law
CoFaB	Convention of Farmers' and Breeders' Rights (India)
COICA	Co-ordinating Body of Indigenous Organisations of the Amazon Basin
CONFEN	National Drug Confederation in Brazil
CRADA	Co-operative Research and Development Agreement
CRRI	Central Rice Research Institute
CSD	Commission on Sustainable Development
CTNBio	National Technical Commission for Biosecurity (Brazil)
DNA	Deoxyribonucleic Acid
DOU	Diario Oficial da Uniao (Brazil's – Federal Official Gazette)
D&PL	American Delta and Pine Land Company
EC	European Community
ECO	Ecooperation Foundation (The Netherlands)

EIA	Environmental Impact Assessment
EMBRAPA	Empresa Brasileira de Pesquisa Agropecuaria (Brazil)
EPO	European Patent Office
ETS	European Treaty Series
EU	European Union
FAO	Food and Agriculture Organisation
GATT	General Agreement on Tariffs and Trade
GEF	Global Environmental Fund
GMOs	Genetically Modified Organisms
GRAIN	Genetic Resource Action International
GRRF	Genetic Resources Recognition Fund (UC Davis)
HSCA	Australian Heritage Seed Curators
IARC	International Agricultural Research Centre
IBAMA	Instituto Brasileiro do Meio Ambiente e dos Recurso Naturais Renovaveis
IBPGR	International Board for Plant Genetic Resources
ICBG	International Co-operative Biodiversity Group
IDEC	Brazilian Institute for Consumer Defence
ILO	International Labour Organisation
IPGRI	International Plant Genetic Resource Institute
ICRISAT	International Crops Research Institute from the Semi-Arid Tropics
IDRC	International Development Research Centre
IIC	International Review of Industrial Property & Copyright Law
ILM	International Legal Materials
INBio	Instituto Nacional de Biodiversidade (Costa Rica)
INPI	National Industrial Property Institute (Brazil)
IPRs	Intellectual Property Rights
IRRI	International Rice Research Institute

IU	International Undertaking
IUCN	World Conservation Union
LMO	Living Modified Organism
MBG	Missouri Botanical Gardens
MINAE	Ministry of Environment and Energy in Costa Rica
NGOs	Non-governmental organisations
OAU	Organisation of African Unity
PBRs	Plant Breeders' Rights
PCT	Patent Co-operation Treaty
PGRs	Plant Genetic Resources
PGRFA	Plant Genetic Resources for Food and Agriculture
POEMA	Programa Pobreza e Meio Ambiente na Amazonia
PPA	Plant Patent Act
PROBEM	Brazilian Program of Molecular Ecology for the Sustainable Use of the Biodiversity of Amazonia
PTO	Patent and Trademark Office (US)
PVPA	Plant Variety Protection Act
RAFI	Rural Advancement Foundation International
R&D	Research and Development
RECIEL	Review of European Community and International Environmental Law
RR soya	Monsanto's Roundup Ready transgenic soybean
RS	Brazilian state Rio Grande do Sul
SDT	Sustainable Development Treaties
SENAD	Secretaria Nacional Antidrogas
SNPC	National Service of Cultivar Protection (Brazil)
TEK	Traditional Ecological Knowledge
TRIPs	Agreement on Tade-Related Aspects of Intellectual Property Rights

UC Davis	University of California at Davis
UKTS	United Kingdom Treaty Series
UN	United Nations
UNCED	United Nations Conference on Environment and Development
UNCTAD	United Nations Conference on Trade and Development
UNEP	United Nations Environmental Program
UNESCO	United Nations Educational, Scientific and Cultural Organisation
UNTS	United Nations Treaty Series
UPOV	Union for the Protection of New Varieties of Plants
U.S., U.S.A.	United States of America
USAID	United States Agency for International Development
USDA	United States Department of Agriculture
USNIH	U.S. National Institute of Health
USNSF	United States National Science Foundation
VPISU	Virginia Polytechnic Institute and State University
WIPO	World Intellectual Property Organisations
WTO	World Trade Organisation
WWF	World Wildlife Fund
YbIEL	Yearbook of International Environmental Law

CHAPTER ONE

INTRODUCTION

The world is experiencing a period of intense changes: the potentially devastating effects of the global warming, the decodification of the human genome and the genetic manipulation of all living beings. Although States have realised that the global warming offers proof that their acts can have a global effect, they have not learned the lesson. There is a confrontation between those that only seek economic power ignoring the large-scale effects of their actions, with those that are fighting to survive. In the field of plant genetic resources, the former are the biotechnological industries which are aiming to monopolise the food, agricultural and pharmaceutical markets. The latter are traditional farmers and indigenous peoples who are suffering the consequences of this monopolisation.

It seems to be that the realisation of the Convention on Biological Diversity objectives, namely the conservation of biodiversity, sustainable use of its components and the equitable share of benefits derived from its use, has been put on hold in order to fully welcome the biotechnology era. Traditional farmers and indigenous peoples around the world have been seeing their plant genetic resources and traditional knowledge monopolised by private enterprises under patents and plant breeders' rights and have not been receiving their equitable share of benefits for their contribution. Furthermore, biotechnology companies have been developing transgenic plant varieties which are genetically uniform, thus jeopardising the conservation of biological diversity. And finally, the privatisation of plant genetic resources and the plundering of traditional knowledge have been widening and exacerbating the economic differences between the biotechnology-rich and biotechnology-poor countries. However, planetary sustainable development cannot co-exist with such wide social and economic inequity.

The purpose of this book is to show that access to plant genetic resources and compliance with the objectives of the Convention on Biological Diversity can only be realised through achieving a balance between the rights and duties of States and stakeholders. Specifically, this book suggests that the global partnership as professed in the United Nations Conference on Environment and Development in 1992 has so far not been reached. It examines the possibility of achieving this global partnership through clear, fair, ethical and equitable biopartnerships in, between and among States. The research is based on the analysis of international instruments dealing with patents, plant breeders' rights, farmers' rights and *sui generis* protection to get a full picture of how they affect one particular developing state chosen as a case-study, namely Brazil.

Therefore, as a first step, Chapter Two will show the continuous evolution of patent law in the United States, Europe and on the international level. In 1980, the United States Supreme Court decided that "everything under the sun made by man is patentable". Nowadays it seems that in the United States, *everything whether made or not made by man is patentable*. Although the European Patent Convention is not so expansive, the European Union adopted in 1998 a directive to regulate biotechnological inventions which allows the patenting of isolated plant genes. On the international level, the Agreement on Trade-Related Aspects of Intellectual Property Rights, known as TRIPs, born out of pressure of the developed countries, especially the USA, obliges countries to adopt a protection system to protect plant varieties either by patents or a *sui generis* system or a combination of both.

Chapter Three will show how the International Convention for the Protection of New Varieties of Plants, known as UPOV, has been expanding the rights of breeders every time it undergoes revision. In addition, a comparison between patents and breeders' rights will be presented. Taking advantage of the international flow of germplasm, breeders' rights have been granted on plant varieties that were collected from international agricultural research centres. Chapter Three will illustrate this point by showing that approximately 118 claims for breeders' rights were granted in Australia in dubious circumstances.

Chapter Four shall examine how patents and plant breeders' rights have been causing alarm to indigenous and farmers around the world who need to maintain free access to these resources, as a means of guaranteeing their food security and basic lifestyle and customs. It will demonstrate how patents and breeders' rights on plant varieties and plant genetic resources have been widening the gap between developed and developing countries and, therefore, run counter to intragenerational equity and thus do not work towards a global partnership. Patents and breeders' rights enrich very few countries, or better expressed, very few people in those countries. Indigenous peoples, farmers and local forest peoples still have not been granted the rights they deserve in regard to their work to conserve and breed plant varieties by traditional methods. Furthermore, examples will be given to show that their traditional knowledge has also been patented. When the benefits to the patentee or the breeder are contrasted with the damaging effects they have on society and the world it is evident that those systems are not effective in enhancing general welfare.

Based upon such criticisms, developing countries are advised not to join the UPOV and not to allow patents on plant varieties. Chapter Five presents proposals of *sui generis* systems to protect plant varieties on the international and national level. Such *sui generis* systems focus mainly on protecting farmers and indigenous rights related to their traditional breeding methods and plant varieties while biotechnologically bred varieties are already protectable by patents and under the UPOV system.

Chapter Six examines how patents are preventing the realisation of the objectives of the Convention on Biological Diversity: conservation of biological resources, sustainable use of their components and the equitable share of benefits that derive from their use. This suggests that great care needs to be taken when creating biopartnerships.

Using information received from institutions in four continents and personal contacts with respondents within the relevant arrangements, Chapter seven examines five particular biopartnerships. Although these biopartnerships were adopted on mutually agreed terms, time will reveal if they in fact managed to reduce global inequity by empowering developing countries rich in biological diversity. Each of the biopartnerships discussed has positive aspects which can serve as examples for other countries willing to undertake similar ventures. However, the complexity of factors and circumstances that influence a biopartnership reveals that each biopartnership is unique, as every country is different from each other. Thus, the continental variety of the biopartnerships analysed is one of the strengths of this study.

The international regimes discussed throughout the book have had great influence on Brazil. The consequences of these influences are critically examined in Chapter Eight. Brazil does not allow patents on plant varieties but has adopted a plant breeders' right law. Furthermore, instead of aiming to be the world's major organic food producing country, it has given into biotechnology. Chapter Eight will show that the United States has been dictating many of Brazil's actions.

However there is still hope for Brazil to wisely use its biodiversity as a vehicle to empower itself scientifically, economically and technologically through fair, ethical and equitable biopartnerships. Chapter Nine shall analyse one of the biopartnerships already in force, known as POEMA. In addition, it will present and analyse a biopartnership proposal made by an Amazon teacher named Moacir Biondo who has gathered vast information on the biological resources of the Amazon forest and associated traditional knowledge.

Having concluded the Brazilian case-study, the last Chapter draws together suggestions and conclusions reached throughout this book. Chapter Ten thus presents biopartnerships as a possible solution to reach intra- and intergenerational equity in this patent era the world is facing. Although considerable research has been undertaken by the author, this book is by no means exhaustive in references and analysis as each Chapter has the potential of being a book on its own. In fact, it is a starting point for further research into solutions of how to compromise the mentioned international instruments in order to achieve a true global partnership where poverty is eradicated and developing countries are empowered.

CHAPTER TWO
PATENT REGULATIONS TO PROTECT PLANT GENETIC RESOURCES AND PLANT VARIETIES

1 - GENERAL INTRODUCTION

Biotechnology involves biological processes which directly or indirectly can control, alter and transfer the genetic information of living organisms in order to achieve a useful end. The world is experiencing a "breakthrough in agricultural technology that may soon enable us to harvest crops from deserts, farm tomatoes in sea water, grow super potatoes in many new localities, and enjoy entirely new crops such as a 'pomato'. We can now isolate and manipulate the genes that constitute the hereditary materials of each species' genetic makeup."[1] Of the intellectual property rights which exist,[2] patents are most commonly preferred by breeders to protect their biotechnological inventions on account of their wide scope of protection. Therefore, this Chapter shall basically focus on patent protection of plant genetic resources and plant varieties.

A patent is a "temporary monopoly granted to the inventor of new technology, to encourage him to exploit it."[3] It grants the patentee the right to exclude others from making commercial use of his invention without his permission for a certain period of years. "Intellectual property is intangible property, like shares in a company or the balance in a bank account. [...] An inventor's patent is not, in any real sense, the piece of paper issued by the Patent Office but the legal rights which enable him exclusively to exploit his invention, his intellectual creation."[4] As the invention is disclosed in the patent claim, through the patent system the public can be aware of the technological advances that are being made. The patent as such is meant to be not only a reward to the patentee for the time and effort dedicated to research and development, but also an incentive to innovation, which consequently stimulates economic activity.[5]

There are those who fear that "patents on genes of wide utilisation in agriculture can block the development of new varieties in a clear contradiction to the objectives for which the (patent) system was designed."[6] However, it is still unknown to what extent a patent holder of a gene can impede the use by farmers who managed to develop the same gene using traditional farming methods. Similarly, there is no international consensus on the patenting of genetically modified organisms. In the United States for instance, "life forms, from bacteria to cows, that are genetically altered to have new and useful characteristics or behaviours, may qualify for utility patents."[7] In Europe, patents are not allowed on plant varieties and developing countries oppose the patenting on all life forms. Although there is a lack of consensus,

---

[1] Myers, Norman; "Draining the Gene Pool: The Causes, Course and Consequences of Genetic Erosion"; in Kloppenburg, Jr. (ed); Seeds and Sovereignty; Duke University Press; London; 1988; at p. 94.
[2] According to the Agreement on Trade-Related Aspects of Intellectual Property Rights, the key international intellectual property right instruments are copyrights, trademarks and geographical indications, industrial designs, patents, integrated circuits, and undisclosed information (trade secrets). See Agreement on Trade-Related Aspects of Intellectual Property Rights, 1994 Final Act of the Uruguay Round, Annex 1C. TRIPs; infra Note 128.
[3] Roberts, Tim; "Patenting Plants Around the World"; 10 EIPR 531, 1996; at 531.
[4] Marett, Paul; Intellectual Property Law; London; Sweet & Maxwell; 1996; at p. 1.
[5] Hart, Tina; Fazzani, Linda; Intellectual Property Law; Macmillan Press Ltd; London; 1997; at p. 9.
[6] Miranda, Santos and Lewontin; "Genetics, plant breeding and patents: conceptual contradictions and practical problems in protecting biological innovations"; Plant Genetic Resources Newsletter, No. 112, 1997; International Plant Genetic Resources Institute (IPGRI); Rome.
[7] Elias, Stephen; Patent, Copyright and Trademark; Nolo Press; Berkeley; 1997; at pp. 186-187.

what is already visible by now is that intellectual property rights are not seen as a "static mechanism for inventions but a changing market mechanism."[8] Therefore, the purpose of this Chapter is to analyse three different legal patent systems - United States, Europe and international - with particular reference to the widening of their scope to allow the patenting of plants and plant varieties.

2 - PLANT VARIETY AND PLANT GENETIC RESOURCE PROTECTION IN THE UNITED STATES

Patent law in the United States has been constantly changing and adapting itself to the evolution of technology, science, and economic trends.[9] Consequently, although initially plant genetic resources and plant varieties were not patentable, they now are.[10] This section shall consider the evolution of patent law in the United States, showing how it reached the point where "everything under the sun made by man"[11] is patentable.

Before 1930, there was no protection for plant varieties in the United States. Plants varieties were regarded as products of nature and could not adequately be described so as to satisfy patent law disclosure requirements.[12] Nevertheless, as the US domestic developments in plant genetic engineering and breeding advanced, the US Congress enacted in 1930 the Plant Patent Act,[13] (hereafter PPA), to "afford agriculture, so far as practicable, the same opportunity to participate in the benefits of the patent system as has been given industry."[14] As such, protection became available to distinct and new plant varieties[15] asexually reproduced[16] and described to a level that is "reasonably possible."[17] The PPA grants the patentee the right to exclude third parties from asexually reproducing the patented plant or from selling and using, offering for sale and importing the plant when it is asexually reproduced.[18] Thus, plant patents did not consider an infringement the reproduction of the protected plant variety by seed.

This changed with the adoption in 1970 of the Plant Variety Protection Act,[19] (hereinafter PVPA), which afforded a patent-like protection to novel varieties of sexually reproduced plants.[20] As most of the commercial crops are sexually reproduced, the PVPA was of more value to commercial agricultural crops than the PPA.[21] The PVPA provides for a certificate of plant variety protection to those that

---

[8] Crucible Group; People, Plants and Patents; International Development Research Centre; Ottawa, Canada; 1994; at xv.
[9] See generally Sibley, Kenneth; "Patent Claims"; in Sibley, Kenneth (ed); The Law and Strategy of Biotechnology Patents; Butterworth-Heinemann; London; 1994; at pp. 11-26.
[10] See generally Bennett, Virginia; "Plant Biotechnology"; in Sibley, Kenneth (ed); Idem; at pp. 171-186.
[11] Diamond v Chakrabarty, 447 US 303, at 309, 100 S.Ct. 2204; at 2207; 206 USPQ 193 (1980).
[12] Adler; "Can Patents Coexist with Breeders' Rights?"; 17(2) IIC 195, 1986.
[13] Plant Patent Act; (1930); 35 USC, Paragraphs 161-164.
[14] "Hearing Before the Subcommittee on Departmental Operations of the Committee on Agriculture"; 91st Cong., 2d Sess. 7 (1970) (statement of Allenby White, Chairman, Breeders' Rights Study Committee, American Seed Trade Association, quoting S. REP. No. 315, 71st Cong. 2d Sess. (1930)).
[15] Plant Patent Act; supra Note 13; Paragraph 161.
[16] Asexually reproduced plants are those reproduced by propagation or grafting.
[17] Plant Patent Act; supra Note 13; Paragraph 162.
[18] Idem; Paragraph 163.
[19] US Plant Variety Protection Act; (1970); 84 Statute 1542, 7 USC. Paragraph 2321 *et seq.*.
[20] Sexually reproduced plants are those reproduced from seed.
[21] Scalise, David and Nugent, Daniel; "International Intellectual Property Protections for Living Matter: Biotechnology, Multinational Conventions and the Exception for Agriculture"; 27 Case W. Res. J. Int'l L. 83, 1995; at p. 88.

breed distinct, uniform and stable plant varieties.[22] The plant variety certificate confers upon the owner an exclusive 18-year right to "exclude others from selling, offering for sale, reproducing, importing, exporting the variety, or using it in producing a hybrid or different variety therefrom."[23] Two exceptions to this rule are provided for in the PVPA: the research exemption[24] and farmers' privilege[25]. Under the research exemption, the protected variety is allowed to be used for *bona fide* research purposes. Farmers' privilege allows farmers "whose primary occupation is the growing of crops for sale for other than reproductive purposes, to sell such saved seed to other persons so engaged, for reproductive purposes."[26]

It was noted that the broad exemption under farmers' privilege "provides for a wide distribution of certified seed without plant breeders receiving compensation for their 'protected' products. In just one crop cycle developers of new plant varieties have essentially lost all exclusive rights to market and sell their innovation."[27] This dissatisfaction of breeders towards the only two forms of protection available to protect their plant varieties continued until a third option was opened: the traditional patent system.[28]

Initially, the American patent law did not allow the patenting of natural products and the forces of nature. The United States Supreme Court decision, Le Roy v Tatham,[29] in 1852, confirmed that no power of nature is patentable. The court held that

> "a principle, in the abstract, is a fundamental truth: an original cause; a motive; these cannot be patented, as no one can claim in either of them an exclusive right. Nor can an exclusive right exist to a new power, should one be discovered in addition to those already known. [...] The same may be said to electricity, and of any other power in nature, which is alike open to all, and may be applied to useful purposes by the use of machinery. In such cases, the processes used to extract, modify, and concentrate natural agencies, constitute the invention. The elements of the power exist; the invention is not in discovering them, but in applying them to useful objects."[30]

Following this line of thought, some say that "discovery is finding the principle, and invention lies in devising a means of applying the principle and making it useful."[31]

By 1939, the principle that a discovery was not patentable under American patent law came under challenge. In the case of Dennis v Pitner,[32] the patentee claimed he had discovered an effective insecticide in an extract from the root of a

---

[22] PVPA; supra Note 19; Paragraph 2401(a).
[23] Idem; Paragraph 2483.
[24] Idem; Paragraph 2544.
[25] Idem; Paragraph 2543.
[26] Idem; Paragraph 2543.
[27] Scalise, David and Nugent, Daniel; supra Note 21; at p. 95.
[28] The PVPA was amended in 1994 to conform with the protection provided by UPOV 1991. See Chapter Three of this book.
[29] Le Roy v Tatham, 55 US (14 How.) 156, (1852).
[30] Idem; at 175.
[31] O'Shaughnessy, Brian; "Patentable Subject Matter"; in Sibley, Kenneth (ed); supra Note 9; at p. 62.
[32] Dennis v Pitner, 106 F. 2d 142, (7th Cir. 1939) (Sparks, J. Concurring), cert. denied, 308 US 606/1939.

plant found in South America.[33] The Supreme Court held that the subject matter of the patent was patentable.[34] To support its position, the Supreme Court observed:

> It would seem to be an unjustifiable distinction to recognise as patentable a machine or other product which puts into novel combination a plurality of old elements producing a new and useful article, and deny to one working in a research field the protection of his discovery, because in his search he finds that a certain article, which we will call a chemical, will act, when taken into the human system or applied to the earth or upon some mineral found therein, in a beneficial way hitherto unknown to man. Clearly the patent law was enacted to benefit society by encouraging discoveries and inventions. That is accomplished by the Government giving to the inventor or discoverer a patent--a legal monopoly for a term of years. [...]
>
> It is true that an old substance with newly discovered qualities possessed those qualities before the discovery was made. But it is a refinement of distinction both illogical and unjustifiable and destructive of the laudable object of the statute to award a patent to one who puts old ingredient A with old ingredient B and produces a cure for ailment C, and deny patent protection to one who discovers that a simple and unadulterated or unmodified root or herb or a chemical has ingredients or health-giving qualities, hitherto unknown and unforeseen.[35]

In a separate opinion on <u>Dennis v Pitner</u>, Judge Sparks disapproved the patentability of the cube roots utilised as an insecticide. Judge Sparks defended the opinion that the:

> statute which authorises the issuance of a patent does not contemplate that a patent shall issue for every new and useful art, machine, manufacture, or composition of matter, or any new or useful improvements thereof. It is not obvious that the disclosures of this patent can be properly classified under any of these subjects. It is certainly not an art or a machine, and I fail to observe how it can be called a manufacture or a composition. The word 'composition' in my mind presupposes a combination of elements. The patent before us is neither a combination nor a process. It is a product and consists only of one natural element. [...]
>
> In any way he uses it, it is nothing more than the pure cube root that is admitted to be an element of nature. We cannot conceive that Congress intended that a patent should issue for the discovery of a mere natural

---

[33] Idem; at 143.
[34] Idem; at 150.
[35] Idem; at 144-45.

element of its properties. If Congress had so intended, it would have been easier to have placed no limitations in the statute.[36]

In <u>Dennis v Pitner</u> the patent was ultimately not granted despite the fact that the subject matter was held to be patentable. The Supreme Court concluded that Dennis was not the first person to discover a new insecticide consisting of the roots of the cube plant. The court held that Dennis had

> doubtless made a discovery of an insecticide, but he was not the first to make it. He helped to develop the industry but patent protection goes only to the first discoverer. If the first does not see fit to apply for a patent, it goes to the public. The discoverer who is second cannot rely on failure of the first to apply for a patent. Only the first inventor may receive a valid patent.[37]

The United States patent legislation is unique in the sense that it is the only country to determine the right to a patent on a "first to invent" basis rather than on a "first-to-file" basis.[38] Under the first to invent system, a patent is granted to the first person who actually makes the invention and not to the one who "wins the race to the patent office."[39]

Although a South American root extract was found to be patentable, in 1948, the US case <u>Funk Bros. Seed Co. v Kalo Inoculant Co.</u>[40] laid down the general understanding that nature was not to be patented. The US Supreme Court held that natural products

> like the heat of the sun, electricity, or the qualities of metals, are part or the storehouse of knowledge of all men. They are manifestations of laws of nature, free to all men and reserved exclusively to none. He who discovers a hitherto unknown phenomenon of nature has no claim to a monopoly of it that is recognisable under the law. If there is to be an invention from such a discovery, it must come from the application of the law of nature to a new and useful end.[41]

However, since 1980, transgenic micro-organisms have been patentable due to the influence of <u>Diamond v Chakrabarty</u>[42] which provided an audacious and innovative basis for US patent law. The case established that a living organism could qualify as a "manufacture" or a "composition of matter" within the context of the US patent statute.[43]

In <u>Diamond v Chakrabarty</u> the United States Supreme Court examined the patent office's refusal to grant a patent to Ananada Chakrabarty for a modified micro-

---

[36] Idem; at 150.
[37] Idem.
[38] See 35 USC, Paragraph 102(f).
[39] Elias, Stephen; supra Note 7; at p. 227.
[40] <u>Funk Bros. Seed Co. v Kalo Inoculant Co.</u>, 333 US 127, (1948).
[41] Idem; at 130.
[42] <u>Diamond v Chakrabarty</u>; supra Note 11; at 2207.
[43] See 35 USC, paragraph 101.

organism that could be used in oil spills on account of its capacity to break down the hydrocarbons in crude oil. The patent office rejected the application on the grounds that micro-organisms are "products of nature" and moreover, that living things are not patentable subject matter under Section 101 of the federal statute. The patent office did not consider the fact that no naturally occurring bacteria had the property of reducing hydrocarbons to a simpler molecular structure to degrade the crude oil. The Supreme Court, however, took the opposite view and held that the

> respondent's micro-organism plainly qualified as patentable subject matter. His claim is not to a hitherto unknown natural phenomenon, but to a non-naturally occurring manufacture or composition of matter - a product of human ingenuity "having a distinctive name, character [and] use."[44]

The Supreme Court rejected the position of the patent office that claimed living things were unpatenteable subject matter, by recalling that in 1873 the patent office had granted Louis Pasteur a patent on "yeast, free from organic germs of disease, as an article of manufacture," and that two patents had been asserted with respect to micro-organisms in 1967 and 1968.[45] The Supreme Court acknowledged that "the relevant distinction was not between living and inanimate things, but between products of nature, whether living or not, and human-made inventions."[46]

The Supreme Court daringly concluded that:

> the Committee Reports accompanying the 1952 Act inform us that the Congress intended statutory subject matter to *include anything under the sun that is made by man.* (emphasis added)[47]

Therefore, the case of <u>Diamond v Chakrabarty</u> determined that living things can be considered statutory subject matter provided that they do not occur naturally. The Supreme Court emphasised in its decision that humanity benefits most from those inventions that

> push back the frontiers of chemistry, physics, and the like.[48] [...] Congress employed broad general language in drafting paragraph 101 precisely because such inventions are often unforeseeable.[49]

In <u>Ex parte Hibberd</u>[50] the Chakrabarty decision was used to reverse the examiner's rejection of patent claims directed to hybrid plant seeds, hybrid plants, and plant tissue cultures. The examiner acknowledged that

---

[44] Diamond v Chakrabarty; supra Note 11; at 2207.
[45] Idem; at 2210.
[46] Idem.
[47] Idem; at 2207-08.
[48] See concurring opinion of Mr. Justice Douglas in Great A. & P. Tea Co. v Supermarket Corp., 340 US 147, 154, 95 L Ed 162, 71 S Court 127 (1950).
[49] Diamond v Chakrabarty; supra Note 11; at 2210. The Supreme Court also stated an abbreviated list of patented inventions which were unforeseeable when Section 101 of the federal statute was drafted: telegraph (Morse, No. 1,647); telephone (Bell, No. 174,465); electric lamp (Edison, No. 223,898); aeroplane (the Wrights, No. 821,393); transistor (Bardeen & Brattain, No. 2,524,035); neutronic reactor (Fermi & Szilard, No. 2,708,656); laser (Schawlow & Townes, No. 2,929,922).
[50] Ex parte Hibberd 227 USPQ 443 Bd. Pat. App. 1985.

in view of the decision in Diamond v Chakrabarty [...] it appears clear that Section 101 includes man-made life forms, including plant life.[51]

Nevertheless, the examiner reinforced and defended the view that as the Congress had enacted legislation specifically for the protection of plants,[52] it intended it to be the only form of protection for plant life. The Patent Office Board of Appeals rejected the examiner's position and reiterated the Supreme Court's decision that statutory subject matter under Section 101 of the federal statute[53] should be given a wide scope to include *anything under the sun that is made by man as patentable*[54], as was determined by the Supreme Court in Chakrabarty.[55] Moreover, the Patent Office Board of Appeals disagreed with the examiner that the enactment of the plant-specific acts excluded the protection for plant life under Section 101. The Patent Office Board of Appeals observed that:

> the overwhelming weight of authority is to the effect that repeals by implication are not favoured and that when there are two acts on the same subject the rule is to give effect to both unless there is such a 'positive repugnance' or 'irreconcilable conflict' that the statutes cannot co-exist.[56]

No positive repugnance or irreconcilable conflict was found between Section 101 of the Federal Statute and the specific US legislation for the protection of plants. As a result, the Patent Office Board of Appeals concluded that plants could fall under statutory scope and a patent was granted.[57]

Thus the idea that patent law does not allow products of nature *per se* to be patented is deceptive in its seeming simplicity.[58] Nowadays, in the United States it is possible to patent plant varieties,[59] genes developed through genetic engineering, or even "substances isolated from a naturally-occurring material"[60] including genes whose prior existence were unknown before the cell or any of its components were modified. Patent applications can refer to "an isolated DNA sequence or DNA constructs and new transformed materials (e.g. plants) derived from them, through claims often include natural DNA sequences without limitations."[61]

These type of patents claims are usually very broad in their scope[62] and cover not only the "described solution but also the outcome (results, function or principle

---

[51] Idem; at 444.
[52] See the Plant Patent Act; supra Note 13; and the Plant Variety Protection Act; supra Note 19.
[53] Title 35 of the US Code, Section 101.
[54] Diamond v Chakrabarty; supra Note 11; at 2207-08.
[55] Ex parte Hibberd; supra Note 50; at 444.
[56] Idem.
[57] After Ex parte Hibberd, the case Ex parte Allen attempted to further extend the scope of the Chakrabarty decision to include animals as well as plants. Nevertheless, the Patent Office Board of Appeals denied the applicant a patent on the basis that his invention was obvious. 2 USPQ 2d 1425, Bd. Pat. App. 1987, aff'd, 846 F. 2d 77 (Fed. Circuit, 1988).
[58] O'Shaughnessy, Brian; in Sibley, Kenneth (ed); supra Note 31; at p. 62.
[59] For examples of patents on plant varieties, plant gene and on purified and isolated DNA sequence see Correa, Carlos; Intellectual Property Rights, the WTO and Developing Countries; Zed books Ltd.; London; 2000; at p. 180-183.
[60] Verma, S. K.; "TRIPs and Plant Variety Protection in Developing Countries"; 6 EIPR 281, 1995; at p. 282.
[61] Correa, Carlos; supra Note 59; at p. 68.
[62] See Agracetus cotton patent; US Patent 5,159,135; Umbeck, Genetic Engineering of Cotton Plants and Lines; 27 October 1992. For more examples on broad patents see: Barton, John; "Patent Scope in Biotechnology"; 26(5) IIC, 1995; at pp. 605-618. See also Noiville, C.; "Patenting Life - trends in the US

behind the solution), even when the applicant has discovered and disclosed only one of several possible solutions to realise a result or function."[63] It can be expected that the use of genetically engineering to improve plant varieties will not only continue but is likely to occur at an ever-escalating pace.[64] However, Crespi notes that "the claims of a patent can only be directed to subject matter which is new [...] and cannot monopolise the known genomic material."[65] Correa clarifies that "the patenting of genes at cell level extends the scope of protection to all plants which include a cell with the claimed gene."[66] Thus, those that hold patents on a gene or DNA sequences will in fact see their patents monopolise the plant variety market.[67]

Another point to consider about US patent law before moving on to European law, is that written description of an invention in the United States or in a foreign country is considered prior art. However, public use of an invention is only considered prior art if such use has occurred in the United States for more than one year prior to the patent application date.[68] As such, several patents have been allowed to claims that use oral traditional knowledge of local and indigenous communities in developing countries.[69] If oral traditional knowledge were considered part of prior art in the United States, as written descriptions are, situations such as granting and revoking the patents concerning such as what occurred to the turmeric could be avoided.[70]

3 - PLANT VARIETY AND PLANT GENETIC RESOURCE PROTECTION IN EUROPE

Although Europe's position on the patentability of plants is still not very clear,[71] this section will describe the current state of European patent law in relation to the securing of a patent for the development of plants and plant varieties under the European Patent Convention.[72]

---

and Europe"; in Baumann et al (eds); The Life Industry; Intermediate Technology Publications; London; 1996; at pp. 78-79.
[63] Meibom, Wolfgang von and Pitz, Johann; "Broad Biotech Claims"; Patent World; August 1996; at p. 30.
[64] See Curry, Judith; The Patentability of Genetically Engineered Plants and Animals in the US and Europe; Intellectual Property Publishing Limited; London; 1987; at pp. 5-7.
[65] Crespi, Stephen; "Patents and Plant Variety Rights: Is There an Interface Problem?"; 23(2) IIC 168, 1992; at p. 182.
[66] Correa, Carlos; supra Note 59; at p. 180.
[67] For the commodification of plant resources in the United States, particularly seeds, see Rappert, Brian; "The US Extension of Plant Variety Protection: a critical evaluation"; 22(2) Science and Policy, April 1995; at pp. 95-105. For the corporate control of the seed industry see Vellve, R.; "The Decline of diversity in European Agriculture"; 23(2) The Ecologist, March/April 1993; at pp. 64-69.
[68] 35 United States Code, Section 102.
[69] See Chapter Four of this book.
[70] See Use of Turmeric in Wound Healing, US Patent No. 5,401,504; issued 28 March 1995. On 14 August 1997, the US Patent and Trademark Office declared the turmeric patent invalid on the absence on novelty. The Council of Scientific and Industrial Research of India, which opposed the patent, managed to provide an ancient Sanskrit text and an article published in 1953 in the Journal of the Indian Medical Association which proved that the use of turmeric as a wound healing agent was already known. These publications were regarded as valid prior art and the turmeric patent was cancelled. See Prakash, S.; "Country Study: India"; 1998; located at World Bank/ WTO Trade and Development Centre website http://www.itd.org/issues/india6.htm; accessed in 1998. See also "India Prevents Patenting of Turmeric"; The Statesman, 23 August 1997.
[71] See, e.g. Eisenberg, E.; "Genes, Patents, and Product Development"; 257 Science 903, 14 August 1992.
[72] European Patent Convention; Munich, 5 October 1973. It entered into force on 7 October 1977. Text found Christie, Andrew and Gare, Stephen; Blackstone's Statutes on Intellectual Property; Blackstone Press Limited; London; 4th edition; 1998; pp. 423-432.

In contrast with the United States' patent legislation, the EPC does not allow *prima facie* the patenting of plant varieties. The position of the European Patent Office, (hereinafter EPO), is that plant varieties are better protected under specific legislation.[73] On this subject, an interesting case, known as the Ciba-Geigy case,[74] came before the EPO Technical Board of Appeals, (hereafter Board of Appeals). The patent claim, which concerned a chemical seed coating, was initially denied on the ground that the claims involved the patenting of plant varieties. The Board of Appeals reversed the decision.

In Ciba-Geigy case, the claims included the following:

> "Claim 13. Propagating material for cultivated plants, treated with an oxide derivative according to formula I in claim 1.
>
> Claim 14. Propagating material according to claim 13, characterised in that it consists of seed."[75]

The board held that:

> If plant varieties have been excluded from patent protection because, specifically, the achievement involved in breeding a new variety is to have its own form of protection, it is perfectly sufficient for the exclusion to be left restricted, in conformity with its wording, to cases in which plants are characterised precisely by the genetically determined peculiarities of their natural phenotype. In this respect, there is no conflict between areas reserved for national protection of varieties and the field of application of the EPC. On the other hand, innovations that cannot be given the protection afforded to varieties are still patentable if the general prerequisites are met. (emphasis added).[76]

The Board of Appeals upheld the above claims, finding that they did not refer to a plant variety *per se*, which could go against the provisions in Article 53(b) of the EPC. Article 53 of the EPC states that patents are NOT available for:

> (a) inventions the publication or exploitation of which would be contrary to "order public" or morality, provided that the exploitation shall not be deemed to be so contrary merely because it is prohibited by law or regulation is some or all of the Contracting States;
> (b) plants or animal varieties or essentially biological processes for the production of plants or animals; this provision does not apply to microbiological processes or the products thereof.[77]

According to this article, patent varieties are not patentable. The Board of Appeals noted that the claims embraced plants propagated from material (e.g. seeds)

---

[73] See Chapter Three of this book.
[74] Ciba-Geigy case; (1979-85) EPOR Volume c 758.
[75] Board of Appeal Decision T49/83, Ciba-Geigy, Official Journal EPO 1984, at p. 112.
[76] Ciba-Geigy; supra Note 74.
[77] EPC; supra Note 72; Article 53(b).

that had been treated with an oxide derivative to confer herbicide resistance. The object of the claims was not considered to be a plant variety and therefore, the patent was allowed. The Board of Appeals stressed that: "No general exclusion of inventions in the sphere of animate nature can be inferred from the European Patent Convention."[78]

A similar case dealt with by the Board of Appeals was the Lubrizol case.[79] Here the Board of Appeals granted Lubrizol patent protection for the method of modifying plant cells with certain Ti-plasmids[80], as well as plants produced from them.[81] The board stressed in this case that exclusions from patentability were to be "construed narrowly". It noted that the generic group of plants produced by the process described in the patent application could not be considered a new variety because it failed to meet the requirements of a plant variety: distinctness, uniformity, and stability. Furthermore, the process by which the group of plants were produced could not be considered "essentially biological" because it involved a variety of human interventions. In this case, it considered steps such as the use of cell culture to maintain heterozygous parents as a technical process and not a biological one. On the other hand, plants produced through "conventional breeding", such as crossing and selection are considered biological, and as such, not patentable. Therefore, since the claim did not relate to the category of plant variety or a process essentially biological, a patent was allowed to Lubrizol.

Another EPO decision of great importance is the one known as the Plant Genetics Systems/Glutamine Synthetase Inhibitors decision (hereafter Plant Genetics Systems).[82] This EPO decision has given a new horizon to Article 53 of the EPC by interpreting it in a unique way. Plant Genetics Systems was granted a patent[83] in respect of its claims concerning a transgenic plant having a foreign nucleotide sequence incorporated into its genome and methods for making and using the transgenic plant.[84] Greenpeace opposed the patent under both Article 53(a) and 53(b). Under 53(a) it argued that it was immoral to patent plant genetic resources because they were part of the heritage of mankind and thus, should remain intact for future generations and available to all without restrictions. Regarding 53(b), Greenpeace argued that said article clearly states that plant varieties, their seeds and the process to make them are not patentable.

When analysing the case, the Board of Appeals found that there was no ground under Article 53(a) to prevent patenting. As the said article does not provide any definition of morality, the Board of Appeals held that it was to be interpreted as to exclude only "inventions the exploitation of which is likely to breach the public peace or social order (for example through acts of terrorism) or to seriously prejudice the environment."[85] The Board found that there was no evidence in the claim or in the case that could prove that the exploitation of the inventive plant would seriously prejudice the environment. Therefore, it concluded that the Plant Genetic Systems

---

[78] Ciba-Geigy; supra Note 74.
[79] Lubrizol case; T320/87 Lubrizol/Hybrid plants (1990); EPOR, 173.
[80] Ti-plasmid is " a plasmid carried by the crown gall bacterium *Agrabacterium tumefaciens*, part of which (T-DNA) becomes integrated into the chromosomes of infected tissue."
Crown gall is "a plant tumour caused by the bacterium *Agrobacterium tumefaciens*".
See Lawrence, E., Jackson, A., Jackson, J.; Longman Dictionary of Environmental Science; Longman; Essex; England; 1998.
[81] Lubrizol Genetics Inc.; Plant Gene Expression; 24 October 1984; EP-B1-122 791.
[82] EPO Decision T 356/93 - Plant Genetics Systems, Official Journal EPO, 1995; at 545.
[83] Plant Genetics Systems; "Plant cells resistant to glutamine synthetase inhibitors, made genetic engineering"; 10 October 1999; European Patent 242,236.
[84] Idem.
[85] EPO Decision T 356/93; supra Note 82; p. 557.

claim was not contrary to morality, and therefore it did not fall under the scope of Article 53(a) of the EPC. In this regard, Drahos noted that "the scope of patentability is expanding while the role of moral standards in the operation of the patent system is being increasingly limited."[86] According to the EPO, the morality concept in Article 53(a) should only be used as bar on patents in "rare and extreme cases."[87]

As regards Article 53(b), the Board found that the claims referring to transgenic plants and seeds *per se* were not patentable under the cited article. However, it did allow a patent on the process for producing herbicide resistant plants by genetic engineering methods, considering that it was not an "essentially biological process"[88] for the production of a plant. Furthermore, the Board regarded the genetically modified plant cells as patentable by considering them as micro-organisms because they were single cells capable of reproduction, just as bacteria yeast, fungi, algae and protozoa. The Board considered the transgenic seeds and cells that resulted from genetic engineering techniques, as products of a microbiological process.[89]

The above cases acknowledge that the EPC does not entirely exempt plant varieties from patentability. Plant varieties are indirectly patented when the biotechnological process that developed them is patented. These are known as "product-by-process" claims as the "product is characterised by the process used for its obtention and not by the elements and structure of the product as such."[90] This 1998 European Biotechnology Directive[91] (hereafter the Directive) has maintained this understanding.

According to the Article 4(1)(a) of the Directive, plant and animal varieties are not patentable.[92] However, according to Article 4(2), "Inventions which concern plants or animals shall be patentable if the technical feasibility is not confined to a particular plant or animal variety."[93] Article 3(2) allows the patenting of plant genetic resources by stating that "biological material which is isolated from its natural environment or produced by means of a technical process may be the subject of an invention even if it previously occurred in nature".[94]

It is thus evident that the patent rights in Europe are slowly catching up with United States standards. On 19 October 1998 the Kingdom of the Netherlands submitted before the European Court of Justice an action of annulment of the Directive.[95] Italy joined this action on 22 February 1999 and Norway followed 19 March 1999.[96] On 14 June 2001, the European Court of Justice Advocate General Francis Jacobs issued his opinion on the legal challenge against the Directive. In his

---

[86] Drahos, Peter; "Biotechnology Patents, Markets and Morality"; 21(9) European Intellectual Property Review 441, September 1999; at p. 442.
[87] European Patent Office Guidelines; Part C, Chapter IV, 3.1.
[88] EPC; supra Note 72; Article 53(b).
[89] For a critical analysis of the Plant Genetic Systems' case see Schrell, Andreas; "Are Plants (Still) Patentable"; 4 EIPR, 1996; at pp. 242-244.
[90] Correa, Carlos; supra Note 59; at p. 70.
[91] European Biotechnology Patent Directive; Directive 98/44/EC of the European Parliament and of the Council of 6 July 1998 on the legal protection of biotechnological inventions; 1998 O.J. L 213; at 0013–0021.
[92] Idem; Article 4(1)(a).
[93] Idem; Article 4(2).
[94] Idem; Article 3(2).
[95] Action brought in October 1998 by Kingdom of the Netherlands against the European Parliament and Council of the European Union; Case C-377/98, O.J. C 378, Dec. 5, 1998.
[96] See Case C-377/98.

opinion he concludes that the motion to annul the directive should be dismissed.[97] The European Court of Justice must now issue its final decision and it is expected that it will probably uphold the conclusion of its Advocate General. If the Directive is considered valid by the Court, all European Union countries will be forced to implement the Directive's provision through national legislation within two years.

4 - THE INTERNATIONAL INTELLECTUAL PROPERTY SYSTEM

Although IPRs fall under the domain of national law and vary from country to country, industrialised countries have slowly been achieving an international harmonisation of patent laws as well as their expansion in scope. Foreign patents have now been filed for biotechnological inventions for more than 100 years.[98] In the 1880s the first international treaties to regulate intellectual property rights on an international level were adopted: the Paris Convention for the Protection of Industrial Property and the Berne Convention for the Protection of Literary and Artistic Works.[99]

This section shall focus on the international intellectual property system and for this purpose shall consider the Paris Convention for the Protection of Industrial Property, the Patent Co-operation Treaty and the Trade-related Aspects of Intellectual Property Rights Agreement.

4.1 - Paris Convention for the Protection of Industrial Property

The first case of industrial property protection occurred in the city of Bordeaux in France, in 1236, when Bonafusus de Sancta and Compania were granted the exclusive privilege to weave and dye woollen cloths, following the Flamengo method, for a period of fifteen years.[100] Also in the 13th century, a few patents were granted for various aspects of the famous glass making products in Venice.[101] However, it was only in 1416, in Venice, Italy, that an industrial privilege was granted with characteristics more similar to the industrial property rights known today. Francesco Petri, who had invented wheat mills that did not need water to operate, was given this exclusive privilege which consisted of rules concerning the express prohibition of third parties to copy or imitate the invention, as well as the transferability and acquisition of the privilege.[102]

In reality, privileges like those consisted mainly of political criteria of convenience and opportunity and it was only with the impulse given by the Industrial Revolution in the 18th and 19th centuries that the privileges were considered as a right to property, namely intangible property.[103] The Paris Convention for the Protection of

---

[97] For the full text of the Advocate's General opinion see http://www.curia.eu.int/jurisp/cgi-bin/form.pl?lang=en. Select Opinion, in the case number search box enter "C-377/98" and click on the submit button.
[98] See, e.g. US Patent No. 141,072, granted to Louis Pasteur in 1873.
[99] Both of these treaties have been updated many times.
[100] Furtado, Lucas Rocha; Sistema de Propriedade Industrial no Direito Brasileiro; Brasilia Juridica; Brasilia; 1996; at p. 16.
[101] Primo Braga, C., Fink, C., Sepulveda, C.; "Intellectual Property Rights and Economic Development"; Background Paper to the World Development Report 1998; at p. 2.
[102] Furtado, Lucas Rocha; supra Note 99; at p. 16.
[103] Idem; at p. 16.

Industrial Property,[104] (hereafter the Paris Convention), was an attempt to internationally harmonise those privileges.

The Paris Convention was concluded in 1883. In 1967 the World Intellectual Property Organisation, (hereinafter WIPO) was created and the Paris Convention fell under its aegis. WIPO regulates, on an international level, the matters concerned with industrial property, including inventions, marks, industrial designs, utility models, trade names, geographical indications and the repression of unfair competition.[105] Brazil, the USA and the European Community are all members of the Paris Union.

The substantive provisions of the Paris Treaty most relevant to this Chapter are those that provide for national treatment, rights of priority and patent rules. Starting with the provisions on national treatment, Article 3 of the Paris Convention provides that, as regards the protection of industrial property, parties must grant nationals of any member country the same protection that they grant to their own nationals.[106] Nationals of Non-member States who are domiciled or have a real and effective industrial or commercial establishment in the territory of a Member State, shall also be granted the same advantages.[107]

The Paris Convention provides for the right of priority for any person who has properly filed an application for a patent, or for the registration of a utility model, or of an industrial design, or of a trademark in one of the contracting States.[108] The right to priority establishes that an applicant who has first duly filed an application in any one of the contracting states, may apply for the protection in any of the other contracting States within a period of 12 months with regard to patents and utility models (six months when it concerns industrial designs and marks).[109] These later applications will be regarded as if they were filed with the date of the first application, thus having priority over any application which may have been filed during the period of time stated above.[110]

Article 4bis of the Paris Convention reveals the territoriality of patents. It states:

> "(1) Patents applied for in the various countries of the Union by nationals of countries of the Union shall be independent of patents obtained for the same invention in other countries, whether members of the Union or not.
> (2) The foregoing provision is to be understood in an unrestricted sense, in particular, in the sense that patents applied for during the period of priority are independent, both as regards the grounds for nullity

---

[104] Paris Convention; 20 March 1883. In 1891 the Paris Convention for the Protection of Industrial Property was completed by an Interpretative Protocol in Madrid. It was then revised at Brussels in 1900, at Washington in 1911, at the Hague in 1925, at London in 1934, at Lisbon in 1958 and at Stockholm in 1967, and it was amended in 1979. U.N.T.S. No. 11851, vol. 828, pp.305-388.
[105] Idem; Article 1(2). The TRIPs Agreement also mentions "layout-designs (topographies) of integrated circuits", (See TRIPs Section 6, Part II), and "undisclosed information" (commonly called "trade secrets"), (See TRIPs Section 7, Part II), among the categories of intellectual property rights. TRIPs; infra Note 128.
[106] Paris Convention; supra Note 103; Article 2(1).
[107] Idem; Article 3.
[108] Idem; Article 4(A)(1).
[109] Idem; Article 4(C)(1).
[110] Idem; Article 4(B).

and forfeiture, and as regards their normal duration."[111]

Thus, it is apparent that a patent is not protected internationally. According to the Paris Convention, a patent claim must be deposited in each Member State where patent protection is sought, observing the right to priority. As such, the duration of each patent is determined by the domestic legislation of each Member State.[112]

Complementing the above provisions, Article 2(1) of the Paris Convention states that:

> "Nationals of any country of the Union shall, as regards the protection of industrial property, enjoy in all the other countries of the Union the advantages that their respective laws now grant, or may hereafter grant, to nationals;"[113]

Therefore, it is evident that the Paris Convention accepts that there are different national patent laws. This means that the Paris Convention placed no obligation on Member States to harmonise their patent laws in accordance to the standards and strictness of the domestic patent laws of the most powerful and influential industrialised countries. The situation is rather different nowadays. Developed countries have been pushing for an international harmonisation of patent law. International treaties, such as the Patent Co-operation Treaty have come into existence and have facilitated the operation of applying for a patent in more than one country.

4.2 - Patent Co-operation Treaty

The Patent Co-operation Treaty,[114] (hereinafter the PCT) is administered by the World Intellectual Property Organisation, (hereinafter WIPO). Its members include countries from the European Patent Convention, various African and Far East countries, as well as former Soviet republic states. The United States and Brazil are also members of the PCT.

This international treaty establishes facilities for applicants wishing to obtain patent protection in more than one State Party to the PCT. The applicant must designate in his claim the Member States or Member Regions with respect to which a patent is desired, facilitating his initial work and reducing his costs. Once the application has been processed, the patent applicant must deal with the local authorities of each of the countries where patent protection is being sought. The applicant has 18 months to decide whether or not to prosecute the PCT application in each of the cited countries. Member States rely on the initial international patent search conducted on the PCT application to check for the novel, non-obvious and prior art requirements.

According to the PCT, orally transmitted traditional knowledge and use only qualify as prior art for purposes of international search if they are substantiated by a

---

[111] Idem; Article 4bis.
[112] Idem; Article 4bis(5).
[113] Idem; Article 2(1).
[114] Patent Co-operation Treaty, 19 June 1970. It was amended 2 October 1979 and 3 February 1984 and is in force since January 1985. Available at World Intellectual Property Organisation website: www.wipo.org/eng/main.htm; accessed in 2001.

written description.[115] However, this written disclosure can serve as valid prior art even if it is published after the "filing date of the international application."[116] The United States is a party to the PCT and thus according to CIEL, orally transmitted traditional knowledge could receive special treatment in order to qualify as prior art even if it were printed in a publication after the patent application date.[117] If this measure were adopted, the US "first-to-invent" patent law provision would also be taken more seriously.

Certainly the PCT has contributed towards the harmonisation of patent law internationally. However, further steps were taken after the PCT. These attempts resulted in the Agreement on Trade-Related Aspects of Intellectual Property Rights.

4.3 - Agreement on Trade-Related Aspects of Intellectual Property Rights

4.3.1 - Introduction

In the late 1970s, when the great depression occurred in the stock market, the practical importance of the industrial property system reduced drastically in the United States.[118] However, in the 1980s, this situation completely changed. The United States realised that its industries had lost competitiveness due to the lack of an adequate intellectual property protection system.[119] In this sense, the United States widened the scope of patents in its territory as much as it could, and took up the task of pressurising other countries to adopt the same standards as it considered adequate. This approach led the United States to launch a world campaign to "link trade and IPRs in order to increase the returns on R&D and to prevent imitation."[120]

At that time, international IPR regulations were adopted through WIPO. However, Industrialised countries were not satisfied with the fact that WIPO "does not have any enforcement abilities and can only suggest revised guidelines for IPR regimes."[121] The Paris Convention, for instance, allows for disputes to be brought before the International Court of Justice; however, it also allows members not to accept this provision if the dispute in question is one with another Member State.[122] Consequently, developed countries, especially the USA,[123] recognising the "growing importance and value of knowledge and information in international trade,"[124] lobbied in favour of by-passing WIPO in favour of the General Agreement on Tariffs and Trade (hereafter GATT). GATT already had its own dispute settlement mechanism,[125]

---

[115] See PCT International Search Guidelines, PCT Gazette, Chapter VI, paragraph 1.2; Special Issue No. 06/1998, 8 October 1998. Available at www.wipo.org/eng/main.htm; accessed in 2001.
[116] Idem.
[117] Centre for International Environmental Law; "Comments on Improving Identification of Prior Art. Recommendations on Traditional Knowledge Relating to Biological Diversity"; Submitted to the United States Patent and Trademark Office; 2 August 1999; at p. 4. Located at http://ciel.org/ayahuascapatentcase.html; accessed in September 1999.
[118] Furtado, Lucas Rocha; supra Note 99; at p. 11.
[119] Correa, Carlos; supra Note 59; at p. 4.
[120] Idem.
[121] Acharya, Rohini; "Patenting of Biotechnology - GATT and the Erosion of the World's Biodiversity"; 25(6) Journal of World Trade 71, December 1991; at p. 73.
[122] Paris Convention; supra Note 103; Articles 28(1) and 28(2).
[123] Bennett, Philippe; "TRIPs - a Victory for US Industry"; Patent World, May 1994; at p. 31.
[124] Dutfield, Graham; "Can the TRIPs Agreement Protect Biological and Cultural Diversity?"; ACTS Press; Nairobi, Kenya; 1997; at p. 2.
[125] See General Agreement on Tariffs and Trade; 30 October 1947; 61 Stat. A-11, T.I.A.S. 1700, 55 U.N.T.S. 194.

a trade-sanction clause that, when activated, blocks the trade in other products with the country considered to be violating GATT provisions.[126]

In November 1982, At the Ministerial Meeting of the GATT in Geneva, the idea to have IPRs fall under the scope of GATT was discussed. No consensus was reached. Four years later, the Ministers met again in September 1986, in Punta del Este in Uruguay. The conclusions to that meeting were only adopted almost eight years later on 15 April 1994 when the Final Act Embodying the Results of the Uruguay Round of Multilateral Trade Negotiations,[127] (hereinafter Final Act), was signed in Marrakech, Morocco, by Ministers from most of the 125 participating governments. The Final Act includes the Agreement Establishing the World Trade Organisation, (hereinafter WTO),[128] as well as the Multilateral Agreements on Trade in Goods; the General Agreement on Trade in Services; and the Agreement on Trade-Related Aspects of Intellectual Property Rights, (hereafter TRIPs).[129] These agreements are binding on the present and future members of the WTO.

Article 3 establishes the national treatment principle and states that "Each Member shall accord to the nationals of other Members treatment no less favourable than it accords to its own nationals with regard to the protection of intellectual property, subject to the exceptions already provided in, respectively, the Paris Convention (1967) [...]."[130] Article 4 provides for the most-favoured-nation treatment principle and reads "With regard to the protection of intellectual property, any advantage, favour, privilege or immunity granted by a Member to the nationals of any country shall be accorded immediately and unconditionally to the nationals of all other Members."[131]

This section shall analyse the international expansion of patents in order to allow, but not require, the patenting of plant varieties.

4.3.2 - Patentable Subject Matter

In accordance with Article 1.1 of TRIPs, Members are not obliged to implement more extensive protection in their domestic law than that required by TRIPs.[132] This provision allows State Parties to adopt intellectual property rights of wider protection than the minimum standards stressed in Article 27 of TRIPs. The only limitation on this possibility is that additional rights do not run counter to rights afforded by the Agreement.[133]

Article 27(1) of TRIPs determines that Member States should declare as patentable subject matter "any *inventions*, whether products or processes, in all fields of technology, provided that they are *new*, *involve an inventive step* and are capable

---

[126] For more information on the WTO dispute settlement see: Jackson, J.; The World Trade Organisation; Royal Institute of International Affairs; London; 1998; pp. 59-104.
[127] Final Act Embodying the Results of the Uruguay Round of Multilateral Trade Negotiations. Marrakech, 15 April 1994. Reprinted in The Results of the Uruguay Round of Multilateral Trade Negotiations - The Legal Texts 2-3; GATT Secretariat (ed); 1994. 33 I.L.M. 1125, 1994.
[128] The WTO replaces the former GATT. Unlike the GATT that was intended to have a provisional existence and had no institutional foundation, the WTO is a permanent institution with its own secretariat. The WTO entered into force on 1 January 1995.
[129] Agreement on Trade-Related Aspects of Intellectual Property Rights, Including Trade in Counterfeit Goods; Annex 1C, Uruguay Round, 1994, WTA/GATT. TRIPs entered into force on 1 January 1996. 33 I.L.M. 1125, 1994.
[130] Idem; Article 3.
[131] Idem; Article 4.
[132] Idem; Article 1(1).
[133] Idem.

of industrial application."[134] (emphasis added) TRIPs does not define "invention". As such, countries willing to totally exclude all living organisms from patentability can adopt a definition of invention that excludes them from its scope and includes them in the scope of discoveries. Members are thus given leeway to determine that all substances found in nature, including genes, are not considered inventions and thus eliminate the possibility of patenting in their territories any organism, genetically modified or not.[135]

Article 27(1) of TRIPs does not provide standard international definitions for the terms "new", "inventive step" and capable of "industrial application". Therefore, States may apply different interpretations of those terms in their domestic patent laws. Oral transmission of knowledge, for instance, could be interpreted as prior art in order to defeat the novelty requirement. Gana questions whether a court in a developing country could "refuse to enforce a patent for a particular drug for malaria, holding that it is not 'new', since traditional native doctors have historically used the components of the drug in more rudimentary forms prior to its 'discovery' by a modern patentee?"[136] By considering oral traditional knowledge as a component of prior art, biotechnological firms would not readily be able to patent traditional knowledge and traditionally bred plants.

In the same way as the concept of novelty, TRIPs does not set an international standard for "inventive activity". Many developing and least-developed countries lag dramatically behind developed nations in technological development. As such, they could frequently be patenting the obvious without realising it. In this sense, Member States could consider that to analyse this criteria, the person skilled in the art could be a true expert, independent of his nationality.

The "capable of industrial application" requirement is a device countries can use to avoid patents on isolated genes the function of which is still unknown. TRIPs does not oblige Members to provide protection for isolated genes or gene sequences, of unknown function. According to Correa, Members should require that the object of the patent be defined precisely, ensuring the practicability of the invention and avoiding broad claims.[137]

Further, patent applicants must fully disclose the invention "in a manner sufficiently clear and complete"[138] so that a person skilled in the art can carry it out. Thus, this provision can be interpreted to mean that "the description should be sufficient to teach the invention to a local expert"[139] of ordinary skills in the pertinent field. Mere translations of patent applications as originally filed in other countries should not necessarily be sufficient.[140] When a patent is claimed in a technologically poor developing country the disclosure must be sufficiently clear and complete to allow local inventors and firms to practise the invention or else there is no advantage for them with the patent.[141] When the description can only be satisfied with the deposit of the material itself, the access to the said material should be made promptly

---

[134] Idem; Article 27(1).
[135] See Correa; supra Note 59; at p.228.
[136] Gana, Ruth; "Prospects for Developing Countries Under the TRIPs Agreement"; 29(4) Vanderbilt Journal of Transnational Law 735, October 1996; at p. 749.
[137] Correa; supra Note 59; at p. 72.
[138] TRIPs; supra Note 128; Article 29.
[139] Correa; supra Note 59; at p.236.
[140] UNCTAD; The TRIPS Agreement and Developing Countries; UNCTAD/ITE/1; United Nations; Geneva; 1996.
[141] Article 7 of TRIPs states that one of the objectives of the agreement is the transfer and dissemination of technology to the mutual advantage of producers and users; supra Note 128.

available with the publication of the application.[142] Thus, given the importance of the disclosure requirement, developing countries should use it to help them increase their technological know-how to improve their competitive position in the world.

While the patent requirements can be adapted to each country's patent law to best suit their individual interests, the TRIPs exceptions to patentability in Article 27(2) can be used as bars to patents on inventions whose use would be contrary to public order and morality.[143] Article 27(2) states that

> Members may exclude from patentability inventions, the prevention within their territory of the commercial exploitation of which is necessary to protect ordre public or morality, including to protect human, animal or plant life or health or to avoid serious prejudice to the environment, provided that such exclusion is not made merely because the exploitation is prohibited by domestic law.[144]

Robin Nott defends the position that morality should not be one of the determinant requirements of patentability. The author holds the belief that "morality is a variable concept which changes with time."[145] Furthermore, Nott defends the point of view that patent law is ineffective in preventing immoral acts and cruelty towards plants and animals. He uses animals to exemplify his point and states that denying patents on animals will not stop any cruelty or ill treatment towards them.[146]

Such reasoning appears to be against the TRIPs principle to safeguard public health, nutrition and socio-economic development.[147] There is a duty on Member States to deny patents on inventions that could harm their economic and environmental welfare.[148] It is well known that even though there are laws that condemn murder, they do not stop people from committing homicides. Following the author's line of thought, it could be said that, as laws that condemn murder do not stop a person from committing a homicide, they should be abandoned and another form of protection against murder developed. This is not the solution. The law should be kept, while further protection can be elaborated to complement it.

Although it is evident that the refusal to patent will not stop its commercialisation[149] the basic intention of patent law, when using morality as a filter to issue patents, is to help mankind to maintain its focus on practising proper social conduct. Nevertheless, this affirmation would probably be disputed by Nott, who, as shown above, believes that morality changes with time.[150] In answer to this argument, it is necessary to examine what is morality.

The concept of morality can be used broadly or narrowly. When seen broadly, on a philosophical or spiritual level, it can be said that morality is a universal mode of conduct that does not depend on creed, time, age, country or person. In this way, it can

---

[142] Correa; supra Note 59; at p.237.
[143] TRIPs, supra Note 128; Article 27(2).
[144] Idem.
[145] Nott, Robin; "Plants and animals: Why they should be protected by patents and variety rights"; Patent World 45, July/August 1993; at p. 47.
[146] Idem; at p. 48.
[147] TRIPs; supra Note 128; Article 8(1).
[148] Idem; Article 7.
[149] Correa; supra Note 59; at p. 63.
[150] Nott, Robin; at p. 47.

even be regarded in a religious context as being a gift of God to mankind[151] because morality can provide peace and order to society. On the other hand, if morality is seen narrowly on a more earthly level, it is regarded as a concept which is defined differently by people, depending on the time period they live in, their culture, their beliefs and in the very consciousness of each civilisation. However, even then, there may be particular principles of morality that are universally shared.

When it is said that it is immoral to patent life, as one of the grounds to reject the patentability of living organisms, morality is used in the universal sense, as an absolute conduct applicable to all human beings. It would not be wrong to use morality in this way to avoid, or prevent, the patenting of life. However, morality in this sense seems to apply only to natural species, and not to all life forms. TRIPs, for example, stimulates countries to adopt a patent system that protects plant varieties,[152] ignoring the fact that plant varieties are also living beings. In this case, morality is given a narrow scope, changeable from country to country, being demarcated by the social function of the plant variety, the economic growth and prosperity of the country. Consequently, the standards of morality are different for natural species and for species genetically modified by man. The latter ones are valued in a different way due to their immediate potential of providing financial gains to the inventor.[153]

Sedjo compares the difficulties of patenting natural genetic resources, with the difficulty of patenting basic knowledge, and uses Einstein's theory of relativity as an example.[154] Einstein's theory of relativity could not be patented because it was the discovery of basic knowledge that already existed, even though it had not previously been discovered.[155] In this sense, McNally and Wheale note that the "legal distinction between the patentable and the unpatentable creates a hierarchy of life forms with a premium on genetically engineered life forms over others. It also creates a hierarchy among social actors, favouring those who have gene technology over those who do not."[156]

This view is confirmed by TRIPs which permits States to patent plant varieties. Article 27(3)(b) of TRIPs states that

> "Members *may* also exclude from patentability:
> (b) plants and animals other than micro-organisms, and essentially biological processes for the production of plants or animals other than non-biological and microbiological processes. However, Members *shall* provide for the protection of plant varieties either by patents or by an effective sui generis system or by a combination thereof."[157] (emphasis added)

This article contains many important issues that differentiate the patent laws in the United States, in the European Patent Convention and in developing countries.

---

[151] Tansey, G.; "Trade, Intellectual Property, Food and Biodiversity"; Quaker United Nations Office; Geneva. Located at http://www.quaker.org.com; accessed in 1998.
[152] TRIPs; supra Note 128; Article 27(3).
[153] For a deeper discussion on the morality of patenting living matter see Sterckx, Sigrid; Biotechnology, Patents and Morality; Ashgate; Hants, England; 1997.
[154] Sedjo, Roger A.; "Property Rights and the Protection of Plant Genetic Resources"; in Kloppenburg, Jr. (ed); Seeds and Sovereignty; Duke University Press; London; 1988; at p. 304.
[155] This is the same case as the discovery of gravity. Neither the definition of gravity in Plato's cosmology, nor Aristotle's theory, nor Newton's theory could be patented.
[156] McNally, Ruth and Wheale, Peter; "Biotechnology and Biodiversity - Comparative Advantages in the New Global Order"; 26(5) The Ecologist, September/October 1996; at p. 226.
[157] TRIPs; supra Note 128; Article 27(3).

The exclusion of plants and animals, as well as essentially biological processes for the production of plants or animals, from the scope of patents is not compulsory. The word *may*, instead of "shall" in the beginning of the article, suggests that Member States are not obliged to exclude them from patentability if they so desire. This means that a patent could be conferred to a plant or an essentially biological process if someone manages to prove to a patent office that the plant or animal referred to in the patent claim is in fact an invention.

According to Carlos Correa, this is not a possibility. He states that it is generally admitted in patent law that "discoveries" are not patentable and this principle can be applied to exclude from patentability substances existent in nature, including genetic material.[158] Furthermore, Correa stresses that countries could interpret TRIPs provisions as excluding from the scope of invention any substance and natural process, like isolated sequences of DNA, although they were transferred from different organisms.[159] He further notes that TRIPs does not refer to any classification of plants, and thus, "countries may exclude the patentability of plant species, varieties, including hybrids and transgenic plants, as well as their cells and seeds."[160] However, if a State adopts this measure, it must provide some form of intellectual property protection for plant varieties.

It should be noted, however, that as regards patentable processes, the exclusion only falls on "essentially biological processes for the production of plants and animals". Article 27(3)(b) allows patents on "non-biological and microbiological processes". This provision, thus, permits the exclusion from patent protection of plant varieties developed through traditional breeding methods. However, it compensates the work of breeders that develop plant varieties through biotechnological methods, genetic manipulation, gene insertion or transfer. Such differentiation is questioned by Correa, who notes that the "concept of 'non-biological process' is very complex and new. How can a plant or an animal be produced by a process that is not totally or partially biological?"[161]

And finally, State Parties are allowed to protect plant varieties through a *sui generis* system they develop that best suits their interests or combine a *sui generis* system with patent protection. This flexibility is permitted due to the lack of consensus among countries in regard to patents for living organisms. The United States, for instance, considers that "everything under the sun, made by man, is patentable"[162] including plant varieties. However, under the European Patent Convention plant varieties are not, in principle, patentable.[163]

Article 27(3)(b) was expected to be reviewed on 1 January 1999 but no consensus was reached and by August 2001 the said article had still not been modified.

4.3.3 - Rights and the Patent Holder

---

[158] Correa, Carlos; "Derechos Soberanos y de Propiedad sobre los Recursos Fitogenéticos"; prepared at the request of the Secretariat of the FAO Commission on Plant Genetic Resources; First Extraordinary meeting of the Commission on Plant Genetic Resources; Rome; 7-11 November 1994.
[159] Correa, Carlos; supra Note 157.
[160] Correa; supra Note 59; at p. 186.
[161] Correa, C.; supra Note 157.
[162] Diamond v. Chakrabarty; supra Note 11.
[163] EPC; supra Note 72; Article 53(b).

TRIPs Article 28 provides for the exclusive rights granted to a patent holder. This article states that when the subject matter of a patent is a product, the patentee has the right to "prevent third parties not having his consent from the acts of: making, using, offering for sale, selling, or importing for these purposes that product."[164] When the subject matter of a patent is a process, the patent holder has the right to "prevent third parties not having his consent from the act of using the process, and from the acts of: using, offering for sale, selling, or importing for these purposes at least the product obtained directly by that process."[165] Patenting a plant variety enables an individual or a company to monopolise the market for that variety for a 20-year patent protection term.[166]

Article 30 of TRIPs provides for exceptions to patent rights conferred. The exceptions allowed for must not conflict with the normal exploitation of the patent and must not unreasonably prejudice the legitimate interests of the patent owner.[167] Member States may, thus for instance, interpret this article to permit exemptions on patentees' exclusive rights for reasons of further research and development. Likewise, "in some countries the use of pharmaceutical inventions is allowed before the expiration of the patent in order for a third party to obtain government approval to commercialise the product immediately after the patent expires."[168]

Article 31(b) stipulates that a Member State may also allow the use of the subject matter of a patent without the authorisation of the right holder "in the case of a national emergency or other circumstances of extreme urgency or in cases of public non-commercial-use".[169] In these situations, the "legitimate interests of the patent owner"[170] are subordinated to the legitimate interest of society. In this sense, the patent holder does not have the right to suppress or distort market forces, and his rights do not prevail over national emergency or other circumstances of extreme urgency.

TRIPs does not limit the grounds for permitting the unauthorised use of a patented object or process. Developing countries can implement provisions in their national law which allow for the unauthorised use of the subject matter of a patent in favour of their national interests and development. In accordance to TRIPs, Members may take appropriate measures to avoid abuse of patents by the right holder, as well as to avoid practices that unreasonably restrain trade or the international transfer of technology.[171] Similarly, Members may adopt provisions to restrict patents in favour of public health and nutrition and to promote the public interest in sectors of vital importance of their socio-economic and technological development.[172] However, the protection, enforcement of and restriction on patents are subject to measures that seek the balance of rights and obligations of producers and users of technological knowledge and in a manner conducive to social and economic welfare.[173]

4.3.4 - Burden of Proof

Article 34 of TRIPs places the burden of proof on the defendant in patent disputes involving process patents. Thus, it is up to the defendant to prove that he has

---

[164] TRIPs; supra Note 128; Article 28(1).
[165] Idem; Article 28(2).
[166] Idem; Article 33.
[167] Idem; Article 30.
[168] UNCTAD; supra Note 139.
[169] TRIPs; supra Note 128; Article 31(b).
[170] Idem; Article 30.
[171] Idem; Article 8(1).
[172] Idem; Article 8(1).
[173] Idem; Article 7.

not violated a patented process.[174] Where plant varieties are concerned, this article ignores two basic issues. The first point to consider is the possibility of two or more breeders developing the same plant variety using different processes. It is a fundamental principle of patent laws that the disclosure of an invention must be sufficient to enable a person skilled in the art to repeat or reproduce it. In the case of plant varieties, where it is impossible to describe the process in sufficient detail and precision as to enable a person skilled in the art to develop an identical plant, patent laws have been allowing breeders to fulfil the disclosure requirement with the deposition of the plant variety or part of its propagating material. Taking this point into consideration, how is a defendant supposed to convincingly describe his own process without being able to use the developed variety in his favour as the claimant is allowed to when requesting a patent?

According to Joseph Straus[175] "Given the ability of living material to reproduce itself, it will only be necessary in the rarest of cases to continue to utilise a particular transfer vector, for instance, which has been used to create a new transgenic plant. On the contrary, it is the plant as such which is used as the initial source for further propagation, selection and so on."[176] Indeed, the difficulty of proving that a process is not same as a patented one is an advantage to patentees. Thus, it is essential for patent offices to deny patents on processes that do not totally fulfil the "industrial application" requirement. In other words, they should refuse claims that do not expressly declare the precise function of the process in order to limit broad process claims.

4.3.5 - TRIPs Implementation

Countries are given the liberty to determine the appropriate method of implementing TRIPs within their own legal system and practice.[177] TRIPs took into consideration the different developmental stages of different countries and in "Transitional Arrangements" it sets forth the period within which members shall be obliged to implement the agreement. All countries are given at least a year to apply the provisions of the agreement.[178] Developing countries are given an additional four years of delay to implement most of TRIPs provisions.[179] In addition, this term is extended to a total of ten years when applying the TRIPs provisions concerning the patent protection to areas of technology not currently protectable in its territory.[180] Least developed countries are granted a transitional period of 10 years to implement the standard patent provisions, and a further extension can be accorded by the TRIPs Council upon duly motivated request.[181] This extension is reasonable because it is likely that an additional amount of time to set up all the appropriate infrastructure, change their laws, train new personnel, and so forth will be necessary in many developing and least developed countries. The transitional periods do not require prior notification by the concerned Members, being automatically applicable.

The transitional periods provided and the additional extensions available reveal that biotechnology and the international harmonisation of patent law are a

---

[174] Idem; Article 34(1).
[175] Joseph Straus was the Head of Department at the Max Planck Institute for Foreign and International Patent, Copyright and Competition Law in Munich in June 1987.
[176] Straus, Joseph; "The Relationship Between Plant Variety Protection and Patent Protection for Biotechnological Inventions from an International Viewpoint"; 18(6) IIC 723, 1987; at p.736.
[177] TRIPs; supra Note 128; Article 1(1).
[178] Idem; Article 65(1).
[179] Idem; Article 65(2).
[180] Idem; Article 65(4).
[181] Idem; Article 66(1).

controversial issue. Therefore, developing and least-developed countries have no obligation under TRIPs to implement plant protection by any method before the extended date for implementation.

Although the United States intellectual property rights are more far-reaching than the ones being adopted by developing countries in general, TRIPs Members are not obliged to implement more extensive protection than the minimum norms it dictates.[182] This is to say that the United States cannot apply its unilateral trade sanctions, as stated in Section 301 of its Omnibus Trade and Competitiveness Act, on a country for not accepting the patenting of plant varieties.[183] A country can opt for a *sui generis* protection system that balances breeders' rights with indigenous' and farmers' rights. Through the *sui generis* option, each country has the right to define the type and of scope of protection granted to breeders of plant varieties as well protect grassroot-level innovations and their economic interests.[184].

Countries can invent a new form of intellectual property protection or adapt the ones already existent such as trademarks, geographic location, utility patents and so forth to protect plant varieties. However, it is not the purpose of this Chapter to discuss forms of protection for plant varieties other than patents.[185]

4.3.6 - Conclusion

TRIPs is an expansion of the Paris Convention. All Members of the WTO must comply with its provisions even if they are not parties to the Paris Convention. This is to say, for instance, that Members who do not adhere to the Paris Convention must comply anyway with the provisions of "national treatment" and "most-favoured nation".[186]

According to TRIPs, Member States may not exclude any field of technology from patentability as a whole and patent laws must confer a minimum of 20 years of exclusive rights to the patentee from the filing date. However, although the implementation of TRIPs favours the growing uniformity of national patent laws, there is still a large amount of controversy and debate over the possibility of patenting living organisms. This makes it impossible, at least at the moment, for there to be a global harmonisation of domestic patent laws.

Countries are allowed not to grant patents in respect of plants or animals, and "essentially biological processes for the production of plants or animals".[187] Member States may also avoid the availability of patents for living organisms by adopting strict standards of interpretation of the concepts of novelty, inventive step and industrial application, while bearing in mind that in accordance with the national treatment

---

[182] Idem; Article 1(1).
[183] Correa; supra Note 59; at p. 10. For the history of all section 301 cases see the Office of the United States Trade Representative website: http://www.ustr.gov.
[184] Bhat, M. G.; "Trade-related intellectual property rights to biological resources: Socio-economic implications for developing countries"; 19 Ecological Economics 205, 1996; at p. 210.
[185] See Chapter Five of this book.
[186] For instance, although India and Pakistan are not party to the Paris Convention, they are Members of the World Trade Organisation, and as such, under Article 2.1 of TRIPs, they must comply with the substantive law provisions of the Paris Convention. However, TRIPs under Article 65, allows developing and "transition" countries to delay, at least until the year 2000, the application of most of the obligations provided for in TRIPs. Obviously developing and transition countries that are part of the Paris Convention cannot use this exception to delay the application of their obligations provided for in the Paris Convention.
[187] TRIPs; supra Note 128; Article 27(3)(b).

principle, these standards must be the same for both nationals and foreigners. However, national policy-makers must weigh the consequences of the standards to be imposed and find the exact measure to maintain technological innovation and environmental protection, as well as the social and economic welfare in all levels of society.

Parties to TRIPs must allow the patenting of micoorganisms, non-biological and microbiological process and provide protection for plant varieties. They are given the option to avoid patenting plant varieties by adopting a *sui generis* system of protection that best suits their beliefs and interests. With this in mind, TRIPs determines that States are not obliged to implement in their laws more extensive protection than it requires. A *sui generis* system may recognise and compensate the contributions made by traditional farmers and indigenous communities to the development of new plant varieties through traditional breeding methods.[188]

TRIPs does not limit the possibilities of compulsory licences,[189] giving Member States the opportunity to control and limit a patentee's right. As such, the national law of a Member State can, for instance, permit compulsory licenses for reasons of public interest. It is recommendable that developing countries take advantage of compulsory licensing to safeguard their national interests, by controlling the monopoly effects of patents on biological material.

Due to the transitional arrangements in TRIPs, developing countries may avoid implementing the standard patent provisions for a period of ten years,[190] while the least developed countries can postpone their implementation for eleven years.

Many developing countries argue that the TRIPs Agreement was a victory for the United States and other industrialised countries. Developing countries feel bullied and pressurised by the competitive position of these industrialised countries which have been using and will continue to use TRIPs to guarantee their own economic growth. In addition, they fear that the agreement will increase their dependency on Northern Hemisphere multinationals. Soon after the adoption of TRIPs, the US Commissioner of Patents and Trademarks announced before the US Senate Subcommittee on Patents, Copyrights and Trademarks:

> "One of the principal ways President Clinton and Secretary Brown are seeking to improve US competitiveness in the international marketplace is by placing increased attention on technology-based economic growth."[191]

Dutfield notes that "The main means employed by the United States to exploit and deepen division within the Third World are through bilateral actions using its Trade Act (1988) Section 301 measures to impose punitive sanctions and tariffs on imported goods from countries considered to have weak IPR laws."[192] However, Correa stresses that US unilateral trade retaliations are illegal under TRIPs because the World Trade Organisation provides its own procedure of dispute settlement mechanism and furthermore, they deprive "developing countries of their right to take

---

[188] See Chapter Five of this book.
[189] See Article 31 of TRIPs; supra Note 128. Through compulsory licences the patentee must allow others to utilise his invention in exchange of a reasonable compensation.
[190] For instance, in the case of the recognition of patents to pharmaceuticals and agro-chemicals.
[191] See, Statement of Bruce A. Lehman before the Subcommittee on Patents, Copyrights and Trademarks Committee on the Judiciary, United States Senate, 9th March 1994.
[192] Dutfield, Graham; supra Note 123; at p. 5.

the necessary time to introduce legal reforms and adopt measures that mitigate their eventual negative economic and social impact."[193]

5 - GENERAL CONCLUSION

As wisely observed by the United Kingdom Environment Minister Mr. Meacher, at the Earth Summit II, held in New York, "a new world order is gradually and painfully coming into play but is confronted by enormous resistance from the old pattern of forces and vested interests."[194] The history of the different development trajectories countries have undergone shows that "there can be decisive winners and losers in international trade; one nation can create advantages in related sets of industries that its rivals cannot match."[195]

As environmental, economic and social conditions are very different from one country to the next, the standard of intellectual property protection to be adopted will inevitably vary from country to country. The United States patent protection in regard to plant genetic resources and plant varieties, as well as the European Patent Convention, were used as examples to demonstrate the different approaches and scope of patent laws. The United States does not consider as an automatic exclusion of patentability the fact that the invention is a living organism or derived from it. After the Chakrabarty case in 1980, where a patent was allowed to micro-organisms, patent scope rapidly expanded in the United States to include whole and parts of living organisms. Although the EPC excludes plant varieties from patentability, the Plant Genetics System case showed that non-biological processes for the production of a plant variety are patentable. Furthermore, the Board of Appeals considered modified plant cells as modified micro-organisms and thus patentable.

The expansion of international trade to encompass intellectual property rights creates too many incentives and gives too much leeway to manufacturers and industrialised countries in general. However, according to TRIPs, countries are allowed to exclude plant varieties from patentability but they must then protect them by an effective *sui generis* system. An international *sui generis* system to protect plant varieties will be examined in the following Chapter.

---

[193] Correa; supra Note 59; at p. 10.
[194] Mr. Meacher; Electronic Telegraph for day June 28, 1997.
[195] Zysman, J., Tyson, L., Dosi, G., & Cohen, S.; "Trade Technology and National Competition"; in Technology and Investment: Crucial Issues for the 1990s; at 187.

CHAPTER THREE

BREEDERS' RIGHTS UNDER THE UPOV

1 - GENERAL INTRODUCTION

As shown in the previous Chapter, the technical difficulties traditionally encountered in protecting new varieties by means of patents resulted in the establishment of special protection for plants in some countries.[1] Furthermore, there was a general concern that the exclusive nature of patents would "impede the common practice of using protected plant varieties for further commercial breeding."[2] This fear resulted in the establishment of special protection for plant varieties, outside the area of patent law. During the decades between the two world wars Czechoslovakia, France, the Netherlands, Austria, Federal Republic of Germany and Spain enacted legislation to protect plant breeders' rights,[3] (hereafter PBRs). At the end of the Second World War, the British Government instituted a system for registering good-quality seed used for agricultural production. A few years later, this idea was expanded to compensate individuals who improved seed further and the concept of PBRs was introduced into the legal system as a reward for new plant varieties bred.[4]

The International Union for the Protection of Plant Varieties, (hereafter UPOV)[5] was born out of the initiative of Italy, Germany, France, Belgium and the Netherlands, which at that time were not parties to the Paris Convention.[6] The Group of Legal Experts at the UPOV Conference of 1961 saw breeders' rights as being very distinct from inventors' rights[7] and they had to decide between a patent law revision and a new law to protect breeders' rights independent of the patent system.[8] They opted for an independent system that was to be regulated by ministries for agriculture rather than patent authorities. Their idea was that a new law could better accommodate the particular characteristics of breeders' plant varieties, as well as suit the technical requirements of breeders' rights.[9]

---

[1] For an analysis on the possibility of expanding the concept of invention to encompass new plant varieties see Moufang, Rainer; "Protection for Plant Breeding and Plant Varieties - A Frontier of Patent Law"; Nordiskt Immateriellt Rattsskydd; 1992; pp 330-348.
[2] School of International and Public Affairs Columbia University; "Access to Genetic Resources: An Evaluation of the Development and Implementation of Recent Regulation and Access Agreements"; Columbia University; Environmental Policy Studies Working Paper No. 4, Prepared for the Biodiversity Action Network; June 1999; at p. 3.
[3] Straus; "Industrial Property Protection: Biotechnological Invention, Analysis of Certain Basic Issues"; World Intellectual Property Organisation BIG/281; at p. 30
[4] School of International and Public Affairs Columbia University; supra Note 2; at p. 3.
[5] UPOV stands for the initials of the original name in French: Union pour la Protection des Obtentions Végétales. UPOV is an intergovernmental organisation with its headquarters is in Geneva.
[6] Ghijsen, Huib; "Plant Variety Protection in a Developing and Demanding World"; Biotechnology and Development Monitor, 36 September/December 2, 1998; at p. 2.
[7] "Group des Experts Juridiques Chargés d'Étudier les Relations entre la Convention de Paris pour la Protection de la Propriété Industrielle et l'Avant-Projet de Convention pour la Protection des Obtentions Végétales", in UPOV, "Actes"; at p. 50.
[8] See LaClavière; "The Convention of Paris of December 2, 1961, for the Protection of New varieties of Plants and the International Union for the Protection of New Varieties of Plants"; 4 Ind. Prop., 1965; at pp. 227-228.
[9] Idem; at p. 227.

It was with the adoption of UPOV Convention in 1961,[10] (hereafter UPOV 1961), that PBRs were recognised for the first time on an international level. UPOV 1961 was amended in 1972 but its first major revision was in 1978, creating the 1978 UPOV Act, (hereafter UPOV 1978).[11] Once UPOV 1978 entered into force, States could no longer accede to UPOV 1961.[12] UPOV 1978 was modified in 1991, which gave origin to the 1991 UPOV Act,[13] (hereafter UPOV 1991). When UPOV 1991 entered into force, UPOV 1978 was closed for further accession except for those States that had already notified their intention to accede to UPOV 1978 and had started that process.[14] Member States bound to earlier UPOV Acts were not obliged to ratify or adhere to a revised Act.

This Chapter will analyse UPOV 1978, as well as UPOV 1991 because they are the only two UPOV Acts in force at the moment.[15] UPOV 1991 is far more expansive in its provisions and protections than UPOV 1978. The purpose of this Chapter is to show how PBRs have been evolving in order to become more similar to patent protection. When a statement in this Chapter refers to the Member States that compose the International Union for the Protection of New Varieties of Plants, the term "Union" is used.

2 - UPOV 1978

2.1 - Introduction

The UPOV Acts are the only the international instruments through which breeders can claim protection of new varieties of plants by means of a *sui generis* intellectual property right. They contain provisions that regulate the requirements for the granting of PBRs, the minimum scope and minimum duration of protection, national treatment, right of priority and the form of protection. The UPOV Acts requires their Member States to adopt plant variety protection systems according to rules prescribed by each act, although States are free to enact more extensive protection through their national law.

This section shall analyse the main elements of UPOV 1978 and make occasional reference to UPOV 1961.

2.2. - Conditions Required for Protection

Although UPOV 1978 does not define variety, the Union considers it "a subdivision within the species of the lowest known rank [...] which promises better quality or yield or other advantages"[16] and is the product of several factors "such as the mode of propagation of the plants, their floral biology and the plant breeding

---

[10] UPOV was first adopted on December 2, 1961.
[11] In November 10, 1972 UPOV 1961 was amended and on 23 October 1978 it was first revised.
[12] UPOV 1978; infra Note 15; Article 33(3).
[13] UPOV 1991, 19 March 1991; Idem.
[14] UPOV 1978; Idem; Article 37(3).
[15] Electronic versions of the 1961, 1978, and 1991 UPOV Conventions can be found at http://www.upov.int/eng/convntns/; accessed in 2000. The texts of these conventions are available in printed form on application to the Office of UPOV: 34, Chemin des Colombettes, CH-1211, Geneva 20, Switzerland.
[16] UPOV; "About UPOV"; located at: http://www.upov.int/eng/content.htm. Available in 2000.

techniques used."[17] To be protectable the variety must be *distinct*, *new*, *homogeneous* and *stable*.[18]

By *distinct*, it is meant that the variety "must be clearly distinguishable by one or more important characteristics from any other variety whose existence is a matter of common knowledge at the time when protection is applied for."[19] The variety must be distinguishable from other varieties known through "cultivation, marketing already in progress, entry in an official register of varieties already made or in the process of being made, inclusion in a reference collection, or precise description in a publication."[20] Therefore, under UPOV 1978, a variety could pass the distinctness test even if it had been simply discovered. The applicant's variety must only be distinct from varieties whose existence is a matter of common knowledege.[21]

To be considered *new*, the variety must not have been offered for sale or marketed, with the concession of the breeder, for longer than one year in the territory of that State[22] or abroad for longer than six years in the case of vines, forest, fruit or ornamental trees, or for longer than four years in the case of all other plants.[23] UPOV 1978 further explains that trials of the variety that do not involve offering for sale or marketing shall not affect the right to protection.[24] It also stipulates that if a variety has become a matter of common knowledge in ways other than through offering for sale or marketing it is still protectable.[25]

To satisfy the requirements of *homogeneity*, a variety must be sufficiently uniform as regards its particular sexual reproduction or vegetative propagation features.[26] To be considered *stable* its essential characteristics must be maintained after repeated reproduction or propagation.[27] Given that a variety must be uniform and stable to be protectable, UPOV encourages the development of genetically uniform varieties which is one of the causes of genetic erosion.[28] Such encouragement, thus, appears to be out of harmony with the CBD objective to conserve biological diversity. It is also noteworthy that the said requirements automatically exclude from protection genetically-diverse traditionally bred varieties.

A final condition required for the protection of a new plant variety is that it has been given a specific denomination[29] that enables it to be identified.[30] The name of the new variety may not be the same or confusingly similar to any existing variety belonging to the same botanical species or a closely related species in any Member State of the Union.[31]

2.3 - Scope of Protection

---

[17] Idem.
[18] UPOV 1978; supra Note 15; Article 6.
[19] Idem; at Article 6(1)(a).
[20] Idem.
[21] Christie, Andrew; "The Novelty Requirement in Plant Breeders' Rights Law"; 19(5) IIC 646, 1998; at p. 651.
[22] UPOV 1978; supra Note 15; at Article 6(1)(b)(i).
[23] Idem; Article 6(1)(b)(ii).
[24] Idem; Article 6(1)(b).
[25] Idem.
[26] Idem; Article 6(1)(c).
[27] Idem; Article 6(1)(d).
[28] UN Food and Agriculture Organisation; The State of the World's Plant Genetic Resources for Food and Agriculture; 1996; at p. 21.
[29] UPOV 1978; supra Note 15; Article 6(1)(e).
[30] Idem; Article 13(1).
[31] Idem; Article 13(2).

The UPOV 1978 covers all plants.[32] Member States are expected to progressively apply the provisions of UPOV 1978 to the largest possible number of botanical genera and species.[33] Article 5(4) of UPOV 1978 allows Member States to confer more extensive rights to breeders in respect of certain botanical genera or species. Therefore, the scope of protection conferred to breeders in UPOV 1978 is the minimum and does not prohibit Member States from granting wider protection through their national laws.[34]

According to Article 5 of UPOV 1978, once the right has been conferred, prior authorisation of the breeder is required to produce, offer for sale or market the reproductive or vegetative propagating material of the variety.[35] This means that the breeder does not have exclusive rights over all possible ways of exploiting the variety, but only as regards those acts that in some way result in the direct or indirect sale of reproductive materials. Other forms of use of a protected variety are not forbidden. One of the motivations of breeders for the revision of UPOV 1978 was to get protection extended at least to cut flowers of their ornamental and fruit-tree varieties.[36]

In this regard, Straus complained that the limited scope of PBRs in UPOV 1978 "leave without protection the entire field of marketing of the end product, whether it be the plant or their parts such as fruit, leaves or roots, or whether it be the products obtained therefrom, such as oil with specific properties, etc."[37] This would mean, for instance, that if a person used the oil of a protected coconut variety to produce a facial anti-ageing cream, and sold thousands of pots of this cream in the market, he would not have infringed the rights of the breeder who developed the coconut variety. The oil of the protected coconut variety is not *reproductive* or *vegetative propagating material*.

As such, at a Union Conference it was suggested that PBRs as offered by UPOV 1978 were not sufficient protection to breeders and they should be expanded to enhance the quality of their protection.[38] In this sense, it was recommended that "the effect of the rights granted to the breeder shall be that his prior authorisation shall be required for the production, offering for sale, placing on the market, use of any kind, importation or holding for the above mentioned purposes of plant material of the variety."[39] UPOV 1991 adopted this recommendation as shall be shown in the following section.[40]

Apart from the limitations found in its scope, UPOV 1978 contains what is known as a *research exemption*. Through this exemption a protected variety is freely available for further research and breeding.[41] Therefore, no authorisation is required from the breeder to market a variety developed as a result of research using the

---

[32] Article 4(1) of UPOV 1978 states "This Convention may be applied to all botanical genera and species"; see supra Note 15.
[33] Idem; Article 4(2).
[34] See Hassan, Sandro; "Ornamental Plant Variety Rights: A Recent Italian Judgement"; 18(2) IIC, 1987; pp. 219-222.
[35] UPOV 1978; supra Note 15; Article 5(1).
[36] Straus, Joseph; "Protection of Inventions in Plants"; 20(5) IIC, 1989; at p. 619.
[37] Straus, Joseph; "The Relationship Between Plant Variety Protection and Patent Protection for Biotechnological Inventions from an International Viewpoint"; 18(6)IIC 723, 1987; at p. 725.
[38] See Greengrass, Barry; "UPOV and the Protection of Plant Breeders - Past Developments, Future Perspectives"; 20(5) IIC, 1989; at pp. 622-636.
[39] UPOV Doc. CAJ/XVIII/6 of July 31, 1986, Appendix – Draft recommendation on the extension and harmonisation of the rights afforded to breeders.
[40] UPOV 1991; supra Note 15; Article 14.
[41] UPOV 1978; Idem; Article 5(3).

protected variety as the primary source.[42] Authorisation is only required if the repeated use of the protected variety is required to produce another variety that is commercialised.[43]

The research exemption, also known as *breeders' exemption*, emerged so that the common practice of using protected plant varieties for further development of new varieties would not be considered a violation of the PBRs.[44] Its existence "prevents the monopolisation of a particular breeding aim. Only the specific variety as such is protected and not the breeding method, nor crops' ingredients or particular traits like disease resistance. Therefore any breeder can follow new developments, without infringing the rights of the previous breeder."[45]

The research exemption of UPOV 1978 did not satisfy everyone. Bernhard Roth, for instance, completely opposed it. "In a relatively short time after the resistant variety has first appeared on market, it is possible for others freely to develop other varieties having the same resistance by using the resistant variety in their breeding work and then, without paying any compensation to the originator of the first variety, commercialise the new variety freely. This is by no means a desirable and equitable situation. Doing the same thing in other technical fields would normally be considered an infringement of property rights."[46] This research exemption was not included in UPOV 1991.

Restrictions in the exercise of rights protected can be applied for reasons of public interest.[47] One could, therefore, imagine that a PBR conferred with respect to a new variety of maize, wheat or rice could be restricted in its scope to protect the general interest of the public which use them intensely for the production of food. So far the public interest restriction has not been used in this way. On the contrary, UPOV 1991 expanded the scope of PBRs and thus, the monopoly granted to breeders over their developed variety is more extensive, even if the variety is an agricultural plant commonly demanded as a source of food. This shall be shown in the Chapter dealing with Farmer's Rights.

2.4- Double Protection

When drafting UPOV 1978, there was a fear of a conflict between the UPOV and the patent systems regarding the requirements and rights under each one.[48] Most European countries at that time excluded from their patent laws either all plants or those that were protectable under the country's breeders' protection law.[49] However, at that time the United States legislation allowed parallel protection for plant varieties. Consequently, due to the influence and pressure of the United States, and in order to

---

[42] Idem.
[43] Idem.
[44] UPOV 1961 also contains the research exemption. See Article 5(3) of UPOV 1961; supra Note 15.
[45] Ghijsen, Huib; supra Note 6; at p. 4.
[46] Roth, Bernhard; "Current Problems in the Protection of Inventions in the Field of Plant Biotechnology – A Position Paper"; 18(1) IIC 41, 1987; at p.51.
[47] UPOV 1978; supra Note 15; Article 9(1).
[48] Remarks o the Representative of BIRPI (forerunner of WIPO) in "Copte Rendu des Travaux du Comité Général, du Comité Juridique , du Comité de Rédaction et du Comité ad hoc pour l Redaction de l'Article 14"; in "Actes des Conférences Internationales pour la Protection des Obtentions Végétales 1957-1961, 1972" (Geneva, 1974); at p. 119.
[49] Czechoslovakia (1921), Holland (1946) and Austria (1946) pursued systems to protect plant varieties. France (1922) and Germany (1934) had enacted not only plant breeders' laws but had also granted utility patents on plants. Italy (1951) did not have a plant breeders' law but, nevertheless, issued utility patent for plants.

facilitate its accession to UPOV 1978, a proviso to soften the ban against double protection[50] was adopted. Thus, Article 37(1), allowed States that provided for double protection on plant varieties to continue doing so by notifying the Secretary-General of that fact when they signed or ratified the act.[51]

2.5 - Duration of Protection

The UPOV 1978 determined that the period of protection may be no less than eighteen years for vines, forest trees, fruit trees and ornamental trees computed from the date of issue of the title of protection and no less than fifteen years for other plant varieties.[52]

2.6 – Conclusion

According to UPOV 1978, authorisation of the breeder is not required for the production of propagating material that is not for commercial marketing. Under this provision, farmers can save seeds gathered from the harvest of a protected variety. The authorisation of the breeder is also unnecessary for the use of a protected variety as the initial variation for creating other new varieties and marketing them. Nevertheless, Member States to UPOV 1978 are allowed to grant more extensive rights to breeders under their national laws.

After more than ten years operating UPOV 1978, and analysing the effects of its provisions, the Union believed that it should be revised to strengthen the protection offered to the breeder. UPOV 1991 thus expanded the scope of PBRs on the international level.[53]

3 - UPOV ACT OF 1991

3.1 - Introduction

UPOV 1991 Convention came into force 24 April 1998. On that date, UPOV 1978 was officially closed for further accession with the exception to those States that had already started their accession process.[54] Those countries were given one year to complete their accession under UPOV 1978. This was the case of Brazil among others.[55]

3.2 - Conditions for the Grant of the PBRs

---

[50] See UPOV 1978; supra Note 15; Article 2(1).
[51] Idem; Article 37(1).
[52] Idem; Article 8.
[53] For comments on the revision process, see Greengrass, Barry; supra Note 38. For an analysis of the major substantive changes made on UPOV 1978 see Greengrass, B.; "The 1991 Act of the UPOV Convention"; 13(12) EIPR, December 1991; pp. 466-472.
[54] See UPOV Press Release, No. 32, 28 September 1998; UPOV, Geneva. Available at http://www.upov.int/eng/prssrlss/32.htm; available in 2000.
[55] Belarus, Bolivia, China, Croatia, Kenya, Morocco, Nicaragua, Panama, Venezuela and Zimbabwe were also given the right to complete the accession to UPOV 1978 in one year.

UPOV 1991 defines a variety as "a plant grouping within a single botanical taxon of the lowest known rank, which grouping, irrespective of whether the conditions for the grant of PBRs are fully met, can be

- defined by the expression of the characteristics resulting from a given genotype or combination of genotypes,
- distinguished from any other plant grouping by the expression of at least one of the said characteristics and
- considered as a unit with regard to its suitability for being propagated unchanged."[56]

The conditions for the grant of PBRs in UPOV 1991 are practically the same as those in UPOV 1978. UPOV 1991 states that to be protected under a breeder's right the variety must be *new, distinct, uniform*[57] and *stable*.[58]

3.3 - Scope of Protection

The scope of protection of PBRs in UPOV 1991 is wider than the scope of UPOV 1978. According to UPOV 1991, the following acts in respect of the propagating material of the protected variety are dependent on the authorisation of the breeder:

(i) production or reproduction (multiplication),
(ii) conditioning for the purpose of propagation,
(iii) offering for sale,
(iv) selling or other marketing,
(v) exporting
(vi) importing
(vii) stocking for any of the purposes mentioned in (i) to (vi), above.[59]

Member States to UPOV 1991 are also allowed to extend the scope of PBRs to other acts not listed above.[60] The acts listed in Article 14(1)(a) also refer to the whole or part of harvested material of protected plants, obtained through the unauthorised use of propagating material.[61] Thus, it is apparent that the breeder is given full commercial control over the propagating material of his variety.[62] Additionally, Members may extend the authorisation of the breeder to acts relating to products made directly from harvested material derived from the unauthorised use of propagating material. For this to be valid, the use of the harvested material must have been unauthorised and the breeder must not have had reasonable opportunity to exercise his right in relation to the said harvested material.[63]

---

[56] UPOV 1991; supra Note 15; Article 1(vi).
[57] UPOV 1978 uses the word homogeneous instead of uniform.
[58] See UPOV 1991; supra Note 15; Article 5.
[59] Idem; Article 14(1)(a).
[60] Idem; Article 14(4).
[61] Idem; Article 14(2).
[62] See Gaia Foundation and GRAIN; "Ten reasons not to join UPOV"; Global Trade in Conflict, No. 2; London/Barcelona; May 1998. Located at: http://www.grain.org/publications/gtbc/issue2.htm; accessed in June 1998.
[63] UPOV 1991; supra Note 15; Article 14(3).

Furthermore, under UPOV 1991, the scope of the PBRs extends to:

1- varieties which are essentially derived from the protected variety;
2- varieties which are not clearly distinguishable from the protected variety;
3- varieties whose production requires the repeated use of the protected variety.[64]

In other words, UPOV 1991 has given breeders the opportunity to gain total monopoly not only over their own variety, but likewise, over the subsequent varieties developed from their variety if the derived variety is commercialised. The breeder of an essentially derived variety can be granted a PBR, but cannot exploit his variety without the authorisation of the breeder of the initial variety.

Certainly Roth would probably have approved this extensive monopoly conferred to breeders through the 1991 UPOV provisions. In regard to UPOV 1978, he emphasised that Article 5(3), which permits the creation and marketing of varieties derived from protected varieties "should be reviewed at least as regards the presently allowed free use of the newly developed varieties. Either this possibility under Article 5(3) should be abolished completely or, if not, it should only come into effect after a certain number of years (e.g. 10 years after grant) at least as far as free commercialisation is concerned."[65] It is noteworthy, however, that if varieties are not essentially derived from the initial variety, authorisation of the first breeder shall not be necessary for all the acts referred to in Article 14(1)(a) of UPOV 1991 in relation to the new varieties.

With a view to deepen insights into the concept of essentially derived varieties, if oral traditional knowledge were part of the filter of common knowledge to test for a variety's distinctness, traditional varieties with only a slight biotechnological modification would be considered essentially derived from the traditionally bred one. Yet, even if this argument were valid it probably would not prevent the former one from being protected under a PBR and the breeder freely exercising his right because traditional varieties are not protectable under PBRs or patents.

UPOV 1991, however, does provide for three compulsory exceptions to the breeder's right by stating that the it does not extend to:

(i) acts done privately and for non-commercial purposes,
(ii) acts done for experimental purposes and
(iii) acts done for the purpose of breeding other varieties.[66]

UPOV 1991 allows States to adopt an optional exception to PBRs, within reasonable limits, and subject to the safeguarding of the legitimate interest of the breeder, in order to permit farmers to re-use harvested material from a protected variety.[67] This is commonly known as "farmers' privilege". Farmers' privilege allows farmers to save and re-use, for the next season's sowing, harvested material, such as seeds, derived from the utilisation of a breeder's plant variety material or seed. Farmer's privilege is not an explicit right in UPOV 1978 because the scope of PBRs

---

[64] Idem; Article 14(5)(a).
[65] Roth, Bernhard; supra Note 46; at p.51.
[66] UPOV 1991; supra Note 15; Article 15(1).
[67] Idem; Article 15(2).

under that Act does not cover harvested material. Consequently, there was technically no reason to institutionalise a possibility for farmers to sow again the protected variety using the seed harvested from the plantation of the protected variety.

It is essential to bear in mind that even if a State Party allows its farmers to save and re-use the seed exclusively on his own holding, this privilege is still subject to *reasonable limits* and to the *legitimate interest of the breeder*. Thus, a Member willing to balance the rights of farmers with those of breeders, may shape appropriate perceptions and attitudes in order to provide a narrow interpretation to what it understands as being *reasonable limits*.

This holds true not only in regard to farmers' privilege, but also with respect to Article 17(1) of UPOV 1991 which determines that apart from the provisions which expressly limit PBRs, there is no reason other than public interest to restrict the free exercise of a breeder's right.[68] Where the public interest is invoked and when a third party is authorised to perform any act for which the breeder's authorisation is required, the breeder has the right to be ensured an equitable remuneration.[69] Although the very aim of this provision is to ensure compensation to breeders, Members could give the concept of public interest a wide interpretation. According to this understanding, the greater the public interest to restrict the exercise of a breeder's right, less would be the compensation owed to the breeder.

3.4 - Double Protection

UPOV has been expanding its provisions and becoming more lenient with regard to double protection. UPOV 1978 forbade double protection in Article 2(1) and allowed a waiver against that ban in Article 37(1). UPOV 1991, goes further and deletes Article 2(1) and consequently, removes the need for Article 37(1). Crespi justified the need for double protection by stating that "a single plant can be a member of particular variety as to its phenotype and at the same time contain a specific functional genetic element by virtue of which it is an embodiment of a patented invention."[70] On the other hand, there are those who acknowledge that patents on plant varieties may prohibit access to propagating material to breed new varieties.[71] Likewise, "if modified plant cells are patented, any plant composed of those cells would infringe the patent."[72]

Thus, State Parties of UPOV 1991 that do not agree with the patenting of plant varieties, genes or gene sequences may exclude from patentability all substances that exist in nature, biological or not, including those that have been isolated and purified.[73] By taking this measure, they can maintain the ban on double protection and determine that the only form of plant variety protection is PBRs.[74]

3.5 - Duration of Protection

---

[68] Idem; Article 17(1).
[69] Idem; Article 17(2).
[70] Crespi, Stephen; "Patents and Plant Variety Rights: Is There an Interface Problem?"; 23(2) IIC 168, 1992; at p. 183.
[71] Correa, Carlos; Intellectual Property Rights and WTO and Developing Countries; Zed books; London; 2000; at p. 177.
[72] Idem.
[73] Idem; at p. 228.
[74] This is the case of Brazil. See Chapter Eight of this book.

The duration of PBRs was expanded in the UPOV 1991 to a period not shorter than 20 years from the date of the grant of the breeder's right.[75] In the case of trees and vines, the duration of the breeder's right is to be no shorter than 25 years from the said date.[76]

3.6 – Conclusion

UPOV 1991 strengthens protection afforded to breeders by including under the scope of PBRs harvested products, including entire plants and parts of plants and essentially derived varieties. Furthermore, States are allowed to include end products of harvested materials as well. According to the Union, the stronger protection offered by UPOV 1991 to breeders is an incentive for plant breeding. "Experience has shown that it is not possible for a breeder to recover his financial investment when he sells his initial supplies in the first years of a new variety's life. The breeder's competitors can secure supplies of propagating material and in a short time compete with him profiting from his many years of breeding effort. It may take between 10 and 20 years to develop new varieties in many species."[77]

With the inclusion of harvested material under PBRs, it became imperative to include the concept of farmers' privilege in the key provisions of UPOV 1991 even though Member States are not obliged to adopt it in their national laws. However, Crucible Group believes that "farmers have the absolute right to save seed, to experiment with exotic germplasm, and to exchange seed with neighbouring communities. To deny these rights is to cut the heart out of global conservation and enhancement of plant biodiversity."[78]

4 - DIFFERENCES AND SIMILARITIES BETWEEN PBRS AND PATENT RIGHTS

Following the example of the Paris Convention, UPOV grants reciprocal rights to national and foreign applicants. A Member State must offer to foreigners the same treatment and terms of protection, and for the same species of plants, as to its nationals.[79]

The Right of Priority is also a general rule in the UPOV, the origins of which can be found in the Paris Convention.[80] For a period of twelve months, this right allows the breeder to use the date of his first application in one of the Member States as the filing date of a subsequent application in another Member State of the UPOV.[81]

UPOV 1978 provides a difference between PBRs and patents which, however, was reduced by UPOV 1991. According to UPOV 1978, breeders have the exclusive right only over the production, sale and marketing of the reproductive or vegetative propagating material of the variety. Thus, a breeder cannot prevent someone from exporting or importing the propagating material and cannot prevent someone from

---

[75] UPOV 1991; supra Note 15; Article 19(2).
[76] Idem.
[77] UPOV; "The Need for Legal Protection for New Plant Varieties"; located at: http://www.upov.int/eng/content.htm; accessed in August 1999.
[78] Crucible Group; People, plants, and patents: the impact of intellectual property on biodiversity, conservation, trade, and rural society; Ottawa, Canada; IDRC; 1994; at p. 87.
[79] See Article 3(1) and 3(2) of UPOV 1978 and Article 4(1) of UPOV 1991; supra Note 15.
[80] Article 4(a)(1) of the Paris Convention. See Chapter Two of this book.
[81] Article 12(1) of UPOV 1978 and Article 11(1) in UPOV 1991; supra Note 15.

marketing parts of the protected variety which are not propagating material. Patent rights, on the other hand, confer exclusive rights on any direct or indirect exploitation of the subject matter.

An illusory difference between patents and PBRs lies in the disclosure requirement. The disclosure requirement for PBRs can be fulfilled by the applicant providing sufficient details to prove that his variety is clearly distinct from all known varieties in at least one important characteristic. The deposit of the variety is also valid for the examination of the application.[82] On the other hand, in patent systems the disclosure of the patented invention must be described clearly enough to enable a person with ordinary skill in the art to develop it.[83] However, nowadays, the disclosure requirement to patent plant varieties is satisfied with the deposit of the plant variety as a substitute to the written description. Thus, it is apparent that patents and PBR are quite similar in the disclosure requirement. This does not mean, however, that the other conditions of protection are similar.

As for patents, an invention must be new, involve an inventive step and capable of industrial application. The requirements for PBRs are that the plant variety be new, distinct, homogeneous and stable. At first sight one might believe that both forms of protection have the novelty requirement in common. However, for PBRs the novelty of the variety is determined on the basis that the propagating or harvesting material has not been offered for sale or marketed with the consent of the breeder. According to patents, an invention is new if it does not form part of the state of art.[84]

Another difference is that the UPOV Convention allows exceptions to the breeder's right, such as acts done for experimental purposes, as well as those done privately with non-commercial purposes. Patents do not offer any exception to their rights apart from compulsory licences.

Notwithstanding these differences showed above, slowly, but steadily, PBRs are becoming more similar to rights conferred under patent laws. UPOV 1991 expands the protective scope of PBRs to give exclusive rights on the direct or indirect exploitation of the plant variety. It is clear that the protection granted by UPOV 1991 regarding monopoly rights over the protected plant variety has become more similar to the exclusive rights conferred upon the patentee through patents.

A wording difference between PBRs and patents can be easily found in the definition of "breeder". According UPOV 1991, "breeder" means

> - the person who bred, or *discovered* and developed, a variety.[85] (emphasis added).

It is essential to bear in mind that this definition makes PBRs more suitable than patents to protect plant varieties because plants cannot be invented. Plants can be discovered in nature and can be bred through natural or biotechnological methods to develop new varieties. However, they are not "invented" for the simple reason that nobody can invent life. Theoretically, patents are not allowed for discoveries, only inventions.[86] However, the international analysis provided for in the previous Chapter reveals that patents in major developed countries have been granted to isolated

---

[82] UPOV 1991; Idem; Article 12.
[83] See Elias, Stephen; Patent, Copyright and Trademark; Nolo Press; Berkeley, US; 1997; at p. 218.
[84] See Chapter Two of this book.
[85] UPOV 1991; supra Note 15; Article 1(iv).
[86] Article 27(1) of TRIPs. See Chapter Two of this book.

genes.[87] Although such achievements were reached through a high input of research and scientific knowledge, the isolated gene is still a discovery.

Tewolde Berhan Gebre Egziabher offers an interesting comment on the patenting of living organisms. He states: "I introduce genes or traits into an organism only if they already exist as such in another organism or organisms. Therefore breeding and genetic engineering reorganise something existing: they do not create anything *de novo*. [...] Even they would only claim that their creativity is reflected in the living thing not that they have made it. [...] If they want reward, they could ask society to develop a system appropriate for their role in the improvement that comes from reorganising. [...] Patenting seems totally inapplicable to life. If we want to reward researchers in the life sciences, we must find another system."[88] As wisely noted, UPOV and patent laws seem to "overlook the fact that these resources did not originate entirely in the laboratory."[89]

Additionally, it must be emphasised that frequently the protection granted to breeders over plant varieties does not consider the "piracy" of traditional knowledge, farmers' and indigenous bred varieties[90] or those stored in international gene banks.[91] When these are the cases, the pirated varieties and knowledge should neither be patented nor protected under PBRs as if they had been developed by the applicant. This merit, if granted to anyone, should be to the true discoverers and traditional developers.

The following section shall exemplify cases of plant piracy in Australia.

5 - PLANT PIRACY IN AUSTRALIA

One of the major inequities and problems of the PBRs and patent protection is that many have been granted to plant varieties acquired from the Consultative Group on International Agricultural Research,[92] (hereinafter CGIAR). According to the Rural Advancement Foundation International (hereafter RAFI)[93], several of these of these now protected varieties are in fact landraces[94] with minimal if any modification. The most widely discussed case in this sense occurred in Australia.[95]

---

[87] See Chapter Two of this book..
[88] Egziabher, Tewolde; "Patenting Life is Owning Life"; Available on http://:www.org.sg/souths/twn/focus.htm; accessed in July 1999. Also available in Third World Resurgence No. 106; June 1999. Tewolde Egziabher is the General Manager of the Environmental Protection Authority in Ethiopia. At the Biosafety negotiations, he was the Chairperson of the African group of delegates.
[89] School of International and Public Affairs Columbia University; supra Note 2; at p.6.
[90] Mooney, Pat; "The Parts of Life. Agricultural Biodiversity, Indigenous Knowledge, and the Role of the Third System"; Development Dialogue, Special Issue; 1998; at pp. 152-154.
[91] The UN Food and Agriculture Organisation and the Consultative Group on International Agricultural Research (CGIAR) called for a moratorium on patents related to germplasm held in trust in international gene banks around the world. See CGIAR Press Release; 11 February 1998.
[92] See Chapter Four of this book.
[93] RAFI is a non-profit international civil society organisation with headquarters in Canada. It dedicates its work to the social and economic impact of new technologies on rural societies.
[94] Landrace is "a variety of a crop plant that has arisen by selection over time by indigenous farmers, and is thus adapted to local conditions." Laurence, E., Jackson, A, Jackson, J.; Longman Dictionary of Environmental Science; Longman; Essex, England; 1998.
[95] See RAFI; "Aussies 'pirate' others genius?"; Press release, 1 February 1998. RAFI; "Doing Well by Doing Little or Nothing? A partial list of varieties under RAFI investigation"; 1998. RAFI; "The Australian PBR scandal: UPOV meets a scandal 'down under' by burying its head in the sand"; RAFI Communique January-February 1998; All RAFI articles in this Chapter could be accessed in September 2000 on RAFI website http://www.rafi.org.

In January 1998, RAFI challenged the claim deposited at Australia's Plant Breeders' Rights Office (hereafter the APBRO) for plant breeder's right on two chickpea varieties taken from the International Crops Research Institute from the Semi-Arid Tropics (hereafter ICRISAT).[96] This challenge led RAFI and the Australian Heritage Seed Curators (hereafter HSCA)[97] into investigating other possible abuses of PBRs in Australia. The final results revealed that at least 118 PBRs may be illegitimate,[98] in other words, taken from CGIAR centres, such as the ICRISAT, or from developing countries.[99]

After this report, APBRO has adopted new measures to prevent further pirated plant varieties from being granted plant patents. Breeders now applying for PBRs in Australia must reveal the origins of the variety and identify its "parent breeding stock."[100] Moreover, applicants for PBRs must submit their varieties to field trials to prove that they are different from their parent lines. This measure was adopted following the HSCA/RAFI report which discovered that 29% of the dubious claims failed to show that their variety was clearly distinguishable from their foreign introduced parents. And finally, provisional protection to applicants waiting to be granted PBRs was limited to a two-year period. This restriction was to stop applicants who, once they gained provisional protection, neglected to present further evidence necessary for PBRs to be granted.[101]

All of these new regulatory changes adopted by the APBRO are not retroactive and thus, concern only new applications. The APBRO has still not acted to investigate these charges and nullify the piracy claims. It has dictated a fee of US $50,000 to be paid by HSCA for the re-examination process of the 118 disputed claims to be opened however, the HSCA is a small civil society organisation and cannot afford to pay this fee. So far less than a dozen of the varieties cited in the HSCA/RAFI study have been cancelled. However, these initiatives were due to the voluntary withdrawal by the applicant.[102]

Under the Australian Trade Practices Act, it is possible for customers who have been paying the breeder to use seeds that are in fact part of the public domain, to sue the owner of the PBR for making false and misleading claims. The owner of the PBR could possibly blame the APBRO for authorising the claims. Due to this hassle, the APBRO has been placing obstacles in the form of high re-examination fees to avoid the initiation of the re-examination process.

Apart from the ICRISAT chickpeas, another of the cases that should be re-examined involves a waratah, (*Telopea speciosissima*), which is an Australian

---

[96] GRAIN; "The Chickpea Scandal: Trust or Consequences?"; Seedling; March 1998; located at http://www.grain.org. RAFI, "Recent Australian Claims to Indian and Iranian Chickpeas Countered by NGOs and ICRISAT"; News Release 1/6/98. See also RAFI; "International Research Centre (ICARDA) Breaks Trust"; News Release 2/2/98; http://www.rafi.org.
[97] HSCA is a non-profit association of heritage seed curators based in Bairnsdale in the state of Victoria, Australia. It works for the conservation and sustainable use of plant genetic resources for food and agriculture around the world.
[98] HSCA/RAFI Report "Plant Breeders' Wrongs"; 16 September 1998. Cited in RAFI News Release; "Plant Breeders' Wrongs Righted in Australia"; 11 November 1998; supra Note 95.
[99] RAFI; "Australia's Unresolved Plant Piracy Problems"; RAFI News 4/12/99; Idem.
[100] See the Australian Government's Plant Variety Journal, Vol. 11, no. 3, 1998.
[101] HSCA/RAFI Report "Plant Breeders' Wrongs"; revealed that 16% of the 118 dubious claims were abuses of this kind; supra Note 98.
[102] In one of the Australian plant breeder's right certificate that was abandoned the applicant refers to a "barnyard millet collected in a market in Pakistan in 1954". The applicant was the St. Lucia, Queensland research station of Commonwealth Scientific and Industrial Research Organisation which was granted a plant breeder's right certificate in Australia in 1995.

ornamental crimson-flowered shrub, colloquially known as, "Pope's Weromba Cardinal". This plant species is the official floral emblem of the Australian state of New South Wales.

There is sufficient evidence that this plant variety dates back at least to 1955. At that date, it grew from a seed planted by Miss Lucelle Pope in her garden at Weromba in New South Wales.[103] The plant, which had impressive flowers, caught the attention of a nurseryman, who took cuttings from the plant. In 1988, he published an article where he described the plant and showed a picture of Miss Pope in front of the plant in her garden. Many propagations of the plant were made in the late 1980s and early 1990s. However, in 1994, after Miss Pope had died, the nurseryman applied for a PBR on the variety that he had asexually reproduced. The PBR was granted in 1997.

The UPOV Convention determines that a variety must be distinct for the breeder to be granted a PBR. This means that the variety must be distinguishable by one or more important characteristics from any other variety known including in a reference collection or precisely described in a publication. The PBR granted to the nurseryman neglected these rules.

The PBRs erroneously granted in Australia provide proof that such monopoly protection, as well as patents, are in fact rewarding biopiracies. Furthermore, they reveal that both the country of origin and the farmers that traditionally bred the varieties are completely excluded from any form of benefit-sharing of the profits derived from their plant varieties. The only ones enjoying such profits are the ones that committed the fraud.

In response to this Australian scandal, the CGIAR called for a moratorium on any form of intellectual property protection over plant germplasm held in CGIAR centres.[104]

6 - GENERAL CONCLUSION

UPOV 1961 was adopted to provide for the first time the international recognition of PBRs. At that time plant breeders found it impossible to comply with the patent requirements of inventiveness and written disclosure of how to make and use the plant variety. UPOV 1978 revised UPOV 1961 and placed limited access restrictions to protected seed. UPOV 1978 provided for a research exemption and allows farmers to collect and plant the seed of protected varieties. On the other hand, UPOV 1991 expands the scope of PBRs to cover not only the propagating material of the protected variety, but likewise, the harvested material obtained through unauthorised use of the said material. As a refuge to such provisions, State Parties have the choice of adopting the farmers' exemption to allow farmers to save seed harvested from the protected variety.

UPOV 1991 also determines that PBRs may fall on varieties that are essentially derived from the protected variety allowing the former to be protected but submitting their commercialisation to the authorisation of the breeder of the original protected variety. Moreover, it allows patents to co-exist with PBR claiming this will

---

[103] RAFI; supra Note 99.
[104] See, RAFI; "CGIAR Urges Halt to Granting of Intellectual Property Rights for Designated Plant Germplasm"; posted on Web 11 February 1998; supra Note 95.

stimulate more research and progress in the field of plant biotechnology and variety development.

With UPOV 1991, agricultural developing countries have started to fear that the next UPOV amendment will determine patents on plants as a rule. As was shown in the former Chapter, TRIPs does not oblige countries to adopt patents for plant varieties but obliges States otherwise to adopt a *sui generis* system to protect them.[105] At the moment, UPOV 1991 is the only international *sui generis* system that specifically protects plant varieties.[106] Nevertheless, States should avoid adhering to UPOV 1991 and alternatively adopt another *sui generis* system that harmonises the rights of breeders with those of farmers, indigenous peoples and local communities who are traditional breeders.

Most developing countries have farmers who traditionally select the desired traits of their plantations through traditional and natural breeding of seed or propagating material. Many traditional crops such as the Neem tree and the Basmati rice have been patented in the USA. On one side there is a need to recognise and compensate biotechnological breeding investments. On the other side, there is an urgent need to stop biopiracy and recognise and reward those that have been traditionally breeding plants for centuries and have thus expanded the world's genetic diversity. The work of traditional farmers has been described as the "longest running and most innovative human research project to date."[107] Superior agricultural products have been "painstakingly accomplished through cross fertilisation and progressive plant and animal selection with the hope that the desired characteristics of the selected parent will surface in its offspring."[108]

As noted by the Union, "The benefits to be derived from the classical selection procedures of plant breeders and from the new biotechnologies are cumulative. The one cannot replace the other. It is accordingly in the interest of society to ensure that systems of incentive be continued or created to encourage investment in both the new biotechnologies and classical plant breeding."[109] Although this is the goal, the following Chapter shall explore farmers' rights and the inequity they suffer in comparison to the rights granted to breeders.

---

[105] Article 27(3)(b) of TRIPs.
[106] See GRAIN; "UPOV: Getting a Free Trips Ride?"; 13(6) Seedling, 1996. Located at: http://www.grain.org/publications/seedling.htm; accessed in 1996.
[107] See Gaia Foundation and GRAIN; supra Note 62.
[108] Scalise, David and Nugent, Daniel; "International Intellectual Property Protections for Living Matter: Biotechnology, Multinational Conventions and the Exception for Agriculture"; 27 Case W. Res. J. Int'l Law 83, 1995; at p. 83.
[109] UPOV; "Modern Biotechnology"; located at: http://www.upov.int/eng/content.htm; accessed in 2000.

CHAPTER FOUR

FAO GLOBAL SYSTEM FOR THE CONSERVATION AND UTILISATION OF PLANT GENETIC RESOURCES FOR FOOD AND AGRICULTURE

1 - GENERAL INTRODUCTION

The Food and Agriculture Organisation (hereinafter FAO), FAO, is the specialised agency of the United Nations responsible for matters involving global food and agriculture, including forestry and fisheries. It is the primary organisation responsible for the global conservation of plant genetic resources (hereafter PGRs). Since 1983, it has been developing a Global System for the Conservation and Utilisation of Plant Genetic Resources for Food and Agriculture (hereinafter the Global System) to internationally conserve and sustainably utilise those resources at the molecular, population, species and agroecosystem levels. Its objectives also include the sharing of the benefits and burdens which arise from the conservation and utilisation of plant genetic resources for food and agriculture (hereinafter PGRFA).

PGRFA are vital to the human race and must be wisely used to cope with the fast growing world population.[1] Every person's livelihood is directly or indirectly supported by such resources. The conservation and sustainable utilisation of PGRFA contributes to national and international development, food security and the alleviation of poverty around the planet.[2] In this field, there are many stakeholders directly involved with PGRFA which pursue their own individual and important roles in the task of better conserving and utilising these resources, *inter alia*, farmers and breeders.[3]

Over the years, the FAO has initiated, in co-operation with other organisations, a series of international technical conferences and meetings on PGRs.[4] On these occasions, concepts and applications of PGRFA, as well as international instruments, codes of practice and guidelines for the sustainable utilisation of PGRs have been developed and adopted.

---

[1] "Eight hundred million people are undernourished and 200 million children under five years of age are underweight. In the next thirty years, the world's population is expected to grow by over 2 500 million to reach 8 500 million." Background Documentation for the International Technical Conference on Plant Genetic Resources, (hereafter Background Documentation); Leipzig, Germany; 17-23 June 1996; at p. 1. It is based on information collected by the Secretariat for the International Technical Conference on Plant Genetic Resources from the 157 Country Reports, the database of the FAO World Information and Early Warning System, the agricultural research centres of the CGIAR, over 50 NGOs, including private sector associations, and numerous individual specialists. See FAO ITCPGR/96/ REP; Report of the International Technical Conference on Plant Genetic Resources; Leipzig, Germany; 17-23 June 1996; at p. 4.
[2] Background Documentation; Idem; at p. 1.
[3] The range of people involved in the conservation and utilisation of PGRFA includes policy makers, planners, scientists, germplasm curators, breeders, rural communities, and farmers. Idem.
[4] See First International Meeting on Crop Genetic Resources; 1961; FAO, Rome. First International Technical Conference on Plant Genetic Resources; 1967; FAO, Rome. Frankel, Otto; "Genetic Resources: The founding years. I. Early beginnings 1961-1966"; 7 Diversity, 1985; pp 26-29. Frankel, O. H.; "Genetic Resources: The founding years. II. The movement's constituent assembly"; 8 Diversity, 1985; pp 30-32. Frankel, O. H.; "Genetic Resources: The founding years. III. The long road to international board"; 9 Diversity, 1986; pp 30-33. Frankel, O. H.; "Genetic Resources: Evolutionary and Social Responsibilities"; in Kloppenburg, Jack Jr. (ed); Seeds and Sovereignty - The Use and Control of Plant Genetic Resources; Duke University Press; London; 1988; at p. 22. Second International Conference on Plant Genetic Resources; 1973; FAO, Rome.

The main institutional components of the Global System are the intergovernmental Commission on Genetic Resources for Food and Agriculture[5] (hereafter CGRFA) and the International Undertaking on Plant Genetic Resources (hereafter IU).[6]

In recent years, in an attempt to become fully operational and in harmony with the Convention on Biological Diversity, principles have been introduced into the Global System context to clarify or revise its original provisions in harmony with binding international instruments which have been adopted subsequently, in particular, the UPOV Acts, and TRIPs.[7] These international instruments provide exclusively for the rights of plant variety breeders and, as such, an evident inequity between farmers and breeders has emerged. "The major factor driving genetic erosion is that traditional farmers who develop and conserve agrobiodiversity, are generating a 'public good', without adequate incentives. They are producing global values for which they obtain no return."[8] On the other hand, breeders are granted plant variety protection rights or patent rights over the plant varieties they develop.

Global food security is threatened by the patenting of plant varieties and other plant variety protection systems such as the UPOV. The free flow of plant genetic resources for food and agriculture is restrained by the barrier of patents or UPOV regulations. Furthermore, plant breeder's varieties, which are genetically uniform cultivars, are depleting genetic raw material by replacing wild varieties on the fields. Due to the vulnerability of these genetically uniform cultivars, a natural disaster, e.g. pest or drought, could cause, and has caused, the total loss of crops, enhancing poverty instead of alleviating it. Patents have even been conceded to plant varieties that are likely to cause great damage to the environment, as in the case of the patent granted to Monsanto's transgenic soy bean.

Facing the urgent need to control this process of extinction, the Consultative Group on International Agricultural Research,[9] (hereinafter CGIAR), established in 1974 the International Board for Plant Genetic Resources (hereinafter IBPGR)[10] as an independent board with a secretariat supplied by FAO. Through the IBPGR

---

[5] One hundred and sixty countries are members of the CGRFA and stand on an equal footing in debates: "one country, one vote." Brazil is a member since August 1984. See CGRFA web homepage: http://www.cgrfa.org; available in May 2000.
[6] The International Undertaking on Plant Genetic Resources was adopted by FAO Resolution 8/83 of the FAO Conference in 1983. So far 113 countries have adhered to the International Undertaking. Brazil has not adhered to it and neither has the United States. For a list of countries that have adhered to the IU see http://www.fao.org/ag/cgrfa/memC.htm#iu; available in May 2000.
[7] See Document C 95/INF/19 of the Conference of the FAO, Progress Report on the Global System for the Conservation and Utilisation of Plant Genetic Resources for Food and Agriculture, 28th Session, 20 October-2 November 1995. Other international agreements which are part of the FAO Global System include the Conference Resolutions on Farmers' rights; the International Code of Conduct for Plant Germplasm Collecting and Transfer; a World Information and Early Warning System on Plant Genetic Resources; Draft Code of Conduct on Biotechnology; the Report of the State of the World's Plant Genetic Resources; the Global Plan of Action; and the International Fund for the implementation of Farmers' rights. For a more complete description of the FAO Global System, see Article 7 of the FAO International Undertaking. See also, Document CPGR-6/95/4 of the Commission on Plant Genetic Resources.
[8] Background Documentation; supra Note 1; at p. 25.
[9] The CGIAR was established in 1971. It describes itself as trustee of global germplasm holdings with the whole world community as beneficiaries. CGIAR; "On Intellectual Property, Biosafety and Plant Genetic Resources"; CGIAR Discussion Paper; 1992; at p. 2; cited in Rose, G.; "International Regimes for the Conservation and Control of Plant Genetic Resources"; in Bowman, Michael and Redgwell, Catherine (eds); International Law and the Conservation of Biological Diversity; Kluwer Law International; London; 1996; at p. 158. The CGIAR is composed of an informal group of donor agencies and developing country members, and is sponsored by the World Bank, FAO, the United Nation Environmental Programme, and the United Nations Development Programme. See Frankel, Otto; supra Note 4; at p. 27.
[10] The International Plant Genetic Resources Institute (IPGRI) is the legal successor to IBPGR.

international plant genetic resources programme, gene banks were constructed and expanded at national, regional and international levels, and the collection of PGRs was accelerated.

The purpose of this Chapter is to show that the Global System is constrained by other international instruments from reaching its objectives of national development, global food security and the alleviation of poverty. The IU will be viewed in the light of its continuous evolution as a means of resolving conflicts with other international environmental instruments which have come into existence. The FAO International Code of Conduct for Plant Germplasm Collecting and Transfer shall also be presented as a guideline for countries when elaborating a *sui generis* system in compliance with TRIPs.

2 - THE INTERNATIONAL UNDERTAKING

2.1- Introduction

Along with the CGRFA, the IU is the other main institutional component of the Global System. It is a non-legally binding instrument, which was adopted in 1983 out of the need to overcome the rapid extinction of diverse farmer landraces. Its provisions establish international guidelines for the collection, conservation and exchange of plant germplasm, particularly for agriculture. Therefore, the objective of the IU is to "ensure that plant genetic resources of economic and/or social interest, particularly for agriculture, will be explored, preserved, evaluated and made available for plant breeding and scientific purposes." [11] The objective of the IU to ensure the availability of PGRs, as well as the definition it provides for PGRs, has caused considerable controversy in the international arena.

Gregory Rose precisely noted that the IU "has been dogged by controversy since its adoption as it deals with the politically explosive issues of PGRs control. Its effectiveness has been hampered by the competing interests of the (mostly developing) countries which have a natural abundance of PGRs and wish to maintain control over them, and, on the other hand, the (mostly developed) countries which have made capital investments in refining PGRs and wish to exercise control themselves. Each also desires unhindered free access to the others' holdings of PGRs."[12]

Therefore, the aim of this section which concerns the IU is to deal with the provisions relating to the definition of and access to PGRs, since these are the issues which have caused most controversy between developing and developed countries.

2.2- Definition of and Access to PGRs

At the time the IU was adopted, technology-rich countries felt constrained by the way PGRs were defined and made available and eight of them expressed reservations with regard to one or both of these issues: Canada, France, Germany, Japan, New Zealand, Switzerland, the United Kingdom and the United States of America.[13] As for the developing countries, most of them signed the IU.

---

[11] International Undertaking; supra Note 6; Article 1.
[12] Rose, Gregory; supra Note 9; at p. 153.
[13] By August 2001 the United States of America had still not adhered to the International Undertaking.

Originally, the IU was regulated by the principle that PGRs are part of the "heritage of mankind and consequently should be available to all without restriction".[14] Therefore, States who have PGRs under their control were expected to "allow access to samples of such resources, and to permit their export, where the resources have been requested for the purposes of scientific research, plant breeding or genetic resource conservation."[15] Furthermore, access to these samples was to be made free of charge, "on the basis of mutual exchange or on mutually agreed terms."[16]

The formal definition of PGRs adopted by the IU is found in Article 2. Thus, PGRs are said to be:

> (a) [...] the reproductive or vegetative propagating material of the following categories of plants:
> (i) cultivated varieties[17] (cultivars) in current use and newly developed varieties;
> (ii) obsolete cultivars;
> (iii) primitive cultivars (land races);
> (iv) wild[18] and weed species, near relatives of cultivated varieties;
> (v) special genetic stocks (including elite and current breeders' line and mutants).[19]

Primitive cultivars, land races, and wild and weed relatives of crop plants have been conventionally considered by plant scientists as PGRs, and have been collected free of charge for preservation in gene banks and for plant breeding programs. Thus the IU in its original form adopted this broader definition of PGRs and included both cultivars in current use and newly developed varieties, as well as elite and current breeders' line and mutants, within its scope.

Therefore, in accordance with this definition and following the IU regulation, which provides that PGRs should be available without restriction for plant breeding and scientific purposes,[20] it is irrelevant if plant varieties and current breeders' line and mutants are developed by private plant breeding companies, as they are still considered PGRs and must be available on demand. This is the issue which industrialised countries strongly opposed at the time they were asked to sign the IU. Developed countries were not (and still are not) willing to renounce the propagating material of their plant varieties or their genetic stock, giving away property rights in their breeders' elite lines.

---

[14] International Undertaking; supra Note 6; Article 1.
[15] Idem; Article 5.
[16] Idem.
[17] In the Background Documentation, *cultivated varieties* were broadly classified as "modern varieties" and "farmers varieties". "Modern varieties" were defined as "the product of plant breeding in the formal system (sometimes called 'scientific breeding') by professional plant breeders working in private companies or publicly-funded research institutes." Furthermore, it was clarified that they are sometimes called "high-yielding varieties or high-response varieties". "Farmers' varieties" were said to be otherwise known as "landraces" and were defined as "the product of breeding or selection carried out by farmers, either deliberately or not, continuously over many generations." See Background Doc.; supra Note 1; at p. 11.
[18] The term "wild" does not necessarily imply the total absence of human influence. Many plant species categorised as "wild" have actually evolved through human influence and management as well as through the relationships with their environments. The human interference in the evolution of wild species is however, less intense than the influence of farmers in the evolution of cultivated species in their fields. Idem, at p. 27.
[19] IU; supra Note 6; Article 2.
[20] Idem; Article 1.

Consequently, although farmers' and breeders' lines are treated alike by the IU, in practice breeders' varieties are tightly sealed under the scope of intellectual property rights or other forms of protection, such as the UPOV. On the other hand, farmers' varieties and their wild relatives are made available to countries through the International Agricultural Research Centres (hereinafter the IARCs).

The IARCs form the global gene banks network and hold PGRs in trust. These centres are governed by boards with an international membership and are co-ordinated and funded through the CGIAR.[21] One of these centres, namely the International Plant Genetic Resource Institute (hereinafter the IPGRI), is concerned solely with PGRs management.[22] The IPGRI is located within the FAO in Rome, but is not constituted as part of the United Nations system. Its duty is to co-ordinate the activities of other IARCs, to establish regional centres for the conservation of PGRs, and to provide financial assistance for other conservation organs not included in the CGIAR.[23]

The IARCs accessions are available on a world-wide level and are distributed abundantly on a regular basis. As noted during the preparatory period for the Fourth International Technical Conference, "the agriculture of virtually all countries is heavily dependent on a supply of resources from other parts of the world [...] North America is completely dependent upon species originating in other regions of the world for its major food and industrial crops, while Africa south of the Sahara is estimated to be 87% dependent on other parts of the world for the plant genetic resources it needs."[24]

Therefore, due to this global interdependence, the international gene banks continuously provide PGRs to countries. Although the work of the IARCs is very important and useful to all countries, developing countries, rich in PGRs, began to regard themselves as victims of the system. The International Undertaking regarded PGRs as the "heritage of mankind"[25] and did not bother to define "heritage", but stated nevertheless, that they should be made freely available to all.[26] This provision gave developed countries easy access to developing countries' resources. On the other hand, developed countries' elite and current breeders' line and mutants were locked in a property rights treasure box and kept distant from the IU. Thus, developed countries rich in biotechnology, such as Germany, Japan, New Zealand and the United States, did not adopt the IU in 1983, when it was adopted by the FAO Conference.

To deal with these concerns, three Resolutions were adopted unanimously and introduced into the Global System as Annexes to the IU.

2.3- Annexes to the International Undertaking

In 1989, two resolutions were formulated by the CGRFA to improve the participation of countries in the IU.[27] FAO Resolution 4/89 provided an Agreed Interpretation of the IU while Resolution 5/89 defined farmers' rights. Two years later, in 1991, a third resolution was adopted, known as Resolution 3/91.[28] This resolution

---

[21] The CGIAR supports 16 IARCs.
[22] See Note 10, supra.
[23] Johnston, S.; "Conservation Role of Botanical Gardens and Gene Banks"; 2 RECIEL, 1993; at p. 175.
[24] Background Doc.; supra Note 1; at p. 13.
[25] IU; supra Notes 6 and 14; Article 1.
[26] Idem.
[27] These two resolutions, known as Res. 4/89 and Res. 5/89 are Annexes I and II respectively of the International Undertaking.
[28] Resolution 3/91 is Annex 3 of the International Undertaking.

recognised the existence of national sovereignty over plant genetic resources, and provided for an international fund for the implementation of farmers' rights.

2.3.1- FAO Resolution 4/89

Resolution 4/89 provided for an Agreed Interpretation of the IU.[29] In this interpretation it qualified, to a certain extent, the concept of "common heritage of mankind" in regard to PGRs and attempted to harmonise the provisions of the IU with the ones provided in the UPOV.

As has already been shown, Breeders have free access to PGRs from developing countries, through the international exchange system. On the other hand, access to breeders' plant varieties is a lot more difficult and expensive owing to breeders' rights and/or patent rights and the fact that the genotype is privately owned or protected. Kloppenburg and Kleinman note that whereas "germplasm flows out of the South as the 'common heritage of mankind,' it returns as a commodity."[30] Therefore, the value of PGRs is recognised as soon as it enters the markets. Once PGRs have undergone biotechnological processing, they are highly priced, whilst raw germplasm is taken for granted.

Although the Commission reaffirmed in Resolution 4/89 that PGRs were a "common heritage of mankind" to be "freely available for use"[31], it made a remarkable rectification by determining that "the term 'free access' does not mean free of charge."[32] This provision qualified the concept of "common heritage of mankind" and brought more fairness and equity to the IU. Even though the IU aims at ensuring the conservation, use and availability of PGRs for plant breeding and scientific purposes, Resolution 4/89 does not allow the pillage of PGRs, and a charge is placed on them. This article is a hope for equity for farmers to receive their share of benefits from the PGRs they have long been providing the world with.

Another point considered by Resolution 4/89 was the compatibility of plant breeders' rights, granted under the UPOV, with the provisions of the IU. Resolution 4/89 declared them compatible.[33] However, Resolution 4/89 only considered the provisions of the UPOV 1978 which allowed farmers to save the seed from their harvest out of the protected variety.[34] With the adoption of UPOV 1991, unlicensed multiplication of propagating material or seed irrespective of the purpose is considered an infringement of the breeder's right. Furthermore, UPOV 1991 considers it an infringement for farmers to save the seed or propagating material from their harvest out of the protected variety.

UPOV 1991 plant variety protection is unsuitable for developing countries whose farmers cannot afford to pay the price of advanced technology and intellectual property rights in order to be able to save and use propagating material or seeds from their own harvest out of the protected variety. If farmers of developing countries, who basically use a subsistence agriculture in small land-holdings as their chief means of

---

[29] FAO Conference Resolution 4/89; Adopted 29 November 1989; 25 Session of the FAO Conference; FAO, Rome.
[30] Kloppenburg, Jack Jr. and Kleinman, Daniel; "Plant Genetic Resources: The Common Bowl"; in Kloppenburg, Jack Jr. (ed); supra Note 4; at p. 10.
[31] Resolution 4/89; supra Note 29.
[32] Idem.
[33] Idem.
[34] See Chapter Three of this book.

income, are not allowed to re-use, sell or exchange seeds among themselves, they face serious complications.

Moreover, the so-called "improved seeds" of breeders require higher inputs of fertilisers and pesticides, which increases the expenses of farmers in developing countries. Thus, the UPOV system barely addresses the issues relating to or affecting farmers. It ignores their farming methods and their very dependency on agriculture as a means of economic and social subsistence.

With the emergence of biotechnology, developed countries, such as the United States, have actively defended their commercial interests with regard to PGRs, and have revealed their private intention to control genetic improvements and processes, disregarding the source countries' rights and needs. The basic point of the breeder's right is to achieve an exclusive monopoly over the economic benefits which arise from the breeder's plant variety. In this case, there is no equity towards farmers, who have contributed greatly to the conservation, improvement, exchange and knowledge of PGRs and hardly receive any benefit at all for their work. It has been noted that "By the end of the eighteenth century, when systematic plant breeding by selection began, the plants grown by farmers were the result of several thousands of years of partly conscious, partly unconscious selection. The art of plant breeding resulted from the realisation by innovative farmers in the eighteenth century that considerable further progress was possible by systematic selection. In this century, the rediscovery of Mendel's laws of heredity contributed to the establishment of plant breeding on a scientific basis."[35] Although farmers have been developing plant varieties for thousands of years and feeding the world with them, they have received less credit for their contributions than breeders for their scientifically developed varieties.

Apart from the fact that traditional farmers should be equitably rewarded for the agricultural contributions they have made using traditional breeding methods, there should also be a halt on the extinction of farmers' varieties. According to the Country Reports submitted by governments for the elaboration of the Report on the State of the World's PGRFA,[36] the major cause of genetic erosion is the replacement of local varieties with new varieties of crops.[37] Therefore, not only is there an evident incompatibility between the provisions which enact breeders' rights and those which grant farmers' rights, but moreover, there is an incompatibility of co-existence of biotechnology-bred cultivars with traditional landraces.

In conclusion, the provision in Resolution 4/89 which declares that "plant breeders' rights, as provided for under the UPOV, are not incompatible with the International Undertaking"[38] are merely words, because when exercised in everyday life, these rights are incompatible with each other. Breeders' rights invade the field of farmers' rights and tend to ignore the great contribution farmers have made towards the conservation and development of PGRs around the world. This contribution provides the basis for the concept of farmers' rights as defined in Resolution 5/89.

---

[35] UPOV; "The Breeding of Plant Varieties"; located at: http://www.upov.int/eng/content.htm; avalilable in May 2000.
[36] FAO; Report on the State of the World's Plant Genetic Resources for Food and Agriculture; prepared for the International Technical Conference on Plant Genetic Resources; Leipzig, Germany; 17-23 June 1996.
[37] Idem; at p. 14. The replacement of local varieties by "improved" varieties is mentioned by 81 countries as being their major cause of genetic erosion. The other main causes noted in the Country Reports are: land clearing, over exploitation of species, population pressure and environmental degradation. Idem, at p. 13.
[38] Resolution 4/89; supra Note 29.

2.3.2- FAO Resolution 5/89

Resolution 5/89,[39] in defining the concept of farmers' rights, described them as the

> rights arising from the past, present and future contributions of farmers in conserving, improving, and making available plant genetic resources, particularly those in the International Community, as trustees for present and future generations of farmers', for the purpose of ensuring full benefits to farmers, and supporting the continuation of their contributions, as well as the attainment of the overall purposes of the International Undertaking.[40]

This definition recognises the critical role farmers possess in the conservation and further development of PGRs. Farmers' varieties usually contain high levels of genetic diversity due to their adaptation to environmental influences, such as soil, climate, rainfall, the interaction with the other species in the environment, and the traditional breeding or selection carried out by farmers. Throughout history, farmers have been selecting "those plants within the species which promised a high yield, good quality or other advantages and which were well adapted to his local environment. Multiple generations of selection resulted in plants giving higher yields, better adapted to the environment in which they were grown and otherwise meeting more closely the needs of mankind."[41] In the Andes region, some communities grow 178 locally named potato varieties, while in the Peruvian Amazon, 61 cultivars of cassava are grown by the Arguarana Jivaro community.[42] It has been noted that peasants in Peru, "with one tenth of the agricultural land, are capable of producing more than half of the nation's food, despite poor market conditions, etc. This performance is not due to ignorance or accident; it is a result of peasants' conscious and careful strategies."[43]

On the other hand, transgenic crops are genetically uniform and pose potential risks to the environment and human health. Dr Mae-Wan Ho[44] explains that there are safety concerns of exotic genes due to the fact that the exotic genes introduced into "transgenic crops are often from bacteria and non-food species, and their expression is greatly amplified by strong viral promoters/enhancers."[45] She further explains that in practice this means that all species that interact with the transgenic crop will be exposed to a large amount of proteins new to their physiology creating the possibility

---

[39] FAO Conference Resolution 5/89; Adopted 29 November 1989; 25 Session of the FAO Conference; Rome.
[40] At the second meeting of the FAO Commission on PGRs, the idea of promoting the concept of "farmers' rights" was raised. Some members of FAO discussed that the term was too broad and therefore, did not adequately characterise the concept. Instead, they suggested the term, "rights of centre of origin countries". Commission on Plant Genetic Resources; Second Session; 16-20 March 1987; Rome; FAO.
[41] UPOV; supra Note 35.
[42] Brush, S. B.; "Farmer conservation of New World crops: the case of Andean potatoes"; 7 Diversity, 1991; pp 75-79.
[43] Salas, Maria; "'The technicians only believe in science and cannot read the sky': the cultural dimension of the knowledge conflict in the Andes"; in Scoones and Thompson, Beyond Farmer First; Intermediate Technology Publications; London; 2000; at p. 65.
[44] Mae-Wan Ho is a geneticist and biophysicist as well as the scientific advisor to the non-governmental organisation Third World Network. She is also the head of the Bio-electrodynamics Laboratory of the Open University in Milton Keynes, United Kingdom.
[45] Ho, Mae-Wan; "Special Safety Concerns of Transgenic Agriculture ad Related Issues"; paper presented at the International Seminar on the Right of Biodiversity held in Brasilia, Brazil; 11-14 May 1999. Located at: http://www.cjf.gov.br/pages/SENbiodiversidade_textos_slides.htm; available in June 1999.

of all sorts of corporal adverse reactions.[46] Safety concerns of unpredictability arise because "interactions between introduced genes and host genes are bound to occur, as no gene functions in isolation, and in particular because the foreign genes are being continuously over-expressed."[47] As regards gene-constructs inserted into the transgenic organism, one of the most frequently used viral promoters is from the cauliflower mosaic virus, "closely related to human hepatitis B virus, and less closely, to retroviruses such as the AIDS virus."[48] And finally, Ho notes that "genes can spread from transgenic plants by ordinary cross-pollination to non-transgenic plants of the same species or related species, and also by secondary horizontal gene transfer to unrelated species."[49]

Therefore, even though biotechnologically altered plants are given a much higher price in the world market, in reality their value remains in part dependent upon traditionally bred varieties or wild species. Biotechnology-bred plants are highly vulnerable in face of their genetic uniformity, and a minor mutation in the pathogen can cause the total loss of the crop.[50] This occurred, for example, in Ireland in 1846-47, where potato was the staple crop of the poor and 1/3 of the population was totally dependent on it for food.[51] The potato was brought from the Andes in the late 1570 and planted in Spain and England. All the potatoes planted in Europe for a period of 250 years descended from the initial plantation from one of those countries.[52] When late blight (*Phytophtora infestans*) attacked the genetically uniform potato plantations in Ireland it wiped out the entire crop and caused the "Great Famine."[53] Another similar devastating incident occurred in the United States in 1946, when derivative lines of the oat variety "Victoria" were attacked by a new disease termed "Victoria blight" causing major crop losses.[54] Therefore, the genetic variability found in wild and domesticated plants makes them vital to mankind. Nevertheless, as is commonly the case, the value of nature is underestimated. Wild and domesticated PGRs are taken for granted in the same way as the two most valuable elements for humanity: clean air and fresh water.

Genetic variability is extremely important in plants. Its value may be divided into three categories, according to their respective functions.[55] The first value of genetic variability is called the "Portfolio Value" which helps provide stability for farming systems through the conservation of a wide range, or portfolio, of crops and intra-crop diversity. The second category of values is known as the "Option Value". Here genetic diversity is seen as a means of insurance against future adverse conditions, as well as adaptability to any change in climatic conditions. The third value of genetic variability is called the "Exploration Value". Genetic diversity is seen as a potentially valuable "treasure chest" which can be explored. As breeders' plant varieties do not exhibit genetic variability, they can not be considered superior to farmers' varieties. Domesticated species and wild species are the parents of breeders' cultivars, as well as their potential "saviours".

---

[46] Idem.
[47] Idem.
[48] Idem.
[49] Idem.
[50] For examples of crops which were lost as a result of monoculture in planting, as well as the uniform characteristics of the plants, see Juma, C.; The Gene Hunters: Biotechnology and the Scramble for Seeds; 1989; London; Zed books; pp 100-103.
[51] Baumann, M., Bell, J., Koechlin, F., and Pimbert, M. (eds); The Life Industry: Biodiversity, People and Profits; Intermediate Technology Publications; London; 1996; at p. 6.
[52] Idem.
[53] Report on the State of the World's PGRFA; supra Note 36; at p. 15.
[54] Kloppenburg, J. Jr, Kleinman, D.; supra Note 30; at p. 6.
[55] Background Doc.; supra Note 1; at p. 15.

Individual traits of landraces have been frequently introduced into existing improved breeding lines. A Turkish wheat landrace, for example, carries resistance genes to various rusts, smuts and other fungal pathogens. Its genes were used in many wheat cultivars which now grow in north-western USA.[56] Other examples include incidents such as when a disease resistance gene provided by wild Asian species prevented the US sugarcane industry from collapse, as well as when genes from the wild Brazilian cassava increased cassava yields in Africa and India up to 18 times.[57]

Another point recognised by Resolution 5/89 is that most PGRs are found in developing countries, yet training and facilities for plant survey and identification and plant breeding are not sufficient or even available in many of those countries. Therefore, the resolution considers that there is a need to strengthen the capabilities of developing countries in the areas of conservation, development and use of PGRs in order to "allow farmers, their communities, and countries in all regions, to participate fully in the benefits derived, at present and in the future, from the improved use of plant genetic resources, through plant breeding and other scientific methods."[58]

The benefits derived from PGRs can be distributed in many ways including through the dissemination of information. Information on PGRs is unevenly distributed around the world. Many developing countries have little or no means of exchanging or accessing scientific and technical information internationally and, although important modern advances have occurred in the developed nations, farmers in the developing world rarely have access to them.[59] International collaboration is necessary to strengthen the scientific basis for the conservation of PGRs world-wide. As noted by Grossmann, "the need for good international training is essential to more equitable exchange and use of germplasm and genetic information."[60] The dissemination of information, coupled with research training in order to build the capacities in national conservation and sustainable utilisation programmes, is the most important step in the technology transfer process. Nevertheless, Grossmann also notes that "it is unfortunate that the current legal and political disagreements over plant breeders' rights, patents, and advanced breeding materials may also inhibit better international training."[61]

The availability of information, as well as technologies were dealt with in Resolution 3/91.

2.3.3- FAO Resolution 3/91

In 1991, the Conference of FAO adopted a third resolution, known as Resolution 3/91.[62] This resolution approached issues such as sovereignty over PGRs, access to breeders' and farmers' materials, as well as the complementarity of information, technologies and funds.

---

[56] Idem; at p. 17.
[57] Idem, at p. 18. For further examples see pp. 17-18.
[58] See Resolution 5/89; supra Note 39.
[59] Approximately 1,4 billion people are dependent on resource-poor farming systems in marginal environments. See Chambers, R.; Introduction; in Scoones, I. and Thompson, J. (eds); supra Note 43; p. xiii.
[60] Grossmann, R.; "Equalising the Flow: Institutional Restructuring of Germplasm Exchange"; in Kloppenburg Jr., Jack (ed); supra Note 4; at p. 270.
[61] Idem, at p. 269.
[62] FAO Resolution 3/91 is the third annex to the International Undertaking. It was adopted 25 November 1991. Report of the Conference of FAO, C91/REP, 26 Session, Rome, 9-27 November 1991.

In Resolution 3/91 the Conference of FAO recognised that "the concept of mankind's heritage, as applied in the IU on Plant Genetic Resources, is subject to the sovereignty of the states over their plant genetic resources."[63] The Conference of FAO once again did not define the concept of "common heritage of mankind", but qualified it by reference to the sovereignty of states over their PGRs.

Therefore, with PGRs being regarded as the "common heritage of mankind" the concern over their conservation and sustainable utilisation is global.[64] As such, the essential characteristics of the Principle of Common Heritage of Mankind, *inter alia*, collective responsibility, sharing of benefits and costs of conservation, and taking into account the interests of future generations are endorsed.[65]

Nevertheless, Resolution 3/91 considers PGRs at a political level and respects the national jurisdiction they fall under, giving States the sovereignty over their PGRs. As countries hold PGRs under their sovereignty they are said to have the stewardship of the PGRs, having to sustainably use them in order to preserve the heritage for themselves, other nations and future generations.[66]

It must be taken into account that sovereignty implies ownership which has to be dealt with at both a public and private level. At the public level, the ownership rights over PGRs rest under the direct control of the government and they can be placed at the disposal of the international exchange system of PGRs, through gene banks, botanical gardens, arboreta,[67] and nurseries[68]. At the private level we find PGRs being used by a company, a community group or an individual in activities such as breeding and farming, for example. At this level, PGRs are only made available through the permission of these private groups.

Although due respect should to be paid to sovereignty, in whatever form it presents itself, this is a very delicate issue when regarding the equitable sharing of benefits coming from the use of PGRs. Nowadays, the PGRs of one country can be found under the sovereignty of another country. The Background Documentation for the International Technical Conference on PGRs identifies that the expansion of agricultural genetic diversity throughout the planet occurred in three phases.

The first phase of the distribution of genetic diversity is correspondent to the time when crops were domesticated.[69] In these cases, researchers have managed to identify that wheat was domesticated in western Asia, rice in East Asia, Maize in Mesoamerica and sorghum in Africa.[70] The centre where a crop was domesticated is "usually the primary centre of *in situ* diversity for that crop and continued gene flow between crops and their wild relatives in these areas underlies their importance as sources of new variability."[71] The second phase came with the voyages of exploration and the trade routes which linked Europe, Asia, East Indies, Africa, Americas, etc.[72]

---

[63] Idem.
[64] The Convention on Biological Diversity provides for the sovereign rights of States over their plant genetic resources and affirms that the conservation of biodiversity is a *common concern* of humankind. The text of the convention is reprinted in 31 ILM 818, 1992.
[65] Peters, P. & Schrijver, N. & Waart, P.; "Responsibility of States in Respect of the Exercise of Permanent Sovereignty Over Natural Resources"; 36 Netherlands International Law Review; 1989; at p. 311.
[66] Weiss, Edith; Environmental Change and International Law; United Nations University Press; Tokyo, Japan; 1992; at 395.
[67] Arboreta are botanical gardens for trees only.
[68] Nurseries are placed where plants are cultivated before they are sold or transplanted.
[69] Background Doc.; supra Note 1; at p. 12.
[70] Idem; at p. 28.
[71] Report on the State of the World's PGRFA; supra Note 36; at p. 10.
[72] Background Doc.; supra Note 1; at p. 12.

During this phase, there was a wide global exchange of PGRFA and secondary centres of diversity originated. Some African countries, for instance, are secondary centres to common bean, maize and cassava introduced from Latin America, and these species show significant diversity.[73] And finally, the third phase of the distribution of agricultural genetic diversity among countries started with the large collection of PGRFA and their conservation in *ex situ* conservation centres.

Summarising, the point in examining the history of the distribution of genetic resources throughout the world is that secondary centres of diversity of PGRs and *ex situ* conservation units have been created. This means that, nowadays, a certain sample of PGRFA can be found and accessed elsewhere than in the country in which they were originally domesticated. In such cases, there are several countries conserving PGRs, through *in situ* or *ex situ* strategies or even both. And although *in situ* conservation areas tend to keep the genetic variability of species high, *ex situ* conservation has prevented, on many occasions, the extinction of certain PGRs.[74]

It is important to note that FAO Resolution 3/91 considers advanced technologies and local rural technologies as "both important and complementary in the conservation and utilisation of plant genetic resources," being *in situ* and *ex situ* conservation strategies "important and complementary [...] for maintaining genetic diversity."[75] Grossmann observes that the "dimensions of strength for the *in situ* approach are the 'weaknesses' of the *ex situ* approaches and vice versa."[76]

In situ conservation strategy enables plant species to have a greater adaptability to environmental hazards, pests or pathogens due to their more varied genetic constitution.[77] Natural genetic evolution and mutation of plants in their natural environments increases their resistance to diseases and environmental changes, giving them greater protection against undergoing a widespread crop loss. Bell and Pimbert noted that "it is impossible to predict what genetic characteristics may become valuable in the future, so allowing our genetic heritage to dwindle is highly dangerous. Climate change, for example, will demand new and adapted plant varieties and animal breeds – derived from natural organisms in order to cope with its impact."[78]

According to Sedjo, "Germplasm, the substance in the plant cells by which hereditary characteristics are transmitted, is the fundamental material of life. The stock of genetic resources comprises a vast reservoir of heritable characteristics that have actual or potential use. The characteristics have potential use in the development of improved crops, pharmaceuticals, and other natural products as well as plant species capable of restoring depleted soils. Germplasm from wild species is used to maintain

---

[73] Report on the State of the World's PGRFA; supra Note 36; at p. 10.

[74] Biodiversity can be lost *inter alia* habitat loss and fragmentation, introduction of exotic species, over-exploitation of plants and animals, pollution, global climate change and industrial agriculture and forestry. See Baumann, M., Bell, J., Koechlin, F., and Pimbert, M. (eds); supra 51; at p. 8.

[75] FAO Resolution 3/91; supra Note 62.

[76] Grossmann points out the advantages of *ex situ* conservation as being: "the accessibility they provide to specific accessions, the strong information linkages that can be established between accessions and evaluation data, their independence from geographical constraints, and, in theory, the higher level of genetic stability that can be maintained in controlled facilities." The *in situ* conservation advantages according to the author are: "the basis of the larger number of species they can maintain, the continuation of evolutionary processes that they permit, the protection they provide for whole ecosystems, and their potential for counteracting the imposition of political control." Grossmann, R.; supra Note 60; at pgs. 262-3.

[77] Brush, Steven; "The issues of *in situ* conservation of crop genetic resources"; in Brush Steven; Genes in the Field; IPGRI; Rome; 1999; at pp. 10-11.

[78] Baumann, M., Bell, J., Koechlin, F., and Pimbert, M. (eds); supra Note 51; at p. 4.

the vitality of most of our important food crops."[79] For instance, California's 160 million dollars crop is protected from the yellow dwarf virus by a gene from a single Ethiopian barley plant.[80] Wheat varieties from Mexico contribute 2700 million dollars crop production in industrialised countries.[81]

The preamble of the Convention on Biological Diversity (hereafter CBD) notes that "the fundamental requirement for the conservation of biological diversity is the *in situ* conservation of ecosystems and natural habitats and the maintenance and recovery of viable populations of species in their natural surroundings."[82] The wording is very clear and shows that conservation of biodiversity at *in situ* level is a "fundamental requirement", as it is the starting point of any search for genetically diversified raw material. It is out of *in situ* environments that solutions can be discovered for challenges to which genetically uniform and vulnerable plant varieties are subject.[83] Nevertheless, the CBD notes "that *ex situ* measures, preferably in the country of origin, also have an important role to play."[84]

In situ conservation is not sufficient to conserve biodiversity and make available PGRs for a rapidly growing population. As a result, *ex situ* conservation strategies have become an important element in the attempt to conserve PGRs before they face extinction.[85] The Report describes the conservation and sustainable use of PGRs as the key "to improve agricultural productivity and sustainability thereby contributing to national development, food security, and poverty alleviation. [...] Improvements in yield on a reliable and sustainable basis will be needed to meet the demands of this growing population."[86] According to UPOV, with the rapidly growing world population "Annual food production will have to go up to over 3,000 million metric tonnes from the current 1,800 million metric tonnes. At the same time, productive farmland is being and will continue to be increasingly diverted to non-farm uses. Such land is often used for urban or industrial development. [...]There is thus no option except to produce more food on less land to meet the needs of the growing population."[87]

---

[79] Sedjo, R.; "Property Rights and the Protection of Plant Genetic Resources"; in Kloppenburg, Jr. (ed); supra Note 4; at p.295.
[80] UNDP; Conserving Indigenous Knowledge Integrating Two Systems of Innovation; New York; 1994.
[81] Idem.
[82] CBD; supra Note 64; Preamble.
[83] For an opposite view, see Frankel, Otto; supra Note 4; at p. 37. Frankel states that "the often-repeated assertion that breeders in developed countries depend on a continuing supply of germplasm from the country of origin of their crop is very largely unfounded. Breeders turn to germplasm collections for exotic materials rather than to the country or countries where landraces of their crop are still in cultivation, and even that is not a common occurrence." Frankel further notes that the claim for access to breeders' material or compensation based on retrospectivity, or in other words, on material collected in the past decades or centuries from "gene-rich" countries is also hard to sustain. He defends his point of view by showing that scientist from the "north" collected most of the germplasm and due to these collections materials that have become extinct on the fields in developing countries, are still available in international and national germplasm collections. See also Swanson, T.; "The Reliance of Northern Economies on Southern Biodiversity: Biodiversity as Information"; 17 Ecological Economics, 1996; pp. 1-8.
[84] CBD; supra Note 64; Preamble.
[85] The Report on the State of the World's PGRFA observes that there has been a high increase in the number of gene banks since the early 1970s when there were less than 10 which held a total of no more that half a million accessions. Nowadays, there are more than 1 300 *ex situ* germplasm collections which hold approximately 6,1 million accessions. These include 527 000 accessions stored in field gene banks. An estimate is made, according to FAO World Information & Early Warning System (WIEWS) database, that fewer than 37 600 accessions are conserved *in vitro*. See the Report; supra Note 36; pgs. 20-21.
[86] Idem; at p. 6. See also Note 1.
[87] UPOV; "The Need for New Plant Varieties"; located at http://www.upov.int/eng/content.htm; available in May 2000.

Thus, it is evident that *in situ* and *ex situ* strategies are complementary to each other. In this sense, Resolution 3/91 recognised that "the availability of plant genetic resources and the information technologies and funds necessary to conserve and utilise them, are complementary and of equal importance."[88] This recognition was an attempt to pacify issues between developing and developed countries. Developing countries, which are rich in biological diversity, have fought, over the years, to legitimise their sovereign rights over their natural resources. Developed countries, rich in technology and funds, seek to preserve their superiority in those matters, and are actively engaged in establishing intellectual property rights over their technology and biotechnology.

Being complementary and equal in importance, PGRs, information, technologies and funds can be interchanged among nations with the purpose of achieving intragenerational equity.

The first Report on the State of the World's Plant Genetic Resources[89] noted that there was loss of diversity in both fields and forests of rural people and in gene banks.[90] Furthermore, it shows that the benefits of PGRs are not being fully realised or shared amongst and within countries. Woodliffe provides a clear and basic solution for this impasse, by declaring that what is necessary is a "legally just accommodation between the interests of the two groups of countries; one that avoids allocating exclusive rights of ownership of products to either side, preserves access to wild genetic resources and the technology that makes use of them and, above all, ensures that indigenous peoples are rewarded for their contribution to the development of a new drug or crop."[91]

2.4 – Revision of International Undertaking

The CGRFA started to revise the International Undertaking in 1994.[92] Negotiations have been addressing the scope of the International Undertaking, realisation of farmers' rights, benefit sharing mechanisms and access provisions to PGRFA. Furthermore, negotiations have been considering regulations for those resources accessed before the entry into force of the CBD, which were mainly collected from developing countries and are now stored in gene banks and frequently used in plant breeding.[93]

Farmers' rights have also been debated, seeking the recognition of farmers as important elements in conserving, sustainably using and traditionally breeding PGRs, which are used as the genetic base in scientific plant breeding. Moreover, the debates

---

[88] FAO Resolution 3/91; supra Note 62.
[89] FAO Fourth International Technical Conference on Plant Genetic Resources; Leipzig, Germany; 17-23 June 1996.
[90] Even though gene banks should be a safe place to store PGRs, the Report noted that only around 30 countries provide secure long-term storage. Consequently, due to the poor conditions of some collections, approximately one million accessions are in need of regeneration.
[91] Woodliffe, John; "Biodiversity and Indigenous Peoples"; in Bowman, Michael and Redgwell, Catherine (eds); supra Note 9; at p. 265.
[92] FAO Conference Resolution 7/93 called for the revision of the International Undertaking in harmony with the CBD. The First Negotiating Draft was reviewed at the First Extraordinary Session of the CGRFA held in November 1994. The Second Negotiating Draft was negotiated at the Sixth Session of the CGRFA, in June 1995. The Third Extraordinary Session of the CGRFA, held in December 1996, discussed the Third Negotiating Draft of the International Undertaking. The Fourth Negotiating Draft was prepared for the Fourth Extraordinary Session of the CGRFA, in December 1997, as well as a Consolidated Negotiating Text; Appendix C of CGRFA-Ex4/97/REP.
[93] For FAO documents relating to the revision of the IU see http://www.fao.org/ag/cgrfa/iu.htm; available in September 2000. See also http://www.ukabc.org/iu2.htm; accessed August 2001.

have also been dealing with the implementation of "Farmers' Privilege" which is the right of farmers to sow seeds from crops they have grown.

There have been proposals to adopt a multilateral international fund as a benefit sharing mechanism for traditional farmers that have enhanced the use of the genetic resources on their fields.[94] Innovations on plant varieties that occur in communities cannot be attributable to a single individual because they take place slowly year after year. This is why they are freely available. Therefore, a multilateral international fund could be an effective mechanism to reward all the contributors.

Negotiations have also focused on the participation of farmers in the decision-making process about agricultural development. "Capacity building is central to this view of Farmers' Rights. [...] Policies should be implemented that will create an environment conducive to the empowerment of local communities and a partnership between institutional and community-based researchers. This means ensuring that local communities are full participants in the definition of national and international R&D priorities."[95]

As States have no obligation to implement IU provisions "The gap between the content of the IU and present international practice, together with the opposition of developed countries and the seed industry",[96] reveals that the IU still has not been given effect. If renegotiated, the revised IU could become a binding protocol to the CBD.[97] Both instruments deal with the similar issues although the International Undertaking covers specifically PGRFA.

2.5 – International Code of Conduct for Plant Germplasm Collecting and Transfer

In 1989, the CGRFA requested the development of an International Code of Conduct for Plant Germplasm Collecting and Transfer (hereafter Code of Conduct). The final draft was adopted in 1993[98] and it forms part of the Global System. The Code of Conduct provides a framework for countries to develop their national laws that regulate access to plant germplasm collection and transfer.

The Code of Conduct is in harmony with the objectives of the CBD: conservation of biodiversity, sustainable use of its components and the fair and

---

[94] Farmers' rights and *in situ* conservation could be financed through a multilateral trust fund. See Brush, S. B.; "Providing Farmers' Rights through *in Situ* Conservation of Crop Genetic Resources"; Commission on Plant Genetic Resources, First Extraordinary Session; 7-11 November 1994; Background Study Paper No. 3.
[95] Crucible Group; People, plants, and patents: the impact of intellectual property on biodiversity, conservation, trade, and rural society; Ottawa, Canada; IDRC; 1994; at p. 46.
[96] Bordwin, H.; "The Legal and Political Implications of the International Undertaking on Plant Genetic Resources"; 12 Ecology law Quarterly 1053, 1985; at p. 1069.
[97] Agenda 21, paragraph 14.60(c), recommended that the Global System on the Conservation and Sustainable Use of Plant Genetic Resources for Food and Agriculture be strengthened and adjusted to be in line with the provisions of the CDB. Article 28 of the CBD provides for the adoption of protocols to the convention. The Conference of the Parties - Decision 11/15 of the Second Session of the Conference of the Parties to the Convention on Biological Diversity, Jakarta, Indonesia, 6-17 November 1995 supported the idea that the IU should be brought into harmony to the CBD. During the Eighth Regular Session of the CGRFA, the adoption of the IU as a binding protocol to the CBD was proposed to be the legal status of the renegotiated Undertaking. See Eighth Regular Session of the CGRFA; Revision of the International Undertaking on Plant Genetic Resources: Legal and Institutional Options; Rome 19-23 April 1999.
[98] Code of Conduct; FAO Conference Resolution 8/93. Adopted by the 27th session of the FAO Conference, November 1993.

equitable share of benefits that derive from their utilisation. According to the Code of Conduct, States should:

> Promote the conservation, collection and use of plant genetic resources from their natural habitats or surroundings in ways that respect the environment and local traditions and cultures.[99]
>
> Promote the sharing of benefits derived from plant genetic resources between the donors and users of germplasm, related information and technologies by suggesting ways in which the users may pass on a share of the benefits to the donors, taking in to account the costs of conservation and developing germplasm.[100]

The Brazilian government was of the view that this objective weakened the concept of fair and equitable share of benefits as stated in the CBD and made a reservation to the text of that objective. It stated that "in disagreement with Article 15, paragraph 7, of the Convention on Biological Diversity, which stipulates that the sharing and development, as well as the benefits of its commercial utilisation, should be carried out on a fair and equitable basis, the text of the Code of Conduct in Article 1, paragraph 7, restricts the concept of fair and equitable sharing of benefits, when it says: 'by suggesting ways in which the users may pass on a share of benefits to donors.'"[101] It is worth noting that this observation is strengthened by the fact that the Code of Conduct makes no reference to the fairness or equity of the distribution of benefits.

Another reservation formulated by Brazil to the Code of Conduct was that it called on States "'to ensure that the collection, transfer and use of plant germplasm is carried out with the maximum benefit to the international community', and with minimal adverse effects on the evolution of crop plant diversity and the environment."[102]

According to the Brazilian government the fact that the collection and transfer of germplasm should be "carried out with the maximum benefit to the international community" rather than to the benefit of the providers precluded a fair return to donor countries.[103]

Moving on to another matter, a further objective of the Code of Conduct is to: "bring recognition to the rights and needs of local communities and farmers, and those who manage wild and cultivated plant genetic resources and in particular to promote mechanisms:

> (a) to facilitate compensation of local communities and farmers for their contribution to the conservation and development of plant genetic resources; and
> (b) to avoid situations whereby benefits currently derived from plant genetic resources by these local communities and farmers are undermined by the transfer or use by others of the resources."[104]

---

[99] Idem; Article 1(1).
[100] Idem; Article 1(7).
[101] See Report of the 27th Session of FAO Conference; Appendix F; 6-24 November 1993; Rome.
[102] Code of Conduct ; supra Note 98; Article 4(1).
[103] See Report of the 27th Session of FAO Conference; supra Note 101.
[104] Code of Conduct ; supra Note 98; Article 1(8).

Although this objective in theory promotes farmers' rights, it restricts the equitable share of benefits with local communities and farmers by recommending countries to promote mechanisms "to facilitate compensation of local communities and farmers..." There is no mandatory provision in the Code of Conduct that stipulates the equitable share of benefits with those stakeholders for their contributions in conserving and traditionally developing plant varieties.

Due to the cited weaknesses of the Code of Conduct, it should be regarded as a framework instrument which can be improved and adapted by each country in order to best serve the interests of its nationals, while promoting the conservation and sustainable utilisation of the biodiversity.

2.6 - Conclusion

The Global System's objective is to conserve and sustainably use PGRs. It focuses on the affirmation that developed and developing countries must work together, complementing each other on PGRs, information, technology and funds. Furthermore, it acknowledges that *in situ* and *ex situ* approaches are complementary conservation strategies to maintain the sustainable utilisation of genetic diversity in all countries. Thus, the Global System works towards intensifying a global partnership.[105]

The International Undertaking is a non-binding international instrument which seeks to grant rights to farmers for their continued contribution over the centuries to the conservation, creation, exchange and knowledge of PGRs.[106] Farmers in developing countries usually posses traditional knowledge over PGRs and ecosystems, as well as simple, traditional techniques to conserve, manage and develop them.[107] However, their financial and technological resources are limited, and the regulations of the 1991 UPOV Act further complicate their situation by restraining them from saving seeds out of the harvest of a protected variety.

Compensation to farmers who provide the "raw" germplasm[108] is neglected and their work is undervalued. Grossmann notes that the "international flow of germplasm has been and is now characterised by inequity. The inequity results from unequal use and abuse of plant genetic resources."[109] This is enhanced by UPOV 1991 and the broadening of the scope of the patent system in order to protect plant varieties.

The Annexes to the International Undertaking sought to bring a balance between the interests of breeders on one the side and traditional farmers on the other. To achieve this, the Annexes had to focus mainly on granting rights to farmers. Breeders already utilise legal systems to protect their cultivars whilst the protection of farmers' varieties and wild varieties in developing countries is far from being substantial.

---

[105] The Declaration of the UN Conference on Environment and Development, (known as the Rio Declaration), determines in Principle 7 that "States have common but differentiated responsibilities" in the global partnership to "conserve, protect and restore the health and integrity of the Earth's ecosystem." Text in General Assembly Resolution 47/190 (1992).
[106] Baumann, M., Bell, J., Koechlin, F., and Pimbert, M. (eds); supra Note 51; at p. 3.
[107] The Report on the State of the World's PGRFA notes that over one billion people live on farms, and the responsibility to manage and improve the plant genetic resources for food and agriculture rests within the family itself; see the Report; supra Note 36; at p. 16.
[108] The expression "raw germplasm" was used by Grossmann, R.; supra Note 60; at p. 255.
[109] Idem; at p. 257.

This can be seen through the loss of traditional varieties, as well as wild species which has increased throughout the years due, *inter alia*, to land clearing, the use of pesticides and fertilisers, the cutting and burning of forests, wars and the introduction of new, high yielding plant varieties. These high-yielding crop varieties are genetically uniform and can require large inputs of fertiliser, pesticide and water. In general, they are very vulnerable to diseases, pest or environmental change. "Even though a modern variety has been bred for resistance to a particular pathogen strain, a minor mutation in the pathogen can often break down that resistance overnight."[110] This fragile condition of breeders' varieties is uncontrollable. The world lacks a comprehensive and co-ordinated system to monitor uniformity in agricultural species, as well as adequate tools to assess related genetic vulnerability.[111]

Advanced technologies and local rural technologies are considered both important and complementary in the conservation and utilisation of plant genetic resources.[112] Likewise, *in situ* and *ex situ* conservation strategies are both important and complementary for maintaining genetic diversity.[113] However, so far, there has not been equitable co-operation and complementarity between them.

The IU is currently undergoing revision with the possibility of being adopted as a protocol to the CBD.[114] The International Undertaking has already undergone some revision through the interpretative and complementary text found in Conference Resolutions 4/89, 5/89 and 3/91, which are now annexes to the instrument. These resolutions established the concept of farmers' rights, attempted to harmonise them with breeders' rights, introduced sovereignty over PGRs and an international fund for the implementation of farmers' rights. The revised International Undertaking will probably incorporate the annexes into its main body, as well as clarify the issues of access to plant genetic resources for food and agriculture and the realisation of farmers' rights. Furthermore, negotiations have been considering possibilities for traditional farmers to participate in the access system and receive their fair and equitable share of benefits for the contributions made from their traditional knowledge and farming techniques.

The following section shall present examples of how farmers are struggling to survive in an era where biotechnology, patents and plant breeders' rights surround them on all sides.

3 - EXAMPLES OF CASES INVOLVING FARMERS AND BIOTECHNOLOGY COMPANIES

3.1- Introduction

According to the Rural Advancement Foundation International, (hereafter RAFI) biopiracy "refers to the use of intellectual property laws (patents, plant breeders' rights) to gain exclusive monopoly control over genetic resources that are

---

[110] The Report on the State of the World's PGRFA; supra Note 36; at p. 15.
[111] Idem.
[112] See FAO Res. 3/91; supra Note 62.
[113] Idem.
[114] At the 27th Session of the FAO Conference in November 1993, Resolution 7/93, which called for the revision of the International Undertaking, in harmony with the CBD, negotiated by the Fifth Session of the Commission, was unanimously adopted. The report on the implementation of Resolution 7/93 is found in document C 95/INF/19-Sup. 1.

based on the knowledge and innovation of farmers and indigenous peoples."[115] There have been many protests from developing countries accusing biotechnological industries of biopiracy. This section shall show examples of cases involving patents in the context of traditional knowledge. Furthermore, it will show how farmers are not only threatened by biopiracy but of also having their crops fertilised by a transgenic gene of a neighbouring plantation.

3.2- Neem Tree

The neem tree, scientifically known as *Azadirachta indica*, is a tree which has been used for centuries in India. In Sanskrit the neem tree is called *Sarva Roga Nivarini*, meaning "the curer of all ailments" and in Arabic it is known as *Shajar-e-Mubarak*, "the blessed tree".[116] Its multiple uses, first discovered by local Indian rural people, include protection against "malaria and internal worms; the leaves are used to protect stored grain from pests and clothes moths, neem oil is used to make candles, soap, a contraceptive, and can even fuel diesel engines; and 500 million Indians reportedly use neem to brush their teeth."[117] It is also commonly used as a natural pesticide for crops.[118] Indian texts 2000 years old mention several of the neem properties.[119] Nevertheless, biotechnological companies have filed dozens of patent claims on the neem tree in the United States[120] and in Europe. All of these patents describe knowledge that is part of prior art in India.

In June 1995, Dr Vandana Shiva,[121] Magda Aelvoet[122] and the International Federation of Organic Agriculture Movements[123] challenged a European patent on the fungicidal effects of neem oil, Patent No. 436 257 B1, owned by W. R. Grace & Co.. On the 30th September 1997, the European Patent Office delivered a favourable interim judgement on the challenge of that patent. The Opposition Division of the European Patent Office held that the patent could not be maintained because, based on the evidence presented by the opponents, the contents of the claim formed part of prior art and lacked an inventive step.[124] On 10 May 2000, the European Patent Office officially revoked the cited neem patent.[125]

However, another patent also owned by W. R. Grace & Co., Patent No. 5124349, granted by the United States patent office, for a storage stable neem formulation, still has not been defeated even though a number of NGOs are opposing

---

[115] RAFI; "1996 Biopiracy Update: US Patent Claim Exclusive Monopoly Control of Food Crop, Medicinal Plants, Soil Microbes and Traditional Knowledge from the South"; RAFI Communique; December 1996. All RAFI articles in this section were available in September 2000 on RAFI website located at: http://www.rafi.org.
[116] Shiva, Vandana and Holla-Bhar, Radha; "Intellectual Piracy and the Neem Tree"; 23(6) The Ecologist 223, November/December 1993; at p. 224.
[117] Posey, D, & Dutfield, G.; Beyond Intellectual Property; International Development Research Centre; Ottawa, Canada; 1996; at p. 80.
[118] Idem.
[119] See International Federation of Organic Agriculture Movements; "Background Paper of the Neem Challenge"; located at http://www.ifoam.org/press/neem_back.html; available in August 2000.
[120] More than 40 patents have been granted to patent claims involving the neem tree in the United States alone. For a list of neem-related patents world-wide see Dutfield, G.; Intellectual Property Rights, Trade and Biodiversity: Seeds and Plant Varieties; Earthscan; London; 2000; at Appendix 1.
[121] Director of the Research Foundation for Science, Technology and Natural Resource Policy; New Delhi, India.
[122] Leader of the Green MPs of the European Parliament in 1995. Now Belgium Environment Minister.
[123] A non-governmental organisation based in Germany.
[124] See International Federation of Organic Agriculture Movements; supra Note 119.
[125] See Goldsmith, E. (ed); "Neem Tree Free!"; 30(4) The Ecologist, June 2000; at p. 8.

it.[126] Many can be the explanations of why the challenge of the European patent was favourable while the challenge of the US patent failed. Basically, the novelty definition as found in the United States patent law allowed the patent.

As shown in Chapter Two of this book, traditional knowledge found in foreign countries can be patented in the United States because it is not recognised as prior art[127] as it is under the European Patent Convention.[128] This provision in the United States patent law is a stimulant for biotechnological companies to simply acquire traditional knowledge from developing countries and patent it in the United States as if it were their own discovery.[129]. In other words, the neem patent is just one example of how industries have received patents for public domain traditional knowledge they accessed and used.[130] "India has protested strongly over Indian materials and associated indigenous knowledge getting patented in the USA as illustrated by turmeric, neem and, more recently, the Basmati rice."[131] "Patents are rewarding biopiracy - not medical innovators."[132]

3.3 – "Terminator Technology"

As patents prohibit the making, using and selling of the invention without the patentee's authorisation, the farmer who buys a transgenic patented seed does not have the right to sell the seeds of his harvest or to save them for the next plantation.[133] For such acts, he would need further authorisation of the breeder which is normally only granted with a royalty payment. However, as the absolute control of unauthorised acts concerning plant varieties is practically impossible, the US Department of Agriculture (hereafter USDA) and the American Delta and Pine Land Company (hereafter D&PL) invented and patented a process that modifies plants in order to prevent seeds from germinating in the next generation.[134] According to the patent, "in this way, accidental reseeding, escape of the crop plant to areas outside the area of cultivation, or germination of stored seed can be avoided."[135] Thus, with this process it is impossible to save, replant or sell seed and patentees increase their monopoly in farmers' fields.[136] In 1998, Monsanto purchased the D&PL and became co-author of the patented process that engineers crops to kill their own seed in the second generation.[137]

Such process has been dubbed "terminator technology" by RAFI which considers that the said technology is a serious threat to the food security of billions of

---

[126] See Kocken, J., Roozendaal, G. Van; "The Neem Tree Debate"; 30 Biotechnology and Development Monitor, March 1997; at pp. 8-11.
[127] Paragraph 102(a) & (b) of 36 USC; see Chapter Two of this book.
[128] Article 54 of the European Patent Convention; Idem.
[129] For more information see Kadidal, S.; "Subject-matter imperialism? Biodiversity, foreign prior art and the neem patent controversy"; 37(2) Idea: The Journal of Law and Technology, 1997; at pp.371-403.
[130] For more examples of biopiracy see RAFI; "1996 Biopiracy Update: US Patent Claim Exclusive Monopoly Control of Food Crop, Medicinal Plants, Soil Microbes and Traditional Knowledge from the South"; December 1996; supra Note 115.
[131] Rana, R. S.; "Access to Genetic Resources and Equitable Benefit Sharing: The Indian Experience"; 1(2) RIS Biotechnology an Development Review; April 1998; at pp.1-2.
[132] RAFI; "No Cure for Patents. Biotech Patents Distort and Discourage Innovation and Increase Costs for Dubious Drugs"; RAFI Newsletter, 2.7.97; supra Note 115.
[133] See Chapters Two and Three of this book.
[134] Lehmann, Volker; "Patents on Seed Sterility Threatens Seed Saving"; 35 Biotechnology and Development Monitor, June 1998; at p. 6.
[135] USDA and D&PL; "Control of Plant Gene Expression"; March 1998; US Patent No. 5,723,765.
[136] RAFI; "US Patent on New Genetic Technology Will Prevent Farmers from Saving Seed"; 11 March 1998; supra 115.
[137] Crouch, Martha; "How the Terminator Terminates"; located at http://www.bio.indiana.edu/people/terminator.html; available in August 2000.

farmers in developing countries.[138] The terminator technology eliminates the age-old tradition of farmers to save and exchange seeds among themselves.

One could argue that farmers are not obliged to buy terminator technology seeds and that they are free to continue planting traditional plant varieties. However, it has been noted that they are also at irk that transgenic crops "may confer or enhance weediness in some crops - that is, they may enhance the crop's capacity to persist in a field, invade new habitats, or both."[139] Thus, transgenic crops pose a risk of becoming weeds[140] in farmers' fields or invading wild habitats. "Once transgenic crops are planted in large numbers near sexually compatible wild/weedy relatives or other crops, transgenes will almost certainly flow via pollen to these other plants."[141]

With the current understanding, it is clear that the biggest threat to farmers with terminator technology seed plantations is not that they will not be able to save, replant or sell transgenic seeds, but that their non-transgenic crops could be contaminated by said seeds. Farmers' crops could be fertilised by the transgenic crop creating unwanted transgenic hybrids.

In face of such possibilities, States should adopt as a duty the right offered by TRIPs to exclude from patentability any inventions whose commercial exploitation could cause "serious prejudice to the environment."[142] Although the terminator technology should be considered in this category of invention, many terminator technology crops have been created and patented. For instance, Monsanto has several patents for a soybean developed with the terminator technology process.[143] According to RAFI, the major biotechnology industries in the world collectively hold more than 30 terminator-type patents.[144]

3.4 - Conclusion

Patent rights over plants and plant varieties have been used by the seed corporations to create a monopoly over PGRs. Nevertheless, patent claims that include plants are commonly piracies of indigenous peoples' or farmers' traditional knowledge.

Big seed companies, in general, claim that they suffer a loss of revenue when farmers save the seed out of the harvest from a protected plant variety seed and sell the harvested seeds to other farmers. The biotechnology companies' claim that the reuse of protected seeds by farmers causes them a reasonable loss of revenue. However, it is

---

[138] RAFI; "The Terminator Technology"; RAFI Communique March-April 1998; supra Note 115. For more on the effects of biotechnology on food security, see Sharma, Devinder; "Biotechnology and Food Security in Third World"; 1(2) Biotechnology and Development Review, April 1998; Research and Information System for the Non-Aligned and Other Developing Countries; New Delhi; at p. 21.
[139] Rissler, Jane and Mellon, Margaret; The Ecological Risks of Engineered Crops; Massachusetts Institute of Technology; Massachusetts; 1996; at p. 34.
[140] According to Rissler and Mellon, the term "weeds" refers to "unwanted plants". In other words "plants that reduce a farmer's yield as well as those that invade non-agricultural habitats such as home lawns, national parks, waterways, and wildlife habitats." Idem; at p. 28.
[141] Idem; at p. 44-45.
[142] Article 27(2) of TRIPs; see Chapter Two of this book.
[143] Patent Co-operation Treaty patent no. W097/44465; Entitled "Methods for Controlling Seed Germination Using Soybean ACYL COA Oxidase Sequences." See also Monsanto's European Patent EPO301749B1 on all soya genetically-modified using an agrobacterium method. Monsanto's request to plant its transgenic soya in Brazil caused great commotion in said country. See Chapter Eight of this book.
[144] RAFI; "Terminator 2 Years Later: Suicide Seeds on the Fast Track"; RAFI Communique February/March 2000; supra Note 115.

a one-sided claim. It is a claim that shows the intention and interests of only one group involved in the situation. The situation involves other groups of people too. This calls all stakeholders to remember an old proverb which teaches that "the liberty of one person stops at the point where it affects the liberty of someone else."

Farmers also have an interest in this biotechnological era the world is facing. They too suffer losses. Farmers suffer an initial loss when their naturally bred products are undervalued in comparison to the genetically engineered products. Moreover, farmers suffer a loss when the biodiversity of their fields is reduced or extinguished as a consequence of the spread and domination of the transgenic seed they planted. Further, farmers also suffer loss of revenue when they are not allowed to save the seed harvested from a crop grown from a protected plant variety. And moreover, "It is feared that over time multinational seed companies will slowly patent most useful genetic seed materials which exist in the international gene banks."[145]

Thus, not only have patents been granted in respect of plant germplasm held in agricultural research centres around the world, they have also been granted in respect of traditional knowledge and biodiversity. Current patent laws do not protect the interests of community innovators, and this could signify a threat to the conservation and improvement of biodiversity world-wide.

4 - GENERAL CONCLUSION

The expansion in intellectual property laws, which accompanied the evolution and commercialisation of biotechnology, now determines which country owns and controls PGRs, creating unfair and difficult obstacles for farmers and source countries. Breeders are interested in the exclusive property rights on their commercial elite and current genetic stocks and mutants, as well as having these exempted from being included in the international network of the exchange of plant germplasm. Farmers, on the other hand, seek primarily that farmers' rights be fully recognised and respected, as well as that their breeding material be excluded from the scope of free access to PGRs. A more equitable international system to protect the interest of different sectors of society and nations is necessary to reach intragenerational equity.

The FAO identified three features to create the strategy for the conservation and utilisation of plant genetic resources for food and agriculture: productivity, sustainability and equity.[146] In order to meet the needs of a growing population, the yield of plant genetic resources must increase, and there must be a continued access to and global exchange of these resources. Effective *in situ* and *ex situ* conservation strategies should guarantee the sustainability of the plant genetic resources. And furthermore, there must be an equitable system of sharing the benefits derived from the utilisation of plant genetic resources, among those responsible for their conservation and development.

So far, this strategy is basically found in words. There is not a global mobilisation to achieve it. What can be seen, on the contrary, are biotechnological countries working to secure their economic benefits from PGRs, while ignoring the social and ecological consequences of their acts. There could be serious implications in genetically altering nature's components. All things in nature are linked to each

---

[145] Bhat, M. G.; "Trade-related intellectual property rights to biological resources: Socio-economic implications for developing countries"; 19 Ecological Economics 205, 1996; at p. 210.
[146] Background; supra Note 1; at p. 26.

other and when one of its elements is altered or manipulated, there is always a reaction.[147]

In this sense, nature can be compared to a motor of a car. The pieces in the motor are all linked to each other. If someone decides to tamper with one piece, another part of the motor will be affected too. For someone who totally understands how the whole mechanism of motors works, this is not a problem. But for someone who has a very limited knowledge of motors, the consequences could be drastic. Comparing this example to genetically manipulating food and agricultural resources, not one man knows fully how nature works. It is more precise to say that all men know hardly anything of this vast divine creation. Consequently, the only way to deal with the conservation and sustainable utilisation of PGRs is to learn from and work with nature. A true partnership can be seen in how nature works as a whole.

Partnerships to prospect biological diversity in a sustainable manner can pay due recognition to all stakeholders that contribute by selecting, discovering or improving seeds and plants that offer secure food sources. Species newly discovered have little current commercial value; nevertheless, they are valuable because they have the potential to become a product which is socially and ecologically in demand.

However, Sedjo noted that "the commercial and social value of these as yet undiscovered species, while often viewed as inherent in the species, typically cannot be released without investments in the development and application of technology. In this respect genetic resources are not unlike other natural resources; it is technology that defines the social and commercial value of the germplasm resource, its suitability in use, and the costs of its utilisation."[148] Following this reasoning, it is evident that partnerships in, between and among countries to conserve and sustainably use natural resources and equitably share the benefits that derive from their use can be the vehicles to achieve intra and intergenerational equity.

Developing countries are advised to adopt a *sui generis* system, in accordance with TRIPs Article 27(3)(b), that favours farmers' rights as a means of avoiding the unauthorised appropriation of farmers' materials and traditional knowledge. Breeders' rights should not annul farmers' rights and both of these rights should be in harmony with the objectives of the CBD. At the moment, plant breeders' rights and patents do not provide for the equitable share of benefits among all stakeholders. Consequently, the solution to implement the objectives of the CBD is through the creation of a *sui generis* system as permitted by TRIPs. The International Undertaking once revised and if adopted as a protocol to the CBD could be a *sui generis* system in harmony with UPOV and the CBD. However, instead of waiting for this to happen, countries should adopt a *sui generis* system that is fair and transparent as regards rights and duties of

---

[147] The Japanese Ministry of Agriculture, Forestry and Fisheries in June 1999 annouced it would adopt more stringent safety regulations on genetically modified crops. This decision is based on a study of Cornell University which shows that pollen from genetically engineered insect resistant B.t. (Bacillus thuringiensis) maize is toxic to monarch butterflies. As such the Agriculture Ministry will suspend the approval of Bt crops in Japan until Japan adopts an appropriapriate biosafety legislation. See RAFI; "RAFI Genotype on Recent Terminator Developments"; 2 July 1999; supra Note 115.

[148] Sedjo, R.; supra Note 79; at p.296.

all stakeholders in the aim of creating fair and fraternal partnerships between developed and developing countries and between different stakeholders.

The following Chapter shall examine some of the *sui generis* systems proposed at the international and national levels.

CHAPTER FIVE

ALTERNATIVE *SUI GENERIS* SYSTEMS TO PROTECT PLANTS, PLANT VARIETIES AND ASSOCIATED TRADITIONAL KNOWLEDGE

1 - GENERAL INTRODUCTION

Many developing and least-developed countries are currently drafting *sui generis* systems in compliance with TRIPs Article 27(3)(b). Such systems tend to reflect in depth the lifestyle, culture and rights of indigenous peoples and traditional farmers in an attempt to create and balance their rights with the extensive rights granted to breeders under the UPOV and patent systems such as the one in United States.[1] As such, they demand fair compensation for indigenous peoples and local communities for their contribution regarding the conservation and genetic enhancement of species through traditional practices and innovations.

This Chapter will provide an analysis of some *sui generis* proposals which focus mainly on the rights of local communities, small farmers and indigenous populations, while others attempt to reconcile both breeders' and farmers' rights. These systems will be analysed with particular regard to the questions concerning how property rights over plant varieties are addressed and who holds those rights, as well as their compatibility with TRIPs and the CBD.

2 - *SUI GENERIS* SYSTEM ON THE INTERNATIONAL LEVEL

2.1 - Introduction

The term *sui generis* means "of its own kind". That is to say that a *sui generis* intellectual property system would have to be different from the main systems of intellectual property protection since those are provided in other articles of TRIPs.[2] TRIPs does not define what it means to be an "effective *sui generis* system" to protect plant varieties. However, it can be deduced that for a plant variety protection system to be "effective" in the eyes of the WTO the holder of the right must be able to exercise and defend his/her right in regard to the variety.

As noted by Dan Leskien and Michael Flitner, for a *sui generis* system to be compatible with TRIPs it should at least:

    1)   provide for an intellectual property right
    2)   provide for the principle of national treatment
    3)   provide for the principle of most-favoured nation
    4)   cover plant varieties of all species
    5)   have an enforcement mechanism

---

[1] See Chapter Two of this book.
[2] Leskien, D. & Flitner, M.; "The TRIPs Agreement and Intellectual Property Rights for Plant Varieties"; in GRAIN; Signposts to *Sui Generis* Rights; February 1998. Located at: http://www.grain.org/publications/signposts.htm; accessed February 1998.

6) and be more than a simple trademark, geographical denomination or protection against unfair competition.[3]

In the first place, the *sui generis* system must define what it is protecting; in other words, define what is a plant variety. The definition of plant variety can differ from country to country depending on each one's national interest. As an IPR it must determine which criteria must be fulfilled for a plant variety to be eligible for protection. For instance, patents require that the invention be new, involve an inventive step and be capable of industrial application, while PBR require that the plant variety be distinct, uniform and stable. Furthermore, both IPR and PBR define the scope of their rights, protectable materials, exemptions and duration of the right. A *sui generis* system in compliance with TRIPs can use either of these sets of requirements, a combination of both or adopt new or additional requirements. It must also clearly define the rights and duties of the right holder, duration of the right and scope of protection.

This section aims to analyse some possibilities of *sui generis* systems on the international level considering the above issues.

2.2 - *Sui Generis* Systems Based on Intellectual Property Rights other than Patents

Proposals have been made to adapt intellectual property rights other than patents to offer protection to community innovation. TRIPS provides the legal basis for countries to develop an original *sui generis* system that goes beyond patents as long as it offers some sort of intellectual property protection to plant varieties developed. What is unknown is how the WTO will react to laws in this sense.

2.2.1 - *Trademarks*

According to the United Nations Conference on Trade and Development, (hereafter UNCTAD) a "trademark is basically a guarantee of a particular set of quality characteristics. [...] Overall, economists are confident that there are significant net benefits to a well functioning trademark system in market economies. Indeed, trademark protection could be particularly valuable in developing countries because of the potential to develop brand recognition for high-quality crafts, clothing and music."[4]

TRIPs defines trademarks as "any sign, or any combination of signs, capable of distinguishing the goods or services of one undertaking from those of other undertakings."[5] "Words including personal names, letters, numerals, figurative elements and combinations of colours as well as any combination of such signs"[6] qualify as trademarks. A trademark confers an exclusive right upon the owner "to prevent all third parties not having his consent from using in the course of trade identical or similar signs for goods or services which are identical or similar to those in respect of which the trademark is registered where such use would result in a

---

[3] Idem.
[4] UNCTAD Secretariat; "The TRIPS Agreement and Developing Countries"; UNCTAD/ITE/1; Geneva; 1997; at Part II, Section IV, Paragraphs 188 and 189.
[5] Article 15(1) of TRIPs.
[6] Idem.

likelihood of confusion."[7] The term of the initial registration shall be no less than seven years which can be renewed indefinitely.[8]

Trademarks could be used as a framework right to create a *sui generis* system. As noted by Crucible Group, "Farmers' varieties are much more genetically variable than breeders' varieties. [...] It is true, however, that it makes varietal identification more difficult for scientists of the industrialised sector. Indigenous farmers, however, have systems of recognising and naming their own varieties, and these systems could be given legal recognition."[9] In India, for instance, the Tea Board of India holds a trademark, which is a special logo, to characterise the genuine Darjeeling tea. Only the packagings that have this logo are allowed to have the words "pure Darjeeling" and "100% Darjeeling".[10] The Swiss organisation Institut fur Marketecologie and the German organisation Naturland-Verband periodically inspect the organic Darjeeling tea gardens to guarantee the genuine production of the Darjeeling tea.[11]

UNCTAD notes that "protection of trademarks benefits producers, traders and consumers in developed and developing countries alike."[12] Trademarks could be used to characterise, for instance, the genuine traditionally bred Amazonian plant species, as well as products derived from them. Furthermore, trademarks could be used to indicate that the traditionally bred plant varieties were developed in an environmentally sustainable manner. The trademark could be, for instance, a green sticker with a unique tree design that would be eligible to characterise every traditional variety that fulfilled certain requirements to be determined. A transgenic plant would have a different type of trademark, a different type of sticker for instance. In this way both traditionally bred and biotechnologically bred plant varieties would be eligible for protection, rather than only the latter as is the case nowadays.[13]

It should be noted, though, that for trademarks to have success in the protection of plant varieties, the public must be successfully informed through efficient marketing strategies. Otherwise, if product labelling is ignored or omitted, genetically altered plant varieties could be sold as if they were organically grown and traditionally bred plant varieties. Furthermore, a *sui generis* system adapted from trademarks would only work if "the producer of a trademarked good maintain a consistent quality over time and across consumers."[14]

Thus, if trademarks were adapted to be used as a *sui generis* system, they would have two main functions. First of all they would offer protection on plant varieties and therefore comply with the TRIPs requirement.[15] And secondly, as trademarks distinguish goods and services in the course of trade,[16] they would also serve as a label which would favour consumers when choosing what to buy. If such a protection worked successfully in a country, the said trademarks could be used on a regional level[17] or globally.[18]

---

[7] Article 16 of TRIPs.
[8] Article 18 of TRIPs.
[9] Crucible Group; People, plants, and patents: the impact of intellectual property on biodiversity, conservation, trade, and rural society; Ottawa, Canada; IDRC; 1994; at p. 37.
[10] Website of the Darjeeling Planters Association. Located at http://www.darjeelingtea.com; accessed in August 2000.
[11] Idem.
[12] UNCTAD Secretariat; supra Note 4; at Part II, Section IV, Paragraphs 188 and 189.
[13] See Chapters Two and Three of this book.
[14] Groves, Peter; Sourcebook on Intellectual Property Law; Cavendish Publishing Limited; London; 1997; at p. 529.
[15] See Article 27(3)(b).
[16] Marett, Paul; Intellectual Property Law; London; Sweet & Maxwell; 1996; at p. 3.
[17] See i.e. Council of the European Union; Council Regulation No. 40/94 of 20 December 1993 on the Community Trademark.

On the other hand trademarks could only prevent others from using the marked varieties. They would not be able to prevent others form selling the plant variety without a mark or under a different mark. Thus, trademarks only have a limited scope of protection and complementary protection would be necessary for a *sui generis* system of this type to work.

2.2.2 - Geographic Indications

Article 22 of TRIPs defines geographical indications as "indications which identify a good as originating in the territory of a member, or a region or locality in that territory, where a given quality, reputation or other characteristic of the good is essentially attributable to its geographical origin".[19] Geographical indications have normally been used on products to identify the place where they come from, its quality or specific characteristics. TRIPs obliges Members to prevent "the use of any means in the designation or presentation of a good that indicates or suggests that the good in question originates in a geographical area other than the true place of origin in a manner which misleads the public as to the geographical origin of the good."[20] Therefore, geographic indications do not protect the traditional knowledge or plant variety as such, but basically prevent the utilisation of a false indication of where the good comes from.

Geographic indications could be adapted to serve as an indicator of the place where the original plant species, used in the development of a new plant variety, was collected: gene banks, wild species, farmer's field, Amazon forest, etc. This could be an important proof to be used in the equitable share of benefits derived from the use of the plant variety accessed in accordance to the CBD. The indication of where the primary plant sources had been accessed could be a signpost to prove that there had been contributions of local farmers to develop the new variety through their traditional breeding techniques. Amazonian plants accessed by foreign companies could be protected under geographic indications which could serve as prior art in order to avoid their patenting abroad just because they are not known in a foreign country. Carlos Correa suggests that in the case of geographic indications, a suitable mechanism could be developed to assure the value of agricultural products and contribute to the prosperity of rural zones.[21]

UNCTAD notes that geographical indications "may have positive effects on rural economies by increasing farmers' income and investments in production and marketing of agricultural products and foodstuffs. Some developing countries have already established valuable geographical indications."[22] Geographic indications could protect traditional knowledge and raise the economic value of plant varieties and herbal formulations developed by local communities or indigenous peoples. The first step to take for this to occur is for the country of origin to protect plant varieties and herbal formulations under geographic indications. TRIPs determines that there is no obligation for States to protect geographic indications which are not protected in the country of origin.[23]

---

[18] See i.e. WIPO; Madrid Agreement concerning the International Registration of Marks; 1891, revised in 1967 and amended in 1979.
[19] Article 22(1) of TRIPs.
[20] Article 22(2) of TRIPs.
[21] Correa, C.; "Derechos Soberanos y de Propiedad sobre los Recursos Fitogenéticos"; prepared at the request of the Secretariat of the FAO Commission on Plant Genetic Resources; First Extraordinary meeting of the Commission on Plant Genetic Resources; Rome 7-11 November 1994.
[22] UNCTAD Secretariat; supra Note 4; at Part II, Section IV, Paragraph 197.
[23] Article 24(9) of TRIPs.

Dutfield notes that the geographical indication system can have retrospective effect.[24] He notes that "For many years Cypriot rivals to the Sherry producers of the Jérez region of Southern Spain were allowed to call their product 'Cyprus Sherry' (Sherry being an English corruption of Jérez). Now the same product must be labelled as 'Cyprus Fortified Wine' if producers wish to export it to EC countries."[25] Thus, the retrospective effect allows products to be protected under geographic indications even though they already form part of common knowledge.

Dutfield also examines the possibility of protection of Basmati rice[26] under geographic indication.[27] Basmati rice is a high quality aromatic rice variety cultivated in areas of Northern India and Pakistan and exported to North America and Europe. Its germplasm was freely accessed by the food company Establissements Haudecoueur La Courneuve and the US company Rice Tec through the International Rice Research Institute,[28] (hereafter IRRI), in the Philippines. Establissements Haudecoeur La Courneuve uses the trademarks "Riz Long Basmati" and "Riz Long Basmati Riz du Monde", while Rice Tec sells its own basmati rice under the name "Texmati" and was awarded in 1998, a patent entitled "Basmati Lines and Grains". Neither company has any obligations to share the benefits that arise from the use of the high reputation of the true Basmati rice with India or Pakistan because the germplasm was acquired prior the CBD entered into force.

Once India and Pakistan have adopted legislation to protect Basmati rice and other of their traditional resources under geographical indications, they could appeal to the WTO on the grounds that TRIPs Article 22(2) had been violated by both companies.

Dutfield, however, expresses the view that the best way for India and Pakistan to favour their Basmati rice growers and make their exportation markets more lucrative is not through litigation but through a competent geographical indication system or certification trademarks and effective marketing.[29] These tools can make it more difficult for competitors to use the reputation of traditional Basmati rice variety to sell their own varieties. This is like "selling a cat as if it were a rabbit".[30]

It is difficult to imagine how geographic indication could effectively work as a *sui generis* system to protect plant varieties. Although it could be used to prevent the false indication of a traditional variety, biopirates could simply choose not to label their products. Therefore, the determination of where the parent of the plant variety was accessed can be **one** of the requirements of the *sui generis* system to protect plant varieties. This would assist to promote the equitable share of benefits with the source country and all stakeholders that contributed to the development of a plant variety. The geographic indication requirement would have to be complemented by other forms of protection.

2.2.3 - Trade Secrets

---

[24] Dutfield, Graham; Intellectual Property Rights, Trade ad Biodiversity: Seeds and Plant Varieties; Earthscan; London; 2000.
[25] Idem.
[26] "Basmati" in Hindi means "the fragrant one".
[27] For an analysis of the Basmati case see Dutfield, Graham; supra Note 24; at p. 76.
[28] The IRRI is one of the International Agricultural Research Centres of the CGIAR system. See Chapter Four of this book.
[29] Dutfield, G.; supra Note 24.
[30] Brazilian proverb.

Trade secrets have also been proposed as a mechanism to protect traditional knowledge.[31] According to TRIPs,

> Natural and legal persons shall have the possibility of preventing information lawfully within their control from being disclosed to, acquired by, or used by others without their consent in a manner contrary to honest commercial practices[32] – so long as such information:
> - is secret in the sense that it is not, as a body or in the precise configuration and assembly of its components, generally known among or readily accessible to persons within the circles that normally deal with the kind of information in question;
> - has commercial value because it is secret; and
> - has been subject to reasonable steps under the circumstances, by the person lawfully in control of the information, to keep it secret.[33]

UNCTAD observed that trade secrets may be applied to major or minor innovations and likewise to "science-based or purely empirical knowledge, as well as to non-technical information that has commercial value."[34] It further adds that frequently "trade secrets are of a 'tacit' nature in the sense that the relevant knowledge is not formalised or codified."[35]

Therefore, traditional knowledge, in regard to medicinal plant properties, known only by the shaman[36] in a tribe could possibly be registered as trade secret. The shaman is customarily in control of the medicinal traditional knowledge that can be secret to other members in the tribe. This knowledge has a potential commercial value. Traditional knowledge registered as a trade secret could be used to negotiate contracts between an indigenous tribe and a pharmaceutical industry, following honest commercial practices and the objectives of the CBD.

Trade secrets do not grant exclusive rights to the holder, as is the case of patents. Its function is to prevent third parties from acquiring and using the protected information in a dishonest commercial manner. Therefore it could be used to impede the utilisation of traditional knowledge related to medicinal plants. However, as noted by Carlos Correa, in order to protect an information as a trade secret, the majority of national laws require that there be deliberate acts of the holder of the information to keep the information secret.[37] In the case of traditional knowledge, this is not always the case.

The lack of secrecy could weaken the possibility of using trade secrets to protect indigenous knowledge. Indigenous people might naively reveal the protected information when offered a gift or simply when asked. As noted by UNCTAD, "third party acquisition of secret knowledge is a violation only when obtained by improper

---

[31] Dutfield, G.; supra Note 24
[32] This footnote is part of Article 39(2). "For the purpose of this provision, 'a manner contrary to honest commercial practices' shall mean at least practices such as breach of contract, breach of confidence and inducement to breach, and includes the acquisition of undisclosed information by third parties who knew, or were grossly negligent in failing to know, that such practices were involved in the acquisition."
[33] Article 39(2) of TRIPs.
[34] UNCTAD Secretariat; supra Note 4; at Part II, Section V, Paragraph 223.
[35] Idem.
[36] Shamans are the healers in an indigenous tribe.
[37] Correa, C.; supra Note 21.

means, that is to say in ways that are excluded by private contractual agreement or that violate a confidential relationship or that otherwise offend public policy. Trade secrets that are voluntarily revealed, insufficiently guarded or reverse-engineered lose all protection and become subject to free competition."[38]

As such, the concept of trade secrets would only be an efficient mechanism to protect traditional knowledge if those in indigenous and local communities in fact made an effort to keep the information secret. "Once information becomes public, no end of confidentiality agreements can restore its confidential status. Any disclosure is fatal to its confidentiality, unless that disclosure is made in circumstances of confidentiality."[39] Nowadays, traditional knowledge is not as well protected as before, and on several occasions it has been appropriated and sealed under patents.

2.3 - UNESCO/WIPO Model Provisions for National Laws on Protection of Expressions of Folklore Against Illicit Exploitation and other Prejudicial Actions

In 1985, the United Nations Educational and Cultural Organisation, (hereafter UNESCO) and WIPO adopted the "Model Provisions for National Laws on Protection of Expressions of Folklore against Illicit Exploitation and Other Prejudicial Actions"[40] (hereafter the Model) to protect expressions of folklore against unauthorised use and distortion.

One of the laudable points of the Model Provisions is to determine that when the use of expressions of folklore is "made both with gainful intent and outside their traditional or customary context", it is subject to the prior informed consent of the respective community or authorisation by a competent authority.[41] Criminal sanctions may be imposed on those who fail to indicate the ethnic and geographic source of an expression of folklore in any type of communication to the public including printed publications.[42]

Another favourable point of the Model is that communities can maintain the exclusive right over their folklore for as long as the community lives. Mihaly Fiscor[43] notes that "folklore is truly a living and still developing tradition, rather than just a memory of the past."[44] According to Posey and Dutfield, "a law that implements the model provisions could include traditional genetic resources as 'expressions of folklore' to be protected if national lawmaking bodies wished to approve such an interpretation."[45] As such, indigenous peoples could keep the exclusive right over their biological inventions forever. The Model proposes that state agencies collect fees from users of folklore. The fees collected ought to be directed towards the protection of

---

[38] UNCTAD Secretariat; supra Note 4; at Part II, Section V, Paragraph 230.
[39] Groves, Peter; Sourcebook on Intellectual Property Law; Cavendish Publishing Limited; London; 1997; at p. 644.
[40] UNESCO/WIPO; Model Provisions for National Laws on the Protection of Expressions of Folklore against Illicit Exploitation and Other Prejudicial Actions; UNESCO/WIPO; Geneva, Switzerland; 1985.
[41] Idem; Section 3.
[42] Idem; Section 6.
[43] Assistant Director General of WIPO in 1998.
[44] Ficsor, Mihaly; "Attempts to Provide International Protection for Folklore by Intellectual Property Rights"; in the codification of the texts of speeches and papers presented at the UNESCO-WIPO World Forum on the Protection of Folklore, held in Phuket, Thailand; 8-10 April 1997; at p. 213.UNESCO Publication No. CLT/CIC/98/1; WIPO Publication No. 758(E/F/S).
[45] Posey, Darrell and Dutfield, Graham; Beyond Intellectual Property; International Development Research Centre; Ottawa, Canada; 1996; at p. 99.

folklore. If this were implemented, it is advisable that this state agency be under sufficient supervision to avoid that the fees collected be misappropriated.

The Model Provisions have attracted little interest from national legislatures. However, they influenced the drafting of the UNESCO Recommendation on the Safeguarding of Traditional Culture and Folklore,[46] (hereafter the Recommendations), which were unanimously adopted by its Member States. According to the Recommendations, folklore is "the totality of tradition-based creations of a cultural community, expressed by a group or individuals and recognised as reflecting the expectations of a community in so far as they reflect its cultural and social identity; its standards and values are transmitted orally, by imitation or by other means. Its forms are, among others, language, literature, music, dance, games, mythology, rituals, customs, handicrafts, architecture and other arts."[47]

The Recommendations emphasise that since "folklore constitutes manifestations of intellectual creativity whether it be individual or collective, *it deserves to be protected in a manner inspired by the protection provided for intellectual productions*. Such protection of folklore has become indispensable as a means of promoting further development, maintenance and dissemination of those expressions, both within and outside the country, without prejudice to related legitimate interests" (emphasis added). In this sense, the manifestations of traditional knowledge are considered part of folklore, and could be protected under IPR.

The Recommendations deserve credit for recognising folklore as having evolutionary nature instead of as fixed and moreover, for admitting that although it has an evolving character, it is still protectable by IPR. UNESCO additionally acknowledges that on account of its "evolving character" folklore "cannot always be directly protected"[48]. As such it recommends Member States to:

(a) establish national archives where collected folklore can be properly stored and made available;

(b) establish a central national archive function for service purposes (central cataloguing, dissemination of information on folklore materials and standards of folklore work including the aspect of safeguarding);

(c) create museums or folklore sections at existing museums where traditional and popular culture can be exhibited;

(d) give precedence to ways of presenting traditional and popular cultures that emphasise the living or past aspects of those cultures (showing their surroundings, ways of life and the works, skills and techniques they have produced);

(e) harmonise collecting and archiving methods;

---

[46] UNESCO Recommendation on the Safeguarding of Traditional Culture and Folklore, adopted by the General Conference at its twenty-fifth session; Paris; 15 November 1989.
[47] Idem; Recommendation A.
[48] Idem; Recommendation C.

> (f) train collectors, archivists, documentalists and other specialists in the conservation of folklore, from physical conservation to analytic work;
>
> (g) provide means for making security and working copies of all folklore materials, and copies for regional institutions, thus securing the cultural community an access to the materials.[49]

By establishing national archives and museums, traditional knowledge, which is not considered part of prior art by some national intellectual property systems because it is transmitted orally, will be documented, conserved and protected from being misused and misappropriated by third parties. According to the Recommendations, States should promote the respect for folklore in "the widest sense of the term" and additionally, promote "a better understanding of cultural diversity and different world views, especially those not reflected in dominant cultures."[50]

According to the UN Draft Declaration on Indigenous Rights,[51] (hereafter Draft Declaration):

> Indigenous peoples are entitled to the recognition of the full ownership, control and protection of their cultural and intellectual property.
>
> They have the right to special measures to control, develop and protect their sciences, technologies and cultural manifestations, including human and other genetic resources, seeds, medicines, knowledge of the properties of fauna and flora, oral traditions, literatures, designs and visual and performing arts.[52]

Furthermore, the Draft Declaration states:

> Indigenous peoples have the right to determine and develop priorities and strategies for the development or use of their lands, territories and other resources, including the right to require that States obtain their free and informed consent prior to the approval of any project affecting their lands, territories and other resources, particularly in connection with the development, utilisation or exploitation of mineral, water or other resources. Pursuant to agreement with the indigenous peoples concerned, just and fair compensation shall be provided for any such activities and measures taken to mitigate adverse environmental, economic, social, cultural or spiritual impact.[53]

---

[49] Idem; Recommendation C.
[50] UNESCO Folklore Recommendations, Recommendation D.
[51] UN Draft Declaration on Indigenous Rights as agreed upon by the members of the Working Group at its Eleventh Session; Published by the United Nations, 23 August 1993. There still has not been a final agreement on the Draft Declaration on Indigenous Rights as of the date of August 2001.
[52] Idem; Article 29.
[53] Idem; Article 30.

Taking into account the Draft Declaration, a *sui generis* system that considers the expressions of traditional knowledge, such as traditional breeding methods and traditional plant varieties, as part of folklore should subordinate access to them to the respective group's prior informed consent. Furthermore, it should adopt the right in the Draft Declaration that determines that indigenous peoples have the right over their *human and other genetic resources, seeds, medicines, knowledge of the properties of fauna and flora, oral traditions*.[54] This could safeguard the true creators and owners of indigenous plant varieties and associated traditional knowledge.

Not only indigenous peoples possess their own folklore, but also rural communities. In this sense, traditional varieties and traditional breeding methods developed by local communities and transmitted orally throughout generations can be considered part of their folklore. Although in the long-run a *sui generis* system based on folklore to protect traditionally bred plant varieties could be adopted, this idea at the moment is still premature as States have still not implemented the Model at national level. Furthermore, two more problems were identified: "the lack of appropriate sources for the identification of the expressions of folklore to be protected and the lack of workable mechanisms for settling the questions of expressions of folklore that can be found not only in one country, but in several countries of a region."[55]

2.4 - Organisation of African Unity Draft Model Legislation on Community Rights on Access to Biological Resources

The Organisation of African Unity, (hereafter OAU), has drafted a Model Legislation on Community Rights on Access to Biological Resources during its Summit of Heads of State and Government during May and June 1998, (hereafter Model Law).[56] The Ministerial Council of the OAU recommended that the Model Law be used as the basis for the elaboration of the national laws of African States, as well as the basis for the creation of a regional convention.

The Model Law was born out of the joint effort of the Scientific Technical and Research Commission of the Organisation of African Unity, (hereafter OAU/STRC), based in Lagos, Nigeria, the Ethiopian Environmental Protection Agency and the Institute for Sustainable Development based in Ethiopia. At the Workshop on Medicinal Plants and Herbal Medicine in Africa, held in Nairobi,[57] the issue of intellectual property rights was identified as the major problem of the regulation of access to medicinal plants and to community knowledge and technologies. The conclusions derived from this workshop led on to the elaboration of the Model Law.

The Model Law reflects the main provisions contained in the CBD reinforcing the rights of local communities over their biological resources. The Preamble of the Model Law states "the rights of local communities over their biological resources, traditional knowledge and technologies that represent the very nature of the livelihood systems and that have evolved over generations of human history, are of a collective nature and, therefore, a priori rights taking precedence over rights based on private

---

[54] Idem; Article 29.
[55] Ficsor, Mihaly; supra Note 44; at p. 223.
[56] OAU Draft Model Legislation on Community Rights and on Access To Biological Resources; Accepted as Doc.CM/2075 (LXVIII) ADD.1; Attached to OAU Resolution on the Draft Law and Convention on Community Rights and on Access to Biological Resources; Ougadougou, June 1998; Doc. CM/2075 (LXVIII).
[57] OAU/STRC/DEPA/KIPO; Workshop on Medicinal Plants and Herbal Medicine in Africa: Policy Issues on Ownership, Access and Conservation; held in Nairobi, Kenya, on 14-17 April 1997.

interest."[58] The CBD superficially mentions the rights of local and indigenous peoples. For this reason, and for the fact that the majority of the people living in Africa are local and indigenous peoples, the Model Law focuses primarily on the interests and rights of those people. Nevertheless, the Model Law recognises that traditional and modern technologies are complementary. "There is the need to promote and support the traditional and indigenous technologies that are important in the conservation and sustainable use of biological resources and to complement them by modern technologies."[59]

The objectives of the Model Law lead to the union of traditional and modern knowledge relevant to the conservation and sustainable use of biological resources.[60] Furthermore, it seeks the equitable share of benefits which derive from their use, for the purpose of improving the biological diversity and life support and health care system in African countries. This is the essence of the CBD that stimulates the creation of equitable ecological and developmental partnerships between developed and developing countries.

The Model Law safeguards the practice related to the traditional exchange of resources and knowledge between local communities and excludes them from its scope, as well as the benefits that derive from those customary practices.[61] These provisions are in line with the FAO International Undertaking.[62]

Collectors have the commitment to provide duplicates of specimens, record of community knowledge collected and information on research and development on the resources.[63] There is also the commitment not to transfer collected biodiversity and traditional knowledge to third parties without prior authorisation of the national competent authority and concerned local community.[64] Furthermore, collectors must commit themselves not to apply for a patent or any other intellectual property right using the collected biological materials and traditional knowledge.

The Model Law creates community rights[65] as Article 5(1) reads:

> The State shall recognise and protect the rights of the local communities over their biological resources and to collectively benefit from their knowledge, innovations and practices acquired through generations and for the conservation and sustainable use of biological resources.[66]

Local communities are to be perpetually recognised as the "sole and legitimate creators, users and custodians of the biological resources, community knowledge, innovations and practices."[67] Furthermore, local communities are entitled to "fifty per

---

[58] Model Law; supra Note 56 Preamble.
[59] Idem.
[60] Idem; Article 2.
[61] Idem; Article 3.
[62] See Chapter Four of this book.
[63] Articles 4(3)(b)(c)and (g) of the Model Law; supra Note 56; Article 15(7) and 17(2) of CBD.
[64] Article 4(3)(d) of the Model Law; Article 15(5) of CBD.
[65] Community rights are based on Articles 8(j), 10(c), 10(d), 15(5) of the CBD, as well as on the decisions taken by the 5th Conference of Parties of the CBD on the implementation of Article 8(j). See 5th Conference of Parties of the CBD, held in Bratislava in June 1998.
[66] Model Law; supra Note 56; Article 5(1).
[67] Idem; Article 5(2).

cent of benefits obtained from any commercial use of biological resources and/or community knowledge and technologies."[68]

African States can use the Model Law when drafting their national laws on access to their biological diversity. The ministerial Council of the OAU unanimously endorsed the Model Law and recommended its adoption by all African States.[69] Furthermore, it recommended that they "initiate a process of negotiation among African countries to formulate and adopt an African Convention on Biological Diversity with emphasis on conditions for access to biological resources and protection of community rights."[70]

The Model Law is rich in rights of local communities towards their traditional knowledge, innovations and practices as well as the African States' developmental aspirations through access to their biodiversity.

2.5 - Conclusion

A *sui generis* system in accordance to TRIPs ought to provide an intellectual property right[71], which excludes others from certain acts in regard to the protected plant variety, and/or obliges them to pay royalties to the developer. So far, as noted by UNCTAD, the existent intellectual property rights are "owned mainly by firms in industrialised countries. While some industrialising nations have begun producing new technologies and technological products, developing countries, in general, are net importers of technical knowledge. [...] Considering developing countries as importers of information, however, one anticipated consequence of their adopting a stronger protection regime would be an increase in royalty payments to foreign title-holders. Furthermore, the exclusive position of title-holders of IPRs allows them to raise the prices paid by consumers and users of industrial technologies. Particularly sensitive products and industrial inputs such as pharmaceuticals and agro-chemicals raise the largest fears as regards significant price increases."[72]

Considering this fact, provided that the new IPR complies to the most-favoured nation principle and national treatment principle, developing States should define and adopt an intellectual property *sui generis* right that best suits their own social and economic development. *Sui generis* systems of this kind should recognise, protect and reward traditional knowledge as well as the development of traditionally bred plants.

A *sui generis* system to plant varieties can be created by uniting different aspects of existing intellectual property systems: trademarks, geographic indications and trade secrets. Such system could protect biotechnologically bred plant varieties with one trademark and traditionally bred varieties with another. Furthermore, they could be qualified with geographic indications "given quality, reputation or other characteristic".[73] Trade secrets could be used to protect confidential traditional knowledge in relation to the plant variety.

---

[68] Idem; Article 5(6).
[69] OAU Resolution on the Draft Law and Convention on Community Rights and the Control of Access to Biological Resources; supra Note 56.
[70] Idem.
[71] TRIPs Article 1(2) states: "For the purpose of this Agreement, the term 'intellectual property' refers to all categories of intellectual property that are the subject of Sections 1 to 7 of Part II." TRIPs Article 27(3)(b), which provides for the *sui generis* system for plant variety protection, falls under Section 5 of Part II.
[72] UNCTAD Secretariat; supra Note 4; at Part I, Section III, Paragraph 44.
[73] TRIPs Article 22(1).

The UNESCO Folklore Recommendations represent a possible means to protect traditional knowledge under the folklore concept. By following the Recommendations, States will help identify, catalogue, protect and disseminate all folklore expressions including traditional knowledge and thus, prevent its misuse and illegal appropriation. A *sui generis* system based on the Recommendations can create an intellectual property right that protects all folklore expressions including the expressions of their traditional knowledge, such as breeding methods and plant varieties. This could be a useful method to oblige those that use traditional knowledge, breeding methods and plant varieties to equitably share the benefits that arise out of their use with the holders of the respective folklore. A code of ethics to access and use folklore could be adopted.

The essential characteristic of an international *sui generis* system to protect plant varieties, is that it ought to facilitate an exchange of information and the integration of all plant breeders, whether biotechnological or traditional. An efficient international *sui generis* system is one that manages to give and balance rights of all those that develop new plant varieties, empowering those sectors of society without empowering others. Unless this is done, the number of unemployed and poor traditional breeders will increase and precious knowledge and fine skill will be lost.

Through the Model Law, African States can regulate access to their biodiversity in a way that respects their interests and traditional knowledge in order to enter fair and equitable partnerships with collectors of biological resources and associated traditional knowledge.

3 - *SUI GENERIS* SYSTEM ON THE NATIONAL LEVEL

3.1 - Introduction

The implementation of *sui generis* systems at the national level should provide real tools and mechanisms to promote and protect local rights. Many manifestations and judicial battles are being fought at national, local and NGO levels to increase peoples' control over their resources and livelihoods. Furthermore, "Article 27.3(b) of the TRIPs Agreement could undermine food security and biodiversity or enhance it depending upon the relative effects of the various provisions".[74] Therefore, TRIPs should allow countries to decide what is an effective *sui generis* system for the protection of plant varieties. An "effective *sui generis* system" should be a system that allows each country to conserve its natural resources and environment and develop economically, and does not start a new colonisation period where biotechnologically rich countries colonise biotechnologically poor countries.

3.2 - *Sui Generis* System Combining Patents And Plant Breeders' Rights

A *sui generis* system combining patents and plant breeders' rights provides the strongest intellectual property rights protection for plant varieties because it allows both types of monopoly rights to be used. IPGRI notes that patents and plant variety protection are likely to exist in the same country and thus, States should include in

---

[74] Tansey, Geoff; "Trade, Intellectual Property, Food and Biodiversity"; Quaker Peace & Service; London; February 1999. Located at: http://www.quaker.org/quno; accessed February 1999.

their laws the prohibition of double protection. It further suggests that national laws can provide different levels of protection for varieties of the same species depending upon their destined use.[75] Those that oppose the patent system for the protection of biological materials suggest that "if nothing else, the world's essential food crops and medicines should remain outside of the patent field."[76] This would avoid corporate monopolies over those vital resources.

The best option is to avoid using the patent system to protect plant varieties, because as the Crucible Group noted, "an international system created almost 125 years ago to patent machines and factory parts may not be the best system for plants, animals, and micro-organisms."[77]

3.3 - Thammasat Resolution

Many traditional communities regard the extension of private ownership rights to biological resources totally inappropriate because they were previously held in the public domain where traditional communities believe they should stay.

The Thammasat Resolution was the final Declaration of the meeting on *sui generis* rights held by the Thai Network on Community Rights and Biodiversity, (hereafter BIOTHAI), and Genetic Resource Action International, (hereafter GRAIN), in Bangkok, Thailand, from 1 to 6 December 1997. "Thammasat" means both "knowledge of nature" and "justice" in Thai.[78] At this meeting, 45 representatives of indigenous, peasant, academic, non-governmental and governmental organisations from 19 countries from Africa, Asia and Latin America met to discuss strategies to overcome the patenting of their biodiversity and traditional knowledge.

The Thammasat Resolution proposes a unique *sui generis* rights system. It denies the *sui generis* rights option proposed under TRIPs which it regards as a new form of monopoly over plant varieties because they will be linked to intellectual property rights. Thus, the resolution affirms that its *"sui generis* rights exist independently of the IPR based *sui generis* systems promoted by the TRIPs Agreement."[79]

Participants in the Thammasat Resolution declared that "Our rights are inalienable, they existed long before IPR regimes were established. As legal, political, economical, social and cultural rights, they are part of people's sovereignty and, therefore, part of human rights."[80] Furthermore, the resolution affirmed that "As community/collective rights, they are indivisible and intergenerational; they include Farmers' Rights and apply to indigenous peoples, peasant and family farmers, fisherfolk and other local communities, which derive their livelihoods from biodiversity."[81]

The Thammasat Resolution excludes all life forms from the scope of intellectual property rights. This opposition to patents on life forms is strictly non-

---

[75] IPGRI; "The Agreement on Trade-Related Aspects of Intellectual Property Rights (TRIPs) – A Decision Check List"; Rome; 1999; Located at: http://www.cgiar.org/ipgri; accessed December 1999.
[76] Crucible Group; supra Note 9; at p. 56.
[77] Idem; at p. 60.
[78] The Thammasat Resolution - Building and strengthening our sui generis rights. Final declaration of the meeting held by the Thai Network on Community Rights and Biodiversity (BIOTHAI) and Genetic Resource action International (GRAIN), in Bangkok, Thailand, from 1 to 6 December 1997.
[79] Idem.
[80] Idem.
[81] Idem.

negotiable. The resolution states: "We reaffirm our total and frontal opposition to the extension of intellectual property rights to life forms, be it on humans, animals, plants, micro-organisms, or their genes, cells and other parts. We are also adamantly against biopiracy[82] and the monopolisation of biodiversity-related knowledge through such IPRs."[83]

Signatories to the Thammasat Resolution not only oppose the patenting of all life forms for not considering them human creations, but moreover, for the belief that any type of IPR is detrimental to local communities. The resolution states that the "overall implication of TRIPS, and for that matter the whole of the WTO, is highly detrimental to people's economies, cultures and livelihoods. [...] While some people look at the *sui generis* option in TRIPS as a window through which other forms of rights over biodiversity can be articulated in legislation, it is our conviction that such rights will be linked to IPR and will result in new and further monopoly rights over plant varieties."[84]

The Thammasat Resolution demands for TRIPs to be revised in order to allow countries totally to exclude all life forms, as well associated traditional knowledge, from intellectual property rights. Moreover, they plead for the CBD to avoid becoming "a mechanism for transnational corporations to trade biodiversity in the name of 'access' and 'benefit-sharing'."[85]

3.4 – Discoverer's Rights

It is well known that indigenous people or traditional farmers in fact discovered many world-wide pharmaceutical and agricultural products that originated from natural products.

Michael Gollin, an American environmental and patent lawyer, suggests a *sui generis* option to protect the rights of those individuals or communities who through their traditional knowledge discover new plant properties. This right would be called the "discoverer's right".[86] He suggests that rights should be granted to individuals, local and indigenous communities who manage to *discover* and make a taxonomic description of any species or varieties, which has not fallen in the public domain.[87]

Such reasoning is in line with Sedjo who believes that "[...] property rights for plant species should be expanded and extended to cover newly discovered natural species and should continue to be applied to special genetic stock, current breeder lines, and genetically engineered organisms. Such an approach would allow the genetically rich Third World countries an opportunity to profit directly from the ownership of genetic resources. Property rights to species would also provide a direct financial incentive to protect and maintain the natural habitat in which rare and as yet unknown species may reside, since their discovery and development at some future

---

[82] On the piracy of the Thai herb kwaao khruea, see Assavanonda, A.; "Experts Want New Bill Passed Soon – Concern Over Piracy by Foreign Companies"; The Bangkok Post; 19 October 1998; Also distributed by GRAIN Los Banos: grain@baylink.mozcom.com.
[83] Thammasat Resolution; supra Note 78.
[84] Idem.
[85] Idem.
[86] Gollin, Michael; "An Intellectual Property Rights Framework for Biodiversity Prospecting"; in Laird, S.A.; Meyers, C.A; Gamez, R.; Sittenfeld, A.; Janzen, D.H.; Gollin, M.A; Juma, C.; (eds); Biodiversity Prospecting: Using Genetic Resources for Sustainable Development; World Resources Institute; Washington, D.C.; USA; 1993; pp. 180-181.
[87] Idem.

time could generate direct financial returns to the owner."[88] The author recognises that "[i]n the absence of property rights to species, even with certainty of future social benefits, neither the individual, the corporation, nor individual countries have any incentive other than altruism to incur costs necessary to protect habitat for unique or endangered plant species."[89]

However, if IPRs were extended to wild species, it is probable that patent offices would receive several claims for plants species whose utility was invented or still unknown.[90] Furthermore, the placement of new plant species in the public domain would facilitate the access of biotechnological companies to those plants which could be tested for medicinal properties or developed into plant varieties.[91] From the public domain those newly discovered plants would fall into the field of private property under the domain of patents. Gollin concludes that the concept of discoverer's right must be further developed in order to be workable.

The "discoverer of a new plant species" can be compared to the "discoverer of a treasure", as provided in ancient Roman law. Ancient Roman law considered a treasure "any precious object, not only money, which remained occult, under earth or in another manner, during the necessary time for the memory of who it belonged to be forgotten, and therefore, becoming impossible to identify the successor."[92] At the beginning of the Roman Republic, a treasure was part of the land where it was found.[93] Several years later, the Constitution of Adrian changed this concept and established that half of the value of the treasure belonged to the owner of the land and the other half belonged to the discoverer.[94]

In the legislation of many countries derived from Roman law, the state is the ultimate owner of all natural resources on its territory. A complimentary status to newly discovered natural resources could facilitate local and indigenous populations to receive an equitable share of benefits derived from the use of the discovered resource. The Spanish Civil Code, for instance, that descends from ancient Roman law, defines "treasure" as the hidden and ignored deposit of money, jewels, gems or other precious objects whose legitimate ownership is not determined.[95] Article 351 of the Spanish Civil Code determined that "the occult treasure belongs to the owner of the land where it is found. However, when it is casually found on a land that belongs to someone else or to the State, half of the treasure belongs to the discoverer. If the discoveries are interesting to science or art, the State may purchase them for a fair price."[96]

A similar concept is also found in English law under the Treasure Act 1996.[97] "Any treasure[98] found on and after 24 September 1997, whatever the nature of the place where the treasure was found and whatever the circumstances in which it was left, including being lost or being left with no intention of recovery, vests, subject to prior interests and rights, in the franchisee, if there is one, or otherwise in the Crown. Treasure so vesting in the Crown is to be treated as part of the hereditary revenues of

---

[88] Sedjo, Roger A.; " Property Rights and the Protection of Plant Genetic Resources"; in Kloppenburg, Jr. (ed); Seeds and Sovereignty; Duke University Press; London, 1988; at p. 294.
[89] Idem; at p. 300.
[90] Gollin; supra Note 86; at p. 180.
[91] Idem.
[92] Iglesias, Juan; Derecho Romano; Editorial Ariel; sixth edition; Barcelona; 1972; at p. 206-207.
[93] Idem.
[94] García, César; "Manual de Derecho Romano"; Editorial Tecnos, S.A.; second edition; Madrid; 1996; at p. 173.
[95] Article 352 of the Spanish Civil Code; Editorial Tecnos, S.A.; seventh edition; Madrid; 1988.
[96] Idem; Article 351.
[97] Treasure Act 1996; 32(s) Halbury's Statute (4th edn.); Open Spaces.
[98] For the meaning of "treasure" see 9(2) Coroners (Reissue), Para. 976.

the Crown."[99] When a reward is payable, it "must not exceed the value of the treasure."[100] "A reward can be paid to the finder, the land occupier or owner or any person who had or has any interest in the land on which the find was made."[101]

Gollin's idea of discoverer's right and the Roman, Spanish and English concepts of "treasure" could be used as a starting point to create a formula to equitably share the benefits derived from varieties bred from species discovered through local or indigenous traditional knowledge. Native medicinal plants and knowledge, for instance, can be regarded as treasures to mankind. A breeder's research and investments can be regarded in a symbolic way as his territory. Applying the Roman distribution of benefits to a discovered treasure, the value of traditional knowledge (treasure) equals to half of the benefits derived from the new variety developed (land).

This idea of "treasure" is presented here not as a means of demanding breeders to give half of their benefits to the local and indigenous communities that directly or indirectly found them a treasure. The use of the Roman concept of treasure, still existent in the Spanish Civil Code, as well as the English Treasure Act rewarding system, is used symbolically to show the value native plants and associated traditional knowledge possess.

As noted by Sedjo, "Rather than limiting property rights for plant species as advocated in the FAO Undertaking, property rights for plant species should be expanded and extended to cover newly discovered natural species and should continue to be applied to special genetic stock, current breeder lines, and genetically engineered organisms. Such an approach would allow the genetically rich Third World countries an opportunity to profit directly from the ownership of genetic resources. Property rights to species would also provide a direct financial incentive to protect and maintain the natural habitat in which rare and as yet unknown species may reside, since their discovery and development at some future time cold generate direct financial returns to the owner."[102]

If the concept of discoverer's right is to work, local communities and indigenous peoples must be awarded a title of ownership over the resources they discover so that they can control access to them. This title of ownership would be a manner to guarantee that access to those resources is subordinated to the prior informed consent of the discoverer and to contracts mutually agreed by the discoverer and the party interested in accessing the resource. A commission could be created to represent the multi-discoverers when more than one person discovers a plant species that cures a particular illness. This body would have to follow a code of ethics and principles, as well as duties and rights previously determined by its founding members. Those farming or indigenous communities that agree to the body's code of ethics and principles as well as its objectives would sign a contract agreeing to those terms and granting authority to that body to negotiate the access contracts to the resources they discover.

Evidently one of the most important clauses of each access contract would be the equitable share of benefits derived from the discovered resources. The benefits would fall into a fund to be distributed to the multi-discoverers. The purpose and objective of the fund must also be previously agreed on by the founding members. The discoverers of new plant species can examine the purpose, objective, duties and rights of the commission and if they are satisfied with all of this they can have their rights

---

[99] Idem; Para. 974. Footnotes omitted.
[100] Treasure Act; supra Note 97; Article 10(4).
[101] Idem; Article 10(5).
[102] Sedjo; supra Note 88; at p.294.

represented by this body. If not, they can seek other ways to negotiate their rights and access contracts independently.

3.5 - Convention of Farmers and Breeders

India is a developing country with a predominantly agrarian economy. It has provided the International Agricultural Research Centres of the CGIAR with valuable contributions of germplasm. The IRRI Gene Bank, for instance, located in the Philippines, stores nearly 18,000 rice seed samples originating in India.[103] The genes of an Indian accession of wild rice, (*Orza nivara*), were used to stunt the growth of virus in rice production in the Asian region.[104] Due to this rich plant genetic resource legacy, India's biological resources attract international interest as a genetic refuge for existing plant varieties as well as the initial source material of breeders.

Private seed corporations see India's freely accessible genetic treasure as presenting an opportunity to gather germplasm of superior varieties of India's agricultural legacy.[105] The patenting of the Indian Basmati rice, tumeric and neem in the United States provides examples of this process. These plants were cultivated by Indian farmers and local communities over centuries and are still traditionally planted in the region.

The United States lodged a complaint with the World Trade Organisation accusing India of not offering an adequate plant variety protection regulation as demanded by TRIPs.[106] In order to comply with the TRIPs regulations, India is studying the possibility of joining the 1991 UPOV system.[107]

Gene Campaign strongly opposes India joining UPOV because "UPOV conditions are for industrial, not agricultural economies where only 2 to 5% of the population practices agriculture and there are no small and marginal farmers."[108] This is not the case in India, where the majority of its farmers practice farming not as a purely commercial activity, but as a livelihood.[109] Suman Sahai of Gene Campaign considers the sheer cost of the UPOV system a barrier for traditional farmers. Considering the figures presented at a seminar organised jointly by the Indian Council of Agricultural Research and the UPOV in Delhi in 1998, he stated that "the figures that were presented for obtaining the UPOV authorised Breeders' Right certificate, [...] will effectively preclude the participation of all but the largest seed companies. There certainly will be no space in such a system for small companies, farmers' co-operatives or farmer/breeders."[110]

Gene Campaign further notes that in industrialised countries, agricultural research is conducted mainly through private investment of the seed companies, while

---

[103] Rana, R. S.; "Access to Genetic Resources and Equitable Benefit Sharing: The Indian Experience"; 1(2) RIS Biotechnology and Development Review, 1998; New Delhi; at p.1.
[104] Idem.
[105] During the second and third Conference of Parties meeting, India stressed the importance of a patent application to reveal the origin of all biological materials, traditional knowledge and practices used in the breeding process, as well as proof that the access to the biological materials was done obeying the CBD regulations of prior informed consent and mutually agreed contract.
[106] Rana, R. S.; supra Note 103; at p.2.
[107] India ratified the CBD on 18 February 1994 and joined the WTO in January 1995.
[108] Sahai; Suman; "An Alternative to UPOV called CoFaB"; 7 March 1999. Available at http://ds.dial.pipex.com/ukfg/UKabc/cofab.htm; accessed in March 1999.
[109] Idem.
[110] Sahai, Suman; Gene Campaign; "Protection of New Plant Varieties: a Developing Country Alternative"; XXXIV Economic and Political Weekly, Nos. 10 & 11; March 1999.

in India agricultural research is financed by public institutions.[111] This change of spectrum from the public to the private domain stimulates seed companies to maximise their profits, creating agricultural market monopolies.[112]

In the attempt to convince the Indian government not to join the 1991 UPOV system, an alternative to the UPOV treaty was developed in India by the Gene Campaign organisation and the Centre for Environment and Development. It is known as the Convention of Farmers and Breeders (hereinafter CoFaB).[113]

According to CoFaB, the breeder who creates a new variety shall be granted a Plant Breeder's Right. The new variety must be clearly distinguishable by at least one characteristic from all other varieties that are already part of common knowledge at the time the plant breeder's right is claimed. "Common knowledge" is understood as "any oral or documented reference in the formal and informal sector, to various factors such as: cultivation, use and marketing already in progress, entry in a register of varieties already made or in the course of being made, inclusion in a reference collection or precise description in a publication."[114] The new variety must be sufficiently homogenous as regards its sexual reproduction or vegetative propagation.[115] And finally, the new variety must be stable in its essential characteristics after repeated reproduction or propagation.[116]

Article 3 of CoFaB establishes that natural and legal persons resident in one of the Contracting States shall enjoy in other Member States the same treatment as that given to their nationals regarding the recognition and protection of Farmers' rights and Breeders' rights.[117] Thus, CoFaB, adopts TRIPs National Treatment Principle.

CoFaB also provides for the "right to priority" for a period of twelve months. Through this right, the breeder of a variety, or his successor in title, who duly filed a plant variety right application in one country, can file another application in another Member State and use the filing date of the first application.[118]

Authorisation of the breeder, who is granted a plant breeder's right, is required for the production of the new variety for the purposes of commercial and branded marketing of the reproductive or vegetative propagating material.[119] The breeder's right shall extend to ornamental plants when they are used commercially as propagating material in the production of ornamental plants or cut flowers.[120] If the new variety is to be used as initial source for the creation of another variety, or for marketing such varieties, the authorisation of the Breeder is not necessary. Nevertheless, if the variety is constantly used as initial source material for the commercial production of another variety, the authorisation of the breeder will be required.[121]

---

[111] Idem.
[112] Idem.
[113] Convention of Farmers and Breeders (CoFaB); Gene Campaign; New Delhi, India; 1999. available on request to Dr Suman Sahai (drsahai@nde.vsnl.net.in) or in the following website: http://ds.dial.pipex.com/ukfg/UKabc/cofab.htm.
[114] Idem; Article 6(1)(a).
[115] Idem; Article 6(1)(c).
[116] Idem; Article 6(1)(d).
[117] Idem; Article 3(1).
[118] Idem; Article 12.
[119] Idem; Article 5(2).
[120] Idem.
[121] Idem; Article 5(3).

An interesting aspect of the breeder's right is that the breeder is encouraged to try to create his/her new, homogenous and stable variety on a broader rather than a narrower genetic base so that the genetic variability on the fields can be maintained.[122] Breeders generally create plant varieties with a narrow genetic base so that their time- and money-consuming creations do not transform from one season to the next through natural evolution and selection as occurs with wild species. However, genetically uniform plantations have been criticised for the possibility of an unexpected pest being able to eradicate not only some of the plants, but the whole plantation.[123] Therefore, it is interesting to see that this risk was implicitly acknowledged in the advice given to breeders to create varieties with broad genetic bases.

There could be two drawbacks to the CoFaB system. The first would be an overflow of claims for the protection of varieties created by nature, thus accidentally intensifying biopiracy. The second drawback would be if a protected plant variety, of a broad genetic base, naturally transformed itself back to its original state or to a new state not predicted by the breeder. CoFaB should consider these issues to make the system more effective.

Article 7(2) determines that the plant variety must be submitted to field trials for at least two cropping years and evaluated by an independent institutional arrangement before a plant variety right can be granted.[124] This article is consistent with the Precautionary Principle that determines that catastrophes should be avoided through prudent analysis of a situation and the elimination of the possible risks. The two-year field trial provides society with some evidence that the new variety will not be harmful to health and agriculture. Article 11 of CoFaB strengthens the precautionary predetermination by stating that each Contracting State "shall require an independent evaluation of performance of the variety before granting protection."

CoFaB stipulates that Farmer's rights are to be granted for an unlimited period of time.[125] On the other hand, breeders' rights duration would be for a period not less than fifteen years.[126] In the case of vines, fruit trees and their stocks, forest trees and ornamental trees the minimum duration of the breeder's right is eighteen years.[127] Periodical evaluations shall be undertaken to prevent the spread of the disease in the appearance of a pest attack. If a pest attacks the variety, the duration of breeder's right can be curtailed.[128]

According to CoFaB, Farmers' rights can not be restricted for any reason. On the other hand, Breeders' rights could be restricted, but only for reasons of public interest.[129] The Breeder's right may become forfeit if the variety created "is not able to meet the demand of farmers, leading to scarcity of planting material, increased market price and monopolies."[130]

Article 1 of CoFaB states that the purpose of the convention "is to acknowledge and to ensure that Farmers have rights ensuing from their contribution to the identification, maintenance and refinement of germplasm and that breeders of new plant varieties have rights over the varieties that they have bred."[131] Farmers' rights

---

[122] Idem; Article 6(1)(d).
[123] See FAO Chapter.
[124] CoFaB; supra Note 113; Article 7(2).
[125] Idem; Article 8(1).
[126] Idem; Article 8(2).
[127] Idem.
[128] Idem; Article 8(3).
[129] Idem; Article 9.
[130] Idem; Article 10(4)(c).
[131] Idem; Article 1.

will be executed through a fee paid by the breeder who uses "land races or traditional varieties either directly or through the use of other varieties that have used land races and traditional varieties, in their breeding program."[132] When applying for a Plant Breeder's right, the breeder must explicitly reveal the name and source of all varieties, including land race or farmers varieties, used in the breeding process.[133] The fees collected will be deposited into a National Gene Fund and a multi-stakeholder body will decide the use of this revenue.[134]

CoFaB was developed with a view of balancing farmers' rights with breeders' rights. For this purpose, it recognises the "need for creating a system where farmers and breeders have recognition and rights accruing from their contribution to the creation of new varieties."[135] As such, CoFaB is compatible with the equitable share of benefits objective of the CBD. On the one hand, CoFaB recognises the importance of breeders to meet nutritional goals and feed the growing world population[136]. On the other hand, CoFaB recognises the importance of maintaining the genetic diversity of species being planted and consequently acknowledges the role of farmers in creating landraces and traditional varieties in their fields.[137]

3.6 - Conclusion

From this discussion, it is possible to identify the overall considerations and requirements of a *sui generis* system to protect plant, plant varieties and traditional knowledge while at the same time being compatible with the provisions in the CBD and TRIPs.

When countries are in the process of drafting *sui generis* systems, they must carefully decide how they are going to manage the benefit-sharing in regard to profit derived from the plant variety originating from genetic resources cultivated by farmers, indigenous or local communities. A number of questions must be confronted. Who owns the genetic resource? Who benefits and how? Who is allowed to freely use the variety? What do the rights granted cover?

The Thammasat Resolution is totally against any form of intellectual property rights over any life form. In this sense, the resolution shows the mistrust towards the intentions of bio-prospecting multi-national industries as well as the plantation of genetically engineered organisms. "Many groups world wide are concerned that patents underpin developments in genetic engineering that risk disturbing a complex pattern of inter-relationships in the natural world that we still only partially understand."[138]

Discoverer's rights present a solution to this problem through the granting of rights to those who discover any unknown plant as well as useful properties it contains. This concept was used to demonstrate a possible equitable share of benefits between discoverers and breeders who further develop the properties of the discovered plant. "The absence of property rights for natural species deny countries and individuals the possibility of benefiting commercially from the presence of unique genetic resources within their jurisdictional boundaries, but the elimination of existing

---

[132] Idem; Article 2(1).
[133] Idem; Article 6(1)(b).
[134] Idem; Article 2(3).
[135] Idem; Preamble.
[136] Idem.
[137] Idem.
[138] Tansey, Geoff; supra Note 74.

proprietary rights to genetically improved stock would eliminate the self-interest that breeders now have to contribute to maintaining genetic diversity."[139]

CoFaB ensures that farmers receive fair accrual of benefits for their agricultural contributions of conservation and genetic enhancement of certain characteristics in the plants. Individual or community farmers in India have been managing to keep the evolutionary process in plants functioning by keeping the genetic diversity in their land-races. Breeders' varieties are genetically uniform and thus CoFaB places some precautionary obstacles for the breeder to be granted a right.

Farmers' rights ought to receive sufficient recognition to be enforceable. Farming is a profession and it is ethical and moral to pay farmers the fair value for crops they have been improving, growing and providing to all. Seed companies must be controlled to avoid their monopoly of the seed market with patents because a large portion of the world population would starve if farmers cannot have access to the seeds to grow the crops.

4 - GENERAL CONCLUSION

Countries should not rush to fulfil the TRIPs obligation by expanding patents to protect biotechnological plant varieties. While there are strong and substantial arguments as to why plants and plant varieties should not be patented there are those who believe that the absence of patent protection benefits only a few people at the expense of many. They defend the point that when there is no patent protection, pirated copies appear in the market and the prices that these pirated copies reach are sometimes even higher than prices in Europe and the United States where the patents are recognised.[140] Moreover, the patent defenders argue that none of the money accumulated through the commercialisation of pirated copies contributes to research dedicated to find cures for diseases.[141] A news report in *Financial Times* about the pirating on plant varieties in France, revealed that the cost to develop a new variety over a 15-year period of research could be up to 10 million francs.[142]

Although the justification of the patent system is to optimise the rate of significant invention and innovation[143] and, consequently it provides society with new choices and a better standard of life,[144] very few individuals in developing countries will benefit from these consequences. Poor developing countries do not have the financial means to pay for the transfer and dissemination of the technology. Developing countries criticise the fact that the monopolies generated by IPRs lead to excessive high prices and unjustifiable restrictions on the use of the patented product or process.[145] Consequently, developing countries that lack highly developed technology, monetary funds, and facilities, such as the personnel and know-how, find themselves excluded from the benefits the biotechnological innovations are supposed to bring.

---

[139] Sedjo; supra Note 88; at p.294.
[140] Third Business Forum of the Americas; Working Group VII: Technology and Intellectual Property Rights; Belo Horizonte, Brazil; May 1997.
[141] Idem.
[142] *Financial Times*, November 1, 1995.
[143] O'Brien, D. P.; "Patents: An Economist's View"; in Phillips, Jeremy; Patents in Perspective, (ed); ESC Publishing Limited; Oxford; 1985; at p. 41.
[144] Aubrey, J.M.; "A Justification of the Patent System"; in Phillips, Jeremy; Idem; at p. 1.
[145] Bhat, M. G.; "Trade-related intellectual property rights to biological resources: Socio-economic implications for developing countries"; 19 Ecological Economics, 1996; at p. 207.

Economically it can be said that property rights constitute the legal supporting structure for the allocation of resources and the distribution of wealth and income.[146] However, Dreyfuss and Zimmerman observed that by "combining the market power of natural competitors with strengthened international intellectual property protection, oligopolists in developed countries seek to make it harder for firms in developing countries to gain access to the most valuable technologies or otherwise to catch up with the leaders in the global market for higher-tech products."[147]

Others argue that although local consumers and local firms pay more for patented products, they also benefit from the possibility of having access to new products, research and technology that may not have been available in the developing country in the absence of a patent system.[148] However, UNCTAD notes other consequences, including "increased royalty payments to foreign innovators; the corresponding loss of investment opportunities in domestic research and development; higher prices for consumer products subject to monopoly rights; and greater dependence on imports in general. Taking the bleakest view, a developing country stands to gain only when a foreign invention affords solutions of particular local utility that would not otherwise obtain sufficient investment in research and development."[149]

UNCTAD further notes that not all developing countries are on the same technological level.[150] Dutfield notes that developing countries are "increasingly heterogeneous in terms of countries' levels of industrialisation, social, and political development."[151] When referring to the compliance of each State with TRIPs UNCTAD states that "there remains scope for countries to implement the Agreement in a manner conducive to promoting dynamic competition within their own economies."[152]

Developing countries are thus advised to enact a *sui generis* system that is in harmony with the minimum global standards for intellectual property protection as provided for in TRIPs. Additionally, the system should best serve their own economic development and help stimulate innovation at the local level. Therefore, the *sui generis* system they adopt should obligatorily protect their farmers' and indigenous knowledge, as well as traditionally bred plants. Furthermore, developing countries should enact laws that avoid biopiracy and promote the equitable share of benefits derived out of the utilisation of their biodiversity. *Sui generis* systems of this kind are intended to recognise and compensate traditional knowledge systems and informal innovations instead of further strengthening biotechnological plant variety protection.

However, as noted by Gana. "The question which continues to plague domestic proprietary regimes and which is aggravated at the international level by the wide gap between rich and poor countries is where to set the balance between access and competition."[153] As provided by Article 7 of TRIPs: "The protection and

---

[146] See Cooter, R. and Ulen, T.; Law and Economics; Addison-Wesley; 2nd ed.; Reading, (Mass); 1997; at p. 69.
[147] Dreyfuss, R. C. & Zimmerman, D. L.; "Conveyors' Introduction: The Culture and Economics of Participation in an International Intellectual Property Regime"; 29 New York University Journal of International Law and Politics, Fall 1996 - Winter 1997; at p. 22.
[148] Adelman, Martin J. and Baldi; "Prospects and limits of the Patent Provision in the TRIPs Agreement: The case of India"; 29(3) Vanderbilt Journal of Transnational Law, May 1996, at p. 510.
[149] UNCTAD; supra Note 4; at Part II, Paragraph 119.
[150] Idem; at Part I, Section IV, Paragraph 79.
[151] Dutfield, Graham; "Can the TRIPs Agreement Protect Biological and Cultural Diversity?"; ACTS Press; Nairobi, Kenya; 1997; at p. 4.
[152] UNCTAD supra Note 4; at Part I, Section IV, Paragraph 83. See also Leskien, D. & Flitner, M.; supra Note 2.
[153] Gana, Ruth; "Prospects for Developing Countries Under the TRIPs Agreement." 29(4) Vanderbilt Journal of Transnational Law; October 1996; at p. 743.

enforcement of intellectual property rights should contribute to the promotion of technological innovation and to the transfer and dissemination of technology, to the *mutual advantage of producers and users of technological knowledge and in a manner conducive to social and economic welfare and to a balance of rights and obligations.*"[154] Countries that adopt *sui generis* systems, which exclusively protect biotechnological breeders' rights contribute to the generation of further poverty in their rural societies. Thus, States should not adopt a *sui generis* system that omits to protect traditional breeders' knowledge and innovations.

An effective *sui generis* system to protect plant varieties is one that offers the balance of rights and obligations of all types of plant breeders and promotes both national and international welfare. It should contribute towards the empowerment of the poor, the conservation of biodiversity and the promotion global food security. Moreover, A *sui generis* system in compliance with TRIPs Article 27(3)(b) must be "complementary and mutually supportive"[155] to the objectives of the CBD and in order to be socially equitable it should be favourable to the International Undertaking.

The link between IPR regimes and access to genetic resources brings us naturally to the Convention on Biodiversity which is be examined in the following Chapter.

---

[154] Article 7 of TRIPs.
[155] Mulvany, Patrick; "TRIPS, Biodiversity and Commonwealth Countries: capacity building priorities for the 1999 review of TRIPS article 27.3(b)"; Commonwealth Secretariat; London; 1998, at p. 30.

CHAPTER SIX

IMPLEMENTATION OF THE CONVENTION ON BIOLOGICAL DIVERSITY: BALANCING THE INTERESTS OF THE SCIENTIFIC AND TRADITIONAL COMMUNITIES

1 - GENERAL INTRODUCTION

The Convention on Biological Diversity, (hereinafter CBD), was negotiated under the auspices of the United Nations Environmental Program, (know as UNEP), and opened for signature in the Earth Summit held in Rio de Janeiro, Brazil, in 1992.[1] The initial motivation for drafting the CBD was to alleviate the global-interest biodiversity conservation burden placed on the biodiversity-rich developing and least developed countries. During the drafting process, negotiations embraced all the aspects related to biodiversity conservation, including such issues as the inequity in international policies regarding flows of genetic resources, basic legal guidelines for the regulation of access to biodiversity, access to biotechnology, and sharing of benefits derived from the use of genetic material. The CBD is a landmark because although there were international[2] and regional conventions[3] that addressed specific questions of biodiversity conservation, it is the first international convention that specifically addresses the global conservation of biodiversity.[4]

The drafting of the CBD was a cumbersome process of balancing the interests of biotechnology-rich, biodiversity-poor developed countries and biotechnology-poor, biodiversity rich developing countries. On the one hand, developing countries desired to exploit their biodiversity economically and did not care much about conservation or sustainable use of the resources. Therefore, they pushed for CBD provisions that would give them the means to demand technology transfer and financial benefits in exchange for the conservation of their natural environments and access to their biodiversity. Developed countries and multinational biotechnology companies, on the

---

[1] The CBD was adopted on 22 May 1992 in Nairobi. It was opened for signature at the United Nations Conference on Environment and Development, (UNCED), on 5 June 1992 in Rio de Janeiro, Brazil and was signed by 150 States. The CBD entered into force on 29 December 1993. Brazil ratified the CBD on 28 February 1994. As of 02 August 2001, the CBD has 181 State Parties. Text in 31 ILM 822, 1992 and 3 YbIEL 663 et seq., 1992.

[2] For instance: Convention Concerning the Protection of the World Cultural and Natural Heritage, text in 11 ILM 1358, 1972; Convention on International Trade in Endangered Species of Wild Fauna and Flora, (known as CITES), unamended text in 12 ILM 1055, 1973; Convention on Wetlands of International Importance, (known as Ramsar Convention), text in 11 ILM 963, 1972; and Convention on Migratory Species of Wild Animals, text in 19 ILM 15, 1980. For full discussions on the conventions see S. Lyster, International Wildlife Law, Cambridge, 1985.

[3] For instance: the 1940 Convention on Nature and Wildlife Preservation in the Western Hemisphere, text in 161 UNTS 193; the African Convention on the Conservation of Nature and Natural Resources, text in 1001 UNTS 3 and in A. Kiss, ed., 1 Selected Multilateral Treaties in the Field of the Environment, UNEP, 1983, at 207, Convention on the Conservation of European Wildlife and Natural Habitats (Berne, 1979), text in ETS 104; UKTS 56, 1982, Cmnd. 8738 and in A. Kiss, ed., 1 Selected Multilateral Treaties in the Field of the Environment 509; and the ASEAN Agreement on the Conservation of Nature and Natural Resources, Kuala Lumpur, 1985, text in I. Rummel-Bulska & S. Osafo, eds., 2 Selected Multilateral Treaties in the Field of the Environment 343, UNEP, 1991, at 343.

[4] The CBD addresses *in situ* and *ex situ* conservation of all species, sustainable use of biological resources, access to genetic resources, access to technology, including biotechnology, access to benefits derived from the use of biodiversity, safety issues related to genetically modified organisms, and financial resources and mechanisms.

other hand, fought for more lenient access measures to biodiversity with the least possible compromise to transfer funds and technology.[5]

Along with the CBD, the Declaration on Environment and Development, (hereafter Rio Declaration),[6] and Programme of Action for Sustainable Development, known as Agenda 21,[7] were also adopted and are of relevance to this Chapter. As known, the CBD is binding on its Member States, unlike the Rio Declaration. However, the Rio Declaration is a complex of 27 important principles, some of them regarding the necessity to eliminate poverty and to create a global partnership promoting the integration of environment and development.[8] Agenda 21 is an instrument that delineates paths to achieve global sustainable development through systematic, co-operative action. It is founded on the principle of sustainable development as the essence of environmental policy. With regard to sustainable development, Agenda 21 links the economic, social and cultural development of societies to environmental preservation as the basis for human existence. Agenda 21, the Rio Declaration and the CBD offer valuable principles and provisions concerning the empowerment of poor people, capacity building, rights of indigenous and local communities in regard to access to genetic resources, associated traditional knowledge and benefit sharing.

The access to a country's biodiversity involves a range of intrinsically linked issues such as ownership, sovereignty and control over biological resources. Furthermore, in order to adopt mutually agreed terms for access, it is necessary to have the prior informed consent of the country providing the genetic resource, as well as the informed consent of the indigenous or local communities affected. In signing the CBD, Member States committed themselves to facilitate access to the biodiversity under their sovereignty in order to achieve the three objectives of the CBD: conservation of biological resources, the sustainable use of their components and the equitable share of benefits which arise from their utilisation.

This Chapter considers the possibility of implementing the CBD objectives by balancing the interests of the scientific and traditional communities. For this purpose, each objective shall be examined individually and contrasted with important obstacles it has to overcome. Furthermore, unresolved issues regarding the access to traditional knowledge and biodiversity, as well as access to biotechnology shall be analysed.

2 - OBJECTIVES OF THE CDB

2.1 - Introduction

The CBD has three main objectives: conservation of biodiversity, sustainable use of its components and the equitable share of benefits that arise from their use. This section shall examine the effect patents and plant breeder's rights have on the objectives of the CBD. However, as already noted by Graham Dutfield, when regarding the possible conflicts and synergies between certain characteristics or effects

---

[5] For a discussion on the heart of the debate between developing and developed countries, see Burhenne-Guilmin, F. and Casey-Lefkowitz, S.; "The Convention on Biological Diversity: A Hard Won Global Achievement"; 3 YbIEL, 1992; pp. 43-59.
[6] Rio Declaration; General Assembly Resolution 47/190; 1992. Reprinted in 31 I.L.M. 874, 1992.
[7] Agenda 21; UN Doc. A/CONF. 151/26/REV. 1, Vols. I-III; 1992.
[8] The Rio Declaration builds on the Stockholm Declaration on the Human Environment, (hereafter Stockholm Declaration), adopted at the United Nations Stockholm Conference on the Human Environment in 1972. Stockholm Declaration, U.N. Doc. A/CONF.48/14 Corr., at 3. Reprinted in 11 I.L.M. 1416, 1972.

of IPRs and achievement of the CBD's objectives "an objective evaluation of the various assertions frequently made pro and contra IPRs is hard to achieve when there is such a dearth of reliable empirical evidence (as opposed to anecdotal evidence and pure speculation)."[9]

2.2 - CONSERVATION OF BIODIVERSITY

Three major assertions have been made in regard to patents and plant breeders' rights regarding plant varieties: 1) they stimulate monoculture plantations which is one of the factors[10] that threatens genetic diversity in species,[11] 2) they are sometimes piracies of traditional varieties,[12] and 3) they make it impossible to achieve the equitable share of benefits that arise out of the use of biodiversity. This section shall examine the first assertion and the importance of biodiversity.

Although the preamble of a convention does not contain binding obligations on the contracting parties, it shows the concerns that motivated States to adopt the legal agreement. The Preamble of the CBD starts out by recognising the "intrinsic value of biological diversity and of the ecological, genetic, social, economic, scientific, educational, cultural, recreational and aesthetic values of biological diversity and its components."[13] The CBD followed the example of the Convention on the Conservation of European Wildlife and Natural Habitats and recognises the *intrinsic value* of biodiversity.[14] The intrinsic value of biodiversity means that all components of biodiversity should be conserved due to their inherent right to exist.[15]

Apart from conserving biodiversity for its inherent right to exist, of particular significance is the fact that conservation of biodiversity is the key for human long-term survival on the planet.[16] The Preamble of the CBD recognises that biological diversity should be conserved "for evolution and for maintaining life sustaining systems in the biosphere."[17] According to the World Charter for Nature, the excessive consumption of natural resources leads to the breakdown of the economic, social and political supporting structure of civilisation.[18] A metaphor can be used to show this more clearly.

"Imagine if suddenly, a musical note disappeared from the keyboard of the piano, the *do*, for instance. The disappearance of the note *do* would cause an enormous disorder. Rarely does note *do* not appear in a musical piece. And, thus, all music

---

[9] Dutfield, Graham; Intellectual Property Rights, Trade And Biodiversity: Seeds And Plant Varieties; Earthscan; London; 2000.
[10] For a chart on other causes of biodiversity loss linked to agriculture, see Dutfield, Graham; Idem.
[11] See the Chapters Three and Four of this book.
[12] See Chapter Four of this book.
[13] CBD; supra Note 1; Preamble.
[14] See the Preamble of the Convention on the Conservation of European Wildlife and Natural Habitats, Berne, 19 September, 1979. Text in ETS 104; UKTS 56, 1982, Cmnd. 8738.
[15] The World Charter for Nature, in its preamble recognised that every life form is unique and warrants respect regardless of its worth to humans. Although the World Charter for Nature has significant political weight as proven through national laws that have adopted its principles, it is not binding on States. World Charter for Nature, G.A. RES: 37/7, U.N. GAOR, 37th Session, U.N. Doc. A/Res/37/7, Supp. No. 51, at 17, 1982, reprinted in 22 I.L.M. 455, 1983.
[16] See International Union for the Conservation of Nature and Natural Resources et al, (hereafter IUCN); World Conservation Strategy: Living Resource Conservation for Sustainable Development, (hereafter World Conservation Strategy); 1980. See also IUCN, UNEP & WWF; "Caring for the Earth: A Strategy For Sustainable Living", (hereafter Caring for the Earth); 1994. Caring for the Earth is the successor to the World Conservation Strategy.
[17] Preamble of the CBD.
[18] World Charter for Nature, supra Note 15; Preamble.

which contained note *do* could not be sung anymore and maybe all the musical instruments would lose their reason of use."[19] If each species is seen as a note, this metaphor shows that all species on this planet have a value. Species are organised in nature in a similar pattern as the musical scale. The extinction of a species initiates a chain where slowly other species follow into extinction. With time, the ecosystem becomes poorer and loses its stability, affecting neighbouring ecosystems.

The importance of biological processes is clearly shown in the "Guide to the Convention on Biological Diversity". The Guide states that "A wide pool of diversity is valuable because it keeps evolutionary options open. Specifically, if populations become small and fragmented, they become vulnerable to inbreeding in which they lose, rather than gain, variability, leading to extinction instead of further evolution. (...) Diversity among living organisms improves the capacity for living systems to adapt to variations in the physical components of the biosphere, such as climate changes."[20] In this sense, the CBD recognises that the conservation of biological diversity is a common concern of humankind.[21] Common concern implies a "common obligation towards an issue that is of paramount importance to the international community."[22]

Birnie and Boyle note that conservation of biological diversity is regarded as one of the "most urgent issues of our time, essential for sustainable development and functioning of the biosphere and thus for human survival itself."[23]

The CBD further notes that "the fundamental requirement for the conservation of biological diversity is the *in situ* conservation of ecosystems and natural habitats and the maintenance and recovery of viable populations of species in their natural surroundings."[24] Traditional knowledge is dependent on *in situ* locations to continue to evolve and be useful.

Walter Reid argues that *in situ* conservation, traditional knowledge and the promotion of research and investment of informal innovation are the effective mechanisms for the long-term maintenance of genetic diversity.[25] However, they are neglected in favour of high-yielding biotechnological, genetically uniform seeds which are protectable under patents and/or plant breeders rights. Some of these biotechnology seeds are hybrids and dependent on agrochemicals to grow.[26] Dutfield notes that the "biodiversity-erosive effects of this IPR-supported bias towards centralised crop breeding programmes are: (i) decreased crop diversity; (ii) decreased spatial genetic diversity; (iii) increased temporal genetic diversity[27]; and (iv) increased

---

[19] Terra Viva (ed); Atlas do Meio ambiente do Brasil; EMBRAPA; Brasilia, Brasil; 1994; at p. 68.
[20] Glowka, L.; Burhenne-Guilmin, F.; Synge, H.; A Guide to the Convention on Biological Diversity; Environmental Policy and Law Paper No. 30; IUCN; Gland, Switzerland; 1994; at p. 9.
[21] CBD; supra Note 1; Preamble. The CBD was the first the first international convention which recognised the conservation of biological diversity as a common concern of humankind. The proposition of biodiversity be regarded as common heritage of humankind was rejected at the early stages of negotiation because most of the worlds biodiversity lies under the sovereignty of States.
[22] Burhenne-Guilmin, F. and Casey-Lefkowitz, S.; supra Note 5; p 47.
[23] Birnie, P and Boyle, A.; International Law and the Environment; Clarendon Press; Oxford;1992; at p. 483.
[24] CBD; supra Note 1; Preamble.
[25] See Reid, W.V.; "Genetic Resources and Sustainable Agriculture: Creating Incentives for Local Innovation and Adaptation"; Biopolicy International No. 2; African Centre for Technology Studies; Nairobi & Maastricht, 1992.
[26] See Chapter Four of this book.
[27] Due to the need to replace cultivars with new ones every few years.

use of external inputs."[28] Kothari and Anuradha share this view and believe that IPRs stimulate the plantation of homogenous modern varieties in favour of traditionally bred heterogeneous varieties.[29]

During the WTO meeting in Seattle,[30] 144 scientists from 25 countries signed up to a letter, the World Scientists' Statement, that was presented to the decision-makers.[31] The letter called for the "immediate suspension of all environmental releases of genetically modified crops and products; for patents on life-forms and living processes to be revoked and banned; and for a comprehensive public enquiry into the future of agriculture and food security for all."[32]

Although World Scientists' Statement probably represents a minority view of scientists, it has great value by elucidating how genetically modified[33] crops compromise healthcare. It noted that the "latest large-scale surveys of GM crops showed they offered no benefits. On the contrary, they yield significantly less and require more herbicides. [...]The broad-spectrum herbicides used with herbicide-tolerant GM crops not only decimate wild species indiscriminately, but are toxic to animals." The World Scientists' Statement acknowledges that glufosinate causes birth defects in mammals. Herbicides that contain bt-toxins kill beneficial insects such as bees and lacewings, pollen from bt-maize is lethal to monarch butterflies and genetically modified potatoes with snowdrop lectin harm ladybirds and are toxic to young rats.[34] Furthermore, it corroborates the affirmation made by the UK Ministry of Agriculture, Fisheries and Food that the "transfer of GM crops and pollen beyond the planted fields is unavoidable and this has already resulted in herbicide-tolerant weeds."[35] The World Scientists' Statement concludes that governments should widely support research into sustainable agricultural methods that do not use genetically modified crops[36] and have proven to result in increased yields and diminished environmental impacts.[37]

Even though the CBD gives emphasis to *in situ* conservation, it also recognises that *ex situ* measures also have an important role to play in the conservation of biological diversity, as a complement to *in situ* measures.[38] *Ex situ* conservation and research of components of biological diversity are preferably to occur in the country of origin of such components.[39] *Ex situ* conservation is an important biodiversity refuge for those cases where *in situ* conservation centres are destroyed by war, fires,

---

[28] Dutfield, Graham; supra Note 9. Graham Dutfield also notes that monocultural agricultural systems are not inherently biodiversity-erosive if they produce higher yields per harvest, and/or harvests per year compared to the polycultural agrosystem it replaced.

[29] Kothari, A. & Anuradha, R. V.; "Biodiversity, Intellectual Property Rights, and the GATT Agreement: How to Address the Conflicts?"; 2 Biopolicy, Paper 4, PY97004, 1997; located at http://www.bdt.org.br/bioline/py; accessed in 1998.

[30] World Trade Organisation's Third Ministerial Conference; Seattle; 30 November-3 December 1999.

[31] From the date of 18 August 2000, 338 scientists had signed the World's Scientist Statement.

[32] The complete letter and the list of signers is located at the website of the Institute of Science in Society. Located at http://www.i-sis.org; accessed in August 2000.

[33] In the World Scientists' Statement, genetically modified is abbreviated as GM; Idem.

[34] See the World Scientists' Statement for more examples and references inclusive on information on the genetically modified bovine growth hormone injected into cows to increase milk yield. This hormone causes excessive suffering and illness to the cows and increases IGF-1 in the milk which is linked to breast and prostate cancer in humans; Idem.

[35] Idem.

[36] The World Scientists' Statement makes reference to the United States Environmental Protection Agency that recommends farmers to plant 40% of non genetically modified crop in order to create a refuge for non-resistant insects pests; Idem.

[37] Idem.

[38] CBD; supra Note 1; Preamble.

[39] Idem; Article 9.

natural catastrophes, and so forth. Timothy Swanson and Timo Goeschl note that *in situ* an *ex situ* conservation "concern the use and management of different forms of information important for the continuance of agriculture."[40]

State Parties to the CBD are expected to establish a system of protected areas destined to conserve biological diversity[41] as well as rehabilitate degraded ecosystems and promote the recovery of threatened species.[42] Furthermore, State Parties must provide measures to prevent the introduction of, control or eradicate living modified organisms which threaten ecosystems, habitats or species.[43] Article 19(3) mandates that parties to the convention shall consider adopting a protocol to regulate the "safe transfer, handling and use of any living modified organism resulting from biotechnology that may have adverse effect on the conservation and sustainable use of biological diversity."[44]

On 29 January 2000, representatives from over 130 countries adopted in Montreal, Canada, a legally binding protocol to the CBD to protect the environment from risks posed by the transboundary transport of living modified organisms, (hereafter LMO), created by modern biotechnology.[45] This Protocol is known as the Cartagena Protocol on Biosafety, (hereafter Biosafety Protocol).[46]

The Biosafety Protocol adopts the Advance Informed Agreement Procedure (hereafter AIA) which obliges the Party exporting transgenic organisms to notify in writing to the importing Party its intentions to export LMOs. The AIA basically only covers LMOs destined for direct introduction to the environment of the importer, such as seeds and micro-organisms. The exporter must prove that the LMOs are not harmful to the environment or human health, and for this he may be required to conduct and/or finance a risk assessment. Liability is not regulated by the protocol.[47]

The adoption of the Biosafety Protocol to control development and plantation and commercialisation of living modified organisms shows the growing international concern about the potential risks of biotechnology. Using the precautionary approach,[48] the biosafety protocol to the CBD aims to help State Parties enjoy the benefits[49] of biotechnology without suffering its risks. States should keep in mind that "the introduction of genetically modified organisms should not proceed faster than advances in scientific understanding."[50]

---

[40] Swanson, Timothy and Goeschl, Timo; "Optimal Genetic Resource Conservation: *in situ* and *ex situ*"; in Brush, Stephen (ed); Genes in the Field; IPGRI; Rome, Italy; 1999; at p. 167.
[41] CBD; supra Note 1; Article 8(a).
[42] Idem; Article 8(f).
[43] Idem; Article 8(h). See also Article 19(4) of the CBD.
[44] Idem; Article 19(3).
[45] Negotiations to the Biosafety Protocol started in 1996, and thus lasted five years. The agreed text of the Biosafety Protocol was opened for signature in UNEP headquarter in Nairobi from 15 to 26 of May 2000 during the Fifth Session of the Conference of Parties to the CBD. After 50 States have ratified it, the Biosafety Protocol will enter into force for its Members. For a detailed history of the Protocol's negotiations see http://www.iisd.ca/biodiv/excop/. Accessed in June 2000.
[46] The Biosafety Protocol received the name Cartagena Protocol on Biosafety because in Montreal States were reassuming negotiations on the text that had been suspended in Cartagena, Columbia, in February 1999 due to a number of outstanding differences including the scope of the protocol.
[47] Article 27 of the Biosafety Protocol determines that the first meeting of the Parties shall initiate the process to elaborate rules and procedures on liability; supra Note 45.
[48] Idem; Preamble, Articles 1, 10 and 11.
[49] According to Biotech Activists, the benefits of biotechnology include new medical treatments and vaccines, new industrial products, improved fibres and fuels. Biotech Activists News Bulletin, 4 January 2000. Received from: biotechactivist@iatp.org.
[50] Idem.

The Biosafety Protocol is an advancement in the process of conciliating trade and environmental objectives. However, there are still many negotiations to go to reach the perfect balance between commercial and public interests.

2.3 - Sustainable Use of The Components of Biological Diversity

The Preamble of the CBD states that "States are responsible for conserving their biological diversity and for using their biological resources in a sustainable manner."[51] Principle 4 of the Rio Declaration proclaims that: "In order to achieve sustainable development, environmental protection shall constitute an integral part of the development process and cannot be considered in isolation from it."[52]

The concept of sustainable development acknowledges that the extinction of natural resources can affect the economies of States and that all States are ecologically[53] and economically[54] interdependent.[55] This section presents different definitions and components of sustainable development because as noted by Sam Johnston, it is a term which is "rather enigmatic, with no one accepted meaning."[56] However, all the meanings converge to a single truth: sustainable development involves the perfect balance of economic, social and ecological conditions. This balance extinguishes poverty and environmental degradation, providing long-lasting welfare and economic growth to society. In this sense, sustainable development provides the improvement of present and future total quality of life.

Sustainable use is defined in the CBD as the "use of components of biological diversity in a way and at a rate that does not lead to the long-term decline of biological diversity, thereby maintaining its potential to meet the needs and aspirations of present and future generations."[57] In its Preamble it states that "conservation and sustainable use of biological diversity is of critical importance for meeting the food, health and other needs of the growing world population, for which purpose access to and sharing of both genetic resources and technologies are essential."[58] The Preamble of the CBD further notes that "ultimately, the conservation and sustainable use of biological diversity will strengthen friendly relations among States and contribute to peace for humankind."[59] The CBD Preamble thus makes it clear that when sustainable development is achieved on a global scale, in other words, both within and among countries, humanity will be closer to living in peace on Earth.[60]

---

[51] CBD; supra Note 1; Preamble.
[52] Rio Declaration; supra Note 6; Principle 4.
[53] Ecological interdependence can be understood through the words of Maurice Strong: "The essential theme of our modern age is interdependence, the interdependence of all the elements which sustain (...) life on the planet, of man with those elements, of the natural system with man's needs and aspirations and most of all man with man." UN Doc. A/C.2/SR. 1466 (1971); quoted in Handl, G.; "Environmental Security and Global Change: The Challenge to International Law"; 1 Yb.I.E.L. 1990; at p. 3.
[54] Economic interdependence can be generally defined as "the direct and positive linkage of the interests of states where a change in the position of one state affects the position of other and in the same direction." Rosecrance, R. et al.; "Whither Interdependence"; 31(3) International Organisation; at 425; 1977.
[55] For analysis on the economic theory of sustainable use see Johnston, Sam; "Sustainability, Biodiversity and International Law" in Redgwell and Bowman (eds); International Law and the Conservation of Biological Diversity; Kluwer Law International; Great Britain; 1995; at pp 51-69.
[56] Idem; at p. 53.
[57] CBD; supra Note 1; Article 2.
[58] Idem; Preamble.
[59] Idem; Preamble.
[60] For the roles of national, state and local governments for institutionalising ecologically sustainable development see Boer, B.; "Institutionalising Ecologically Sustainable Development: the Roles of National, State, and Local Governments in Translating Grand Strategy into Action"; 31 Willamette Law Review, 1995; at p. 307-351.

Article 10(c) of the CBD states that each State Party to the convention shall, as far as possible and as appropriate, "protect and encourage customary use of biological resources in accordance with traditional cultural practices that are compatible with conservation or sustainable use requirements."[61] Furthermore, the CBD also encourages Contracting Parties to "support local populations to develop and implement remedial action in degraded areas where biological diversity has been reduced."[62] Traditional knowledge and the customary use of biological resources of indigenous peoples and traditional farmers are extremely valuable.[63]

In the case of the Amazon indigenous peoples, it has been recognised that their management of territory, knowledge of nature and traditional technology result from their harmonious coexistence and adaptive evolution to the diversity and heterogeneity of the tropical forest.[64] Amazon Indians know that the Amazon forest is a "planetary reserve"[65] and have played a perfect role in its conservation and sustainable use. However, rarely are they consulted about plans and projects to be implemented in the Amazon forest although the projects seek the economic, scientific and agricultural benefits from the forest and could be greatly enriched through indigenous advice.[66]

Principle 22 of the Rio Declaration states: "Indigenous people and their communities, and other local communities, have a vital role in environmental management and development because of their knowledge and traditional practices. States should recognise and duly support their identity and interests and enable their effective participation in the achievement of sustainable development."[67] Indigenous and local people possess the view of what actually occurs inside the rainforest and are capable of formulating more precise and appropriate strategies and programmes than those people who impose solutions based on outside analysis and observations.

Edith Weiss appropriately noted that sustainable development implies intra and intergenerational equity.[68] That is to say that intragenerational equity is the first step to reach intergenerational equity and thus, sustainable development. According to Ben Boer, intragenerational equity means that "all people are entitled to basic needs, which may be taken to include a healthy environment, adequate food and shelter, and cultural and spiritual fulfilment."[69] However, Ben Boer also recognises that the concept of intergenerational equity is confronted with political, social and practical difficulties.[70]

David Hurlbut believes that sustainable development means that "current generations must leave future generations an environment and a stock of natural

---

[61] CBD; supra Note 1; Article 10(c).
[62] Idem; Article 10(d).
[63] For world case studies on how traditional communities conserve and improve crops *in situ* see Brush, Stephen; Genes in the Field; IPGRI; Rome, Italy; 1999.
[64] Cardenas, M., Correa, H., & Baron, M. (eds); Derecho Territoriales Indígenas y Ecología del America; Bogota; CEREC and Gaia Foundation; London; 1991; at p. 12.
[65] Hosken, L. & Steranka, K.; A Tribute to Forest People, Gaia Foundation; London; 1990; at p. 31.
[66] For development projects which had negative impacts on Indian People see Hitchcock, R. K.; "International Human Rights, the Environment, and Indigenous Peoples"; 5 Colorado Journal of International Environmental Law & Policy 1, 1994; at p. 12.
[67] Rio Declaration; supra Note 1; Principle 22.
[68] Weiss, Edith; Environmental Change and International Law; United Nations University Press; Tokyo, Japan; 1992; at 385.
[69] Boer, B.; supra Note 60; at p. 320.
[70] Idem.

resources that is as good and as plentiful as those it received from past generations."[71] Jeremy Carew-Reid et al concluded that sustainable development has not yet been accomplished. "Sustainable development means improving and maintaining the well-being of people and ecosystems. This goal is far from being achieved. People need to improve their relationships with each other and with the ecosystems which support them, by changing and strengthening their values, knowledge, technologies and institutions."[72] This view is similar to a traditional Asian story about civilisation. According to the story, one day a disciple asked his master:

> "What do you think about civilisation?"
> The Master responded:
> "It is a good idea, someone should put it into practice!"

Sustainable development is the harmonious conjunction of economical, social and ecological actions. This harmony is still not visible in governmental actions. "Sustainable development includes not only ecologically sound co-ordination of economic processes in such a way that they are in conformity with the carrying capacity of the ecological systems, but also encompasses relevant processes of social equalisation among the various national economies where the gap of performance is becoming ever greater."[73]

The Third Session of the Commission on Sustainable Development, (hereafter CSD),[74] reiterated the importance of substantiating the partnership between developing and developed nations established at the UNCED, where each one recognises its contribution towards unsustainability of the world and accepts duties and responsibilities to cease and reverse this process.[75] The outgoing Chairman Klaus Topfer wisely noted that world peace required an end to poverty.[76] Many times has the world testified that social need generates the irresponsible handling of resources, and reproachable actions in the desperation for the satisfaction of daily basic needs. Empowering the poor is a necessary foundation for sustainable development.

As stated by the CSD, "There is an urgent need to formulate or strengthen policies and strategies geared to substantially reducing overall poverty in the shortest possible time, and reducing inequalities, and to eradicate absolute poverty[77] by a target date to be specified by each country in its national context. Such strategies should also incorporate measures to ensure environmental sustainability."[78] The Rio Declaration likewise notes that the essential task of eradicating poverty is an indispensable requirement for sustainable development and all States and all people ought to co-

---

[71] Hurlbut, David; "Fixing the Biodiversity Convention: Toward a Special Protocol for Related Intellectual Property"; 34 Natural Resource Journal 379, 1994; at 380.
[72] Jeremy Carew-Reid et al., Strategies for National Sustainable Development: A Handbook for Their Planning and Implementation; IUCN, IIED, Earthscan; 1994; at xiii.
[73] Extracts from the 1994 Environmental Report of the German Council of Environmental Adviser, translated to English "In Pursuit of Sustainable Environmentally Sound Development", in 25(3) Environmental Policy and Law, 1995; at 90.
[74] The CSD was constituted by Resolution 47/191, 1992 q.v. to promote incorporation of the principles of the Declaration in the implementation of Agenda 21.
[75] UN E/CN.17/1995/14; Third Session of Commission on Sustainable Development; 11-28 April 1995.
[76] Idem. The CSD reiterated that all major UN conferences held since 1990 launch a global attack on poverty: World Summit for Children, International Conference of Nutrition, World Conference on Human Rights, International Conference on Population and Development and the World Summit for Social Development. And recommended that the forthcoming 1995 World Conference for Women emphasises poverty eradication similarly.
[77] Absolute poverty is known to be the severe deprivation of essential needs at a basic level. For instance: nutrition, housing, health services, safe drinking water and sanitation.
[78] CSD; supra Note 75.

operate in this essential task.[79] Sustainable development may quantitatively be measured in terms of "increased food, real income, educational services, health-care, sanitation and water supply, emergency stocks of food and cash, etc., and only indirectly concerned with economic growth at the aggregate, commonly national level."[80]

"The primary concern of sustainable economic development is ensuring that the poor have access to sustainable and secure livelihoods."[81] The CSD stressed the importance of maintaining poverty eradication on a long-term. For this purpose the promotion of full employment and the sustainable use of resources is essential. "Many environmental problems in developing countries originate from the lack of development, that is from the struggle to overcome extreme conditions of poverty."[82] Along with this strategy, empowering the poor with the right to participate in the design, planning and implementation of poverty eradication projects was also noted by the CSD as a way of ensuring the effectiveness of the system. Indigenous and local communities are important elements in conserving and sustainable using biodiversity. Grassroot participation and the equitable and fair remuneration for their contribution are crucial in areas of rich biodiversity.

Although some authors regard the sustainable development concept as elaborated in the CBD as deficient in normative content of the obligations[83], States have different development goals, "common but differentiated responsibilities"[84] and the "sovereign right to exploit their own resources pursuant to their own environmental policies."[85] As such it is reasonable that the CBD declined to deepen and generalise sustainable development commitments on a global level.

2.4 - Equitable Share of Benefits Derived from the Utilisation of its Components

Two of the most debated international topics and the main reasons for the elaboration of the CBD are the access to genetic resources and fair and equitable share of benefits arising from the use of those resources. Developing countries have freely shared their abundant biodiversity components with the rest of the world for purposes of research and germplasm collection in the International Agricultural Research Centres.[86] However, breeders and biotechnological industries, on the other hand, took the opportunity to collect the freely available biodiversity materials from germplasm collections and *in situ* locations, such as tropical forests, to isolate and manipulate their genes. The cycle is ongoing. Biotechnological industries work to highlight or change a trait of the original plant to increase its economic value by protecting it under IPRs[87] since they can be described and utilised with the precision of manufactured objects.[88] This involves a drastic limitation on their access.

---

[79] Rio Declaration; supra Note 6; Principle 5.
[80] Barbier, E.; "The Concept of Sustainable Economic Development"; 14(2) Environmental Conservation, summer 1987; at p. 103.
[81] Idem; at p. 101.
[82] Bartelmus, P.; Environment and Development; Allen and Unwin; London; 1987; at p 18.
[83] See Johnston, Sam; supra Note 55; at p. 54.
[84] Rio Declaration; supra Note 6; Principle Seven.
[85] CBD; supra Note 11; Article 3.
[86] International Agricultural Research Centres are part of the Consultative Group on International Agricultural Research, CGIAR. See Chapter Four of this book.
[87] See Chapter Four of this book.
[88] See School of International and Public Affairs Columbia University; "Access to Genetic Resources: An Evaluation o the Development and Implementation of Recent Regulation and Access Agreements"; Environmental Policy Studies Working Paper no. 4; Environmental Policy Studies Workshop; 1999.

How can there be a fair and equitable share of benefits on a patented plant genetic resource? Patents do not oblige the patentees to share the benefits of their investment with the source country or the indigenous community that revealed the medicinal property in the patented plant. There is a contradiction between the objective of the CBD and the result of patenting plants and plant varieties.

Although Article 16(2) of the CBD states that access to patented technology shall be provided on terms that recognise and are consistent with IPRs,[89] it further determines that Members should take measures to "ensure that such rights are supportive of and do not run counter to its objectives."[90]

The CBD further determines that technology in the CBD includes biotechnology and other technologies that are relevant to the use and conservation of biological diversity and that make use of genetic resources.[91] As such, countries should facilitate their access and transfer. However, little progress has been made in this regard and there is much inequity with the country of origin of the accessed biodiversity.

Patents and plant breeder's rights fail to consider the contribution of indigenous peoples and farmers to the traditional breeding of plants, the enhancement of desired traits, and the maintenance and management of the environment throughout years of cultivation and husbandry.[92] This situation has caused the protest of traditional farmers, indigenous peoples, activists in particular and developing countries in general.

Another disadvantage suffered by indigenous peoples and traditional communities at the hands of technological breeders, is that some countries with a strong IPR system do not consider traditional knowledge transmitted orally as prior art, and thus leave a wide leeway for traditional knowledge to be pirated.[93] In these cases, the equitable share of benefits with the true inventors of traditional plant varieties and discoverers of medicinal plant properties is completely jeopardised.

There are numerous examples of the misappropriation of traditional knowledge and the patenting of plants that have been traditionally used by indigenous and local peoples over centuries.[94] "Transnational pharmaceutical companies send researchers to the developing countries with the greatest bio-genetic diversity -- in the Americas, Africa and Asia -- to seek information on traditional curative plants, unknown to the industry in industrialised countries."[95] These researchers include doctors, sociologists and other experts.[96]

One clear example of misappropriation and non-compensation of traditional knowledge refers to the medicinal plant cat's claw, (*Uncaria tomentosa*). Indigenous people in the Amazon region discovered long ago that cat's claw's bark strengthens and invigorates the human immunological system. Due to its healing properties, cat's

---

[89] CBD; supra Note 1; Article 16(2).
[90] Idem; Article 16(5).
[91] Idem; Article 16(1).
[92] Glowka, Lyle; Burhenne-Guilmin, Françoise; Synge, Hugh; supra Note 20; at p. 5.
[93] See Chapter Two of this book.
[94] See Chapter Four of this book.
[95] Lama, Abraham; "Ills of Unregulated Medicinal Plant Exports"; IPS News Wires; February 2000; located at http://www.ips.org; accessed in April 2000.
[96] Idem.

claws has been effective in treating several types of cancer and AIDS.[97] Cat's claws has been patented by two European pharmaceutical labs.

In 1993, 200 kilos of unprocessed cat's claws were exported to the United States. This quantity was small in comparison to the 20,000 kilos exported in 1994 and more than 800,000 in 1999 for a very low price.[98] The indigenous discoverers of the medicinal properties did not receive their equitable share of benefits for their valuable contribution that is already being of great benefit to humanity.

Although Article 8(j) of the CBD recognises the role of indigenous and local communities in conserving and sustainable using biological diversity, it only *encourages* Member States to equitably share the benefits with the indigenous peoples when their knowledge, innovation and practices are used. This provision is a stimulus for the pirating of indigenous knowledge and customs because the equitable share of benefits with indigenous peoples is based on an encouragement rather than a duty or obligation.

Another point to consider is that patents on genetically modified seeds intensify corporate monopoly. According to the World Scientists' Statement, genetically modified crops "will cause unemployment, exacerbate Third World debt, threaten sustainable farming systems and damage the environment" resulting in famine for the poorest countries.[99] The World Scientists' Statement stresses that it "is on account of corporate monopoly operating under the globalised economy[100] that the poor are getting poorer and hungrier."[101] It is evident from this observation that patents on life forms hinder equity and sustainable development.

Patents on life forms also block breeding directed to research and development in the public sector. A survey was conducted to determine how widespread were the difficulties for public sector plant breeding operations in obtaining genetic material under patent or plant breeder's right protection.[102] Out of the responses, the survey noted: "Forty-eight percent indicated that they had experienced difficulty in obtaining genetic stocks from private companies, 45% indicated that this had interfered with their research, 28% felt that it had interfered with their ability to release new varieties, and a shocking 23% reported that it had interfered with the training of graduate students."[103] This reveals strong opposition to patents and plant breeder's rights.

---

[97] Idem.
[98] A kilo of cat's claw in the jungle is worth two US cents. In Lima, the capital of Peru, a kilo is sold for twenty-eight US cents. In Europe, a bottle of 100 capsules of 300 mg of cat's claw is sold for 18 dollars. Idem. Although it is logical that the price be higher due to the added value of the capsules and bottle, the initial forest price of cat's claw, 2 US cents and the export price 28 US cents is far too low to control over-exploitation of the species and stimulate sustainable use.
[99] See World Scientists' Statement; supra Note 32.
[100] For instance, four corporations currently control 85% of the world trade in cereals. According to Rural Advancement Foundation International, (RAFI), world agriculture is controlled by 10 seed companies: 1. Pioneer Hi-Bred International (United States), 2. Novartis (Switzerland), 3. Limagrain (France), 4. Advanta (Netherlands), 5. Grupo Pulsar (Mexico), 6. Sakata (Japan), 7. Takii (Japan), 8. Dekalb Plant Genetics (United States), 9. KWS (Germany), 10. Cargill (United States). See RAFI Communiqué November/December 1997; Located at: www.rafi.org; accessed in 1998.
[101] See World Scientists' Statement; supra Note 32.
[102] Ken Frey at Iowa State University conducted the survey which occurred from 1990 to 1994. The survey was sent to 187 public plant breeders and forwarded to others. The actual number of how many breeders received the survey is unknown. The total of responses was 86, representing 25 US universities and 41 crops. See Price, S.; "Public and Private Plant Breeding"; 17 Nature Biotechnology, October 1999; at p. 938. Located at: http://biotech.nature.com/; accessed in January 2000.
[103] Idem.

According to UPOV 1978, authorisation of the breeder is not required for the utilisation of the variety as an initial source of variation for the purpose of creating other varieties.[104] UPOV 1991 determines that breeder's right shall not extend to acts done privately and for non-commercial purposes, for experimental purposes and for the purpose of breeding other varieties.[105] Furthermore, the breeder's right may be restricted for reasons of public interests.[106] TRIPs mandates that the protection and enforcement of intellectual property rights should be to the mutual advantage of producers and users of technological knowledge and should promote technological innovation and the transfer and dissemination of technology.[107] The survey reveals that intellectual property rights limit the access of the public sector to breeding the protected variety for experimental and research purposes. This is in direct violation of UPOV 1978, UPOV 1991 and TRIPs. As the public sector is being harmed, intellectual property rights are not to the mutual advantage of producers and users of the technology and furthermore, they do not favour the transfer and dissemination of technology.

Seen in this light, the intellectual property rights on technologically bred plant varieties, parts of plants and seeds are in opposition to the implementation of the equitable share of benefits that arise from the utilisation of biodiversity as determined by the CBD.

The CBD states that access to and transfer of technology is equally important as access to biodiversity and associated knowledge to ensure conservation and sustainable use of biodiversity.[108] Moreover, the CBD determines that there should be a fair and equitable sharing of the benefits arising out of the utilisation of genetic resources, as well as transfer of technology. With this in mind, Article 15(6) of the CBD should be more demanding and enforce the compulsory participation of the source country in the scientific improvements on genetic resources. Article 15(6) of the CBD reads: "Each contracting Party shall endeavour to develop and carry out scientific research based on genetic resources provided by other Contracting Parties with full participation of and, where possible, in such Contracting Parties."[109] The article lacks force and the obligation is not as strongly worded as might be desirable.

The CSD stressed the importance of international financial and technological aid to developing countries while noting that poverty is a multidimensional problem for the solution of which no single measure will suffice. It stressed that a "Favourable international economic environment, and the critical provision of financial and technical assistance flows are essential catalysts towards poverty eradication. Better terms of trade, better access to markets, particularly for labour-intensive products, for agricultural and agro-based products, and those of medium and small-scale enterprises, access to and transfer of environmentally sound technology on favourable terms, including on concessional and preferential terms, as mutually agreed, taking into account the need to protect intellectual property rights as well as the special needs of developing countries are, therefore, also important conditions for sustainability."[110]

Many developing countries, especially the least developed, lack the economic and technological capacity to achieve sustainable development. Therefore, technology transfer and know-how to those countries is a condition precedent to the

---

[104] Article 5(3) of UPOV 1978; see Chapter Three of this book.
[105] Article 15(1) of UPOV 1991; Idem.
[106] Article 9(1) of UPOV 1978 and Article 17(1) of UPOV 1991; Idem.
[107] Article 7 of TRIPs; see Chapter Two of this book.
[108] CBD; supra Note 1; Article 16(1).
[109] Idem; Article 15(6).
[110] CSD; supra Note 75.

accomplishment of sustainable development. Nevertheless, some of those countries are so poor that they lack the proper infrastructure to install the relevant technology. As such, the most important benefit that can be given to those countries is not the payment of royalties for any product that derives from their biodiversity, but the construction of adequate technological, scientific, educational and health infrastructures in their territories, and empowering their own nationals.[111]

A true and effective equitable share of benefits that arise from the utilisation of biodiversity must occur on three levels: local, national and international. Stakeholders vary tremendously on the local level to include bio-prospecting multinational corporations, small locally based industries, local communities, indigenous communities, all of which reflect different needs, objectives and areas of work. On the national level, governments like Brazil, with a federal system, negotiate not only with other nations on the international level, but also within themselves with the different states which compose the country. This is also the case of the United States. State Parties to the CBD can create a national central funding system to collect charges, taxes and donations for the use of traditional knowledge and native plants. The central funding system would invest in the conservation of the native plants, their ecosystems, the cultivation of traditional knowledge and the equitable share of benefits with all stakeholders.

The central funding system is not an easy task to accomplish with ambition and financial greed invading people's hearts like a weed. Corruption is a serious problem in developing and least developed countries and the central funding system would have to be constantly supervised and investigated in order to demonstrate transparently that the collected funds were in fact distributed fairly and equitably among all stakeholders. In this way, national seed systems can be developed that are responsive to the needs and rights of farmers, local communities and indigenous populations.

On the international level, a financial mechanism under the guidance of the Conference of the Parties is responsible for providing financial resources to developing country Parties on a grant or concessional basis.[112] This mechanism is to operate "within a democratic and transparent system of governance."[113] Article 39 of the CBD proposes that as long as it has been fully restructured to fulfil the requirements of Article 21 of the CBD, the Global Environmental Facility, (hereafter GEF),[114] shall be the institutional structure operating the financial mechanism.[115]

Furthermore, another point to consider is that Article 15(3) of the CBD excludes from the scope of the convention those resources that were stored in gene banks and other *ex situ* conditions before the entry into force of the CBD.[116] Much of this vast biological material originated in the developing and least developed countries. "World-wide holdings of crop germplasm in *ex situ* collections (including

---

[111] For ways and methods on how to potentialise local level seed activities, see Cromwell, E.; "Local-level Seed Activities: opportunities ad challenges for regulatory frameworks"; in Tripp, Robert; New Seed and Old Laws (ed); Intermediate Technology Publications; London; 1997; at p. 214.
[112] CBD; supra Note 1; Article 21(1).
[113] Idem.
[114] The GEF was established in the International Bank for Reconstruction and Development, also known as World Bank, for the assistance in the protection of the global environment and promotion of environmentally sound and sustainable economic development. The United Nations Development Programme and the United Nations Environment Programme assisted in its establishment and along with the World Bank, are the implementing agencies of GEF.
[115] In March 1994, representatives of the States participating in the GEF, at their meeting in Geneva, Switzerland, agreed on the instrument that restructured the GEF.
[116] CBD; supra Note 1; Article 15(3).

wild relatives) amount to about 4.2 million accessions, including over two million accessions of cereals and about half a million of food legumes."[117] There are several proposals being negotiated in the FAO to subject these collections to the CBD principles. These proposals include: "bringing international collections under intergovernmental control; repatriating samples from both national and international collections to the countries of origin; ensuring prior informed consent and mutually agreed returns for the commercial use of the stored material; ensuring that IPRs are not applied to any such materials without the consent of the country of origin."[118]

2.5 - Conclusion

It can be said that IPRs tend to stimulate an increase in the plantation of monocultural agriculture and pesticide-resistant transgenic crops that are a threat to genetic diversity and the natural balance of the ecosystem. Furthermore, when traditional knowledge or wild species are used to develop a plant variety, IPRs promote social inequity by disabling the possibility of providing the equitable share of benefits to all the stakeholders.

Biotechnology is a new field and little is known about the potential and actual damaging effects and adverse impacts it might have on the environment. The Cartagena Protocol on Biosafety has been adopted as a protocol to the CBD for protecting the environment from risks posed by the transboundary transport of living modified organisms created by modern biotechnology. State parties to the CBD should adopt a biosafety law to regulate the existence and commercialisation of genetically modified crops in order to avoid poverty, social disruption and the increase of foreign debt.

There is an urgent need to better regulate the access to biodiversity, as well as the equitable share of benefits with all the stakeholders involved in the improvement of the plant variety.

3 – MECHANISMS AVAILABLE FOR STATES TO NEGOTIATE THE EQUITABLE SHARE OF BENEFITS DERIVED FROM THE USE OF THEIR BIODIVERSITY

3.1 - Introduction

The Preamble of the CBD recognises that States have the sovereign right over their natural resources. In addition to the preamble, Article 3 and Article 15 of the CBD reaffirm this sovereignty.[119]

With this in mind, the CBD subordinates access to genetic resources to the prior informed consent of the Contracting Party providing the resources and on mutually agreed terms of both parties. These two access requirements are golden opportunities for developing countries to enforce conservation and sustainable use of

---

[117] Nijar, Gurdial Singh; "In Defence of Indigenous Knowledge and Biodiversity"; Third World Network; Malaysia; 1995. Copies can be ordered by the following e-mail: twn@igc.apc.org.
[118] Kothari, A. & Bhatia, S.; "Access to Biological Resources: Some Proposed Actions by Countries and COP2"; Indian Institute of Public Administration; 1995. This article can be ordered through the following e-mail: akothari@unv.ernet.in.
[119] CBD; supra Note 1; Articles 3 and 15(1).

biodiversity, as well as negotiate issues concerning intellectual property rights, royalty payment, transfer of technology and the empowerment of local people.

3.2 - Prior Informed Consent

Prior informed consent is a mechanism State Parties pursue to control and regulate access to the genetic resources in their territory.[120] Through this legal procedure, governments can determine the requirements to be fulfilled to permit access to their genetic resources. In this sense, governments can and should impose all the requirements that promote the conservation of biodiversity, sustainable use of its components and the equitable share of benefits that derive from their use. The CBD applies to those biological resources that will be used for their functional units of heredity[121] "of actual or potential value".[122] Therefore, no prior informed consent is necessary for a person to access flowers or fruits on public land for purposes other than using their genes.

States are sovereign over their own natural resources in their jurisdictions. However, many of these resources are under private ownership so a State's sovereignty may not be sufficient to determine access to all of the materials. Therefore, when analysing the prior informed consent requirement, it is essential to examine it in conjunction with the State's sovereignty over its biodiversity, and private ownership of resources. Does a State's sovereignty over its biodiversity affect indigenous peoples control over the biological resources located on their lands? If indigenous people hold the ownership of the biodiversity on the lands they traditionally occupy, then the "prior informed consent requirement" of article 15(5) ought to be applicable not only to the Contracting Party providing the resources, but also to the respective indigenous community.[123]

Access to traditional knowledge implies primarily access to the biological resources to which the knowledge is associated. Access to biological resources on indigenous land is not a well-solved issue in most countries. Mexico and the signatories to the Andean Pact assign tenure of biological resources to communities but reserve exclusive property rights for the state, thus limiting the distribution of benefits through a state-owned property regime while obligating communities to preserve the resources.[124] Other countries, such as Brazil, have forcibly removed indigenous peoples from their lands and or territories to construct a road which was never completed and nowadays is completely abandoned and covered with vegetation. Traditional knowledge, culture, folklore beliefs and heritage are inextricably connected with traditional lands and territories of each community. Therefore, when indigenous communities are removed from their lands, their traditional knowledge in regard to biodiversity is sentenced to a death penalty.

---

[120] Idem; Article 15(5).
[121] See definition of "genetic material"; Idem.
[122] See definition of "genetic resources"; Idem.
[123] According to the ILO Convention Concerning Indigenous and Tribal Peoples in Independent Countries, (hereafter ILO Convention 169), governments shall recognise the ownership and possession of indigenous peoples over the lands they traditionally occupied. It further states that governments shall consult indigenous peoples before undertaking any programme for the exploration or exploitation of minerals, sub-surface resources or other resources encountered in indigenous territory. See Articles 14(1) and 15(2) respectively of ILO Convention 169; ILO International Labour Conference, 7th Session; Geneva; 27 June 1989. Reprinted in 28 ILM 1384 et seq., 1989.
[124] School of International and Public Affairs Columbia University; supra Note 88; at p. 10.

Therefore, although the CBD requires Member States to facilitate access to genetic resources for environmentally sound uses by other Contracting Parties,[125] Member States must consider the impacts that access could have on local and indigenous communities. It is important to consider likewise that access to biological diversity for the purpose of bioprospecting usually requires access to land or waters to obtain biological resources. Sufficient care and respect towards the nation's sovereignty, indigenous culture, and traditional lands have to be taken into account to allow for the sustainable use of economic, cultural and ecological diversity. Clearly, these issues are very closely linked and are to be considered as steps in a process of access, collection and use.

Several guidelines and legislative drafts have highlighted the role of indigenous communities in the conservation and sustainable use of biological resources on their lands.[126] The United Nations has drafted a Declaration on the Rights of Indigenous Peoples.[127]

Through their national laws, governments can define how they are willing to exercise sovereignty over biodiversity.[128] In other words, a State can define what overall approach it will develop to allow access to its natural resources in order to guarantee that the relevant stakeholders can have the right to deny or allow access as well as receive their equitable share of the benefits for their contribution.

3.3 - Mutually Agreed Contracts

Article 15 of the CBD encourages Member States to provide access to their genetic resources to other Member States. At the same time, it also recognises their right to deny access.[129] Through mutually agreed access contracts,[130] providing countries can exercise their sovereign rights over their genetic resources, as well as ensure the formal process of benefit sharing, transfer of technology and results of research.

Indigenous and local peoples, for instance, should not sign a contract whereby they permit a single company to have exclusive rights to prospect their traditional plant varieties and associated traditional knowledge. No biotechnology, pharmaceutical or other corporations should obtain a monopoly over traditional local and indigenous knowledge or resources. Likewise, no State should have a monopoly over its citizens' traditional knowledge or traditionally bred varieties. Contracts allow indigenous peoples to bypass the State and negotiate their own interests and terms for access to their own knowledge on medicinal plant properties, agricultural biodiversity, conservation and sustainable use techniques and so forth. In this way, indigenous people would not only be contributing to society with their traditional knowledge, but

---

[125] CBD; supra Note 1; Article 15(2).
[126] The draft Organisation of African Unity legislation proposal, in Article 5(2) considers communities as "sole custodians of the relevant knowledge, innovations and practices" arising from genetic resources "for perpetuity". Ethiopian Ministry of Foreign Affairs; Draft legislation on community rights and access to biological resources; Draft model legislation tabled for OAU Ministers conference; 1998. See Chapter Five of this book.
[127] Draft Declaration on the Rights of Indigenous Peoples; UN E/CN.4/1995/2. E/CN.4/Sub.2/1994/56; 26 August 1994. This draft declaration contains provisions devoted to protection of indigenous rights which include: collective, cultural and ethnic rights; rights to land and resources which are all relevant issues to the conservation and sustainable use of biodiversity.
[128] Glowka, Lyle; Burhenne-Guilmin, Françoise; Synge, Hugh; supra Note 20; at p. 77.
[129] CBD; supra Note 1; Article 15(4).
[130] CBD; supra Note 1; Article 15(4).

would also enjoy the contractual benefits that arise from such contributions, instead of the State treasury.

The equitable share of benefits that arise out of the utilisation of biodiversity must be clearly and fairly provided for in the contract. The way the benefits will be shared, their duration, quantity, and form depends on the contracting parties. Developing and least developed countries are advised to negotiate, as part of their share of benefits, the transfer of technology and know-how, and demand that research on the accessed resources occur in their territory. As noted by Naomi Roht-Arriaza, "so long as communities in Southern countries continue to act as mere providers of raw materials for processing elsewhere, they forfeit the value-adding possibilities of in-country processing of such materials and reproduce the cycles of dependency that have characterised South-North relationships since colonial times."[131] Therefore, developing and least developed countries should negotiate contracts which provide them with financial as well as technological and scientific benefits in order to build their capacity to add value, research and commercialise their biodiversity.[132] In this way they can empower and motivate their own nationals to conserve and enhance biodiversity and avoid being colonised by multinationals. However, for this to occur, there must be a clear established system of rights that guarantees the equitable share of benefits with all stakeholders.

Biodiversity prospecting contracts and partnerships shall be considered in more detail in the following Chapter of this book which deals specifically with those issues.

3.4 - Conclusion

The CBD provides two big opportunities for State Parties to better achieve equity in the distribution of benefits arising from the use of biodiversity: prior informed consent to access and mutual agreement. These two legal provisions are follow ups to the principles of a State's sovereignty over its natural resources and will determine their access requirements. Although the expression "mutually agreed terms" seems to suggest an *ad hoc* contractual arrangement, it does not preclude the possibility of States adopting national legislation to regulate access to their genetic resources consistent with the CBD.

States should enact laws that guarantee that local and indigenous communities are able to safeguard their biological and intellectual resources, deny or negotiate access terms and receive the benefits derived from their use. This would be a powerful incentive for local communities to conserve biodiversity and a far-reaching step towards benefit-sharing with all stakeholders.

Costa Rica has adopted a comprehensive national biodiversity legislation, that provides the regulations on access, intellectual property rights, community rights, safety concerns, conservation and sustainable use of biodiversity. The relevant aspects of that law in regard to this Chapter will be examined in the following section.

---

[131] Roht-Arriaza, Naomi; "Of Seeds and Shamans: the Appropriation of the Scientific and Technological Knowledge of Indigenous and Local Communities"; 17 Michigan Journal of International Law, 1996; at p. 961.
[132] See Article 15(6) and 15(7) of the CBD; supra Note 1.

4 - COMPREHENSIVE NATIONAL BIODIVERSITY LEGISLATION- COSTA RICA

The Costa Rica Biodiversity Law, Biodiversity Law no. 7788, has been considered a revolutionary development in the area of incorporating the objectives of the Biodiversity Convention. It is a good example of how a national legislation can identify the benefits of conserving and sustainably using biodiversity, develop principles which regulate the access, management, development and export of its biodiversity, as well as to the associated traditional knowledge.

4.1 - Definition of Biodiversity

Costa Rica's Biodiversity law defines biodiversity as follows:

Variability of living organisms of any source, found in terrestrial, air, maritime, aquatic ecosystems or in other ecological complexes. It comprehends the diversity within species, as well as between species and of ecosystems in which they form a part.

For the purposes of this law, the term biodiversity shall be understood to include the intangible elements which are: the knowledge, the innovation and the traditional practice, individual or collective, of real or potential value associated with biochemical and genetic resources, protected or not by the intellectual property systems or sui generis systems of register.[133]

The first paragraph of Article 7 of the Costa Rican Biodiversity Law is quite faithful to the wording of the definition of biodiversity in the CBD. Subsequently, Costa Rica expands on the definition and extends its scope of interpretation to cover intangible components associated with biochemical and genetic resources. According to Costa Rica, individual and collective knowledge, innovation and traditional practice of actual or potential value to humanity linked to the genetic resource, its derivatives, or the biological resource containing them, are comprehended as part of biodiversity as well. Costa Rica safeguards its interests and its interpretation of the definition of biodiversity by stating that the components it introduces into the definition are valid in its State regardless of whether or not they are protected by intellectual property rights systems or *sui generis* systems thereof.

The Costa Rican biodiversity definition is pioneer in including intangible components. By doing this, it provides the legal protection to safeguard its national development when conserving, utilising or allowing access to its biological diversity. The Law of Biodiversity in Costa Rica provides that the "State shall exercise complete and exclusive right over the elements of biodiversity"[134] which are "under the sovereignty of the State."[135] The exceptions to this rule are found in Article 4 of the same law, and they include *inter alia* the access to biochemical and human genetic material, as well as the exchange of biochemical and genetic resources and the knowledge associated with them resulting from practices, uses and customs, without the aim of profit, among the indigenous peoples and local communities.[136]

---

[133] Costa Rica Biodiversity Law; Ley de Biodiversidad, No.: 7788; April 1998; at Article 7.
[134] Idem; Article 2.
[135] Idem; Article 3.
[136] Idem; Article 4.

4.2 - Objectives

Article 1 of the Costa Rica Biodiversity Law states that the major objectives of the law are the conservation of biodiversity, the sustainable use of resources and the fair distribution of the benefits and costs which derive from the utilisation of the resources.[137] It can be easily noted that those are also the objectives of the CBD.

In Article 10 of its biodiversity law, Costa Rica sets the secondary objectives to be met. It initially demonstrates its willingness to use its biological diversity and the knowledge associated with it as a means to contribute to its economic development without endangering the nation's social and cultural development, as well as the protection of the environment.[138] Costa Rica acknowledges that different sectors of society depend upon or have interests in biodiversity. Therefore it promotes the active participation of all social sectors in conservation and ecological sustainability.[139] By promoting the active participation of all social sectors, Costa Rica recognises that they have a contribution to make towards the conservation and sustainable use of biodiversity. For instance, one of society's sectors contributes with its traditional knowledge, another sector through technological knowledge, and a third sector provides financial assistance. Consequently, each form of participation is compensated. The law defines knowledge as a whole as the "dynamic product generated by society over time and by different mechanisms comprehending what is produced by traditional methods as well as what it generated by scientific practice."[140]

Although Costa Rica has complete and exclusive rights over the elements of biodiversity in its territory,[141] when they generate profit Costa Rica's biodiversity law provides for the equitable share of benefits among all social sectors, with special consideration being given to local and indigenous communities. The equitable distribution of benefits encompasses the benefits that arise in the social, environmental and economic sectors.

Costa Rica's law, in common with most Roman-derived legal systems, provides that biodiversity is part of the State's patrimony. As such, the Costa Rica Biodiversity Law determines that the State shall "authorise the exploration, the investigation, the bioprospection, the use and the utilisation of the elements of biodiversity which constitute property of public domain, as well as the utilisation of all genetic and biochemical resources."[142] It is important to recall here that according to Article 3, the State has complete and exclusive right over the elements of biodiversity under its sovereignty.[143] However, this rule does not apply to the exchange of biochemical and genetic resources among indigenous peoples and local communities, as well as their traditional knowledge resulting from practices, uses and customs, when they are not used for commercial purposes.

Environmental security is also regulated by the Biodiversity Law.[144] A full chapter deals mainly with the investigation, development, production, liberation or introduction of genetically modified organisms in Costa Rica.[145] The law establishes

---

[137] Idem; See Article 1.
[138] Idem; Article 10.
[139] Idem.
[140] Idem; Article 7(6).
[141] Idem; Article 3.
[142] Idem; Article 6.
[143] Idem; Article 3.
[144] Idem; Chapter III - "Garantias de Seguridad Ambiental".
[145] Idem; Article 44.

the mechanisms and procedures to regulate the access to the elements of biodiversity located under its sovereignty when they are used in any of the actions cited above, in order to "avoid and prevent present and future damages and prejudices to human, animal or plant health, or to the integrity of the ecosystems."[146]

4.3 - Access To Genetic Resources

Costa Rica stipulates that one of the basic requirements to be fulfilled in order to obtain the permission for access to the biodiversity under its sovereignty is the prior informed consent of the representatives of the place where the access would occur.[147] This provisions not only maximises Costa Rica's control over its genetic resources, but also correctly delegates authority to private proprietors, as well as local and indigenous communities, to grant or withhold access to resources located on their lands, as well as to the knowledge associated to the resources.

The transfer of technology and an equitable share of benefits which arise from the utilisation of the elements of biodiversity is a fundamental requirement to allow access to its biodiversity. In this case, the terms for the transfer of technology and equitable share of benefits should be agreed in the permissions, agreements and concessions regarding access of the genetic or biochemical resource.[148] The permissions, agreements and concessions should also contain the type of protection demanded by the representatives of the area from which the resource was extracted in regard to the knowledge associated to the resource.[149]

4.4 - Conclusion

The Costa Rican government has been obedient to the CBD's provisions. Its Biodiversity Law aims to facilitate access to Costa Rica's biodiversity, the traditional knowledge of all of its peoples, but simultaneously, it imposes restrictions to avoid actions which run counter to the objectives of the CBD.[150] The law also attempts to avoid restriction on the provisions of the CBD that can occur through intellectual property rights on genetically modified organisms.

Pharmaceutical and biotechnological firms are allowed access to Costa Rica's biological diversity through binding mutually agreed contracts where intellectual property rights and profits are regulated clearly and the benefits of the access are shared equitably among all parties.

The Costa Rica Biodiversity Law is not a framework law. On the contrary, it is practical and introduces nationally the rights and duties provided for in the CBD. It recognises the CBD's basic objectives, expands them in order to recognise and compensate indigenous and local knowledge, and designs the path for the fulfilment of all the objectives. By improving education, recognising and compensating the use of indigenous knowledge, regulating access to the elements of biodiversity, having all social sectors jointly working on the conservation and sustainable utilisation of biodiversity, encouraging international co-operation, promoting transfer of technology and so forth, the three basic objectives of the CBD are likely to be reached.

---

[146] Idem.
[147] Idem; Article 63(1).
[148] Idem; Article 63(3).
[149] Idem; Article 63(3).
[150] CBD; supra Note 1; Article 15(2).

As Costa Rica's Biodiversity Law exemplifies, it is advisable for countries to adopt a biodiversity access law that protects both community and scientific development. In this sense, States should encourage the full participation of all the sectors in society for the conservation and safe enhancement of biodiversity, as well as promote the balance of their rights and duties. Dutfield notes that Costa Rica's Law shows that "biodiversity legislation rather than IPR laws *per se* may provide the most appropriate framework to subordinate IPRs to biodiversity conservation and to develop *sui generis* systems through such a process."[151]

5 - GENERAL CONCLUSION

Sustainability, as a way of living, presents a choice of values. What do we want from plant genetic resources. What value do we want to give them? What value do they really have? Is the lack of property rights on biotic and genetic material of unprocessed biodiversity leading to the undervaluation of these resources, and consequently to their unsustainable use? To what extent do we want genetic material to provide commodities and to what extent do we want them to provide environmental benefits? To what extent do we want to conserve the natural species as they are and to what extent do we want do genetically modify them? Developed and developing countries have different choices because they have different economic conditions. Thus, in summary, the challenge is to discover a balance in the choices to be made.

Member States to the CBD must urgently find a way to harmonise TRIPs with the provisions of CBD objectives. When considering both the access to genetic resources and the patentability of life forms it is essential to consider the respective ethical, economic, environmental and social implications because if any of those aspects is ignored, it is impossible to achieve conservation, sustainable use and the equitable share of benefits. Sustainable development is inconsistent with environmental degradation, cultural disruption and social and economic instability.

However, breeders and biotechnological companies feel that their effort, time and financial investment expended in the development of new distinct varieties from medicinal plants, for instance, should be compensated and are totally in favour of patents and plant breeders' rights on plant varieties. Nevertheless, on the other side stand the local and the indigenous communities who also feel their conservation methods and their traditional knowledge should also be compensated. Although the CBD recognises that States have sovereign rights over their biological diversity, ownership of these resources varies from country to country and in many countries remains an issue to be clarified. The United States, for instance, has a very strong intellectual property system, which permits the monopolisation of biological resources under patent rights. Other countries, such as Brazil, must deal with a wide horizon of internal stakeholders when determining who owns a selected set of biological resources: the indigenous community, local community, large industries, government, and so forth.[152]

There are sufficient objectives in the CBD and sufficient moral ground to be codified into a practical system of equitable and fair partnerships between stakeholders. The CBD asserts the sovereignty of nations over their biological diversity as well as their right to establish legislation regulating access to genetic resources. Access is subordinated to prior informed consent of the source country and

---

[151] Dutfield, G.; supra Note 9.
[152] See the Chapters on Brazil, Eight and Nine of this book.

to a contract mutually agreed by the parties. In the elaboration of this contract the source country can demand from collectors an up-front payment for access to biodiversity and a fee to enter into contractual agreements, negotiations of royalty payments as well as the equitable share of all benefits which derive from the use of the collected biodiversity. Furthermore, partnerships can create opportunities to empower the poor providing them with the means to live sustainable and secure livelihoods. In this context, there is more possibility for the CBD objectives to be met and for equity to be accomplished in present and in future generations.

Through biodiversity prospecting and biopartnerships countries can exercise their right to development and simultaneously conserve biological diversity, sustainably use its components and reduce poverty. To maintain the sustainable livelihood of the poor in the long term, they must have access to education, training, technology and health systems. All of these measures would economically empower the poor and enable them to lead themselves out of poverty.

The CBD pursues several articles that can serve as frameworks for the construction of partnerships between countries, *inter alia*, Article 15 (Access to Genetic Resources); Article 16 (Access to and Transfer of Technology); Article 20 (Financial Resources); and Article 21 (Financial Mechanisms). The implementation of the above articles can be used as a starting point for countries to achieve the fair and equitable share of efforts and benefits to conserve, manage, research and commercialise biological diversity and derived products, transfer technology and know-how and improve basic human needs. As economic, social and ecological conditions vary from country to country, the more particular terms of biopartnership contracts will be formulated on a case by case basis based on mutually agreed terms of the Contracting Parties. Partnerships dealing with biodiversity prospecting are dealt with in the following Chapter.

CHAPTER SEVEN

BIOPARTNERSHIPS

1 - GENERAL INTRODUCTION

Global sustainability depends on the effective co-operation of all States. Global partnership is basically a partnership where all countries work together to improve the general quality of human life on Earth. Both the CBD and the Rio Declaration contain provisions related to a global partnership of all states "to conserve, protect and restore the health and integrity of the Earth's ecosystem."[1] The Rio Declaration, for instance, declared that all States "shall co-operate in the *essential task of eradicating poverty as an indispensable requirement for sustainable development*, in order to decrease the disparities in standards of living and better meet the needs of the majority of the people of the world"[2] (emphasis added).

Principle 3 of the Rio Declaration provides for intergenerational equity by stating that the "right to development must be fulfilled so as to equitably meet developmental and environmental needs of present and future generations."[3] Likewise, the CBD in its preamble declares that the Contracting Parties are "determined to conserve and sustainably use biological diversity for the benefit of present and future generations."[4]

One of the first tasks of the global partnership is to reduce poverty processes in order to avoid further environmental degradation. Logically, poor people are concerned mainly with their basic and immediate survival and will not refrain from using biodiversity unsustainably. Poor nations will only join this partnership, and thus recognise and accept that they have intergenerational obligations, once they themselves have reached the standards developed States already pursue. Poverty eradication can contribute substantially towards the use of biodiversity in a way and at a rate which allows both present and future generations to meet their needs and aspirations.[5] Thus, intragenerational equity is the first step to intergenerational equity.

Intragenerational equity suggests that countries broaden their limited competitive view and start working together to improve their citizens ecological, social and economic living standards. "Partnership between generations is the corollary to equality."[6] Intragenerational equity implies social, technological and economic empowerment of poor people through research, training and education.[7] It is worth stressing Article 20(4) of the CBD which states "that *economic and social development and eradication of poverty are the first and overriding priorities of the developing country Parties.*"[8]

Public education and awareness of the importance of the conservation of biological diversity and sustainable use of its components are integral parts of the

---

[1] Principle 7 of the Rio Declaration; UN. Doc. A/CONF. 151/5/Rev.1 (1992).
[2] Idem; Principle 5.
[3] Idem; Principle 3.
[4] Preamble of the CBD.
[5] See CBD definition of sustainable development in Article 2 of the CBD.
[6] Weiss, Edith; Environmental Change and International Law; United Nations University Press; Tokyo, Japan; 1992; at 396.
[7] See Article 12 of the CBD.
[8] Article 20(4) of the CBD.

global partnership programme. Article 13(b) of the CBD states that Contracting Parties shall "co-operate, as appropriate, with other States and international organizations in developing educational and public awareness programmes, with respect to conservation and sustainable use of biological diversity."[9]

Another important aspect of the global partnership is the recognition of the contribution of indigenous and local communities to the conservation, sustainable use and general knowledge about plant properties.[10] It is relevant to remember that the Rio Declaration declared that States have common but differentiated responsibilities.[11] The principle of common but differentiated responsibilities also applies to all stakeholders undertaking a biopartnership. Likewise, the participatory approach of all stakeholders must start at the establishment of the partnership and be carried out throughout the whole process in order to ensure mutual benefits and achieve the realisation of the objectives of the CBD.

The preamble of the Rio Declaration acknowledges the necessity of "establishing a new and equitable global partnership through the creation of new levels of co-operation among States, key sectors of societies and people."[12] This is an incentive for different stakeholders, who are experts in different areas of knowledge, to form partnerships that mutually benefit all parties.

2 - GLOBAL INEQUITY

According to the World Bank, "progress in poverty reduction appears to have stalled in the past few years, with a resulting increase in the total number of poor people in many regions."[13] The 1999 Human Development Report, (hereafter the Report), revealed that the gap between nations, including that between people in developed nations,[14] has been increasing.[15] Furthermore, the report notes that the average income in the richest five countries in the world is 74 times the level of the five poorest.[16] This reveals the world is facing the widest economic and social development inequality gap ever seen.

The Report further notes that patents and technology are rapidly becoming a monopoly of a few countries and companies. Companies and institutions of only 10 countries in the world hold 95% of all the patents issued in the US over the past 20 years.[17] Moreover, the prices of items "from new drugs to better seeds" are unaffordable to poor nations.[18]

---

[9] Article 13(b) of the CBD.
[10] See Articles 8(j), 10(c) and 18(4) of the CBD.
[11] Rio Declaration; Principle 7.
[12] Idem; Preamble.
[13] World Bank; "Strengthening Infrastructure for Social Development"; Paper submitted by the by the World Bank in January 2000 to the World Summit for Social Development Five Year Review, in Geneva; June 2000; at p. 4. Located at: http://www.un.org/esa/socdev/geneva2000/docs/wbinfra.pdf; accessed in June 2000.
[14] Especially United States, Britain and Sweden.
[15] See the 1999 Human Development Report prepared by the U.N. Development Program. Researchers that prepared this report examined income, education, life expectancy and health care in 174 countries. The 1999 Human Development Report can be found on the UNDP website, at http://www.undp.org/hdro; accessed in September 2000.
[16] Idem.
[17] Idem.
[18] Idem.

Bell and Pimbert note that a "gross imbalance of wealth, power and natural resource utilisation is inherent in the modern world order. Industrial countries, which contain only 26% of the world's population, consume 80% of its energy and 40% of its food. [...] The excessive demands of the industrialised countries threaten biodiversity throughout the world. [...] The affluent North has come to depend on the developing South to provide it with cheap raw materials such as timber, cotton, cocaine, and plant and animal genes."[19]

Through all of the above statements and examples it is clear that the idea of a global partnership has not been effective in action. As such, a new movement has been emerging. Citizens from developing countries are not willing to wait for their governments to take action and work together globally towards the common goal of better social welfare and environmental protection. Furthermore, local, indigenous and tribal communities have been acknowledging that the sustainable use of biodiversity associated with their traditional knowledge is sought *inter alia* by institutions, industries and botanical gardens due to the recognition of the value and potential of biodiversity in biotechnology.[20]

Partnerships involving traditional knowledge and natural resources are called biopartnerships. Local people in developing countries have been adopting biopartnerships as a means of improving their living standards. In this sense, while governments postpone the compliance of their duties to realise the so far theoretical concept of "global partnership", **fair**, **ethical** and **equitable** biopartnerships can play an important role in poverty eradication, preservation of traditional knowledge and environmental protection. The words **fair**, **ethical** and **equitable** are highlighted because their existence in biopartnerships is the only way biopartnerships can help eradicate poverty. Their absence would mean that a "traditional-knowledge-natural-resource" colonisation period, on the verge of emerging, would gain force and rule the destinies of biodiversity rich countries and control the use of traditional knowledge of indigenous and local communities. Thus, to prevent such negative happenings, any biopartnership accorded should be founded on fairness, ethics and equity.

3 - BIOPARTNERSHIPS

3.1 - Introduction

Biopartnerships can be achieved by uniting scientific and technological knowledge with traditional knowledge of local communities and indigenous populations. This unified knowledge can be used to empower the local population, improve their living conditions through the generation of jobs and income, discover the various uses of the native species, share results and benefits and disseminate innovation and information. The fight against poverty and environmental destruction can be accomplished through the creation of biopartnerships at the local, national and international levels.

Through fair and balanced biopartnerships with developed countries, developing countries can sustainably use their natural resources in order to gain the economic incentive they seek. Likewise, the private sector of both developed and developing countries can also create biopartnerships with local communities and indigenous populations to add value to biological resources and the associated

---

[19] Bell, J. and Pimbert, M.; in Baumann, M., Bell, J., Koechlin, F., Pimbert, M., (eds); The Life Industry. Biodiversity, people and Profits; Intermediate Technology Publications; London; 1996; at pp. 6, 10.
[20] Idem; at p. 16.

traditional knowledge in the market. The effectiveness of these biopartnerships depends on fair, direct and clear contractual terms. This is to say that the biopartnership should not be like a competitive tennis match where one player through clever movements tries to eliminate the other player in order to win the game. It should be as a racket ball game on the beach where one player tries to help the other player so that the game can continue. A partnership created to conserve biodiversity, sustainably use its components and equitably share the benefits that arise from their use must be a win-win game where all parties in the biopartnership succeed.

Partnerships must be built on the mutual satisfaction of all parties. Local and indigenous peoples should refuse to provide cheap raw material and labour to developed countries. Instead, they should enter into fair and equitable partnerships which are formalised through mutually agreed contracts. The General Secretary of UNCTAD, Rubens Ricupero, stated "let the new perspective be: conservation and the knowledge from it brings value, value means business, as well as more value, in turn, for conservation."[21]

The Preamble of the CBD stresses "the importance of, and the need to promote, international, regional and global co-operation among States and intergovernmental organizations and the non-governmental sector for the conservation of biological diversity and the sustainable use of its components."[22] Local and indigenous communities, for instance, are deeply familiar with local plant species, the environment and climate. These qualities could be potentialised in biopartnerships.

In Mexico, for example, the Huastec indigenous peoples cultivate around 300 different plants.[23] Local communities in Indonesia cultivate around 100 plant species for purposes of food, medicine, building materials, fuelwood and so forth.[24] Industries interested in accessing those plant species, and associated traditional knowledge could enter into mutually agreed partnerships with those communities.

There are three main reason why pharmaceutical companies are increasing their research into natural products:

1- Screening techniques have become more efficient and thus extensive natural product screening has become more affordable.
2- Tapping into traditional medicinal knowledge has drastically reduced research cost and investigation time in finding a valuable medicine.
3- There is a growing demand in developed countries for natural medicines.[25]

In the United States, 25% of the prescriptions refer to drugs whose active ingredients were extracted or derived from plants.[26] Sales of plant-based medicines in the United States amounted to approximately $15.5 billion in 1990.[27] However, the market value of products derived from the use of genetic and biochemical resources

---

[21] Poematropic; Os Desafios do Desenvolvimento Sustentavel, Numero 1, Janeiro/Julho de 1998; at p. 10.
[22] Preamble of CBD.
[23] Bell, J. and Pimbert, M.; supra Note 19; at p. 3.
[24] Idem.
[25] Bell, Janet; "Genetic engineering and biotechnology in industry"; in Baumann, M., Bell, J., Koechlin, F., Pimbert, M., (eds); supra Note 19; at p. 33.
[26] Reid, W., Laird, S., Gámez, R., Sittenfeld, A., Janzen, D., Gollin, M., Juma, C.; "A New Lease on Life"; in Reid, W., Laird, S., Meyer, C., Gámez, R., Sittenfeld, A., Janzen, D., Gollin, M., Juma, C.; Biodiversity Prospecting: Using Genetic Resources for Sustainable Development; World Resources Institute; USA; at p. 7.
[27] Idem.

provides "little indication of the potential market value of the unimproved genetic material in the source country."[28]

Developing countries that are rich in biological diversity are hopeful that the access to their genetic resources can be the mechanism they need to obtain the capital for their development. "Currently, however, there is little infrastructure, few researchers, and practically no budget for basic biological research in most tropical, developing countries."[29] "The loss of biodiversity is due above all to economic factors, especially the low values given to biodiversity and ecological functions such as watershed protection, nutrient cycling, pollution control, soil formation, photosynthesis and evolution. Biodiversity is a cross-sectorial issue, and virtually all sectors have an interest in its conservation and the sustainable use of its components."[30]

According to Kloppenburg, bioprospecting deals "are characterised by inadequate compensation, inadequate consultation with the stewards of the resources, and the extension of the reach of the global market. I know of no case of bioprospecting that I would regard as just, in the sense of informed consent by all parties and adequate compensation for all parties."[31]

Even though biopartnerships have a lot to improve in the areas of equity and transparency, in this Chapter, various international biopartnerships between countries, as well as between different sections of society, are described and analysed. The partnerships were selected not only for their efficiency, originality and clarity, but moreover, for the availability of information and compliance to the objectives of the CBD.

3.2 - Biopartnership Contracts

Contractual agreement is the most practical way through which equity can be achieved. Biopartnership contracts allow parties to mutually decide on biodiversity access terms, the form in which benefits are to be shared, the interests and priorities of each party and the duration of the agreement.

Government, scientific bodies, specific indigenous communities, individuals, non-governmental organisations, and so forth, can all be parties to biopartnerships. Indigenous and local communities can act on their own behalf or delegate powers to organisations that represent their true interests. The agency, non-governmental organisation or governmental body that would most faithfully and honestly represents indigenous interests will vary from country to country.

Benefits in biopartnerships can be monetary or non-monetary. Both forms of benefits are important and complementary. Monetary benefits should include an upfront payment once the partnership is sealed and subsequent payments on the supply of natural resources, as well as fees per sample of natural resource. Parties providing natural resources should definitely negotiate short-term benefits as it is it not certain if

---

[28] Idem; at p. 15.
[29] School of International and Public Affairs Columbia University; "Access to Genetic Resources: an Evaluation of the Development and Implementation of Recent Regulation and Access Agreements"; Environmental Policy Studies Working Paper no. 4; 1999; at p. 10.
[30] Glowka, Lyle; Burhenne-Guilmin, Françoise; Synge, Hugh; A Guide to the Convention on Biological Diversity; Environmental Policy and Law Paper No. 30; IUCN; 1994; at p. 18.
[31] Kloppenburg, Jack; "Changes in the Genetic Supply Industry"; in Baumann, M., Bell, J., Koechlin, F., Pimbert, M., (eds); supra Note 19; at p. 29.

researchers will discover a new pharmaceutical of agricultural product nor how long such activity would take.

However, if the research is undertaken on a plant traditionally used to cure certain diseases, for instance, the short-term benefits should be much higher than if nothing was known of the accessed plant. The possibility of a pharmaceutical company of developing a medicine from a traditionally used medicinal plant is very high, thus reducing the costs of the whole process of discovering, screening and producing a new drug.

Biopartnership contacts should also negotiate long-term benefits as royalty payments based on the net sales of the developed product. The percentage of each royalty to the provider of the raw material and/or associated knowledge will depend on the contribution made by that party to the development of the final product.

Non-monetary benefits refer mainly to the capacity building of developing countries "by improving scientific understanding through exchanges of scientific and technological knowledge, and by enhancing the development, adaptation, diffusion and transfer of technologies, including new and innovative technologies."[32] Article 18(2) of the CBD determines that Contracting Parties shall "promote technical and scientific co-operation with other Contracting Parties, in particular developing countries, in implementing this Convention, *inter alia*, through the development and implementation of national policies. In promoting such co-operation, special attention should be given to the development and strengthening of national capabilities, by means of human resources development and institution building."[33]

Non-monetary benefits for biodiversity rich countries should be targeted towards their immediate and long-term development and social needs. They can take various forms such as the construction of health services, schools, contribution to scientific or institutional infrastructure, training in collection and specimen-identification techniques, technology transfer and associated know-how, sharing of lab results, agreement to provide drugs at cost price, and so forth. Host-countries can also negotiate screening for tropical diseases. Non-monetary benefit negotiations and choices will depend on the preferences and necessities of each contracting party providing raw materials and associated traditional knowledge.

Training, skill formation and enhancement of self-organisation will help the poor communities to improve their earning capacities. Likewise, biopartnerships that provide local communities with market links, finance, training, management, and so forth, are fundamental for the empowerment of poor people.[34]

4 - BIOPARTNERSHIP CASE-STUDIES

4.1 - Introduction

The following case studies describe biopartnerships undertaken in different countries.[35] They have been chosen as case-studies because they not only represent

---

[32] Principle 9 of the Rio Declaration.
[33] Article 18(2) of the CBD.
[34] See Baumann, M., Bell, J., Koechlin, F., Pimbert, M., (eds); supra Note 19. See also Reid, et al.; supra Note 26.
[35] There was a great difficulty of accessing information on existent biopartnerships. Most of the information in this section was provided by parties involved in the biopartnerships.

different countries and continents, but also different stakeholders and types of arrangements. Merck-INBio was the first biopartnership to be adopted and served as a model for others that followed. After the Merck-INBio, Costa Rica has been forming other biopartnerships, such as the one with the Netherlands, Bhutan and Benin. The Bioresources Development and Conservation Program has initiated biopartnerships between African tribes and pharmaceutical companies. Suriname has also undertaken a biopartnership with pharmaceutical companies. And finally this section will also analyse a partnership undertaken by the University of California. This section will examine how far these partnerships have gone to recognise the rights of holders of traditional knowledge, as well as accomplish the CBD objectives.

4.2 - Merck-INBio Agreement

Costa Rica is a small Central American country. Its diverse geographical landscape has generated a vast quantity of biological resources. The conservation of its biological resources is a common responsibility of the government and the civil society and is based on three concepts: save, get to know and use.[36]

Costa Rica's Ministry of the Environment and Energy (hereafter MINAE)[37] has signed a Co-operation Agreement[38] with the Instituto Nacional de Biodiversidad (hereafter INBio), in Costa Rica where they committed themselves to prepare Costa Rica's biodiversity inventory[39] and not to commercialise the samples taken for that purpose.[40] INBio, however, is allowed to collect biological samples for the purpose of bioprospecting.[41] Fifty percent of the economic and material benefits INBio gains from bioprospecting are transferred to MINAE for the management and conservation of wildlands.[42]

INBio was created on 25 October 1989 on the recommendation of a National Planning Commission. As a "non-government, non profit, scientific research institute of social orientation and for the public good"[43] its main objectives are:

(1) To assume responsibility for developing and executing a national biodiversity inventory.
(2) To locate national collections within one physical space under a single administration.
(3) To centralise biodiversity information.
(4) To put information on biodiversity in easily understandable form for a wide variety of users and promote its use by Costa Rican society.[44]

---

[36] See Mateo, Nader, Tamayo; "Utilización de la biodiversidad con Fines Económicos"; Prospección de Biodiversidad; INBio; Costa Rica; Received by e-mail by Carolina Roldan (croldan@inbio.ac.cr).
[37] MINAE is the abbreviation of Ministerio del Ambiente y Energia.
[38] The Co-operation Agreement between INBio and MINAE was signed 7 October 1994 and is valid for a period of five years from the signed date. On 7 October 1999 it was automatically renewed for the same period.
[39] Scientists in Costa Rica estimated that the country has 12,000 plant species of which 80% have been documented. INBio's biological inventory estimated that Costa Rica has over 500,000 species of plants, animals and micro-organisms.
[40] Co-operation Agreement; supra Note 38; Clause 1.
[41] Idem.
[42] Idem; Clause 12.
[43] INBio; "INBio-Merck Research Agreement Renewal/Questions and Answers". Sent as electronic mail attachment by Priscilla Hurtado, askinbio@inbio.ac.cr; 1999.
[44] Idem.

Only 15% of INBio's total yearly budget is derived from agreements with private companies. The other 85% of its budget come from project grants provided by different sources.[45] INBio has undertaken inventories and catalogued Costa Rica's biological diversity through a database of species names, conservation status, distribution, and potential commercial use of over 80% of Costa Rica's plants species.[46] In addition, INBio has been training its nationals in paratoxonomy.

On 1 November 1991, INBio signed a three-year agreement with Merck, a multi-national pharmaceutical industry dedicated to research and bioprospecting.[47] The agreement was renewed in July 1994, and again in August 1996. It includes confidential information that is only allowed to be disclosed after a period of seven years.

According to the agreement, INBio supplies Merck with samples of plants, insects and micro-organisms collected from Costa Rica's protected forest. Furthermore, INBio hires and trains staff for the necessary activities related to access to the biological samples. Merck has temporarily the exclusive right to screen, develop, and commercialise new pharmaceutical products derived from the samples provided by INBio. Patents on such products are allowed, but there must be a clear definition of sample and patent ownership and the payment of royalties on net sales.

When the research of the biological resources yields a commercially viable product, Merck is committed to pay INBio up to ten percent in royalties. MINAE receives five percent of these royalties. In addition, Merck has been transferring technology[48] and training the Costa Rican scientists and paratoxonomists[49] in species identification and collection. As an up-front payment, Merck paid one million dollars to INBio in order to analyse an agreed number of species.[50] Moreover, INBio stresses that pharmaceutical research and development be carried out in Costa Rica. Merck also commits itself to financially contribute to the conservation of Costa Rica biological resources as an alternative to deforestation.[51]

Some authors have questioned whether Merck paid the true value for Costa Rica's biodiversity.[52] The answer is most likely "no". However, in the situation Costa Rica was at the time it signed the Merck-INBio partnership, it was the best it could achieve. Nowadays, after Costa Rica has increased its scientific and technological capacity, due to the technology and know-how transferred by Merck, and having been able to conserve and sustainably use its biodiversity, as a consequence of the agreement, Costa Rica's potential has expanded. It has empowered itself and has more

---

[45] Including United Nations Environmental Programme, (UNEP) and the Swedish International Development Agency.
[46] The text of the Merck INBio Agreement is unavailable. Therefore, the information presented were derived through personal contacts with INBio, as well as through the standard Summary of Terms for the INBio-Merck & Co., Inc. Collaboration Agreement.
[47] Much of the information on this biopartnership was received from first source, in other words, from INBio which respected the confidential terms of the contract.
[48] For instance, Merck provided $180,000 in equipment to INBio for chemical extraction. Merck also provided materials valued at $135,000. See Zerner, C. And Kennedy, K.; "Equity Issues in Bioprospecting"; in Baumann, M., Bell, J., Koechlin, F., Pimbert, M., (eds); supra Note 19; at p. 101.
[49] Paratoxonomists are field collectors.
[50] Ten percent of this initial one million dollars will be transferred to MINAE to be invested in biodiversity conservation.
[51] About twenty-eight percent of Costa Rica's forest was lost between 1966 and 1989. Species were being reduced at a rate of half a percent a year due to deforestation. The government of Costa Rica, however, has managed to reverse that situation and more than thirty percent of the country's territory has been declared conservation areas. See Mateo, Nader, Tamayo; supra Note 36.
[52] See Zerner, C. and Kennedy, K.; "Equity Issues in Bioprospecting"; in Baumann M., Bell, J., Koechlin, F., Pimbert, M., (eds); The Life Industry. Biodiversity, people and Profits; Intermediate Technology Publications; London; 1996; at p. 103.

competence to enter into more lucrative deals and biopartnerships or even be more independent or "self-employed". Another point to consider is that if a first deal had not been made, the value of the accessed biodiversity would have continued unknown, as Costa Rica did not have the technical capacity and scientific knowledge to investigate its own biodiversity alone.

The Merck-INBio agreement involves local people in the projects and assists in the human rights of the local peoples. It has been used an example by other countries to set their own biopartnerships with industries interested in researching biological diversity. This agreement is a win-win partnership even though Merck's profits are higher than those of INBio when a Costa Rican plant drug is developed and commercialised. What characterises the success of this partnership is the mutual satisfaction of the parties involved. Another positive aspect of this biopartnership is that it was renewed two or three times. At the end of each term, Costa Rica had empowered itself a bit more and could renegotiate the contractual terms. The renewal of the contract shows INBio's satisfaction with the biopartnership and thus, shows it to be fair.

It is important to note, however, that Costa Rica is not characterised by a wide range of indigenous communities and its applicability to developing countries with many diverse indigenous and local communities is limited.[53]

The Dutch government made an important financial contribution to INBio in the framework of the sustainable development treaties they have adopted. This biopartnership is the following case study to be examined.

4.3 - Sustainable Development Treaties between the Netherlands and Costa Rica, Bhutan and Benin

"By generating a sense of symbiotic partnership, undesirable practices like biopiracy can give way to an era of biopartnerships based on procedures like co-patenting and credit and profit-sharing. South-South partnership is as important as North-South partnership for using biodiversity for public good, since the centres of diversity of most economic plants occur in the South."[54]

In 1988, Bhutan was identified as one of the 10 countries of highest species density (species richness per unit area) in the world.[55] It holds some of the most endemic species of the eastern Himalayas and has the highest proportion of forest cover and protected area of any Asian country. Bhutan has increased its forest area from 64% in the early sixties to 72.5% nowadays and has declared 26.23% of its land as protected area.[56] However, Bhutan faces many problems which are a threat to the conservation of its biodiversity and ecosystems. The main problems are overgrazing, illegal hunting, unsustainable farming, agricultural and logging practices, uncontrolled extraction of non-timber forest products, unsound road building

---

[53] Idem; at p. 105.
[54] Swaminathan, M. S.; "South and Southeast Asia Regional Workshop on Access to Genetic Resources and Traditional Knowledge"; Chennai (Madras), India; 22-25 February 1998; in I(2) Biotechnology and Development Review, 1998; New Delhi; at p. 35.
[55] Biodiversity Action Plan for Bhutan; December 1997; at p. 29. - Located at http://www.biodiv.org/natrep/Bhutan/Bhutan.pdf; accessed in May 2000.
[56] Idem.

practices and the introduction of exotic species.[57] These problems are exacerbated by the increasing human population.[58]

According to its Biodiversity Action Plan, Bhutan is constrained from further conserving its biological wealth and expanding the country's economic benefits from the use of its biodiversity due to the "shortage of basic scientific knowledge of the identity, status and distribution of species and genetic resources in the country, the status and distribution of habitats, the ecological requirements of various species, and the ecological functioning of ecosystems. [...] The management of protected areas is constrained by incomplete surveys of species and poor knowledge species requirements. Marketing of herbal medicines is constrained by incomplete information on status of wild populations of medicinal plants and information on how to cultivate threatened species. Bioprospecting is constrained by incomplete knowledge of what species are present, inability to assure potential 'clients' of the validity of the taxonomic identification of the sample, inability to assure the re-collection of a sample, and lack of knowledge of the potential ecological role of particular species."[59]

Benin, located in West Africa, is mainly an agricultural country with 90% of its income based on cotton exports.[60] Benin's most important crops include corn, sorghum, millet rice, sugar cane and exotic and endemic vegetable species.[61] Even though a complete inventory of Benin's fauna has not yet been conducted, it is estimated that there are at least 80 species of mammals, 300 bird species and 10 reptile species.[62]

Protected areas cover 11% of Benin's national territory which "represent a significant ecological, economic, social and cultural potential."[63] However, they are under threat from the cotton plantation activities that have reached their borders.[64]

Both Bhutan and Benin have started to form biopartnerships to gain the scientific knowledge and technological expertise to conserve their biodiversity. Bhutan has recognised that "nothing will be more important to human well-being and survival than the wisdom to appreciate that, however great our knowledge, our ignorance is also vast."[65]

In 1994, the Netherlands signed Sustainable Development Treaties, (hereafter SDT), with both of these countries, as well as with Costa Rica.[66] By 1996 all of these countries had ratified the treaties with the Netherlands where they express their conviction "of the necessity to establish a new and equitable global alliance aiming at the creation of new forms of co-operation between states, between key sectors of society and between individuals."[67]

---

[57] Idem; at p. 58.
[58] Idem.
[59] Idem; at p. 121.
[60] Benin, Bhutan, Costa Rica and the Netherlands Joint Report on Biological Diversity; Report presented to the Conference of the Parties to the Convention on Biological Diversity in Bratislava, Slowakia, 1998. Provided by Ecooperation Foundation, Netherlands, through personal contact by the following e-mail: Ecooperation@antenna.nl.
[61] Idem.
[62] Idem.
[63] Idem.
[64] Idem.
[65] Biodiversity Action Plan for Bhutan; supra Note 55; at p. 3.
[66] Sustainable Development Treaties between the Netherlands, Costa Rica, Bhutan and Benin. For information about the Sustainable Development Treaties contact Mr. Lammers from Ecooperation Foundation at Ecooperation@antenna.nl.
[67] Idem.

Through the SDT, all four of these countries agree "to establish long-term co-operation between their countries based on equality and reciprocity as well as consultation and mutual assistance in order to pursue effectively and efficiently all aspects of sustainable development, thereby promoting the participation of all interest groups in their respective societies."[68] According to the Dutch agency established to implement the SDT,[69] the Ecooperation Foundation, (hereafter Eco), the underlying idea of this biopartnership is that "sustainable development cannot be achieved by governments alone, it needs the involvement of civil societies."[70]

Although Eco is responsible for managing the thematic programmes and projects, it offers SDT parties joint ventures where each country makes its own business decision, as the "purse strings for the development budgets are held in their own country."[71] The goal is to explore new grounds to add value to the products originating from the three Southern parties to the SDT. This creates new opportunities for small and medium sized southern producers since their relationship is direct in the industrialised country, allowing them to become more independent of intermediate parties.[72] As the Netherlands has lost a major part of its biodiversity, it also benefits from these SDT biodiversity projects.

The funding for the implementation of the SDT was initially provided by the development and environment budgets of the Netherlands.[73] Gradually, the funding shifted from Overseas Development Aid to private funding organisations set up in each of the four countries for this purpose.[74] More than 160 projects are in progress involving hundreds of organisations, including civil societies, businesses, research institutes, non-governmental organisations, and governmental organs of the four treaty countries.[75] Biodiversity projects between all four countries include research on the possibilities of elaborating socio-economic valuation of biodiversity within their territories.[76]

The SDT provide an innovative type of biopartnership which can be seen as a "people to people" biopartnership based on the principles of reciprocity, equality and participation.[77] According to Eco, the SDT are aimed to build a "two-way street instead of reinforcing the traditional one-way street from donor to recipient."[78]

The basic difference between this biopartnership and the Merck-INBio Agreement is that the latter was a bilateral agreement, while this biopartnership is among four countries in four different continents, giving an idea of globalisation in biopartnerships. Three of the parties are developing countries, which shows that if

---

[68] Idem.
[69] All Member States parties to the SDT have created autonomous organisations to implement the treaties. The organisations are: in Bhutan the Sustainable Development Secretariat; in Benin the Centre Beninois pour le Developpement Durable, and the Fundecooperacion in Costa Rica. Anne Bourjailly, Dale; "Market-Driven Instruments for a New era Adding Value to Bio-Resource Based Business"; paper presented at the conference "BIOTRADE Initiative --Bio-partnerships for Sustainable Development: commercialisation and the bio-industry challenge"; organised by UNCTAD; held 10-12 November 1998 in Lyon, France.
[70] Quote taken from material sent by Ecooperation Foundation.
[71] Anne Bourjailly; supra Note 69.
[72] Idem.
[73] Idem.
[74] Idem.
[75] Information sent by Ecooperation Foundation; supra Note 60.
[76] The main themes of action of the SDT are: energy/climate change, agriculture, biodiversity, economic relationships and culture.
[77] Anne Bourjailly; supra Note 69.
[78] Information sent by Ecooperation Foundation at Ecooperation@antenna.nl.

such States unite they can also empower themselves. This biopartnership is thus of great importance as it provides an example of international co-operation among developing countries. Each party offers what it has. The Netherlands does not have a rich biodiversity, so it offers funds, technology and training. The other countries contribute with their biodiversity and associated traditional knowledge. In addition, 160 projects have developed from this biopartnership, operating as if they were small business and research partnerships inside the global one adopted by the four countries themselves. This biopartnership is a landmark to be used as an example by other countries.

4.4 - The Bioresources Development and Conservation Program

Maurice Iwu is an Igbo traditional healer in Nigeria, past professor of pharmacognosy[79] at the University of Nigeria, Nsukka, and is currently president of the International Society of Ethnobiology. Furthermore, Iwu is the founder and director of the Bioresources Development and Conservation Programme, (hereafter BDCP), an international NGO operating in several African countries.[80] Through the BDCP, Iwu has been working on building up the technical skills of Africans and using biological resources and traditional knowledge as vehicles to sustainable development.

According to Iwu, instead of developing countries exporting unprocessed vegetable drugs and crude extracts, they should "process the plant materials themselves as phytomedicines and other standardised but low-tech herbal products."[81] Iwu believes this is the only solution in face of patents for developing countries, local and indigenous people to receive their equitable share of benefits from the profits derived from medicines originating from their biodiversity and traditional knowledge.[82] For this purpose, the BDCP encourages "'win-win' partnerships between communities and commercial users of medicinal plants that emphasise the establishment of long term relationships, capacity building and institution strengthening in source countries."[83]

In collaboration with national and international agencies, the BDCP has started inventories of west and central African forests.[84] The BDCP focuses on medicine discovery programs that cure African tropical diseases such as malaria, leishmaniasis, and trypanosomiasis. It has formed a biopartnership with the Walter Reed Army Institute of Research, (hereafter Walter Reed), the Smithsonian Tropical Research Institute, universities in Nigeria and Cameroon and thirteen other institutions in the development of treatment of those diseases. This group is called the African International Co-operative Biodiversity Group, (hereafter ICBG) which is sponsored by the US National Science Foundation, (hereafter USNSF), US Agency for International Development, (hereafter USAID), and the US National Institute of Health, (hereafter USNIH).[85] According to the BDCP, the "main focus of the African

---

[79] According to the Chambers Dictionary, "pharmacognosy" is the study of drugs of plant and animal origin. The Cambers Dictionary; Chambers Harrap Publishers Ltd; Edinburgh; 1993.
[80] The information contained in this section was taken from the paper "Development of Medicinal Plants Through Strategic Business Alliances: Case Study from West Africa", presented by Maurice Iwu at the conference "Bio-partnerships for Sustainable Development: commercialisation and the bio-industry challenge"; supra Note 69. Additionally, information was also accessed from the BDCP website: http://www.bioresources.org; accessed in May 2000.
[81] Iwu, Maurice; paper presented at the Bio-partnership Conference; supra Note 80.
[82] Idem.
[83] Idem.
[84] See http://www.bioresources.org/about.htm; accessed in May 2000.
[85] The International Co-operative Biodiversity Groups (ICBGs) Program was initiated in March 1992 in collaborative effort of the US National Institute of Health (NIH), US National Science Foundation (NSF)

ICBG project is the establishment of an integrated program for the discovery of medicinally active plants for drug development and the conservation of biodiversity, while ensuring that local communities and source countries derive maximum benefits for their biological resources and intellectual contributions."[86]

The benefit-sharing mechanism adopted for the BDCP-African ICBG biopartnership is a 3-phase compensation model presented by the BDCP:[87]

1 - Short term and immediate benefits effected in three modes:
    a)   small cash payment to the informant and collector;[88]
    b)   assistance with community development projects;
    c)   medical help to treat severe illnesses.

2 - Long-term benefits in the form of royalty payments. Traditional healers and scientists in the developed countries who contributed intellectually to the development of the medicine are all grouped in the same category. Thus, depending on the extent of the contribution, a traditional healer, informant or a member of a community will receive royalty payments for the derived product.

3 - Training and capacity building. This non-monetary benefit trains African ecologists, biologists, chemists, pharmacologists, ethnobiologists and field taxonomists.

The benefits derived from the biopartnership are distributed among individuals, communities, traditional healer associations and local institutions. When the biopartnership projects are in an advanced state of research and development, a Co-operative Research and Development Agreement, (hereafter CRADA), is adopted.[89] The purpose of the CRADA is to address issues concerning the administration, scope of the research, intellectual property rights, licensing and distribution of royalties.[90] CRADA establishes:

- "provisions of funds for research on tropical country diseases;
- reward of actively-involved scientists' intellectual contribution;
- requirement of prior informed consent of individuals providing ethnomedical or ethnobotanical knowledge to direct the research, which will likely result in the return (not detailed in the CRADA)."[91]

---

and the US National Agency for International Development (USAID). Funding for this program is provided by six institutes of the NIH, the Foreign Agriculture Service of the United States Department of Agriculture (USDA) and the Biological Sciences Directorate of the NSF. The co-operating NIH institutes are the Fogarty International Center (FIC), National Cancer Institute (NCI), National Institute of Allergy an Infectious Diseases (NIAID), National Institute of Mental Health (NIMH), National Institute on Drug Abuse (NIDA) and the National Heart, Lung, and Blood Institute (NHLBI). The ICBGs are currently working in ten countries in Africa, Latin America and Asia.

[86] See BDCG website supra Note 80.
[87] See BDCP; "ICBG Drug Development and Conservation of Biodiversity in Africa: A New Standard of Collaboration with Indigenous People"; in 1(1) Biological Resources, April 1996; Idem.
[88] See Iwu, Maurice and Laird, Sarah; "The International Co-operative Biodiversity Group Drug Development and Biodiversity Conservation in Africa: Case Study of a Benefit-Sharing Plan"; February 1998; case-study submitted in response to the Call for Benefit Sharing Case Studies by the Secretariat of the Convention on Biological Diversity; posted on CBD website in 1998: http://www.biodiv.org; accessed February 1999.
[89] Idem.
[90] See http://www.bioresources.org/!01icbgd.htm; accessed in May 2000.
[91] See Iwu, Maurice and Laird, Sarah; supra Note 88.

In the case of the BDCG-African ICBG biopartnership, all royalties and other benefits derived from licenses of IPRs are distributed in the following manner:

- 20% will be equitably shared among those that intellectually contributed to the IPR. This distribution takes into account the amount each stakeholder contributed towards the creation of the invention. Inventors receive no less than 15% of this 20% share of royalties.
- 50% will be donated to BDCP. A Trust Fund will distribute this 50% royalty payment as follows:
    - 20% BDCP-International to be used in the conservation and development activities throughout Africa.
    - 10% Acquisition of general supplies and equipment to support graduate student research and training in Nigeria.
    - 10% Acquisition of general supplies and equipment to support graduate student research and training in Cameroon.
    - 10% National Botanical Gardens and Herbaria of Nigeria and Cameroon.
    - 50% Traditional healers' organisations, community development funds, etc.[92]
- 30% will be donated to the Tropical Disease Drug Development Program based at Walter Reed that will be used in research on diseases in the developing countries.[93]

CRADA further provides that access to confidential information will only be allowed after the traditional healer, in particular, or the source country, sign an Informed Consent Form. And finally, CRADA requires that if future supplies of raw material are needed, companies must seek as the first source of raw material the country of the original sample collection.

African members of the ICBG participate in all the stages of the drug development process, thus enhancing their technical capacity, scientific infrastructure and knowledge to engage on their own in similar ventures in the future. BDCP has created and been expanding the first African off-line database on the economic botany of African plants, containing their "taxonomic identification, (including local names), traditional medicinal uses, chemical constituents, potential industrial application, reported pharmacological activities and toxicity profiles."[94]

According to the BDCP, with the help of Shaman Pharmaceutical,[95] the "ICBG has developed a highly selective plant selection which has led to a hit rate of more than 85%. The project has led to the identification of indole, alkaloids of *Picralima nitida* as a new type of chemical in the treatment of chloroquine-resistant malaria and possibly the first broad-spectrum antiprotozoan agent for the treatment of leishmaniasis and trypanosomiasis."[96]

This biopartnership is an example of intelligence and initiative. Maurice Iwu is from an African tribe, but has also learned from developed countries and applies his accumulated knowledge and negotiating techniques in favour of his own tribe and other African tribal communities and universities. This biopartnership empowers and

---

[92] See Note 90.
[93] Idem.
[94] Idem.
[95] Shaman Pharmaceuticals, Healing Forest Conservancy and BDGP have created the Fund for Integrated Rural Development and Traditional Medicine that allocates funds for conservation, drug development and the socio-economic well-being of rural communities. See BDCP website; supra Note80.
[96] Idem.

enhances the capacity of local people, African universities and industries scientifically, technologically and intellectually. It offers an interesting share of benefits with an up-front payment, high royalty payment to traditional healers' organisation and the research on African diseases. As traditional knowledge is fully recognised and compensated, it stimulates tribal people not only to preserve their age-old wisdom, but to keep it evolving. Another favourable point of this partnership is that biological resources are processed before they are exported, increasing their market value and the commercial gain of the source country. Developing countries should follow this example, take the initiative, learn from developed countries and use such knowledge in their own favour. Biopartnerships of this type could help promote sustainable economic development in developing countries rich in biodiversity and traditional knowledge.

4.5 - ICBG Biopartnership Project in Suriname

The Republic of Suriname is located in the northern part of South America, between Guyana and French Guyana. Suriname is one of the countries that has a share of the Amazon Forest.

In 1993, the ICBG awarded a grant to various institutions that submitted a joint project proposal for Suriname: the Virginia Polytechnic Institute and State University, (hereafter VPISU),[97] Conservation International, (hereafter CI),[98] Bedrijf Geneesmiddelen Voorziening Suriname, (hereafter BGVS),[99] Missouri Botanical Gardens, (hereafter MBG),[100] and Bristol-Myers Squibb Pharmaceutical Research Institute, (hereafter BMS).[101] Through this grant, the ICBG biopartnership project in Suriname, (hereafter the Suriname ICBG), was formed. The Suriname ICBG works with the Bushnegros and Maroons[102] which hold extensive knowledge of medicinal properties of the forest plants in Suriname.[103]

The Suriname ICBG's objective is to promote drug discovery based on the natural resources in Suriname while conserving its biodiversity and ethnobotanical knowledge. Arrangements between the various stakeholders occurred through oral and written agreements. In 1993, a multilateral contract was signed between CI,[104] BMS,[105] BGVS,[106] VPISU[107] and MBG[108] which specified each of the participant's rights to the licensing and royalties of any drug derived from the Suriname ICBG activities. This

---

[97] The Suriname ICBG is led by Dr. David Kingston of the VPISU, a state-funded university in the US.
[98] The CI is an international non-governmental conservation organisation.
[99] The BGVS is a pharmaceutical company owned by the government of Suriname.
[100] The MBG is an US botanical research institution.
[101] The BMS is and US pharmaceutical company.
[102] The Maroons transmit their knowledge matrilineally and orally. Each shaman in a Maroon family is specialised in one or more illnesses.
[103] All the information on the Suriname ICBG was taken from the case study submitted to Executive Secretary of the Conference of the Parties under compliance to various decisions of COP-3. See Guérin-McManus, M., Famolare, L., Bowles, I., Malone, S., Mittermeier, R., Rosenfeld, A.; "Bioprospecting in Practice: A Case Study of the Suriname ICBG Project and Benefits Sharing under the Convention on Biological Diversity"; posted on CBD website in 1998: http://www.biodiv.org; accessed in February 1999.
[104] In the Suriname ICBG project CI is responsible for carrying out ethnobotanical collections, documenting traditional knowledge and conservation initiatives.
[105] BMS is responsible for most of the screening and drug development.
[106] BGVS is in charge of the biodiversity extraction and carries out in-country screening.
[107] VPISU is responsible for the overall co-ordination of the project, as well as performing cancers screens and isolating active compounds.
[108] MBG is responsible for random botanical collections for both floristic inventory and drug discovery. Furthermore, it provides training in botanical collecting techniques for herbarium staff, university students and members of tribal communities.

contract is known as the International Co-operative Biodiversity Grant Research Agreement. In early 1994 a Letter of Intent between the Granman[109] of the Saramaka tribe[110] and CI staff was executed. Through the Letter of Intent, the Granman granted permission for CI to conduct ethnobotanical research in co-operation with the Saramaka people and CI committed itself to represent the interest of the Saramaka people. By the end of the first year VPISU and BGVS had made plant extraction in Suriname possible, MBG had carried out several general botanical collections and CI had gathered the first ethnobotanical samples. In face of such results, the Granman and village captains signed a co-operative agreement permitting CI to take measures to conserve and collect biodiversity samples in their communities for a period of ten years.

CI frequently travels to the Saramaka region for three-week expeditions. Before initiating any expedition, the Granman is updated on the project and gives his informed consent to continue the ethnobotanical research with one of the shamans of the tribe. The shaman then takes CI to his own plantation of medicinal plants and reveals their medicinal properties, which diseases it cures, the medical potion, dosage, side effects, etc. All of this valuable information is recorded by CI in an encoding system developed for this purpose to secure the traditional information during the initial screening process. Coded plant samples are sent to BGVS, ICBG partners in the United States and to the National Herbarium of Suriname. If a party is interested in acquiring more samples of a specific plant, BGVS is contacted and the sample is requested through its code number. BGVS notifies CI, which returns to the shaman to ask for his help for further collection in the same area the shaman had taken his representative. This coding procedure prevents BMS from collecting the samples elsewhere and ensures tribal communities receive their equitable share of benefits for their contributions.

The Centre for Agricultural Research, a scientific agricultural research foundation based at the University of Suriname, prepares the samples to be sent to BGVS which stores them for future tests and screening. The prepared samples are also sent to VPISU and BMS for the screening process. BMS must test all samples for anticancer and anti-infective properties and must confidentially inform VPISU whether the extracts are active or inactive. VPISU sends copies of such reports to BVGS, CI and MBG. Furthermore, BMS must provide a confidential written list of the therapeutic areas in which the samples will be tested. If BMS loses interest in the sample, it becomes available to other potential partners. If the sample has medicinal properties, its biologically active substances are isolated. Such a process is known as fractionation and is undertaken by BMS, BGVS or VPISU, or by more than one of these parties. Until the fractionating process the name of the plant from which the sample derives is unknown. CI only reveals such information after the shaman gives his consent.

The compensation granted to tribal communities for their contribution includes an up-front payment, sharing of information, technical and scientific training on plant collection, forest taxonomy, biotechnology, extraction, management and technology transfer provided throughout the whole project. Furthermore, the Suriname people will also receive direct economic benefits in the form of royalties from any drug derived from their medicinal plants or knowledge. The up-front payment, known as the "Forest People's Fund", was established in 1994 with a $50,000 grant from BMS, followed by another $10,000 donation in 1996. It is administered by the Forest

---

[109] Granman is the supreme chief of the Saramaka tribe.
[110] The Saramaka tribe is composed of 17,000 Maroons living in villages along the Suriname River.

People's Foundation[111] and is used to fund small-scale, sustainable economic development projects in the tribal communities and provide social, educational and health assistance.[112]

In accordance with the ICBG contract, a joint ownership patent is filed when the product is resultant from the collaborative work with the shaman. However, BMS alone has the option of exclusively pursuing a world-wide license to all the inventions developed out of the Suriname ICBG. The fees and royalties of such licence are negotiated between BMS and the other parties. Royalties are payable until the end of the life of the patent, or if there is no patent, for five years after the first commercial sale. The royalty percentage given to Suriname is kept confidential among the parties. If within one year from the date of the first patent application BMS does not exercise its licensing right, or if within six months the parties do not manage to reach an agreement on the license terms, the sole or joint patent holders are allowed to offer the license to other parties. Prior to such action, BMS must be informed of the offer made to other parties and is given 30 days to decide whether to take the offer itself.

This is a complex biopartnership with many control mechanisms to preserve the confidentiality of traditional knowledge. Although this aim is noble, it could cause excessive delays in the process. Another unfavourable feature of this biopartnership is that the up-front payment of $50,000 is extremely low. A positive aspect of this biopartnership is that it provides joint patents that recognise the importance and utility of traditional knowledge and ethnobotanical collections. However, it is unknown what benefits the indigenous communities receive for their contribution as many terms of this biopartnership are kept confidential. The Suriname ICBG project can provide ideas to other countries, communities and institutions to develop biopartnerships. It is important to stress however, that each country, indigenous and local community have their own particularities which must be recognised and respected when parties mutually prepare any biopartnership contract.

4.6 - The Genetic Resources Recognition Fund of the University of California, Davis[113]

The case to be analysed in this section is not a typical biopartnership. It has been included in this section because it offers an original and voluntary benefit-sharing mechanism to compensate the source country for the benefits derived from the use of a traditional plant variety.

Oryza longistaminata, (hereafter *OL*), is a rhizomatous, perennial, wild rice species from the African mainland and Madagascar. Dr. Devadath of the Central Rice Research Institute, (hereafter CRRI)[114], evaluated an OL specimen from Mali for its

---

[111] The Forest People's Foundation is headquartered in Paramaribo, the capital of Suriname. Its Board of Directors is composed by five members: one Ameridian, one Maroon, the President of CI, based in Washington, the director of CI-Suriname, and one member nominated by BGVS. Their mandate lasts five years.

[112] Any tribal person in Suriname, community or foundation can submit project proposals to the Forest People's Fund Foundation. Upon request, CI-Suriname can assist in the project design and proposal. The Board decides whether to grant funding.

[113] Kerry ten Kate and Amanda Collis; "The Genetic Resources Recognition Fund of the University of California, Davis" case-study was prepared by Kerry ten Kate and Amanda Collis on behalf of the Royal Botanic Gardens, Kew in London, and submitted to the Executive Secretary of the Convention on Biological Diversity. All information in this section, referring to this benefit-sharing case study, was taken from a copy of their paper which was obtained through personal contact with Kerry ten Kate of the Royal Botanic Gardens, Kew.

[114] The CRRI is based in Cuttack, India.

resistance to rice blight *Xanthomonas oryzae* pv. *oryzae*, (hereafter Xoo). In 1976, Dr. Devadath informed Dr. Khush, of the International Rice Research Institute, (hereafter IRRI),[115] that the species had proved resistant to several strains of bacterial blight in India. Between 1978 and 1990, the IRRI bred the *OL* rice blight resistance into rice variety IR24 and discovered that the blight resistance was caused by a DNA section, found on a single chromosome, that they termed *Xa21*. The new resistant variety of IR24, containing the *Xa21*, was named IRBB21.

In 1991, Professor Pamela Ronald and her colleagues at Cornell University started their research to find the location of *Xa21* in the IRBB21 sample she had obtained from IRRI.[116] In 1992, Professor Ronald moved to the University of California at Davis,[117] (UC Davis), and continued her research on the *Xa21* with her UC Davis colleagues.

After five years of work, in 1995 the UC Davis team[118] identified and cloned the *Xa21* and filed a patent on its sequence. In 1996, UC Davis established the Genetic Resources Recognition Fund, (hereafter GRRF), with the assistance of Professor John Barton of Stanford University.[119] The GRRF is a benefit-sharing mechanism that funds fellowships for scholars from source countries, which in this case is Mali. Licensee companies that commercialise a product based on a gene isolated by UC Davis, will have to make a lump-sum payment into the GRRF one year after commercialisation takes place.[120] In July 1996 and January 1997, two agricultural biotechnology companies adopted licensing agreements with UC Davis.[121] The first company agreed with UC Davis to pay US$52,000 to the GRRF a year after its commencement of sales of a successful product involving the *Xa21*. The second company committed itself to pay US$30,000. These quantities were calculated to cover the costs of Fellowships for visiting scholars rather than representing a percentage of the financial benefits derived from the commercialisation of a successful product incorporating *Xa21*. This latter option would have provided a fairer and more equitable benefit-sharing mechanism to the source country.

Since the creation of the GRRF, Professor Ronald has not been negotiating with the representatives of the countries of origin. In the case of the *Xa21*, she has been corresponding with the Director-General of the University of Mali, Dr. Aboubacar Toure, who is also the head of Mali's Sorghum Breeding Programme and has offered to propose students for the GRRF Fellowship.

---

[115] The IRRI is based in Los Banos, Philippines.
[116] Kerry ten Kate and Amanda Collis stress that Professor Ronald obtained a sample of IRBB21 from IRRI prior to the entry into force of the CBD. Furthermore, it was prior to the 1994 agreements between the FAO and the Centres of the CGIAR where it was declared that any person or institution that accessed germplasm and/or related information from any CGIAR Centre could not claim legal ownership over designated germplasm or seek IPR over the germplasm or related information. See FAO-CGIAR Agreement; October 1994; FAO; Rome. And finally, Professor Ronald accessed IRBB21 sample prior to the IRRI adopting in 1996 material transfer agreement, (hereafter MTA) procedure where recipients of IRRI material commit themselves not to claim ownership over the accessed material and/or seek IPR over the germplasm or related information. For more on MTA see Cohen, J.; Falconi, C.; Komen, J.; and Blakeney, M.; Proprietary Biotechnology Inputs and International Agricultural Research; Briefing Paper 39 of the International Service for National Agricultural Research; May 1998; located at http://www.cgiar.org/isnar/publications/briefing/bp39.htm; accessed in December 1999. See also IPGRI: APO Newsletter - Regional No. 27, December 1998. Located at http://www.cgiar.org/ipgri/regional/apo/news/news27/27reg_1.htm; accessed in December 1999.
[117] Professor Ronald is Assistant Professor of Plant Pathology at UC Davis.
[118] Professor Ronald, Wen-Yuan Song and Guo-Liang Wang.
[119] Professor John Barton is a Professor of Law at Stanford University.
[120] The benefit-sharing payment was settled on the commercialisation of a successful product in view of the low percentage rate of research that actually invents a successful commercial product.
[121] Kerry ten Kate and Amanda Collis did not reveal the name of the companies in their case-study because the companies did not wish to be identified.

In addition to the GRRF benefit, researchers and institutions in source countries can undertake a material transfer agreement to access, at cost price, genes and transgenic varieties produced by UC Davis, committing themselves to only commercialise the accessed material after prior written consent of UC Davis.

The mission statement of Professor Ronald's laboratory states that the objective of research into plant genetic resources is "to investigate the fundamental bases of plant-microbe interactions"[122] in order to increase "food production, renew the genetic diversity of the world's crops and reduce inputs of pesticides and herbicides."[123] Since the isolation of gene *Xa21*, scientists in several institutions have been working on the transformation of *Xa21* into African and Asian rice varieties. The trials of these varieties at UC Davis are subject to the US Department of Agriculture regulations that demand compliance with biosafety standards[124] and environmental impact assessments.

Although the Xa21 should not have been patented as it is a chromosome found in nature, the GRRF of UC Davis represents an innovative benefit-sharing mechanism for genetic resources in *ex situ* collections acquired prior to the entry into force of the CBD. Given that Professor Ronald had acquired the sample of IRBB21 before the entry into force of the CBD, she had no legal obligation to adopt any type of benefit-sharing mechanism. The GRRF was based on her own initiative to provide some sort of compensation to the source country. It is expected, however, that the FAO International Undertaking in revision will provide formal mechanisms for biotechnology scientists and industries to share, with the country of origin and traditional farmers, benefits derived from the use of plant genetic resources for food and agriculture, including those in *ex situ* collections acquired prior to the CBD.

4.7 - Conclusion

The demand for access to biological resources is intensifying year by year and it has become fundamental to integrate the interests of all stakeholders involved with the objectives of the CBD: conservation of biodiversity, sustainable use of its components, fair and equitable share of benefits which derived from their use. Quite a few countries have started to form biopartnerships to interact combined interests of bioprospecting and developing. Combining the different knowledge and interests of different stakeholders can be a time-consuming task when formulating an agreement. However, the mutual benefits can be abundant.

While the Merck-INBio agreement focuses on the allocation of benefits at a national level, the ICBG biopartnerships concentrate on returning benefits to local and indigenous communities. All the biopartnerships presented empowered biodiversity-rich developing countries with information, training programs and technology giving them more opportunity to develop sustainable industries based on their biodiversity. Furthermore, they have helped record, secure, value and pay indigenous and local communities for the use of their traditional knowledge, which in some countries is rapidly disappearing.

---

[122] See http://indica.ucdavis.edu/default.htm.
[123] Idem.
[124] One of the requirements is that plant varieties be tested at a distance from other plants to avoid cross pollination. Furthermore, plant varieties containing blight cannot be tested other than in special quarantine conditions.

The Genetic Resources Recognition Fund is a purely voluntary initiative of Professor Ronald to reward source countries and traditional farmers for their earlier efforts in the conservation and traditional breeding of plant varieties. With the adoption of the revised International Undertaking and national genetic resources access legislation, benefit sharing for the use of plant genetic resources for food and agriculture may become compulsory in many currently unregulated circumstances.

The formation of the Merck-INBio Agreement, SDT and the ICBG biopartnerships show compliance with several CBD provisions: Article 5, related to the co-operation of international conservation organisations; Article 10(e) referring to co-operation between governmental authorities and the private sector; 18(5) in regard to co-operation through joint research and joint ventures; Articles 8(j) and 10(c) showing the preservation of traditional knowledge, innovations and practices and the promotion of their wider application in the sustainable use of biological resources; Article 11 which calls for economically and socially sound measures that serve as incentive to conserve and sustainably use biodiversity components; Article 12 requiring the establishment of scientific and technical education and training in measures for the identification, conservation and sustainable use of biodiversity; Article 16 referring to the transfer of technology; Article 17 in regard to exchange of information; and Article 18 requiring technical and scientific co-operation.

Industrialised countries who enter into biopartnerships with developing countries should implement the technology sharing provisions of the CBD, thus empowering the poor by building their scientific, technical and technological capacity and adding value to genetic resources used as raw material. Rana notes that "value-addition and benefit-sharing will help to end the prevailing paradoxical situation where the conservers of genetic resource continue to live in poverty in marked contrast to the prosperity of those who have utilised their materials and associated knowledge."[125]

It is advisable that a code of conduct be annexed to biopartnerships contracts. This code of conduct will regulate morally and ethically the questions of access to the biological materials and associated traditional knowledge, academic and scientific research, commercialisation of the products, transfer of technology and access to all information discovered, and equitable share of benefits.

Biopartnerships are not made from one day to the next. They require time-consuming negotiations to be accorded. To form fair and equitable partnerships, a widespread of stakeholder participation in the source country is recommended in order to empower the local population, eradicate poverty and guarantee the conservation of the environment.

5 - GENERAL CONCLUSION

According to Vandana Shiva, "Biodiversity prospecting is the first step towards accepting the dominant system of monocultures and monopolies, and thus accepting the destruction of diversity. Taking knowledge from indigenous cultures through bioprospecting means developing an IPR-protected industrial system which must eventually market commodities that have used local knowledge as an input but are not based on the ethical, epistemological or ecological organisation of that

---

[125] Rana, R. S.; "Access to Genetic Resources and Equitable Benefit Sharing: The Indian Experience"; I(2) RIS Biotechnology and Development Review, April 1998; New Delhi; at p. 9.

knowledge system."[126] However, from the above biopartnership case studies, it is clear that biodiversity prospecting can be used in a positive way.

As such, biopartnerships will only be directed to monocultures and monopolies if the contracting parties mutually agree to this. Biodiversity-rich countries can decide only to enter into biopartnerships concerned with the development of pharmaceuticals or the production of organic crops; the licensing terms of the products derived from their natural resources, the form, quantity and scope of benefits, and so forth. In other words, the owners of biodiversity and traditional knowledge must be the masters of the deal because bread cannot be made without the wheat. Developing countries and indigenous communities have the right to say no to biopartnerships they do not agree to. They have the right to refuse biopartnerships that do not regard them as equal partners in the deal, or that are a threat to the conservation of the environment and to the sustainable use of its components.

With the already known negative consequences related to transgenic crops, and partially proven fears of their harm to human health and biodiversity, it is advisable for people, communities, institutions, organisations, and so forth, to avoid forming biopartnerships which involve commercial agricultural biotechnology. On the contrary, biopartnerships which potentialise and add value to traditional knowledge, raw material and derived products, develop medicines, conserve the environment and empower poor people should be stimulated.

When considering the formation of fair, equitable and ethical biopartnerships, four major elements ought to be highlighted. The first element is the right recognised with respect to technological inventions. Nobody should be denied the right to research and the right to be compensated for their inventions because this would mean a stoppage of technological development related to plant properties and the positive aspects it could offer. The second point concerns traditional knowledge, which should likewise be recognised and duly compensated. This is a good way for indigenous and local communities to improve their economic situation and for society to value and fairly profit from knowledge accumulated throughout generations. Moreover, recognising and compensating traditional knowledge is a form not only of protecting traditional knowledge but also of avoiding its disappearance. The third point relates to the paths to unite both rights. There must be a path to unite the rights offered to breeders and to traditional communities to avoid incompatibilities or overlaps. This union can be accomplished in many ways as was shown in the different biopartnerships presented in this Chapter. And finally, there is a common right to enjoy the equitable share of benefits derived from biopartnerships. This common right can be baptised as the "**Partners' right**".

"Partners' rights" are not stone-rigid, pre-determined rights. They ought to be mutually negotiated by all stakeholders in every biopartnership contract. The adoption of this "partners' rights" concept on an international level should be linked to a code of ethics to guarantee the respect and proper use of traditional knowledge. "Partners' rights" can be an important element in the achievement of the aspired goals of poverty eradication, sustainable development, conservation of biodiversity and global peace.[127]

"Underlying the Earth Summit agreements is the idea that humanity has reached a turning point. We can continue with present policies which are deepening

---

[126] Shiva, V.; "The Losers' Perspective"; Baumann, M., Bell, J., Koechlin, F., Pimbert, M., (eds); The Life Industry. Biodiversity, people and Profits; Intermediate Technology Publications; London; 1996; at p. 127.
[127] See Principle 25 of the Rio Declaration and Paragraph 21 of the CBD Preamble.

economic divisions within and between countries--which increase poverty, hunger, sickness and illiteracy and cause the continuing deterioration of the ecosystem on which life depends. Or we can change course. We can act to improve the living standards of those who are in need. We can better manage and protect the ecosystem and bring about a more prosperous future for us all. No nation can achieve this on its own. Together we can--in a global partnership for sustainable development."[128]

---

[128] Introduction to the Final Text of Agreements Negotiated by Governments at the United Nations Conference on Environment and Development (UNCED); 3-4 June 1992, Rio de Janeiro, Brazil (United Nations Department of Public Information, 1992).

CHAPTER EIGHT

THE EFFECTS OF INTERNATIONAL REGIMES IN BRAZIL

1 - GENERAL INTRODUCTION

The Amazon rainforest extends its beauty and natural richness throughout eight South American countries: Brazil, Bolivia, Colombia, Ecuador, Guyana, Peru, Surinam and Venezuela. Sixty percent of the Amazon forest is located in Brazil.[1] Fourteen Germanys and twenty Englands could fit into the Brazilian Amazon.[2] Many species found in Brazil cannot be found in any other country;[3] however the exact number of species in the Brazilian Amazon is still unknown. Very few plant species have been examined and named. Those that have already been identified by a genus and a species name sum up to 30,000 and represent 10% of the planet's plants.[4]

Although Brazil's biodiversity can be an important factor in the country's sustainable economic development, access to biological and genetic resources is an extremely complex issue, for there are important ecological, social, cultural, economic, political and legal implications to consider. This Chapter shall examine how these issues are dealt with in Brazilian legislation and will highlight the benefits to be gained by the Brazilian government and its nationals through the sustainable management of Brazilian biodiversity. This Chapter will also examine the level of clarity and efficiency of the provisions which regulate the protection of biological safety when its biodiversity undergoes biotechnological transformation.

Thus, this Chapter shall examine the influence and effect of the CBD, the UPOV, FAO International Undertaking and TRIPs have had on Brazil. As means of illustration, an analysis shall be presented in regard to the patented transgenic soya which was prohibited to be planted in some European countries due to its uncertain effects upon the environment. The patentee requested permission from the Brazilian government to plant the transgenic soya on Brazilian territory. This example provides an expansive view of the effects those international instruments can cause to a developing country and to the different sectors of its population.

2 - SOCIAL EQUALITY, ENVIRONMENTAL AND INTELLECTUAL PROPERTY PROTECTION IN THE BRAZILIAN CONSTITUTION

The current Brazilian Constitution[5] (hereafter the Constitution) entered into force in 1988 with the following words constituting its preamble:

---

[1] EMBRAPA; Atlas do Meio Ambiente do Brasil; Terra Viva; Brasilia, Brazil; 1994; at p. 82.
[2] Alvarenga, T.; "A Destruiçao da Amazonia"; in the supplement Veja Especial Amazonica, 24 December 1997, of the Brazilian Magazine Veja Ano 30-No. 51; at p. 8.
[3] Ministério do Meio Ambiente, dos Recursos Hídricos e da Amazônia Legal; Primeiro Relatório Nacional para a Convençao sobre Diversidade Biológica: Brasil; Brasilia, Brazil; 1998; at p. 35.
[4] Varella, Flavia; "Calderao da Vida"; in the supplement Veja Especial Amazonica, 24 December 1997, of the Brazilian Magazine Veja Ano 30-No. 51; at p. 32.
[5] The translation of the 1988 Brazilian Constitution presented in this Chapter, is the official translation. Constitution of the Federative Republic of Brazil; Central Graphic of Brazil's Federal Senate; Brasilia; 1990.

> We, the representatives of the Brazilian People, (...) for the purpose of ensuring *well-being, development, equality and justice* as supreme values of a *fraternal, pluralist and unprejudiced society, founded on social harmony* (...) promulgate, under the protection of God, this Constitution of the Federative Republic of Brazil.[6] (emphasis added).

Article 3 of the Constitution reinforces the preamble and states that the fundamental objectives of Brazil are:

> I - to build a free, just and solidary society;
> II - to guarantee national development;
> III - to eradicate poverty and substandard living conditions and to reduce social and regional inequalities;
> IV - to promote the well-being of all, without prejudice as to origin, race, sex, colour, age and any other forms of discrimination.[7]

As the highest law in the country, all other laws must harmonise with the Constitution to be valid. That is to say that any law or action in the country which opposes the social *well being, development, equality and justice* of the Brazilian people is unconstitutional. Even though the Constitution is 10 years old, and preaches *well being, development, equality and justice as supreme values of a fraternal, pluralist and unprejudiced society*, reality shows that the gap between rich and poor people in the country has widened and environmental degradation increased.

Despite the fact that the Amazon Forest has colloquially been called the lungs of the planet, a very precious library, and a natural pharmaceutical lab, its richness still has not been used wisely enough by the government. Furthermore, local populations do not hesitate to practise slash-and-burn techniques of shifting agriculture as a means to support themselves and their families. Once the original floral cover is gone, these poor people migrate to another virgin land in the forest and repeat the whole process. Alternatively, poor people work for predatory and non-ecologically-minded companies for a meagre allowance, which does not guarantee their bare subsistence. The results of these acts are clearly noticeable: extensive devastation of the Amazon forest, acceleration of the process of soil degradation, extinction of numerous natural medicines, short term benefits to the business community and the increase of poverty in the region.

Article 225 of the Constitution states "All have the right to an ecologically balanced environment which is an asset of common use and essential to a healthy quality of life, and both the Government and the community shall have the duty to defend and preserve it for present and future generations."[8] According to the Constitution, this implies a need to "preserve and restore the essential ecological processes and provide for the ecological treatment of species and ecosystems."[9]

However, in the last three decades the Brazilian government has utilised the Amazon forest in an irrational and compulsive manner in an attempt to promote the

---
[6] The Constitution; Preamble.
[7] Idem; Article 3.
[8] Idem; Article 225.
[9] Idem; Article 225(I).

country's economic development. The Amazon forest has suffered exhaustive logging,[10] poisoning the rivers with mercury in the search for gold and provoking fires to clear the land for farming,[11] to raise cattle[12] and so forth.[13]

For these reasons, contrasting Article 225 of the Constitution with reality, it is clear that Jordan E. Erdos is right when noting that "on paper, Brazil has some of the most progressive environmental legislation in the world. But in practice, bureaucracy, corruption, lack of resources and an underdeveloped infrastructure have often prevented the country from achieving its environmental aims."[14]

Another point to consider in the Constitution is the right to industrial property. Article 5(XXIX) acclaims that

> The law shall ensure the authors of industrial inventions of a temporary privilege for their use, as well as protection of industrial creations, property of trademarks, names of companies and other distinctive signs, *viewing the social interest and the technological and economic development of the country.*[15] (emphasis added).

Consequently, the Constitution conditions the existence of the industrial property right upon the fulfilment of its social, technological and economic functions. One of the principles that constitutes the country's economic order refers to the social function of property, including thus, intellectual property. Article 170 of the Brazilian Constitution reads:

> The economic order, founded on the appreciation of human work and on free enterprise, is intended to ensure everyone a life with dignity, in accordance with the dictates of social justice, with due regard to the following principles: [...]
>
> III - the social function of property;
> IV - free competition; [...]
> VI - environment protection;

---

[10] There is a high foreign demand for Amazon wood. Additionally, a vast area of the forest was cleared to construct a road, Perimetral Norte, to cross through the Amazon forest. The construction never finished and the road, which ends in the middle of nowhere in the forest, is gradually being covered by the forest's vegetation. See Magalhaes, Juraci; A Ocupaçao Desordenada da Amazonia e Seus Efeitos Economicos Socias e Ecologicos; Gráfica e Editora Competa Ltda.; Brasilia, Brazil; 1990.

[11] The Amazon soil is poor of nutrients. The trees do not feed themselves from the soil but from their own organic material, leaves, branches, seeds, fruits, insects, fungus, and so forth. All of this settles and rots on the ground and then absorbed by the superficial capillaries of the roots. Idem.

[12] Part of the Amazon forest was cleared to plant grass to raise herds of cattle. The Amazon soil is so poor that the grass did not grow and the project was a failure. Idem.

[13] In the past three decades, a forest area bigger than France was devastated by fires and electric saws. However, although the Amazon region has suffered such great devastation, the population in the region is still low and completely virgin forest areas, of the size of some European countries, can still be found. See Alvarenga, T.; supra Note 2; at p. 8. Furthermore, the first national report about the Brazilian implementation of the CBD states that 85% of the Brazilian Amazon forest still remains standing. See Ministério do Meio Ambiente, dos Recursos Hídricos e da Amazônia Legal; supra Note 3.

[14] Erdos, Jordan E.; "Current Legislative Efforts in Brazil to Regulate Access to Genetic Resources"; December 1999. Located at: http://www.sustain.org/biotech/library/admin/uploadedfiles/Current_Legislative_Efforts_in_Brazil_to_Regul.htm; accessed in January 2000.

[15] The Constitution; Article 5(XXIX); supra Note 5.

VII - reduction of regional and social differences; [...][16]

As was shown in earlier Chapters, patents on plant varieties do not consider social, environmental and economic order principles. Thus, it can be stated that in accordance with the above constitutional provisions, if the monopoly granted by a patent increases the gap between rich and poor, is a threat to the environment or if it annuls the possibility of free competition, it should be considered unconstitutional. The Brazilian patent office could and should use this ground to control the patenting of living organisms, especially those which are destined for alimentary and pharmaceutical purposes.

3 - PATENT LAW

3.1 - Introduction

As was shown earlier in this book,[17] the United States has the patent law of widest scope and accordingly, it has been pressurising other States to adopt patent laws it considers adequate, that is to say, similar to the US patent law. Brazil surrendered to United States pressure and adopted new industrial property legislation long before the closing date offered by TRIPs.[18]

In April of 1991, the Brazilian IPR bill was drafted in consultation with the United States government and sent to the Brazilian Congress to be examined.[19] That same year, in October, a Special Commission on Industrial Property was created in the Chamber of Deputies in the Congress. This commission became in charge of drafting a bill which compromised the various interests that were manifested in public hearings and closed meetings held by the commission. In June 1993, the Chamber of Deputies approved a version of the bill which stated that natural biological material and processes were not inventions and, thus not patentable. Senator Marina Silva proposed additional clauses to guarantee the equitable share of benefits to indigenous and local communities for patents related to their knowledge, innovation and practices.[20] Nevertheless, the proposals were rejected. In May 1995, the Senate and Justice Commission introduced a second version of the bill which also prohibited the patenting of naturally occurring life forms and biological materials and processes. In the same year, the Economic Affairs Commission of the Congress presented its own bill, which adopted demands made by the United States and the pharmaceutical sector. This third bill resulted in Brazil's industrial property Law no. 9.279/96.[21]

Under the new patent law plants, animals and essentially biological processes for the production of plants and animals are excluded from protection. However, the law allows patents on pharmaceuticals, chemicals and food products which were previously excluded from protection in Brazil.

---

[16] Idem; Article 170.
[17] See Chapter Two of this book.
[18] According to Article 65 of TRIPs developing countries had until 1 January 2000 to implement TRIPs.
[19] See Tachinardi, Maria Helena; A Guerra das Patentes; Paz e Terra; Sao Paulo, Brazil; 1993; at p. 20.
[20] Arcanjo, Francisco Eugênio M.; "Convenção sobre Diversidade Biológica e Projeto de Lei do Senado Nº 306/95: Soberania, Propriedade e Acesso aos Recursos Genéticos"; in Benjamin, Antonio H. V. (ed) 5 Anos após a ECO-92; proceedings of the 1997 International Conference on Environmental Law held by the Lawyers for a Green Planet Institute; São Paulo, Brazil; 1997; at p. 43.
[21] Brazilian Industrial Property Law; Law no.: 9.279/96; enacted on 14 May 1996. This law entered into force on the 15 May 1997. The official English translation of Law 9.279/96, provided by the National Industrial Property Institute in Brazil, will be used in this book.

This section shall analyse Law 9.279/96, and the effects it will have on Brazilian development and on the owners of traditional knowledge.

3.2 - General Principles

By virtue of the Paris Convention, Brazil must treat nationals of other Member States in the same way as it treats its own nationals.[22] This is also in conformity with the National Treatment principle as provided in TRIPs.[23] Brazil also adopts the Principle of Reciprocity in Article 3(II) by upholding the same or equivalent rights of Brazilians to nationals and domiciled persons of countries which grant Brazilians the same reciprocity.[24]

Law 9.279/96 provides for the "first to deposit" principle. As such, the first person to deposit the patent claim for an invention shall have priority even if he was not the first to invent it.[25] The right to priority is also provided for. During one year from the filing date in Brazil, the applicant may request the right to priority of his application using an earlier date of the same patent claim applied for in one of the Member States of a convention Brazil is a party to.[26]

And finally, Law 9.279/96 adopted Article 34 of TRIPs by stating that the burden of proof falls on the owner of a new process. As such, the rights to a patented process shall be considered infringed "if the holder or owner of a product fails to prove, by a specific judicial ruling, that his product was obtained by a manufacturing process different from the process protected by the patent."[27] Therefore, a third party cannot make, use, offer for sale, sell or import for these purposes a product he cannot prove to have obtained from a process different from the patented one.

3.3 - Patentable Subject Matter

According to Law no. 9.279/96, an object or process must fulfil three fundamental requirements in order to be patentable it must:

1) be a **novelty**;
2) result from an **inventive activity**;
3) have an **industrial application**.[28]

By novelty it is understood that the object was not accessible to the public by written or oral description, or by use or any other means, in Brazil or in a foreign country, before the patent application date.[29] Therefore the scope of prior art in Brazil is wider than that in the United States. As was shown in earlier Chapters of this book, prior art in the US excludes oral description as a means of challenging the novelty of a particular invention for which a patent is currently being sought or enforced. As such, patents based on traditional knowledge of indigenous and local communities around

---

[22] Idem; Article 3(I).
[23] Article 3 of TRIPs; see Chapter Two of this book.
[24] Law 9.279/96; supra Note 21; Article 3(II).
[25] Idem; Article 7.
[26] Idem; Articles 16 and 17.
[27] Idem; Article 42, paragraph 2.
[28] Idem; Article 8.
[29] Idem; Articles 11 and 11(1).

the world have been granted in the United States.[30] In Brazil, Law 9.279/96 adopted the concept of absolute novelty to determine the state of the art. Absolute novelty has been described by Brazil's National Industrial Property Institute, (hereafter INPI)[31] as:

> "everything that has been made available to the public anywhere in the world, in any branch of activity, by any means of communication and/or through usage, prior to date of filing the application for privilege or, as the case may be, of the oldest priority."[32]

The invention is considered to have resulted from an inventive activity when a person skilled in the art acknowledges that it was not derived evidently or obviously from the state of the art.[33] The invention is susceptible of industrial application when it can be used or produced by an industry of any kind.[34]

Although Law 9.279/96 does not directly define invention, Article 10 enumerates that the following shall not be considered inventions or utility models:

> I - discoveries, scientific theories and mathematical methods;
> II - purely abstract concepts; [...]
> VIII - techniques and methods for operations or surgery or methods for therapy or diagnosis applied to human or animal body; and
> IX - all or part of *natural* living beings and biological materials *found in nature*, or isolated therefrom, including the genome or germplasm of any *natural* living being and the *natural* biological processes.[35] (emphasis added)

Article 10(IX) gives leeway to consider that non-natural living beings could be considered an invention. For instance, a transgenic plant that due to direct human intervention in its genetic composition, expresses a characteristic that cannot be normally achieved by the species under natural conditions.

However, Article 18 determines that the following are not patentable in Brazil:

> I - anything contrary to morality, decency or public safety, order and public health; [...]
> III - living beings, whole or in part, except for transgenic microorganisms meeting the three requirements of patentability - novelty, inventive step and industrial application - provided for in article 8 and which are not mere discoveries.
> Sole Paragraph[36] - For the purposes of this law, transgenic microorganisms are organisms, except for plants or animals, whole or part, that due to direct human intervention in their genetic composition, express a characteristic that cannot be normally achieved by the species under natural conditions.[37]

---

[30] See Chapter Four of this book.
[31] INPI stands for Instituto Nacional de Propriedade Industrial. It is the organ responsible for granting patents in Brazil. INPI was created in 1970 by law 5.648/70 and is linked to the Ministry of Industry and Commerce in Brazil.
[32] See INPI website: http://www.inpi.gov.br; accessed in June 2000.
[33] Law 9.279/96; supra Note 21; Article 13.
[34] Idem; Article 15.
[35] Idem; Articles 10(I), 10(II), 10(VIII), 10(IX).
[36] In Brazilian Legislation, articles in a law may have paragraphs . When there is only one paragraph, it is named "Sole Paragraph".
[37] Law 9.279/96; supra Note 21; Article 18.

Two points ought to be considered here. First of all, Article 18(III) states that the only living beings that are patentable are transgenic micro-organisms. All other living beings, including natural and non-natural plants and animals and their parts are non-patentable. As such, according to Article 10(IX), non-natural organisms could be considered as inventions but nonetheless Article 18(III) states they are not patentable. TRIPs allows this exclusion of patentability. Therefore even if a transgenic plant fits into the requirements of novelty, inventive step and industrial application INPI should not grant a patent on it.

The second point to consider is even though Article 18(III) prohibits plants from being patented, Article 230 allows protection to *"foodstuffs* and chemical-pharmaceutical substances, matter, compounds or products, and *medicines of any kind*, and the respective process for obtaining or modifying them by the person who holds protection afforded under a treaty or convention in force in Brazil."[38]. In this sense there is a possible anomaly in the law which could create doubt as to whether crop plants and medicinal plants, which are definitely living beings, are allowed to be patented. To clarify this issue and completely exclude plants, transgenic or not, from patentability INPI should give primacy to the provision declaring the non-patentability of living beings apart from transgenic micro-organisms over the provision that allows patents on food crops and medicines of any kind. As a support to this measure, it could interpret the concept of "morality" widely as to consider it immoral to patent all plants, their parts including their genes in isolated and purified form. Such interpretation of morality could receive judicial support from the Constitutional provisions which subordinates patents to social, environmental and economic order principles.[39]

It is possible that INPI will interpret Article 230 as only referring to the laboratory process to obtain the active principle in the medicinal plant, the final medicine developed by a laboratory, the process to develop foodstuffs, and the foodstuff developed by industries. However, if this is the case, if an indigenous or local community plays the main role in the development of a medicine or foodstuff by discovering and traditionally developing the plant properties, the law only protects those who terminate the work by adorning the final product and process. Law 9.279/96 does a good job to protect and compensate those who dedicated time, effort and money to develop foodstuffs and medicines. Nevertheless, for this law to succeed in its social function, Brazil must enact an effective law to protect traditional knowledge and traditionally bred plants.

Time will show the real scope of Law 9.279/96 and how much US influence it absorbed. In any way, INPI will be deciding patent applications on a case-by-case basis and will have time to see the short and long-term consequences of the US patents on living organisms. As such, INPI will only follow US patent practice if it wants to.

3.4 - "Prior User" Concept

Apart from the usual restrictions placed on patents,[40] Law 9.279/96 further limits the patentee's right by providing for the "prior user" concept.

Article 45 states:

---

[38] Idem; Article 230.
[39] See the Constitution; supra Note 5; Articles 5(XXIX) and 170.
[40] For instance, the patent scope does not apply to acts carried out by unauthorised third parties when those acts are for non-commercial purposes as well as those for experimental purposes. See Article 43 of Law 9.279/96; supra Note 21.

A person who in good faith, prior to the filing or priority date of a patent application, used to exploit the subject matter thereof within the Country, shall be entitled to continue such exploitation under the same form and conditions, without liability.

This Article can safeguard the rights of local and indigenous communities in Brazil if a plant variety they traditionally bred and habitually use is patented, as occurred to the Basmati rice[41] and the neem tree in India.[42] As noted by UNCTAD, this exception on the patentee's rights "('*bona fide* prior use') aims at preserving the rights of prior users of a subsequently patented invention in order to allow them to continue their use of that invention in their own enterprises."[43] However, the "prior user" concept is incompatible with the novelty requirement. A patent can only be granted if the subject matter is completely new. If the patented subject matter was being exploited by a third party, as provided for in Article 45, the subject matter cannot be considered new and thus, the patent should never have been granted or should be cancelled once a prior user is discovered. Lucas Rocha Furtado[44] states that the "prior user" concept "constitutes an anachronism of the law which, eventually, will give margin to endless controversies."[45]

Although the prior use concept could be a solution to allow local and indigenous communities the continuous access to and use of their traditional plants patented by third parties, it fails to prevent biopiracy and is completely at odds with the CBD provisions which determine the equitable share of benefits and their prior informed consent.

3.5 - Term of Protection

In accordance with TRIPs, Law 9.279/96 adopted in its Article 40 a 20 year patent term of protection for inventions.[46] This term is counted from the day the patent application is made. Due to the fact that a long period can elapse from the day the application is made to the day the actual patent concession is granted, Law 9.279/96 fixed a minimum period of 10 years for the duration of a patent from the day it is granted.[47] The law also determines that the patent term shall be the longest period resultant either by counting the days from the application date or counting the days from the point the patent is actually granted.

3.6 - Conclusion

As Brazil excludes from patentability materials found in nature, even if isolated therefrom, and considers oral description part of prior art it is evident that traditionally bred plants are not patentable and neither is traditional knowledge of

---

[41] See Chapter Five of this book.
[42] See Chapter Four of this book.
[43] UNCTAD; The TRIPS Agreement and Developing Countries; UNCTAD/ITE/1; United Nations, Geneva, 1996.
[44] Lucas Rocha Furtado is a sub-general attorney of the public prosecution service in Brazil.
[45] Furtado, Lucas R.; Sistema de Propriedade Industrial no Direito Brasileiro; Brasília Jurídica, Brasília, 1996; at p. 55.
[46] Article 40 of Law 9.279/96; supra Note 21. According to the revoked Brazilian Industrial Property Code, Law no. 5.772, of 21 December 1971, in the patent-term for an invention was for a period of 15 years. If the application was for an industrial model and design or an utility model, the duration of the protection was of 10 years.
[47] Sole Paragraph of Article 40; Idem.

medicinal plants. Traditional knowledge, transmitted orally from one generation to the next, is commonly known by more than one person, and frequently, by more than one community.

The Brazilian patent system determines that the object of the patent must be completely disclosed to the public. If it is not possible to reproduce the patented product or process with the information contained in the patent claim, the patent will be nullified. This is compatible with the objectives of patents: to disseminate technologies that benefit society economically and technologically.

The World Bank warns that IPRs can be disadvantageous to developing countries "by increasing the knowledge gap and by shifting bargaining power toward the producers of knowledge, most of whom reside in industrial countries."[48] In this sense, it is worth following Furtado's advice when he stresses that although Brazil has adopted patent legislation that fulfils national standards, this legislation should be applied in conjunction with the Constitutional provisions which condition IPRs to the accomplishment of its social function, as well as to Brazil's economic and technological development.[49]

4 - PLANT VARIETY PROTECTION LAW

In 1997, Brazil adopted the Cultivar Protection Law, Law No. 9.456/97, (hereafter the Cultivar Law).[50] This law allowed Brazil to become a party to the 1978 UPOV Act[51] before it was closed for new ratification.[52]

The Cultivar Law grants protection to the breeder of a new plant variety[53] for a certain amount of time by an intellectual property system, known as "cultivar protection certificates", (hereafter cultivar certificates). The period of protection is 18 years for vines, forest trees, fruit trees and ornamental trees and 15 years for other species.[54] The breeder's authorisation is required for the production for purposes of commercial marketing, offering for sale, and marketing of the reproductive or vegetative propagating material of the protected variety.[55]

In line with UPOV 1978, the Cultivar Law allows farmers to save and plant the seed obtained from the harvest of a protected variety.[56] Furthermore, the small farmers are allowed to exchange among themselves seeds of protected cultivars.[57] And finally, the breeder's authorisation is not required for the utilisation of the variety as an initial source of variation for the purpose of creating other varieties.[58]

---

[48] World Bank; "Knowledge for Development – World Development Report"; 1998/99 OUP; 1998; at p. 35.
[49] Furtado, Lucas R.; supra Note 45; at p. 23.
[50] Cultivar Law; Law no. 9.456/97; April 1997; Diario Oficial da Uniao; 28 April 1997.
[51] On May 23 May 1999 Brazil joined UPOV 1978. To see the status of ratification of States Party to the UPOV visit the following website: http://www.upov.org/eng/ratif/pdf/ratifmem.pdf; accessed in September 2000.
[52] The Brazilian government, in the fear of being forced to sign UPOV 1991 after the closing date of UPOV 1978, decided to join the later.
[53] Plant varieties are referred to as cultivars in the Cultivar Law; supra Note 50.
[54] Cultivar Law; Idem; Article 11.
[55] Idem; Articles 8 and 9.
[56] Idem; Article 10(I).
[57] Idem; Article 10(IV).
[58] Idem; Article 10(III). Article 10, paragraph 2, clarifies that the breeder's authorisation is required when the repeated use of the variety is necessary for the commercial production of another variety. Likewise, the breeder's authorisation is also required to commercialise a variety characterised as essentially derived from the protected variety.

The National Service of Cultivar Protection, (hereafter SNPC)[59] is the agency responsible for granting cultivar certificates[60] to plant variety breeders.[61] According to the Cultivar Law, a cultivar is a plant variety which is distinct, homogeneous and stable.[62] By distinctness it is understood that the plant variety is clearly distinguishable from other known plant varieties by a minimum margin of descriptors.[63] A cultivar is considered homogeneous if it presents minimum variability in its descriptors when planted on a commercial scale.[64] And finally, the cultivar is stable when it maintains its homogeneity after successive generations.[65]

The Cultivar Law distinguishes between cultivars, in general, and new cultivars. Only new cultivars or essentially derived cultivars,[66] of any plant genus or species are protectable.[67] A new variety is a cultivar which has not been offered for sale in Brazil more than 12 months before the application date and has not been offered for sale in foreign countries, with the breeder's consent, more than 6 years in the case of trees and vines, and 4 years for the other species.[68] Essentially derived cultivars are varieties that fulfil all of the following characteristics:

> 1- It is predominantly derived from the initial cultivar, or from another cultivar essentially derived, while retaining the expression of the essential characteristics that result from the genotype or combination of genotypes of the initial cultivar, except for the differences that result from the act of derivation.
> 2- It is clearly distinguishable from the initial cultivar by minimum variability in its descriptors, in accordance to the criteria established by the competent organ.
>
> 3- It has not been offered for sale in Brazil more than 12 months before the application date and has not been offered for sale in foreign countries, with the breeder's consent, more than 6 years in the case of trees and vines, and 4 years for the other species.[69]

Janet Bell wisely notes that descriptors of protectable plant variety "pay no attention to objectives of improvement, and place value on morphologic characteristics rather than agronomic qualities."[70]

According to the Cultivar Law, a cultivar certificate is the only form of cultivar protection and legal protection that can impede the free utilisation of plants or

---

[59] Decree No. 2.366 of 5 November 1997 regulates the Cultivar Law and disposes about the SNPC.
[60] See Cultivar Law; supra Note 50; Article 2.
[61] Article 3 of Decree no. 2.366 provides for the functions of the SNPC; supra Note 59.
[62] Cultivar Law; supra Note 50, Article 3(IV).
[63] Idem; Article 3(VI).
[64] Idem; Article 3(VII) of the Cultivar Law.
[65] Article 3(VIII) of the Cultivar Law.
[66] See Chapter Three of this book.
[67] Cultivar Law; supra Note 50; Article 4.
[68] Idem; Article 3(V).
[69] Idem; Article 3(IX).
[70] Bell, Janet; Brazil's Transgenic Free Zone; Seedling; September 1999; located at: http://www.grain.org/publications/set99/set991.htm; accessed in September 2000.

of their reproductive or vegetative propagating material. In this sense, one could deduce that INPI will not grant patents on plant varieties.

However, if Brazil follows the same patent trajectory as the US, history reveals that it has been expanding the scope of patents gradually. Asexually propagated plants started to be patentable in the US in 1930 and sexually propagated plants started to be eligible for protection under the Plant Variety Protection Act in 1970. In 1980, with the Diamond vs Chakrabarty Supreme Court decision, the patenting boom on living organisms, their traits and genes began in the US. Therefore, the fact that plant varieties and their parts are not patentable in Brazil at the moment does not mean that Brazil has liberated itself from US influence. The Cultivar Law stimulates the development of plant varieties. The adoption of Law 9.279/96 and the Cultivar Law show that Brazil is interested in protecting its own biotechnological developments and such protection is liable to expand if it progresses in the field.

The Brazilian national organ of agriculture and stock raising research, known as EMBRAPA[71] notes that the biotechnology is a great investment, the potential market of biotechnological crops being valued at 30 billion dollars. As such, EMBRAPA has been developing genetically modified corn, wheat, potato and sugar-cane which are resistant to herbicides, insects and viruses.[72] EMBRAPA has also developed a soybean variety which has made Brazil the world's second soybean producer.[73] However, a Brazilian newspaper warned at the end of 1999 that the "spread of soybean plantations is the main threat to the Amazon forest because they require large properties and strong financial and technological investments."[74] Furthermore, EMBRAPA has developed a transgenic bean process, considered at the moment the most efficient process to transform bean culture. It has claimed a patent for this process which it is using to develop a transgenic bean tolerant to herbicide and resistant to certain pests.[75]

EMBRAPA is already commercialising 30 cultivars (hybrids and varieties) of corn all over Brazil. One of the corn hybrids developed is highly tolerant to acid soils and has a higher yield than normal corn. According to EMBRAPA, these corn cultivars have generated more profit to farmers, created more jobs and increased corn yield.[76] These are not conclusive arguments for Brazil to surrender to crop biotechnology because if the same financial input and research dedicated to develop transgenic crops were invested in traditional farming, there would also be an increase in profits, more jobs would be created and the yield would not only be in terms of quantity, but also of quality. Furthermore, by investing in traditional farming and permaculture, for instance, Brazil would avoid devastating its biodiversity and forest.[77]

It seems ironic that Brazil, a country with so much land still to farm, has also given into biotechnology. Organic products, which are usually more expensive than

---

[71] EMBRAPA stands for "Empresa Brasileira de Pesquisa Agropecuária". EMBRAPA, which was created on 26 April 1973, is linked to the Agriculture Ministry.
[72] See the following EMBRAPA website: http://www.cenargen.EMBRAPA.br/biotec/biotec.html; accessed September 2000.
[73] Idem. See also Adeodato, Sérgio; "O Vigor do Campo"; in the Brazilian magazine Época No. 102, 1 May 2000.
[74] Savini, Marcos; "Florestas Tropicais Fora dos Eixos"; Correio Braziliense; Brasilia; 5 December 1999; Mundo, p. 4.
[75] For more this transgenic bean process and examples of other transgenic crops being developed by EMBRAPA, see the EMBRAPA website; supra Note 72.
[76] Idem.
[77] Trees have been frequently chopped in the Amazon region, with the purpose of transforming the forest in agricultural land.

non-organic products, are nevertheless widely sold in Europe.[78] Roger Bate notes that "in the United Kingdom, demand for organic food is growing at over 40 percent a year. This demand amounted to nearly US$ 1.6 billion in 1999, with a third of the population buying organic food."[79]

Moreover, biotechnological companies have been seeing a reduction in sales growth that has been attributed to recession, increased research costs resultant from the growth of environmental controls over product development and farm policy reforms in developed countries.[80] Developing biotechnological products is far more difficult and expensive than anyone had anticipated.[81] Furthermore, another unfavourable consequence of biotechnology is that the dissection of organisms into their genetic components permanently removes them from the natural world altogether.[82] Taking into account these factors, it is a pity that the Brazilian government has been ignoring Brazil's golden opportunity to be the world's greatest organic food exporter and has also been developing transgenic plants and animals.

Janet Bell notes that "Until 1996, seed production in Brazil was nationally-based. Since adopting life patenting legislation and joining UPOV, the private sector has increasingly been profiting from knowledge which was previously in the public domain and has progressively being taking control of seed production. One of the direct consequences has been a flood of take-overs of Brazilian companies by the transnational agbiotech giants in the last few years."[83]

In the face of so much inequity towards traditional farmers, the most urgent thing the SNPC must do to safeguard the interest of local farmers[84] is introduce certificates of origin of the initial plants used in the development of a new cultivar as an attachment to the cultivar certificate. If this mechanism were adopted, it would be possible to locate, if existent, the traditional breeders who initiated the development of the cultivar using traditional techniques. Likewise, it would be possible not only to identify the traditional breeding part of the process, but moreover the traditional intellectual knowledge that discovered the specific plant property if that were the case. As such, the share of benefits derived from the use of the protected cultivar could be distributed equitably and fairly among all stakeholders.

---

[78] For a list of European supermarkets which have committed themselves to eliminate genetically modified ingredients from their own brand products see Bell, Janet; supra Note 70.

[79] Bate, Roger; "Organic Myths: The retreat from science"; 41 Biotechnology and Development Monitor, March 2000; at p. 24.

[80] Bell, Janet; "Genetic engineering and biotechnology in industry"; in Baumann, M., Bell, J., Koechlin, F., Pimbert, M., (eds); The Life Industry. Biodiversity, people and Profits; Intermediate Technology Publications; London; 1996; at p. 41. Jack Kloppenburg notes that the bovine growth hormone, bovine somatotropin, cost more than $500 million to develop and the genetically engineered tomato, Flavr Savr, $25 million. The bovine somatotropin, also known as BST, has shown to have serious negative effects on the cows treated with the hormone, as well on humans through meat and dairy products. The genetically engineered tomato has a mere 3 to 5 day shelf-life advantage over existing commercial tomatoes. See Kloppenburg, Jack; "Changes in the Genetic Supply Industry"; in Baumann, M., Bell, J., Koechlin, F., Pimbert, M., (eds); Idem; at p. 29.

[81] Kloppenburg, Jack; Idem.

[82] Bell, Janet; supra Note 80; at p. 45.

[83] Bell, Janet; supra Note 70. Janet Bell, with the following examples, shows how the seed production scenery in Brazil has changed after Law 9.279/96 and the Cultivar Law were adopted. Monsanto has bought the Brazilian company Agroceres and has gained the monopoly of 60% of the Brazilian corn market. Monsanto has also bought Brazil's largest soybean seed producers: FT Sementes, Monsoy, and Terrazawa. Moreover, other US companies which have been totally or partially bought by Monsanto have also implanted their roots in Brazil: Cargill seeds, Asgrow, DeKalb. Du Pont has established a branch in Brazil and has acquired the Brazilian company, "Sementes Dois Marcos". AgrEvo has bought the Brazilian seed companies "Sementes Ribeirão" and "Sementes Fartura".

[84] Traditionally bred varieties normally do not meet plant variety protection requirements due to their broad genetic base.

5 - BIOSAFETY REGULATIONS

5.1 - Introduction

According to Furtado, "modern biotechnology presents enormous beneficial potential in the development of new medicines or genetically improved plants. However, for its enormous capacity to transform life, its application should be submitted to judicial criteria of evaluating risks and prevention of harmful accidents to man and the environment."[85]

The growing concern on possible negative effects of modern agriculture biotechnology[86] has led countries into adopting safety regulations on biotechnology products, known biosafety regulations. The Constitution provides that the Brazilian government has the duty to "preserve the diversity and integrity of the genetic patrimony of the country and to control entities engaged in research and manipulation of genetic material."[87] Furthermore, the State has the duty to "control the production, sale and use of techniques, methods or substances which represent a risk to life, the quality of life and the environment".[88]

Brazil adopted a Biosafety Law in 1995 to establish security norms and supervision methods relating to genetic engineering techniques in the production, cultivation, manipulation, transport, commercialisation, consumption, release and eradication of genetically modified organisms.[89]

5.2 - Biosafety Law

Law 8.974/95 is Brazil's Biosafety Law. Decree 1.752 supplements the Biosafety Law and created the National Technical Commission for Biosecurity (hereafter CTNBio), which is Brazil's biosafety agency.[90]

Several articles in the Biosafety Law provide for measures to be taken in the case of eventual incidents related to GMOs that could cause damage to human health or the balance of ecosystems.[91] Article 14 of the Biosafety Law states that the author[92] is obliged to indemnify or repair the damages caused to the environment or to third parties affected by activity involving GMOs. As such, an element of uncertainty towards the effects of GMOs is present in the law. The CTNBio is the competent organ to further regulate issues relating to food security such as the commercialisation and labelling of transgenic food. These new regulations to be adopted will contribute significantly towards the awareness of the safe use of biotechnology.

---

[85] Furtado, L.; supra Note 45; at p. 173.
[86] See Chapter Four of this book.
[87] The Constitution; supra Note 5; Article 225(II).
[88] Idem; Article 225(V) of the Constitution.
[89] Biosafety Law No. 8.974/95; adopted 5 January 1995. Published in the D.O.U. of 6 January 1995, section I, p. 337. The Biosafety Law can also be found at the following site: http://www.mct.gov.br/ctnbiotec/lei8974.htm; accessed October 2000.
[90] Decree No. 1.752 of 20 December 1995 created the CTNBio.
[91] Article 10 of the Biosafety Law, for instance, refers to the occurrence of accidents and diseases related to the GMO; supra Note 89.
[92] In this case, the "author" is the person responsible for the environmental damages.

One of the most important environmental provisions in the Constitution is the requirement for the prior environmental impact assessment, (hereafter EIA), "for the installation of works and activities which may potentially cause significant degradation of the environment".[93] However, Article 2(XIV) of Decree 1.752 determines that the CTNBio has the competence to "require, *if it believes necessary*, additional documentation, *Environmental Impact Assessment and the Report on the Impact on the Environment* of projects and applications that involve the *liberation of genetically modified organisms in the environment*, besides the specific requirements applicable to the level of risk."[94] (Emphasis added)

Aurélio Virgílio Veiga Rios, regional attorney general in Brazil, stated that the EIA is extremely important in the application of the precautionary principle in order to predict the possible risks of releasing GMO in the environment.[95] Furthermore, Rios noted that a constitutional requirement such as the obligation of performing EIA could not be limited by a decree, and thus, declared that Article 2(XIV) of Decree 1.752 was unconstitutional.[96] On the other hand, one could argue that there is no inconsistency between the Constitution and the Decree because someone has to judge whether there is a risk of environmental harm as the Constitution refers to "activities which may potentially cause significant degradation." Thus, it could seem that this function has been allocated to CTNBio.

In any case, the lack of EIA allowed Monsanto's transgenic soya to be planted in Brazil. However, Greenpeace and the Brazilian Institute for Consumer Defence, (hereafter IDEC), representing Brazilian citizens, managed to nullify Monsanto's access concessions through public civil actions. Through such actions, the Public Ministry, Brazilian state governments or citizen associations can legally oppose works or activities which can potentially degrade the environment.[97] This case will be examined in the following section.

5.3 - Transgenic Soya Case

"Brazil is the world's second-largest soybean producer after the US, harvesting 31 million tons in 1998. [...] One US analyst has predicted profits of $US 1 billion if Monsanto captures 50% of the Brazilian soybean market, let alone the benefits it will reap from the train of other GM products that it plans to introduce in the transgenic bean's wake."[98]

In this section, the introduction of Monsanto's Roundup Ready transgenic soybean, (hereafter RR soya) in Rio Grande do Sul, a Brazilian state, will be

---

[93] The Constitution; supra Note 5; Article 225(IV).
[94] Article 2(XIV) of Decree 1.752; supra Note 90.
[95] Veiga Rios, A. V.; "Biossegurança - Aspectos Jurídicos e Políticos"; paper presented at the International Congress on the Right of Biodiversity held in Brasilia, Brazil; 11-14 May 1999.
[96] Idem.
[97] Brazilian Law no. 7.347,of 1985 constituted the public civil action of responsibility for damages caused to the environment. For an analysis of the use of public civil actions see Fernandes, Edesio; "Collective Interests in Brazilian Environmental Law"; in Dunkley, John (ed); Public Interest Perspectives in Environmental Law; Chancery Law Publishing Ltd; West Sussex, England; 1995; pp. 118-129. See also Machado, Paulo Affonso Leme; Direito Ambiental Brasileiro; Malheiros Editores Ltda.; Sao Paulo, Brazil; 1992; at pp. 227-231. See also Freitas, Vladimir Passos and Freitas, Gilberto Passos; Crimes Contra a Natureza; Editora Revista dos Tribunais Ltda.; Sao Paulo, Brazil; 1992; at pp. 158-162. For the use of public civil actions by the Public Prosecution Service see Araujo, Rosalina Correa de; Direitos da Natureza no Brasil; Liber Juris; Rio de Janeiro, Brazil; 1992; pp. 117-123.
[98] Bell, Janet; supra Note 70.

analysed.[99] Rio Grande do Sul, (hereafter RS), is the second-largest soybean-producing state[100] in Brazil.[101] On 1 January 1999, RS declared itself a transgenic-free state.[102] Several European countries have denied the plantation of the RR soya in their territories for the fear that it can be prejudicial to the environment. In this case, however, the CTNBio gave permission for the RR soya to be planted in Brazil without demanding an environmental impact assessment because the Biosafety Law does not determine that the environmental impact assessment is compulsory. On the contrary, Decree 1.752 gives authority to the CTNBio to decide whether the environmental impact assessment is necessary on a case-by-case basis.[103] In regard to the plantation of Monsanto's transgenic soya in Brazil, it decided that the environmental impact assessment was not necessary.

One year after the adoption of the Biosafety Law, biotechnological industries claimed authorisation to release genetically modified organisms in the environment for experimental purposes. The CTNBio authorised all of the claims. On 15 June 1998, Monsanto claimed CTNBio authorisation to *inter alia* test, plant, transport, store, commercialise, consume, import and release the RR soya. IDEC filed an interlocutory injunction also in 1998 against the plantation of the RR soya alleging the lack of an EIA.[104] Judge Raquel Perrini, from the eleventh Federal Circuit of São Paulo, granted a temporary restraining order preventing it from being commercialised until the government issued biosafety and labelling regulations for genetically-modified organisms.

Neglecting this order, CNTBio released its final opinion in favour of the liberation of the RR soya on Brazilian territory. By this time IDEC's interlocutory injunction had been annexed to a similar judicial process opened by Greenpeace which was running at the sixth Federal Circuit of the Federal District.[105] On 26 November 1998, Judge Antônio Oswaldo Scarpa from that circuit revoked the temporary restraining order relating to the suspension of RR soya plantations, but demanded its segregation from other soybeans, its proper labelling and demanded that Monsanto keep the courts informed of who bought the RR soya. In March 1999 Consumer Protection organs all over the country communicated their motion where they demanded that biosecurity be regulated and transgenic crops labelled. Monsanto drew back its claim to register the RR soya alleging lack of technical information. Also in March the interim Minister of Agriculture, Benedito Rosa do Espírito Santo,

---

[99] The RR soya case information were accessed from the following websites: http://www.uol.com.br/idec/campanhas/crono.htm and www.idec.org.br; accessed in October 2000.
[100] Six million tones of soybean are produced by RS every year over and area of 3.1 million hectares. Half of this production is exported and sixty percent of the exportation is imported by European countries. Fifty percent of soybean production in the US is from RR soybean plantations. Many of the biggest European supermarkets are suspicious about the RR soybean, and consequently US soy exports to Europe in 1999 dropped by 46 % in comparison to 1998. See Bell, Janet; supra Note 70.
[101] Parana is Brazil's first soybean producing state.
[102] Article 25 of the Constitution allows the Brazilian states to be governened by the constitutions and laws they may adopt, in harmony with the Constitutional principles. Article 24(VI) of the Constitution grants states the power to legislate *inter alia* on the "preservation of nature, defense of the soil and natural resources and protection of the environment" and Article 24(XII) allows them to legislate on "social security, protection and defense of health."; see supra Note 5. For a deeper analysis on the competence of the Brazilian government and the Brazilian states concerning environmental matters see Silva, Jose Afonso da; Direito Ambiental Constitucional; Malheiros Editores Ltda.; Sao Paulo; 1994; at pp 48-53.According to the RS government, transgenic crops are a risk to the state's sovereignty, the environment and people's health. Furthermore, RS being a state where small-scale farmers dominate the agricultural setting, the RS government fears that patented seeds would not be appropriate or affordable for most of the state's farmers. See Bell, Janet; supra Note 70.
[103] Decree 1.752; supra Note 90; Article 2(XIV).
[104] Interlocutory injunction no. 98.34.00027681-8; IDEC v. Federal Union.
[105] Public civil action no. 97.00036170-4; Greenpeace v. President of CTNBio. Public civil action no.98.00.027682-0; IDEC v. Federal Union.

announced that Monsanto would be granted authorisation to plant RR soybean on a commercial scale once it redeposited its claim.

On 14 May 1999 the National Service of Cultivar Register and the Agriculture Ministry authorised the RR soybean to be planted on commercial scale. Greenpeace and IDEC filed a suit against this decision claiming that the Constitution required that any work or activity which may potentially cause significant degradation to the environment must be subjected to an environmental impact assessment.[106] They further claimed that Brazilian Consumer's Law requires the labelling on transgenic food and no law had yet been adopted to regulate this matter. On 18 June 1999, the federal judge Antônio de Souza Prudente, holder of the sixth circuit of the Federal District, released a temporary restraining order on the cultivation and commercialisation of the RR soya. On 10 August 1999, in a judgement on the merits, judge Prudente confirmed the order and prohibited the RR soya to be planted or commercialised until biosecurity were appropriately regulated in Brazil and the RR soya had been submitted to an EIA.[107] In his ruling, Judge Prudente stated that, *"I believe that the irresponsible haste in introducing the advances of genetic engineering is inspired by the greed of economic globalisation."*

As was shown in previous Chapters of this book, transgenic plant species are genetically uniform in order to contain the genes and characteristics determined through the biotechnological process. By allowing the plantation of Monsanto's transgenic soya without demanding an environmental impact assessment, the CTNBio acted imprudently towards the preservation of the diversity and integrity of Brazil's genetic patrimony and failed to control Monsanto's actions in Brazilian territory concerning manipulation of genetic material.[108] Likewise it was negligent towards the preservation of the essential ecological processes.[109] In one of his speeches, Deputy Fernando Ferro, of the Labour Party in Brazil, commented on the necessity of investigation and research for scientific development, but emphasised that Brazil should not be transformed into a laboratory where Brazilians are the guinea-pigs and used in experiments which could cause problems to the environment through the production of animal and plant species aberrations.[110].

In the RR soya case, Brazilian citizens opposed the Brazilian governmental organ, CTNBio, in favour of the environment and their own health. This is an excellent example of how Brazilian nationals are not willing to accept environmentally harzardous projects dictated by their own government or foreign companies.

5.4 - Labelling Genetically Modified Foods

There is not a unanimous opinion in Brazil in favour of the ban on the RR soybean. There are those who are in favour of transgenic crops and state that only proved scientific facts should be a restriction on the plantation, commercialisation and

---

[106] The Constitution; supra Note 5; Article 225(IV).
[107] For a complete summary on the RR soya case in Brazil see IDEC website: http://www.uol.com.br/idec/campanhas/crono.htm; accessed in October 2000.
[108] See the Constitution; supra Note 5; Article 225(1)(II).
[109] Idem; Article 225(1)(I).
[110] Taken from the speech given by Fernando Ferro in the Deputy Chamber on 24 June 1999. Located at: http://www.informes.org.br/notas/seminario.htm; accessed in July 1999. The Labour Party in Brazil campaigns in favour of Brazil being a transgenic free country. Janet Bell notes the lack of a biosafety system in developing countries "can lead to biotechnological colonialism, whereby Southern lands are used to carry out field tests in conditions that would never be allowed in the North." Bell, J.; supra Note 80.

use of genetically modified organisms. Others argue that the lack of full scientific certainty should be a reason to halt the production and commercialisation of products that pose a threat to the environment and human health.

There are those such as Bate who believe that if the growing European boycott on genetically modified foods were followed by the rest of the world, the impact on the poor people in developing countries and on the environment could be devastating.[111] More land is needed to plant organic food because the yield is usually inferior to transgenic crops, and it would be considered a problem if diverse ecosystems were ploughed up to provide for the population.[112] "Six billion people inhabit Earth now. In 2050, it is predicted that figure will double to twelve billion. How do we meet the needs of a growing population in a suitable way?"[113] "The benefits of agricultural biotechnology are of particular importance to people living in developing nations. There, genetically improved seeds and other products will improve crop yields and quality and make farming possible in areas previously unsuitable for food production."[114]

Dr Mae-Wan Ho, on the other hand, completely opposes the idea that transgenic agriculture is needed to feed the world. According to Ho, the "intensification of corporate monopoly on food is going to cause famine. It also diverts us from implementing the sustainable, organic agriculture that can truly guarantee food security and improvement of health for all." She notes that transgenic agriculture "has the potential to destroy all life on earth."[115]

There are fears, predictions and short-term outcomes in favour of and against transgenic crops. Probably the only certain fact about genetically modified crops is that not enough time has gone by to show their medium and long-term effects and counter-effects for human health and the environment. As it does not seem probable that biotechnological seed companies will abandon their research, production and commercialisation of transgenic agriculture, transgenic food must be properly labelled giving consumers the choice of ingesting it or not. Cigarette packets inform smokers that cigarettes can cause cancer, nevertheless cigarettes are still smoked. Information and education on genetically modified foods should be provided so that people can consciously decide whether to eat or avoid transgenic crops.

Article 2(V) of Decree 1.752 confers upon CTNBio the competence to regulate the commercialisation and consumption in Brazil of genetically modified organisms. Through its public civil action IDEC requested the court to oblige CTNBio to disallow all commercial plantation of transgenic crops until food safety, commercialisation and labelling of transgenic crops were regulated.[116] Article 9 of the Brazilian Code in Defence of the Consumer, (hereafter Consumer Code), states:

> "The provider of products or services potentially harmful or dangerous to health or security must inform in an ostensive and adequate way on labels and marketing messages, about the harm or danger,

---

[111] Bate, Roger; supra Note 79.
[112] Idem.
[113] See DuPont website located at www.dupont.com/corp/whats-new/newsfile/todo/food/food.html; accessed in September 2000.
[114] Posted on Monsanto's website http://www.monsanto.com; accessed January 2000.
[115] Ho, Mae-Wan; "Special Safety Concerns of Transgenic Agriculture ad Related Issues"; paper presented at the International Seminar on the Right of Biodiversity held in Brasilia, Brazil; 11-14 May 1999.
[116] For the public civil action proposed against CNTBio see IDEC website located at www.idec.org.br.

without the impairment of the adoption of other measures appropriate in a specific case."[117]

Dr Eliana Fontes, Marcelo Varella and Fernando Galvao da Rocha indicate, *inter alia,* the following ways in which the public should be informed about transgenic organisms:

> 1- Inform local residents living near areas where transgenic organisms will be released and educate them on the safety measures they should undertake.
> 2- Label products as transgenic organisms, as well as those derived from them.[118]

Article 6(III) of the Consumer Code states that the consumer has the basic right to adequate and clear information about products in regard to their quantity, characteristics, composition, quality, price, guarantee and risks they present.[119]

As some governmental organs in Brazil seem to have adhered to the transgenic movement, it is imperative that all transgenic crops, derived products and processes in Brazil should be labelled in harmony with the Consumer Code provisions prior to their marketing and commercialisation. However, on 19 July 2001 a presidential decree was published in Brazil's Official Gazzette[120] which states that only food products containing more than 4% of transgenic ingredients must be labelled.[121] According to Article 31 of the Consumer Code, ALL genetically modified products must be labelled. The federal public prosecution service, representing IDEC, has filled a public civil action against the federal government stating that the decree violates the Consumer Code. Once again the lack of consensus among governmental organs on matters referring to transgenic products is visible. In the same way it is visible that Brazilian citizens are fighting against governmental actions that jeopardise their rights to health, security and information.

The label on all transgenic products should provide "true, clear, precise, ostensive information in Portuguese about its characteristics, qualities, quantities, composition, price, guarantee, validity and origin"[122] for consumers to have the necessary knowledge to take a conscious decision.[123] Access to education and to information is not only a right of citizens, but also a powerful tool a nation should use to enter a constant progressive process of sustainable development.

5.5 - Conclusion

It is logical that there must be some discretion regarding the imposition of the environmental impact assessment because most human actions have some sort of

---

[117] Article 9 of the Consumer Code. See Alvim; Código do Consumidor Comentado; 2 edition; RT; Sao Paulo; 1995.
[118] Varella, M., Fontes, E., Rocha, F.; "Biossegurança e Biodiversidade: Contexto Científico e Regulamentar"; Del Rey Editors; Belo Horizonte, Brazil; 1999; at pp. 96-97.
[119] Consumer Code; supra Note 117; Article 6(III).
[120] See Decree 3.871, published in the Diário Oficial da Uniao on 17 July 2001. The Decree can be found in the Brazilian government's website www.planalto.gov.br. Click on "Legislaçao", and then on "Decretos", and on the year "2001". On the list of decrees of 2001 find Decree 3.871.
[121] See Article 1 of Decree 3.871.
[122] Consumer Code; supra Note 117; Article 31.
[123] See the Technical Ruling on Labelling of Genetically Modified Foods and Ingredients prepared by the Consumer Defence and Protection Department of the Economic Law Secretary of the Justice Ministry in Brazil; 1999. Located at: http://www.mct.gov.br/ctnbiotec/consultapublica2.htm; accessed in May 2000.

impact on the environment. For instance, a person who drives to work pollutes the air with carbon dioxide. There is no need for every person who drives to be submitted to an environmental impact assessment although his/her driving does have an impact on the environment. On the national level, there are environmental impact assessments and targets to reduce CO2 level emissions into the air. In the case of the transgenic soya, the environmental impact assessment was necessary because it was imperative to know how the transgenic soya would react to Brazilian land, weather, climate, and so forth. As it turned out, the transgenic soya could not resist the Brazilian sun.[124]

The victory of NGOs and IDEC in preventing Monsanto from planting and commercialising the RR soybean as well as IDEC's persistent action for the proper labelling of transgenic products are good examples of how the Brazilian citizens are eager to use their Constitutional right and duty of protecting the environment and their own health.

6 - PROPOSED LEGISLATION TO REGULATE ACCESS TO BRAZIL'S GENETIC RESOURCES AND DERIVED PRODUCTS

6.1 - Introduction

Access to genetic resources and derived products should involve a balance of rights and duties of all stakeholders, as well as a balance of social, economic and ecological implications and issues. As such, for a genetic resource access law to be effective and fair, it should provide for such balances.

The management of and access to Brazil's genetic resources, ensuring that benefits which arise from the use of these resources are shared, fall under the scope of Bill of Law, no. 306/95 (hereinafter Bill 306/95).[125] This bill has been undergoing procedural steps in the Congress since 1995. The initial legislative proposal was presented by Senator Marina Silva and subsequently modified by Senator Osmar Dias. There is also another bill of law being analysed by the Brazilian Congress,[126] Bill of Law no. 4.579/98, (hereafter the Deputy Bill), which was elaborated by the Federal Deputy Jacques Wagner and has also been directed to the Legislative Power for analysis.[127] Both Bill 306/95 and the Deputy Bill were drafted with public input and

---

[124] According to Bill Vencil of the University of Georgia in Athens, Monsanto transgenic soya is not suitable to be planted where the climate is very warm. Under intense heat, the stems of the transgenic soya open, causing a loss of 40% of the harvest. After farmers in the USA, who planted Monsanto's soya, had great losses in the harvest due to two very hot springs where the soil temperature was between 40 and 50 degrees Celsius, Vencil researched into the problem. The results he found revealed that until 25 degrees Celsius RR soya grew as well as and normal soya. However, when the temperature was 45 degrees Celsius, the RR soya growth was visibly less than the normal soya and the stems of the RR soya opened when the first leaves started to appear. Information taken from the article "Monsanto's Altered Soya Does not Resist to Warm Climates", (Soja Alterada da Monsanto Não Resiste a Clima Quente) in the Brazilian newspaper Estadao; 22 November 1999.

[125] The bills of laws in Brazil are given an initial identification number. This number changes as the bill undergoes procedural steps on its course through the Congress to become a law.

[126] Article 61 of the Brazilian Constitution states that any of the following parties has the competence to initiate supplementary and ordinary laws in accordance with the constitutional provisions: any member or committee of the Chamber of Deputies and the Federal Senate or the National Congress, the President of the Republic, the Supreme Federal Court, the Superior Courts, the Attorney-General of the Republic and the citizens. See the Constitution; supra Note 5.

[127] A bill of law approved by one House in the Brazilian Congress shall be reviewed by the other. If the bill is amended, it shall return to the Chamber where it was proposed for modification. If the bill is approved by the reviewing Chamber, it is sent to the President of the Republic for sanctioning. The President has the power to veto fully or partially the bill if he considers it unconstitutional or contrary to

participation.[128] A third bill was negotiated behind closed doors and had no public participation. This third bill was an initiative of the Executive Power, and is known as Bill no. 4.751/98, (hereafter the Executive Bill).[129] The Executive Bill was a response to Bill 306/95, which for the Executive Power was too bureaucratic. The Executive Bill aims to provide a fast and modern operational juridical base for access to Brazil's biodiversity.

The Bill of Law to be analysed here will be the one proposed by the Senator Marina Silva, Bill 306/95 because it was the first one to be developed and generated the interest for the other two proposals to arise. However, its provisions will be contrasted and compared to the Deputy Bill and the Executive Bill to reveal the main intentions of each and the degree and manner which each complies with the provisions of the CBD.[130] At the moment, it is not known which of these bills will become Brazil's law to regulate the access to Brazilian biodiversity or if all three bills will be combined into a final bill.

6.2 - Objectives of Bill 306/95

Brazil was the first State to sign the CBD at the United Nations Conference on Environment and Development, held in Rio, in June 1992. The CBD has been the main guideline[131] for the elaboration of Bill 306/95, in accordance with the country's particular interests, conditions and capabilities.[132]

Article 1 of the Bill 306/95 states that its objective is to regulate "the rights and duties regarding the access to genetic resources, genetic material and derived products, in *ex situ* or *in situ* conditions, existent in the national territory or those of which Brazil is the country of origin, to traditional knowledge of indigenous communities and traditional or local populations associated with genetic resources or derived products and agricultural cultivations, domesticated and semi-domesticated, in Brazil."[133]

The Sole Paragraph of Article 2 of Bill 306/95 provides that it shall be guaranteed to the proprietors and holders of properties and rights the fair and equitable share of the benefits derived from the access to genetic resources and derived products, to traditional knowledge of indigenous communities and traditional and local populations.[134]

---

public interest. The veto is then examined by the Congress and may only be rejected by the absolute majority of the Deputies and Senators, by secret voting. If the veto is not withheld, it is sent back to the President for promulgation. See Articles 65 and 66 of the Brazilian Constitution.

[128] The draft of Bill of Law no. 306/95 analysed in this section was the one numbered as Bill of Law no. 4.842/98 when sent to the Chamber of Deputies for revision in November 1998. The text of the Deputy Bill is Bill of Law no. 4.579/98 as approved by the Chamber of Deputies in June 1998.

[129] Execute Bill; Bill of Law 4.751/98; August 1998.

[130] Bill 306/95, the Deputy Bill and the Executive Bill have only been published in Portuguese. Therefore the translations offered here are not formal official translations.

[131] This is also true in regard to the Rio Declaration. The CBD was then ratified by Brazil´s National Congress in February 1994 by the legislative Decree no. 2/94.

[132] Article 6 of the CBD states: "Each Contracting Party shall, in accordance with its particular conditions and capabilities: (a) Develop national strategies, plans or programmes for the conservation and sustainable use of biological diversity or adapt for this purpose existing strategies, plans of programmes which shall reflect, *inter alia*, the measures set out in this Convention relevant to the Contracting Party concerned."

[133] Bill 306/95; supra Note 125; Article 1.

[134] Idem; Article 2.

There are two points to consider here. First of all, Articles 1 and 2 of Bill 306/95 visibly show that the bill's objective is mainly to guarantee all stakeholders the fair and equitable share of benefits derived from the access to genetic resources, derived products and traditional knowledge. The stakeholders are the proprietors and holders of properties and rights. Those that have rights such as the State, which holds the sovereign right over its biodiversity, or patentees, who hold the patent right over their patented object or process, are clearly covered by this Article. However, indigenous communities and traditional communities have no official right over genetic resources and derived products they traditionally use, although indigenous peoples have the exclusive usufruct of the riches of the soil, the rivers and the lakes existing on the lands they traditionally occupy.[135] Therefore, for the access law to fulfil its objective to promote the fair and equitable share of benefits, Brazil would have to officially adopt a *sui generis* system to provide rights such as farmers' rights and traditional knowledge rights and balance them with breeders' and patentees' rights.

The second point to note is that conservation and sustainable use of genetic resources are not stated as objectives of Bill 306/95. At first sight, this could be considered a significant omission, however, from Article 5 onwards of Bill 306/95, there are provisions regarding the conservation of the genetic resources, as well as the regulation of the sustainable use of the components of biological diversity. Certainly, the strength of Bill 306/95 to conserve Brazil's biological diversity, use it in a sustainable manner, and provide for the fair and equitable share of the benefits derived from use of the countries biological resources, would be increased if these provisions were set out simply and transparently in Article 1 of Bill 306/95 which deals with its objective. The conservation and sustainable use of natural resources are essential to guarantee future generations the access to at least the same quantity and quality of biodiversity as that found on the planet today. An indigenous proverb teaches that we are not owners of the natural resources, rather we borrow them from our grandchildren.

Article one of the Deputy Bill, which also deals with the objectives of the law, is identical to Bill 306/95. However, the Executive Bill is worded differently. Article 1 of the Executive Bill reads:

"This law regulates the rights and duties relating to the access to components of the Genetic Patrimony existent in the national territory, on the continental shelf, territorial sea or in the exclusive economic zone, to traditional knowledge associated to it and relevant to the conservation of biological diversity, to the sustainable utilisation, and the fair and equitable share of the benefits derived from its exploration."[136]

Genetic Patrimony is defined as "information of genetic origin, contained in all or in part of the plant, microbial or animal species, in substances derived from the metabolism of these living beings and extracts obtained from these live or dead organisms, found in *in situ* conditions or kept in *ex situ* collections, as long as they were collected from *in situ* conditions in the national territory, the continental platform, the territorial sea or the exclusive economic zone."[137]

Therefore all three bills regulate the access to the totality of genetic resources originating in the Brazilian territory and the associated traditional knowledge.

---

[135] The Constitution; supra Note 5; Article 231, Paragraph 2.
[136] Executive Bill; supra Note 126; Article 1.
[137] Idem; Article 7(I).

6.3 - Scope of Bill 306/95

Although the access bills related to access to genetic resources, they also regulate the access to biological resources because they are the ones which contain genetic resources. The definition of genetic material in Bill 306/95 includes biological material. "Genetic material" is defined as "all *biological material* of plant, animal, microbial or other origin which contains functional units of heredity."[138] (Emphasis added). "Genetic diversity" is defined as the "variability of genes and genotypes among species and in species; part or whole of genetic information contained in the *biological resources*."[139] (Emphasis added). Any part of a biological resource can be seen as a genetic resource. Stating the obvious, Bill 306/95 regulates access to Brazil's biodiversity through provisions which regulate access to its genetic diversity. This measure is in line with the CBD.

Article 8 of the Bill 306/95 states the genetic resources which are excluded from the Bill:

> Article 8 - This Law does not apply:
>
> I - to genetic material or any component or substance of human beings, all collection and use of these resources, components and substances being dependent on the approval of the Executive Power, after prior informed consent of the individual, until a specific law to regulate this mater enters into force.
>
> II - to the exchange of genetic resources, derived products, traditional agricultural cultivations or associated traditional knowledge, done by the local communities and indigenous populations, among themselves, for their own purposes and based on customary practice.[140]

Article 8(II) can be seen as a reflection of the 1978 UPOV Act which allows farmers to save the seed from their protected variety's harvest. Brazil is a signatory of the 1978 UPOV Act and therefore, it has maintained the right of farmers and indigenous populations to exchange resources, a traditional practice they have been doing for centuries.

6.4 - Who Can Access Brazil's Genetic Resources

Bill 306/95 applies to all those interested in accessing Brazilian biodiversity as Article 15(I)(a) states that the entity seeking access to Brazil's genetic resources must be a natural person or a legal entity with juridical capacity to sign contracts and proven technical capacity.[141] Nevertheless, it determines that when the access is requested by a foreign industry, it is compulsory for the process of collecting genetic material to involve a Brazilian research or teaching institution.

The Executive Bill takes a different approach and states that access to genetic resources existent in *in situ* conditions shall only be authorised to public or private

---

[138] Bill 306/95; supra Note 125; Article 4(XIV).
[139] Idem; Article 4(XI).
[140] Idem; Article 8(II).
[141] Idem; Article 15(I)(a).

Brazilian institutions which promote activities of research and development in biological and similar areas.[142] The participation in the gathering of genetic resources or traditional knowledge by legal entities based in a foreign country shall only be allowed when it is undertaken in conjunction with a public Brazilian institution, which must compulsorily co-ordinate the activities.[143]

At first glance, one could think that the Executive Bill is denying foreign investment in Brazil. However, the Brazilian Constitution states that Brazilian industries are those "constituted under Brazilian laws and which have their headquarters and administration in Brazil."[144] According to this understanding, private foreign industries established in Brazil are considered Brazilian industries and have therefore been receiving national treatment.[145]

Thus, the Executive Bill provision that determines that only Brazilian industries can access Brazilian genetic resources can be economically and technologically beneficial to Brazil. Foreign industries interested in accessing Brazil's biodiversity would have to consent to Brazilian legislation and establish their headquarters in Brazil, as determined by the Brazilian constitution. The establishment of foreign industries suggests the entry of foreign investment in Brazil which generates wealth, employment and technology. In addition, part of the benefits produced by the industry revert back to Brazil through taxes.

Although this requirement could provide significant economic and technological benefit to Brazil, it could also be a definite obstacle to those foreign industries which are not interested in establishing their headquarters in Brazil. This could generate a loss of foreign investment which is the very opposite to the aim of the Executive Bill. Therefore, the bill to be adopted could allow foreign industries to decide whether or not they want to constitute their headquarters in Brazil but simultaneously offer fiscal benefits and more access concessions to those that do.

6.5 - Access Contracts

According to Bill 306/95, the access contract is the legal mechanism to ensure the fair and equitable share of benefits derived from the access of Brazil's genetic resources or traditional knowledge.

An access contract, which is basically an adhesion contract, establishes the duties and the obligations of each party in the access proceedings. An adhesion contract is a contract where "one of the parties to the contract succeeds by complete acceptance of a series of clauses formulated previously, in a general and abstract way, by the other party, to constitute the normative and compulsory content for concrete future relations."[146]

That is to say that all natural persons or legal entities, nationals or foreigners, which want to access Brazilian genetic resources will have to agree to minimum conditions and requirements previously established, which regulate the access, management and destiny of genetic resources collected in *in situ* and *ex situ* conditions

---

[142] Executive Bill; supra Note 126; Article 9.
[143] Idem; Article 9(2).
[144] The Constitution; supra Note 5; Article 171(I).
[145] This is the case of Monsanto. See the Brazilian Monsanto website http://www.monsanto.com.br; accessed in September 2000.
[146] Gomes, Orlando; "Condicoes Gerais dos Contratos"; De. Revista dos Tribunais; Sao Paulo, Brazil; 1972; at p. 3.

in Brazil. This type of contract does not infringe the CBD provisions which states that access contracts must be elaborated on mutually agreed terms. The prior access determinations are only minimum access provision requirements. Article 22 of Bill 306/95 reads:

> Article 22 - The access contract, determined by the terms and clauses mutually agreed by the parties (...).[147]

Therefore, only the previously determined access provisions are generic, uniform and directed to the collectivity . The more substantial and case-by-case access clauses are to be determined mutually by all parties to the contract. Similarly, differentiated clauses can be established when the objects of access are genetic resources for agricultural cultivations. The final aim of the contractual negotiations is to reach a balanced and fair partnership of reciprocal rights and duties.

6.5.1 - Responsible Organ for Access Proceedings

All access requests regulating Brazil's genetic resources made by a natural person or a legal entity, national or foreigner, must be directed to the Competent Authority which shall be an organ designated by Brazil's Direct Administration.[148]

The decisions of the competent authority in relation to the national policies of access and access authorisations will be countersigned by a Commission of Genetic Resources, (hereafter the Commission), which will be created by the Executive Power.[149] This countersignature represents an opportunity to avoid a legal appeal or a social protest against a decision of the Competent Authority.

The Commission will be composed of representatives of the "Federal Government, state governments and the Federal District, scientific community, local communities and indigenous populations, agencies of access, non-governmental organisations and private enterprises."[150] Members of the Public Power, local communities and non-governmental institutions, which include teaching and research institutions, shall have representatives on the same level.[151]

Although the Commission of Genetic Resources is to be democratically representative of different sectors in society one can imagine that it would still be possible to out-vote local communities, NGO, and indigenous communities. None of the representatives of the Commission of Genetic Resources has a veto power against access authorisations at this stage. However, according to Article 17(3) of Bill 306/95 this is not true at an earlier stage where access to resources located on indigenous land will depend on the authorisations of the competent authorities, as well as on the prior informed consent of the indigenous community in question. Furthermore, local and indigenous communities can request the competent authority to deny access to genetic resources on their land when they consider that the access activities will threaten the integrity of their natural and cultural integrity.[152]

The Deputy Bill differs from Bill 306/95 in this last point by stating that indigenous and local communities *have the right to deny access* to genetic resources

---

[147] Bill 306/95; supra Note 125; Article 22.
[148] Idem; Article 10.
[149] Idem; Article 11.
[150] Idem.
[151] Idem.
[152] Idem; Article 46, Sole Paragraph.

on the lands they occupy, as well as the associated traditional knowledge, when they judge that such access activities are a threat to the integrity of their natural and cultural patrimony.[153] As indigenous and local communities are the owners of their own traditional knowledge and are the custodians of the biodiversity on the lands they occupy, they should have the right to deny access to both. They should not have to request the competent authority to deny access because they should have the right to deny access to what is theirs.

The Executive Bill does not grant the right to local and indigenous communities to deny access to genetic resources on the land they occupy. It grants indigenous communities exclusively the right to be heard before access to genetic resources on their lands and to the associated traditional knowledge is authorised.[154] They do not have power to deny access; this right is granted to the official indigenous organ.[155]

6.5.2 - Pre-established Requirements of the Access Contracts

According to Bill 306/95, a person or entity requesting access to Brazilian genetic resources must present an access project along with his claim fulfilling an extensive list of requirements. This section shall focus on the main ones as well as the pre-established provisions of access contracts.

The access project must provide for a detailed and specific description of the genetic resources, derived products or traditional knowledge to which access is claimed.[156] This includes their present and potential use and the risks to which they would be vulnerable to with the access.[157] Where access to traditional knowledge is claimed, the access project must be accompanied by a visit authorisation to the local community and indigenous population in question, as well as authorisation to access information, in oral or written form, relating to the traditional knowledge.[158] Furthermore, an access contract to traditional knowledge or a domesticated agricultural cultivation will establish fair and equitable compensation for all stakeholders to the benefits derived from the utilisation of the accessed component.[159]

Once the application and access projects are completed, an extract of the claim and access project are published for three consecutive days in the official newspaper of the federal government[160] and in the most widely read newspaper of the region where the access shall take place.[161] During 60 days following the publication, anyone can object to the access.[162]

As soon as the access project is approved, negotiations to adopt an access contract commence. Access contracts must determine the possible intellectual property rights and the commercialisation of products and processes derived from the accessed genetic resources and the conditions for licence concessions.[163] Furthermore, they must require that samples of all genetic resources and derived products which are the

---

[153] Deputy Bill; Article 46, Sole Paragraph.
[154] Executive Bill; Article 9, Paragraph 4.
[155] Idem. The official indigenous organ is the National Foundation of the Indian, known as FUNAI.
[156] Bill 306/95; supra Note 125; Article 15.
[157] Idem.
[158] Idem; Article 15, Paragraph 1.
[159] Idem; Article 20.
[160] The official gazette of the federal government is called "Diario Oficial da Uniao".
[161] Bill 306/95; supra Note 125; Article 16.
[162] Idem; Article 18, Paragraph 2.
[163] Idem; Article 22.

object of the access contracts, including all associated knowledge, be deposited in a Brazilian institution designated by the Competent Authority.[164] Access contracts shall have a maximum validity of three years but may be renewed for similar periods.[165]

Confidential information is allowed in access contracts when the publication of the information can be unfairly used commercially by third parties.[166] However, if the publication of the information is necessary to protect the public interest, the environment or rights relating to traditional knowledge, the information will not be accepted as confidential.[167] Furthermore, confidentiality is not permitted in regard to the precise location where the access will take place[168] nor in relation to the indication of the destination or subsequent use of the collected material.[169]

Compulsorily, all access processes shall be accompanied by a Brazilian public or private research or teaching institution, which is recognised for its expertise regarding the object of the access contract. This institution, along with the Competent Authority, has the duty to ensure compliance to the access contract terms, guaranteeing that the genetic resources and derived products accessed are exclusively the ones which were authorised[170] and that the environment is conserved in the area where the access occurs.[171]

Apart from the remuneration and distribution of benefits agreed by the parties, the country must be assured fair compensation, which shall be monetary or in the form of commercialisation rights.[172] The monetary benefits will constitute a special fund that will be used for the conservation, research and inventory of the genetic patrimony.[173] This fund will be a financial support to projects relating to the access to and conservation of genetic resources, as well as the associated knowledge[174] which will be selected by the Competent Authority and counter-signed by the Commission.[175] Thus, ideally the fund will be administered by the government and representatives of indigenous and local communities.

Bill 306/95 provides for a full supervision and follow-through of the access process in order to guarantee economic and social benefits to the country. The Deputy Bill is quite similar to Bill 306/95 in the points mentioned. The Executive Bill does not expressly list the requirements to access genetic resources. It does, however, determine that if a foreign industry based in a foreign country wants to access Brazilian genetic resources, it must enter into an agreement with a Brazilian institution which will co-ordinate the activities. The Executive Bill does not require visit authorisations of indigenous communities as in the case in Bill 306/95 and the Deputy Bill. Furthermore, it does not require any type of publication for the access claim or the access authorisation.

Bill 306/95 is detailed and precise in regard to the content of the access contracts. The Executive Bill lists in a single article, in the simplest way possible, the essential clauses for access contracts: object, duration, manner to fairly and equitably

---

[164] Idem.
[165] Idem; Article 23.
[166] Idem; Article 24.
[167] Idem.
[168] Idem; Article 15(IV).
[169] Idem; Article 15(V).
[170] Idem; Article 34(I).
[171] Idem; Article 34(II).
[172] Idem; Article 35.
[173] Idem; Article 36.
[174] Idem.
[175] Idem; Article 36, Sole Paragraph.

share the benefits, rights and responsibilities of the parties, intellectual property rights, rescission, and penalties, forum.[176] The Executive Bill does not stipulate a maximum duration for the access contracts and therefore, this issue will have to be dealt with during the contract negotiations. It is advisable, though, for Brazil to follow Costa Rica's example in the Merck-INBio agreement and adopt a short-term renewable contract. This allows Brazil to renegotiate the terms of the contract if it is not satisfied with the outcome of the access process.

Regardless of which of the bills turns out to be the access law, one of the main requirements of access contracts should be the guarantee that inventions involving Brazilian natural resources be developed in Brazil. As such, Brazil will be empowering its nationals, generating jobs, developing technologically, scientifically and thus truly receiving the benefits from its own biodiversity. Furthermore, Brazil's access law should provide for the conservation and sustainable utilisation of genetic resources and the equitable share of benefits derived from their use with all stakeholders of the contract.

With this in mind, the Brazilian government has created the Brazilian Program of Molecular Ecology for the Sustainable Use of the Biodiversity of Amazonia, known as PROBEM.[177] With PROBEM, the government aims to develop biotechnology and industries in Brazil by undertaking research in the Amazon forest in search of useful active principles in the development of new medicines and other products.

To implement PROBEM, the Brazilian Association for the Sustainable Use of the Biodiversity of Amazonia, known as BIOAMAZÔNIA was created.[178] BIOAMAZÔNIA is a non-profit company of public interest which develops projects of social value involving research and development of products derived from the Amazon forest, and trains and empowers local inhabitants to perform the program's jobs.[179] At the moment PROBEM and BIOAMAZÔNIA are working on the construction of the Amazonia Biotechnology Centre, (hereafter ABC) in Manaus.[180] The ABC will be the largest biotechnology complex of laboratories in South America dedicated to the research, development and production of forest products such as "pharmaceuticals, body care items, essences, cosmetics, foodstuff, bioinsecticides, enzymes of technological interest, essential oils, anti-oxidants, natural dyes, aromatizers and others."[181] As part of its BIOTRADE Initiative program,[182] UNCTAD created a US$ 150 million Amazon Biodiversity Permanent Fund,[183] to be co-ordinated by BIOAMAZÔNIA and Banco Axial, a private bank, in order to finance PROBEM's biotechnology research and development activities.[184] This Amazon project will be implemented between 2000 and 2002.

---

[176] Executive Bill; supra note 126; Article 17.
[177] PROBEM is a joint initiative of the scientific community, private sectors, and national and regional governments. The Secretary of Co-ordination of Amazonia, in the Ministry of Environment, is the organ responsible for PROBEM.
[178] Presidential Decree of 18 March 1999 created PROAMAZÔNIA and qualified it as a social organisation.
[179] See PROBEM website located at: www.bioamazonia.org.br; accessed in August 2000.
[180] Manaus is the capital of the Brazilian state Amazonas.
[181] See PROBEM website located at: www.bioamazonia.org.br.
[182] For information on UNCTAD's BIOTRADE Initiative see the following address www.biotrade.org. Accessed August 2001.
[183] The financial support comes from the United Nations Foundation which was created in 1997 to fund United Nations goals and activities. For more information on the United Nations Foundation see www.unfoundation.org.
[184] See BIOTRADE Initiative website: www.biotrade.org. For more information on the BIOTRADE Amazon project contact biotrade@unctad.org.

6.6 - Conclusion

It is already commonly known that Brazil is the richest country in the world as regards biodiversity. Likewise, in Brazil it is commonly said, generation after generation, that Brazil is the country of the future. It should be recognised that "the future is now" and that the opportunity to start to consummate this saying lies in the adoption of what can be one of Brazil's most important laws. Brazil is in the process of elaborating a law which will regulate access to its vast known and unknown biological diversity and associated traditional knowledge and this has the potential to generate great wealth to the country.

Considering the creation of conditions to facilitate the access to Brazil's genetic resources,[185] the Executive body decided that the scope of Bill 306/95 and the Deputy Bill were too broad and the provisions in those bills which restrict, guide, manage and supervise access to Brazil's genetic resources were too many. Consequently the Executive Bill is said by the Executive Power to be a means of providing "a quick-moving, solid and modern juridical and operational base to guarantee a better insertion of Brazil in the growing globalisation of the world, protecting and valuing the components of its rich biodiversity."[186]

Through repeated examples among developing countries, biodiversity as raw material is accessed easily and cheaply, if not freely, by enterprises of developed countries for *inter alia*, biotechnological inventions, pharmaceuticals, and agrochemicals. The natural resources are then processed, if possible patented or protected under other rights such as plant breeder's rights. The access to those processed or biotechnological products, rather than being fast and modern, is slow and costly due to the value added by the monopoly rights of the patents.

As noted by Erdos, the "Executive Bill, drafted behind closed doors with no public participation, is clearly not interested in incorporating stakeholder interests and concerns."[187] As such, if the Executive Bill were adopted as Brazil's Access Law, it is unlikely that it will be efficient in safeguarding Brazil's social, environmental and economic interest. Once again it is worth citing Erdos when he states that "implementation and enforcement of any resulting access to genetic resource legislation will depend upon the involvement of various actors and stakeholders."[188] Thus, it must be stressed that the enforcement of any access law will depend on public participation in many stages of the biodiversity access process. Considering that a single leaf contains the whole genetic code of the plant, it is practically impossible to control access to genetic resources without public participation being motivated by receiving their share of benefits.[189]

The Executive Bill reveals the domination of a short-term planning horizon jeopardising the longer term concerns of sustainable development, such as the eradication of poverty and food security. As such, the government shows more political willingness to make alliances with biotechnological enterprises in developed countries than to make some stricter regulations towards its natural resources conservation, management, mobilisation and allocation.

---

[185] See Article 15(2) of the CBD.
[186] Executive Bill; supra Note 126; Annex Mensage no. 978/98.
[187] Erdos, Jordan E.; "Current Legislative Efforts in Brazil to Regulate Access to Genetic Resources"; December 1999. Located at: supra Note 14.
[188] Idem.
[189] José Sarney Filho, the current Minister of the Environment in Brazil, noted that around 20,000 natural extracts a year are illegally smuggled from Brazil. See "Madeira: R$ 10 mil em Multas"; in the Brazilian newspaper Jornal da Tarde, 20 August 1999; at p. 18A.

Bill 306/95 and the Deputy Bill provide opportunities for the participation of local and indigenous communities in the access undertakings on their lands, as well as protection and compensation for the access to their traditional knowledge. This stimulates a continuous and transparent dialogue in the decision-making process, as well as in the multi-stakeholder deliberation regarding access to Brazil's biodiversity.

7 - GENERAL CONCLUSION

While Brazil's biodiversity was economically unimportant and dormant for centuries, with the awareness of the actual and potential value of genetic resources, it is now seen as an opportunity to advance the country's development. The CBD recognises the multiple values of biodiversity[190] and the world has acknowledged that the Amazon forest provides a vast quantity of products and services which include *inter alia* sources of food, clothing, medicines, building material, precious stones and minerals, ecological tourist sites and the absorption of carbon dioxide from the air.

Although Brazil's biodiversity is a real potential source for the country's scientific, commercial, environmental and social benefit, Brazil has so far failed to effectively take the opportunity to sustainably use its natural resources for the nation's own development. Likewise, it still has not succeeded in receiving an equitable share of benefits from the biological resources and associated traditional knowledge accessed from its territory by the biotechnologically-rich developing countries.

The law that Brazil will adopt to regulate access to its genetic resources, should not limit itself to short-term benefits because long-term benefits are more important for Brazil's economic, technological and social development. In other words, Brazil should not be a party to biopartnerships and contracts where it loses the sovereignty over its genetic resources. Therefore, Brazil's law on access to genetic resources should require Brazilian participation in the discovery of useful properties and compounds of its biodiversity, as well as the transfer of all relevant technology and know-how determining that all research and development on Brazilian biodiversity occur in Brazil. Additionally, as it is frequently the case that natural extracts and active compounds are modified to achieve a new compound of more efficiency, Brazil must impose through its access law, the fair and equitable distribution of benefits derived from the final product.

There are currently three Bills of Laws, on access to genetic resources being discussed in the Brazilian congress. While the bills are being discussed and modified, biological resources are being degraded at a rapid pace, devalued by poor people and extracted from the country without adequate legal control. Although the first bill proposed, Bill 306/95, was issued in 1995, consensus in the congress still has not been reached, making the process quite fastidious.

Brazil has adopted a new IPR law and a plant variety law in compliance with TRIPs. Thus, it has adopted the means to protect biotechnological knowledge and the investment that goes with it. As traditional knowledge and traditionally bred varieties do not fulfil the requirements of the new IPR and Cultivar Law, it is necessary for Brazil to take a step further, and search for ways and means to legally protect the traditional knowledge and innovations of its indigenous and rural people. Bill 306/95 envisages the creation of a register where indigenous and local communities could

---

[190] See Preamble of CBD.

officially register their traditional knowledge to avoid biopiracy. It further states that the lack of registration does not prevent a patent being denied or cancelled in cases of biopiracy. In its search for ways of implementing the provisions of the CBD, Brazil ought to properly regulate access to the information contained in its genetic resources, as well as access to traditional knowledge in its own right. Sometimes, access to traditional knowledge is access to the resource itself. This is the case with access to landraces which have been traditionally bred by generations of farmers.

The implementation of the CBD in Brazil, as in most developing countries, is a delicate balance of interests, rights and duties among a wide range of stakeholders and diverse areas of protection. For instance, the State's sovereignty over its biodiversity is limited by its duty to protect the environment for present and future generations, rights of farmers, local and indigenous communities, indigenous land, protected areas, and so forth. Thus, issues of ownership of resources and knowledge must be completely clear in the law to be adopted.

Without a multi-sectorial approach and improved co-ordination and collaboration among all stakeholders to conserve, sustainably use natural resources and alleviate poverty it is impossible to achieve sustainable development. This is not only a Brazilian problem. It is a global issue and thus, a global battle because there is a mutual dependence between developing and developed countries.

The following Chapter shall examine issues Brazil should consider when undertaking biopartnerships and two good examples of Brazilian biopartnerships which originated at grass root level.

CHAPTER NINE

BRAZILIAN BIOPARTNERSHIPS

1 – GENERAL INTRODUCTION

As was seen in Chapter Seven of this book[1], every country has its own particularities which must be acknowledged and respected when forming biopartnerships. In the case of Brazil, some of its plants are used religiously by indigenous and local communities. Thus, due protection must be granted to safeguard and respect their religious beliefs when the plant genetic resources of those plants are accessed for bioprospecting purposes.

All resources are generally treated as if they are open to scientific investigation and possible commercialisation. Brazil, like most countries which are in the process of adopting or have adopted a law to regulate access to their natural resources, do not exclude from commercial exploitation those resources that are integral to the cultural and/or spiritual integrity of local people. Bill 306/95, the Deputy Bill and the Executive Bill (hereafter Access Bills), all regulate plant genetic resources on a general basis. Thus, this Chapter shall propose modifications to the Access Bills in order to provide special protection to the indigenous and religious communities which use certain plants in their religious ceremonies.

This Chapter shall also examine two examples of sustainable development biopartnerships in the Amazon region, namely POEMA and Building the Scenery of Traditional Knowledge. They can be pictured as tangents drawn from TRIPs and the CBD which offer the possibility of complying with the provisions of those instruments through biopartnerships. These biopartnerships show that different sectors of society are slowly awakening to the conservation and sustainable use of the forest's rich biodiversity, as well as the preservation of traditional knowledge of local and indigenous communities.[2]

2 - ACCESS TO PLANT GENETIC RESOURCES OF PLANTS OF TRADITIONAL SPIRITUAL VALUE: CASE-STUDY THE AYAHUASCA PLANTS

2.1 - Introduction

Although indigenous communities consider all plants sacred, some of them are used in their religious ceremonies and are considered by their members to be of particularly high spiritual value. This section shall take as an example the case of two Amazonian plants, which are used to prepare a tea called Ayahuasca,[3] which is the primary element of religious ceremonies of some indigenous and religious communities in Brazil and in other countries. One of the plants is a vine known

---

[1] Biopartnerships Chapter.
[2] A West African proverb states that an old man dying is like a library going up in flames.
[3] The Ayahuasca is prepared by boiling together those two plants for several hours under very high temperature. Consequently, the chemical compositions of the Ayahuasca are different from the chemical composition of each of the two plants. See Campos, Otavio & Brito, Glacus; "Ayahuasca (Hoasca): Historico, Botanica, Fitoquimica, Farmacologia, Efeitos Clinicos e Neuropsicologicos"; provided by the Centro de Estudos Médicos - UDV; Sao Paulo, Brazil.

scientifically as *Banisteriopsis caapi*. The other plant used to prepare the tea is scientifically named as *Psychotria viridis*. It is important to note that different indigenous and religious communities use the term Ayahuasca to refer either to the vine *Banisteriopsis caapi* or alternatively to refer to sacred tea prepared out of those two plants.

The Ayahuasca tea was first studied and described by Richard Spruce, an English botanist, who discovered that the indians of the tribe Tukanos in the valley of the river Uaupés and Villavicencio, in the Brazilian Amazon, made use of the Ayahuasca.[4] In Quechua, which is the language used by the ancient Inca population and still used by half of Peru's population,[5] Ayahuasca comes from two words: "aya" meaning spirit and "huasca" meaning vine. In other words, "vine of the spirit". They call the sacred tea as Yage. The sacred tea has been named by different indigenous and religious communities in several ways.[6] The most commonly heard names are: Hoasca,[7] Ayahuasca,[8] Caapi,[9] Mihi,[10] Dápa,[11] Pildé,[12] Daime,[13] Vegetal.[14] Luna cited around 72 groups of indigenous tribes which used the tea and 42 native names to refer to it.[15] In Brazil, the terms Vegetal, Ayahuasca and Hoasca, are most commonly heard when referring to the sacred tea. When referring to the vine used in the tea, the word Mariri is used, and the word Chacrona refers to the other plant whose leaves are used to prepare the tea. Therefore, as this Chapter relates particularly to access to Brazilian biodiversity, the terms Hoasca, Ayahuasca, Mariri and Chacrona shall be used, except if otherwise explained in the case of citing an author who uses different terminology.

2.2 - Access Bills and Access to the Sacred Plants Mariri and Chacrona

Access to the Mariri and to the Chacrona is not meant to generate material benefit, which is the explicit intention of the Access Bills being discussed in Brazil. These plants are used to prepare the tea Hoasca, which is drunk by the believers in a spiritual context. Some indigenous and religious communities use the Ayahuasca for divination, spiritual communication, social interaction and the treatment of illnesses[16] and others use it as a vehicle of spiritual evolution.[17] The Access Bills do not contain

---

[4] Spruce, Richard; "On Some Remarkable Narcotics of the Amazon Valley and Orinoco, Ocean Highways"; 1(55) The Geographic Review, 1873; pp. 184-193.
[5] Stated under the definition of the language "Quechua" in the Oxford English Reference Dictionary; Oxford University Press; Oxford; 1996.
[6] Grob, McKenna, Callaway, Brito, Neves, Oberlander, Saide, Labigalint, Tacla, Miranda, Strassman, Boone; "Farmacologia Humana da Hoasca, Planta Alucinógena Usada em Context Ritual no Brasil: Efeitos Psicológicos"; 15(2) Informaçao Psiquiatrica, 1996; at pp. 39-45.
[7] Denomination used by the religious entity Centro Espírita Benificente Uniao do Vegetal (CEBUDV). See Centro Espírita Benificente Uniao do Vegetal; Uniao do Vegetal: Hoasca, Fundamentos e Objetivos; Sede Geral; 1989.
[8] This denomination is used by the indigenous peoples of the Peruvian and Bolivian mountains. Idem; at p. 134.
[9] Used among the oriental Tukanos of the Uaupés, an indigenous Amazonian tribe. Idem.
[10] Used by the Cubeos indigenous people. Idem.
[11] Term used by the indigenous people Noanamá do Chocó. Idem.
[12] Used by the indigenous people Emberá. Idem.
[13] Used by the followers of the religion Daime. Idem.
[14] Term used by the members of the religion Centro Espírita Benificente Uniao do Vegetal. Idem.
[15] See Luna, L. E.; "Appendices"; 46(1) America Indigena, 1986; pp. 247-251. Luna, L. E.; "Vegitalismo: Shamanism Among the Mestizo Population of the Peruvian Amazon"; Almquist and Weiskell International; Stockholm; 1986.
[16] See Dobkin de Rios, Marlene; Visionary Vine: Psychedelic Healing in the Peruvian Amazon; Chandler Publications for Health Sciences; San Francisco; 1972.
[17] The Centro Espirita Benificente Uniao do Vegetal uses the tea as an instrument to achieve mental concentration in order to reach a higher state of consciousness. See CEBUDV; supra Note 7; at p. 34.

any provision which prevents plants used for religious purposes by certain indigenous and religious communities from being exploited commercially.

Laboratories in different countries have started to study the properties of the two plants which compose the sacred tea, as well as of the Hoasca as a whole. The danger lies in the possibility of creating medicines out of this sacred tea and furthermore, that the derived medicines be patented. If this occurred, the demand for these sacred plants would increase, jeopardising their sustainable use and conservation. Consequently, religions which use the Hoasca as their communion, would be at risk of losing their main ceremonial component. This would be like taking the holy bread out of the Roman Catholic mass which is the main element of that ceremony.[18]

Another point to consider is that the National Drug Council in Brazil (hereafter CONFEN),[19] after intensive research on the Hoasca publicly declared that it was not considered a drug[20] and allowed the continuation of its use in a religious context.[21] However, the Brazilian doctor, Otavio Castelo de Campos, warns that it is one thing to synthesise the Hoasca and to distribute it in a disco and a completely different thing to use it in a religious context, where it is seen as a sacred vehicle, surrounded by a cultural context and a set of values.[22] To prove their compliance to the CONFEN regulation, which allowed the use of the Hoasca only for religious purposes, Ayahuascan religious entities in Brazil presented CONFEN with a Letter of

---

[18] This would be a violation of the right to religion provided under the Universal Declaration of Human Rights. Article 18 states: "Everyone has the right to freedom of thought, conscience and religion; this right includes freedom to change his religion or belief, and freedom, either alone or in community with others and in public or private, to manifest his religion or belief in teaching, practice, worship and observance." The Universal Declaration of Human Rights can be found at: http://www.hri.org./docs/UDHR48.html.

[19] CONFEN is an abbreviation for Conselho Federal de Entorpencentes. In June 1998 CONFEN was replaced by the National Anti-drug Secretary, known as SENAD which stands for Secretaria Nacional Anti-drogas.

[20] In 1985, the Ayahuasca tea was listed as a drug by the Health Ministry in Brazil. See Administrative Ruling 02/85, of the National Division of the Sanity Vigilance, organ of the Health Ministry. In 1986, the Ayahuasca was taken off that list in view of a legal opinion presented by CONFEN after the properties of the tea, as well as the effect it had on its users, had been extensively analysed by a multi-disciplinary group of professionals selected by CONFEN. See CONFEN Resoluçao No. 6, of 4 February 1986, published in the Diario Oficial da Uniao (the Federal Official Gazette in Brazil), on 5 February 1986. In 1992, CONFEN reaffirmed its legal opinion that the Ayahuasca was not considered a drug. See the CONFEN Resolution published 24 August 1992 in the Diario Oficial da Uniao, section 1, p. 11.467.

[21] See Fabiano, Ruy; "Chá Hoasca É Inofensivo À Saúde"; in the Brazilian newspaper Correio Braziliense; 10 July 1996. This article provides the results of a multinational scientific research project on the Hoasca between 1993-1995 which were presented in the International Conference on Hoasca Studies, held in Rio de Janeiro in 1995. The investigation involved the following universities and institutions: Escola Paulista de Medicina, Universidade do Amazonas, Universidade de Campinas, National Institute of Research in the Amazon - (INPA), University of California, University of New Mexico, University of Miami, University of Kuopio, Finland. The conclusions of this research reaffirmed the conclusion of CONFEN that the Ayahuasca is innocuous to people's health. Furthermore, the tests, which disclose the lethal dose of each substance, known as test of DL-50, revealed that Ayahuasca's DL-50 is 7.8 litres very similar to the DL-50 of passion fruit juice which is 8 litres. The DL-50 of whiskey is 1 litre. Jace Callaway is one of the main scientists of University of Kuopio, Finland, who has been studying the properties of the Hoasca. His report on the International Conference of Hoasca Studies held in Rio de Janeiro, Brazil, November 1995 is located at http://www.maps.org/news-letters/v06n3/06336udv.html. Callaway's report on the current status of the Hoasca Project is located at http://www.maps.org/news-letters/v05n4/05404aya.html. For further results of this scientific investigation see Grob, Mckenna, Callaway, Brito, Neves, Oberlander, Saide, Labigalint, Tacla, Miranda, Strassman, and Boone; supra Note 6. See also Andrade E. N., Brito, Andrade E. O., Neves, Cavalcante, Oberlander, Cardoso, Okimura, Callaway, Mckenna, Grob et al.; "Farmacologia Humana da Hoasca, Chá Obtido de Plantas Alucinógenas Usado em Contexto Ritual no Brasil: parte clínica"; Copy obtained through personal contact with the Centro de Estudos Médicos-UDV, Brasil.

[22] Lerrer, Débora; As Portas de Uma Outra Dimensao; Revista Planeta; 23 April 2000. Located at http://www.terra.com.br/planetanaweb/transcendendo/mente/outra_dimensao.htm.

Principles where they committed themselves not to commercialise the Ayahuasca and to use it only in a religious context.[23]

With this in mind, some questions emerge. The Letter of Principles states that the tea would not be commercialised, but nothing was decided about the products derived from the Hoasca as a whole or from either of the two plants. Can those be sold? Who should receive the benefits from those products? On a financial analysis, ignoring the morality of deriving money from plants used religiously by some indigenous and religious communities, and considering only the fair and equitable share of benefits derived from the use of the medicines originated from the Mariri, Chacrona or Hoasca, it is not easy to determine who, which religious community or what country should be included in the distribution of the benefits.[24] In Brazil, for example, the Hoasca is prepared and drunk by more than 10 religious communities and several indigenous tribes. As such, should all those indigenous and religious communities and all the Amazonian countries be included in the fair and equitable share of benefits? How can their rights be safeguarded?[25] How should the distribution of benefits occur? These questions must be answered in lights of the access bills being elaborated in Brazil.

Bill 306/95 and the Deputy Bill provide for the fair and equitable distribution of benefits derived from the access to genetic resources and derived products. Both of these Bills include products derived from traditional knowledge as "derived products" and allow plant varieties to be interpreted as derived products of the original plant.[26] The Executive Bill does not define derived product. Therefore, the access law to be adopted should explicitly declare that the varieties of the Mariri and the Chacrona, and other plants traditionally considered sacred, are not to be commercialised either. This safeguard is to restrict the monopoly trap of the patent system and basically to respect the spiritual value those plants have to their users.[27] Mariri, the vine, has already been patented once. In the plant patent claim, the vine was referred to as Ayahuasca. The

---

[23] Among other provisions in the Letter of Principles, the signatory entities committed themselves: to only allow a minor, (less than 18 years old), participate in a ceremony with the authorisation of the parents or the person responsible, not to use the sacred tea mixed with prohibited substances, not to commercialise the tea, only use it in a religious context under supervision of an experienced spiritual guide, not to serve the tea to mentally-ill people, and not stimulate the practice of quackery. See Letter of Principles, signed 23 and 24 November 1991 in Rio Branco, capital of the Brazilian state Acre.

[24] The Ayahuasca is commonly used by the indigenous tribes in the Amazon forest which is part of eight South American countries.

[25] The Yurayaco Declaration of the Union of Indigenous Yagecero Doctors of the Colombian Amazon, adopted in Yurayaco, Colombia, June 1999, shows that communities from other South American countries are also concerned about the misappropriation of their sacred plants. The Yurayaco Declaration, refers to the Mariri as yagé. The declarations states: "Here in the foothills of Amazonia, indigenous groups still survive, and we have inherited from our ancestors great wisdom, our medicinal plants, with the knowledge of our forests and the use of the sacred vine: the yagé. [...] Our motivation is not economic or political. [...] Non-indigenous people are finally acknowledging the importance of our wisdom and the value of our medicinal and sacred plants. Many of them profane our culture and our territories by commercialising yagé and other plants. [...] Others want to declare yagé a narcotic plant and prohibit its use for the good of humanity. We also denounce those anthropologists, botanists, business people, doctors and other scientists who are experimenting with yagé and other medicinal and sacred plants without taking into account our ancestral wisdom and our collective intellectual property rights. We denounce the abuse committed against our Tatuyo brothers from the Yapú area of the Vaupes, who in transit to the Gathering were held by the authorities and dispossessed of the yagé they were bringing to ceremonially share at the Gathering. [...] Our medicine looks beyond the physical and seeks the wellbeing of the mind, the heart and the spirit. [...] We declare that yagé and other medicinal plants we use are the patrimony and collective property of the indigenous people. It's use in the name of mankind must be carried out with our participation and we should enjoy any other benefits that derive from its exploitation." The Yurayaco Declaration can be ordered from the following e-mail: Info@AmazonTeam.org.

[26] Article 4(XVI) of Bill 306/95 and Article 4 of the Deputy Bill.

[27] There is a wide leeway in the Access Bills which allows the patenting of inventions based on traditional knowledge.

patent belonged to an American scientist, Loren S. Miller, who claimed to have invented a variety of the vine and was granted a plant patent in the United States.[28]

According to CIEL, after the Ayahuasca case in the US, biodiversity rich countries and indigenous peoples should not be afraid of losing the sovereignty over any of their natural resources if they are patented in the United States as plant varieties. The PTO adopted a narrow interpretation of the scope of a plant patent in the re-examination proceedings of the Ayahuasca case. According to the PTO's interpretation, the plant patent holder can only enforce his right against those who attempt to market or make use of plants directly descended from the patented plant by asexual reproduction.[29] However, it is not certain if other patent offices around the world would adopt the same interpretation.

To avoid the misappropriation and disrespect to religious beliefs related to plants, it is possible to adapt certain articles of Bill 306/95 and the Deputy Bill to protect plants of traditional spiritual value. For instance, one solution to give special protection to sacred plants could be by expanding the exclusions of Article 8 of both bills.[30] The following inclusion could be added to the article to exclude from the scope of the law:

> *III - plants and derived substances, of spiritual value and crucial elements in religious ceremonies of indigenous and/or religious communities.*

---

[28] On 17 June 1986, Loren S. Miller was granted the US Plant Patent 5,751 for his alleged variety of the *Banisteriopsis caapi*, dubbed as "Da Vine". In this case of the "Da Vine" plant patent, Ayahuasca refers only the vine, which in the text above is called Mariri. In his patent application, Loren Miller claimed he had invented a new and unique variety distinct from other forms of the vine by: leaves of different sizes, shapes, and texture; different size pedicels; greater pubescence; different flower colour and size; and absence of samaras or nuts. Furthermore, he added that he was investigating the possibility of medicinal properties of the plant. Loren Miller stated that he had obtained a cutting of the vine from a "domestic garden in the Amazon rain-forest of South America." In 1994, the Co-ordinating Body of Indigenous Organisations of the Amazon Basin (hereafter COICA), discovered that their sacred plant had been patented and that Miller intended to set up a pharmaceutical laboratory in Ecuador for the purpose of researching the Ayahuasca and other plants. COICA feared that bilateral intellectual property reciprocity agreement between the United States and Ecuador would force the traditional users of the Ayahuasca to recognise the Miller's proprietary rights over their sacred plant. Thus, on 30 March 1999, on behalf of COICA and the Coalition for Amazonian Peoples and Their Environment, (hereafter Amazon Coalition), the Centre for International Environmental Law, (hereafter CIEL), filed a Request for Re-examination of US Plant Patent 5, 751 (hereafter the Request). The Request revealed that there was sufficient prior art to prove that that the "Da Vine" cultivar was not distinguishable from typical forms of *Banisteriopsis caapi* that occur naturally in the Amazon forest, cultivated by indigenous peoples, or from *Banisteriopsis caapi* specimens found in US herbarium collections. Furthermore, the Request argued that the "Da Vine" patent did not meet the utility requirement of the Patent's Act because patenting a plant considered sacred, which is used for religious and medicinal purposes by a large number of cultural and ethnic groups in South America, was against the public policy and morality aspects of the utility requirement. On 28 May 1999, the Request was granted by the US Patent and Trademark Office, (hereafter PTO). The PTO cancelled Miller's "Da Vine" patent on 3 November 1999. The rejection was founded on the narrowest basis possible. PTO stated that the colour of the flowers in the "Da Vine" cultivar, which was the main aspect of the plant patent claim, were indistinguishable from those of specimens of *Banisteriopsis Caapi* located in the Field Museum in Chicago, as was proved by accessioned specimen sheets from that museum. Thus the PTO recognised herbarium specimen sheets as "printed publications". Section 102(b) of 35 USC prohibits patents to be granted when the invention was described in a printed publication more than one year prior to the date of the patent application. Therefore, as the plant variety already existed, it did not fulfil the novelty requirement. CIEL, COICA and the Amazon Coalition have sent comments and recommendations to the PTO to improve identification of prior art. The Request for Re-examination, an analysis of the Ayahuasca case, and the comments to the USPTO recommending changes to their investigation of prior art can be found on the CIEL website at: http://ciel.org/ayahuascapatentcase.html; accessed in July 2000.

[29] See Wiser, Glen; "PTO Rejection of the 'Ayahuasca' Patent Claim"; November 1999; located at http://ciel.org/ayahuascapatentcase.html; accessed in July 2000.

[30] See Chapter Eight, Section 6.3 of this book.

It must be noted, however, that it is unlikely that the Brazilian Congress would adopt a law which would completely exclude from its scope the access to plants which are integral to religious ceremonies. The reason is that scientists willing to research into the genetic resources of those plants or a person eager to use them in an innovative way other than making the tea, would not necessarily be infringing the rights of those that use the plants in a religious context. This right would only be violated if the practice of their beliefs were jeopardised through the over-exploitation of those plants, or the patenting of the Mariri, Chacrona and Hoasca as well as the associated traditional spiritual knowledge. As such, special protection should be provided by Brazil's access law to safeguard for indigenous and religious communities the permanent continuation of their religious use of these plants and the Hoasca.

All Access Bills determine that access to Brazilian biodiversity shall be done through access contracts.[31] The Executive Bill refers to these access contracts as "Contracts for the Utilisation of Genetic Patrimony and the Distribution of Benefits" but does not give it a formal definition.[32] Bill 306/95 and the Deputy Bill define "access contract" as an:

> agreement between the *competent authority* and natural person or legal entity, which *establishes the terms and conditions of access* by those persons or entities to genetic resources and the *subsequent utilisation*, compulsorily including the share of benefits and the access and transfer of technology, in accordance to the provisions of this Law.[33] (emphasis added).

Therefore, the first step for religious and indigenous communities to have some authority over access to the sacred plants is that they be represented by an "Ayahuascan" body.[34] The second step would be that this body gained the status of *competent authority* to *establish the terms and conditions of access* to the Mariri, Chacrona and Hoasca, as well as *subsequent utilisation*. The Ayahuascan body would be formed by representatives of indigenous and religious communities which drink Ayahuasca in their ceremonies. As such, they would be able to express their views and

---

[31] See Chapter Eight, Section 6.5 of this book.
[32] Article 16 of the Executive Bill.
[33] Article 4(IX) of Bill 306/95 and Article 4 of the Deputy Bill.
[34] CONFEN Resolution 1992, published 24 August 1992 in the Diario Oficial da Uniao, section 1, p. 11.467 recommended that the use of the Ayahuasca in a religious context should be regulated by a mixed commission formed by members of CONFEN and representatives of entities that use the Ayahuasca in their spiritual ceremonies. The recommendation stated that the purpose of the mixed commission is to consolidate the principles and basic rules on use of the Ayahuasca common to all religious entities that make use of the tea. According to the CONFEN Resolution published on 9 May 1995, in the Diario Oficial da Uniao, section 1, p. 6.533, CONFEN decided that the mixed commission should establish control mechanisms to realise the intentions contained in the Letter of Principles signed by the religious entities. This mixed commission, for instance, could be reorganised and adapted to expand its scope in order to be the Ayahuascan body referred to in the text. The religious entity Uniao do Vegetal, considered by the Brazilian government as an entity of public utility, proposed in a letter dated 19 April 1996, to the then president of CONFEN, Mathias Flach, the creation of a Justice Chamber under the jurisdiction of the mixed commission to assure the fulfilment of the Letter of Principles. At that time, as well as nowadays, some of the other religious entities disregard their commitment under the Letter of Principles and commercialise the tea, among other infractions. As such, if the mixed commission were to be the Ayahuascan body referred to in the text, the Ayahuascan body would have to adopt the Justice Chamber proposal of Uniao do Vegetal as a means of guaranteeing the proper use of the Ayahuasca as authorised by CONFEN. A copy of the above-mentioned letter was provided by a member of the Uniao do Vegetal through personal contact.

concerns regarding the plants when they are to be accessed for bioprospecting purposes. Furthermore, they could contribute with their traditional knowledge concerning the plantation, cultivation and gathering of the Mariri and the Chacrona. Certain powers could be delegated to those committees to negotiate access contracts to the Mariri and the Chacrona in order to avoid the over-exploitation and degradation of those plants.

The distribution of benefits derived from products developed from the Mariri and the Chacrona could be used in the conservation of the Amazon Forest and the plantation of the Mariri and the Chacrona, as well as other medicinal plants.[35] This could satisfy the interest of all the people who are interested in those plants for religious purposes, researching their properties, or who make medicines or other products out of them. The basic link between all of these people is that without those plant species there would be no Ayahuasca for the religious ceremonies, no research and no medicine or other product derived from them. Therefore, the conservation of the Mariri and the Chacrona is a basic interest.

Other than through an Ayahuascan body, indigenous and local communities could also protect their religious use of the Mariri, the Chacrona and the Hoasca under the definition of "traditional knowledge". "Traditional knowledge" in Bill 306/95 is defined as:

> every knowledge, innovation or individual or collective practice of an indigenous population or local community, with real or potential value, associated to genetic resource or derived products, protected or not by intellectual property regime.[36]

Several provisions in Bill 306/95 and the Deputy Bill grant authority to local communities and indigenous populations to negotiate access to genetic resources on their lands and to associated traditional knowledge. Article 5(III) of both Bills, for instance, states the:

> necessity of prior informed consent of local communities and indigenous populations to the access activities to genetic resources located in areas they occupy, to their domesticated and semi-domesticated agricultural cultivations and to the traditional knowledge they hold.[37]

Article 45 of Bill 306/95 and the Deputy Bill state that local and indigenous communities hold the exclusive right over their traditional knowledge.[38]

Bill 306/95 defines "local community and indigenous population" together as a:

> human group distinct for its social, cultural and economic conditions, which totally or partially

---

[35] An administrative ruling of Brazilian Institute of the Environment and Renewable Resources (IBAMA) gives special protection to the exploration of forest resources used for religious or research purposes. See Administrative Ruling, No. 44N, published 17 August 1998, in section 1 of the Diario Oficial da Uniao.
[36] Article 4(V) of Bill 306/95. This definition in the Deputy Bill differs only in the use of words, but not in meaning.
[37] Article 5(III) of Bill 306/95 and the Deputy Bill.
[38] The Executive Bill fails to mention this.

organises itself with its own customs and traditions or by a special legislation and that no matter what is its juridical situation, conserves its own social, economic, cultural institutions or part of them."[39]

The problem in this case is that the definition of "local community and indigenous population" could satisfy the interests of indigenous communities, but not of the religious communities which drink the Hoasca. The definition is too narrow to encompass religious conditions. It is hard to classify everyone who drinks the Ayahuasca in a religious context as a person who is distinct for its social, cultural and economic conditions. The people who drink Hoasca vary from indigenous people to medical doctors and judges. In the same way, the nationalities of those who drink Hoasca also vary a lot.

Therefore, alternatively, the words *"or spiritual"* when classifying the conditions which make local communities and indigenous populations a distinct human group could be added. The definition would thus read:

a human group distinct for its social, cultural, economic *or spiritual* conditions, which totally or partially organises itself with its own customs and traditions [...].[40]

Likewise, another possibility would be to leave the definition of local community and indigenous population as it is and add to the Bill the term: *"spiritual communities"*. The definition of spiritual communities could relate to those religious communities which use the plants they consider sacred as the crucial elements of their spiritual services. The definition of spiritual communities could give some authority to the religious communities, such as their prior informed consent to commercialise for instance their sacred plants. In regard to the Ayahuasca, these communities could supervise the extraction activities on national territory, guarantee that the Mariri and the Chacrona are sustainably used, and thereby conserving them for the possible continuation of their own religious acts and beliefs.[41]

It is important to stress that religious and indigenous communities would not have a police power to control the gathering, management and use of their sacred plants. The competent authority would exercise this police power. Nevertheless, they already have general powers to control access to their sacred plants, through the provisions of Article 5 of both Bill 306/95 and Deputy Bill which determine that it is:

"incumbent on all natural persons and juridical entities and to the Public Power, in particular, to preserve the genetic patrimony and biological diversity of the country, promote its study and sustainable use and control the activities of access to genetic resources, as well as supervise the entities dedicated to prospecting, collection, research, conservation, manipulation, commercialisation, among other activities related to these resources."[42]

---

[39] Article 4(VI) of Bill 306/95. The Deputy uses the terms "indigenous societies" and "local or traditional population" and defines them separately. See Article 4 of the Deputy Bill.
[40] Idem. This term is not defined in the Deputy Bill neither in the Executive Bill.
[41] Both the Mariri and the Chacrona can be found completely undomesticated, semi-domesticated and in cultivated states throughout Brazil.
[42] Article 5 of Bill 306/95 and the Deputy Bill.

This is a general stimulus for all Brazilians to initiate public civil suits against industries which degrade the environment, and so forth. The Executive Bill fails to provide this.

And finally, an easier and probably more effective alternative to give special protection to plants of spiritual value would be to create an ANNEX to the adopted law to declare which plant and animal species are not allowed to be commercialised. This appendix would include the Mariri, the Chacrona, the Hoasca as a derived product, animals and plants in extinction, and so forth.

2.3 - Conclusion

The Access Bills being drafted in Brazil can be modified in several ways to give special protection to plants and substances of traditional spiritual value. When the access to genetic resources involves plants of spiritual value, the access to bioprospection, biotechnology and commercialisation must be restricted and controlled. There should be a ban on the patenting of sacred plants and their active compounds. A representative body of the indigenous and religious communities could be created to supervise the access and use of the sacred plants that are crucial to their religious ceremonies. These communities should have unrestricted access to their sacred plants.

3 - POEMA: PROGRAM POVERTY AND ENVIRONMENT IN AMAZONIA

The Program Poverty and Environment in Amazonia, (hereinafter POEMA), is a special program established in 1991 by the Federal University of Pará.[43] POEMA believes that the "university, using technical- and economically feasible means must establish a productive dialogue with its social and political environment thereby supporting the struggle against the trends of socio-environmental destruction that currently are underway in the region."[44] The initial idea of the program was to study the living conditions of the inhabitants of the poor communities of Bengui in Belem, capital of Pará. The results of the research motivated POEMA to help those communities to meet their basic needs.

The ideas which led to the development of POEMA rose out of a research project on the precarious conditions of the low income groups which live in the slums of Belem, the capital of Pará. From the general results of the research, innovative forms of co-operation were sought to meet the basic needs of the poor people and to build their capacity to increase their economic opportunities.[45]

3.1 - Sanitation and Nutrition

---

[43] Para is a state in the North of Brazil.
[44] Mitschein, Thomas, Miranda, Pedro; POEMA: A Proposal of Sustainable Development in Amazonia, Belem-Para-Brazil; Federal University of Para; 1996; at p. 17. See also POEMA, Development and Conservation in the Brazilian Amazon: Inventory and Analysis of Projects; Tratado de Cooperaçao Amazônica. For a copy of this publication send and e-mail to: poema@ufpa.br.
[45] Mitschein, Thomas, Miranda, Pedro; Idem; at p. 8.

The basic principles of POEMA are **integration** and **interdisciplinarity**. Through integration POEMA aims to achieve the "co-operation for the development of integrated activities involving:

> 1 - poor people from the Amazonian interior regions and their organisations;
> 2 - public agencies: municipal, state and federal;
> 3 - non-governmental organisations;
> 4 - institutions of science and technology;
> 5 - private sector."[46]

POEMA integrates the areas in which the basic needs of the local people are not met with the areas which can generate employment and income. As basic sanitation, health, nutrition and social organisation are precarious in the region, POEMA focuses on agroforestry, the processing of natural products, and foodstuffs, production of inputs for pharmaceuticals, and alternative forms of energy generation. In addition, it programs potable water treatment and supply systems, sanitary sewage disposal and adequate use of domestic gardens to provide harvests for the families have been implemented.

POEMA trains community agents for the dissemination of basic activities regarding environmental sanitation and offers training and technical assistance so that local populations can manage the sanitation programs themselves. By doing this, POEMA has managed to reduce the cost of implementation to provide people with access to potable water and water treatment systems. Moreover, the incidence of water-borne diseases has been reduced, domestic water supply has been improved and the local communities have been empowered.

Along with the improvement of basic sanitation, POEMA has been evaluating the nutritional status of the local inhabitants and developing preventive activities in the areas of health and nutrition to overcome the severe nutritional deficiencies, well below the minimum standard of food consumption acknowledged by the World Health Organisation. An inventory of the natural resources available in the region was made and a diversified diet and home remedy practices containing regional flora and fauna were elaborated. Once again, community agents were trained to disseminate basic information and to implement the health and nutritional programs. The results of the dissemination of the use of foodstuffs were obviously positive: family diets were enriched, malnutrition levels of children from 0 to 5 years of age dropped, and the nutritional status of pregnant women improved.[47]

Instead of the customary migratory agriculture and high predatory exploitation with low levels of sustainability practised by thousands of small holders in the Amazon region, POEMA introduced alternative forms of use in the three productive areas of small rural holders: the domestic garden, the cultivated field and the forest. Fruits and vegetables are planted and small animals are raised in domestic gardens to provide the families with a regular food supply.

3.2 - AGRICULTURE IN LAYERS, COMMERCIALISATION OF FOREST PRODUCTS AND BIOPARTNERSHIPS

---

[46] POEMA, Alliances in Defence of Life; Universidade Federal do Para, Nucleo de Meio Ambiente; at p. 3.
[47] Idem; at p. 5.

In conjunction with the home gardens program, an efficient agroforestry system is being implemented in cultivated fields in cleared forest areas. POEMA's agroforestry system, known as "agriculture in layers", unites the knowledge of indigenous Kayapo agriculture, technical scientific knowledge and experiences of small holders of land.[48] It is based on the cultivation of natural products of the Amazon region which are planted in association, without the use of chemical products, and thus adapt perfectly to the regional soil and climate conditions. At the same time, the remaining forest areas undergo recuperation and sustainable management of their natural products.

However, Amazonia is a fragile ecosystem which can be degraded by agricultural activities. With this in mind, POEMA's agroforestry system respects the balance of the forest and interacts with it to maintain productivity in agricultural areas without degrading them.[49] Technical assistance and training of workers are provided to the local small rural holders. New and balanced alternatives of exploration of the natural resources in the region are disseminated, improving the production systems by decreasing costs and optimising commercialisation.

One of the issues POEMA works on is the verticality of the productive process which brings the farmer with the raw material nearer to the end consumer. In general, approximately 80% of the ultimate prices are added to the product after it leaves its original location when the merchandise is processed and commercialised. This is to say that local farmers, working as direct agents of the production through the processing and commercialisation parts, can gain a greater appropriation of the ultimate prices. Consequently, their income and living conditions would substantially improve. POEMA creates an improved base for economic production of rural communities by carrying out research on technical processes for natural products and opening access to markets. Of the species studied, POEMA selected the following:

"a) In the area of fibres
- Curaua (*Ananas erectifolius*)
- Piteira (*Furcraea gigantea*)
- Aninga (*Montrichardia arborescens*)
- Buriti (*Mauritia flexuosa*)
- Banana plant (*Musa sp*)
- Coconut (*Cocos nucifera*)

b) In the area of natural oils and resins
- Buriti (*Mauritia sp.*)
- Andiroba (*Carapa guianesis*)
- Copaiba (*Copaifera multijuga*)
- Brazil nut (*Bertholletia excelsa*)
- Colza (*Brassica campestris*)
- Palm oil (*Elaeis guineensis*)
- Açai (*Euterpe orelacea*)
- Bacabi (*Oenocarpus minor*)
- Castor oil (*Ricinus communis*)
- Jutaicica (*Himenea courbaril*)

c) In the area of latex-rubber
- Rubber tree (*Hevea brasiliensis*)

---

[48] Mitschein, Thomas, Miranda, Pedro; supra Note 44; at p. 24.
[49] Idem; at p. 28.

- Jutai-mirim seeds (*Hymenaea parvifolia*)
- Jutai-acu seeds (*Hymenaea courbaril*)

d) In the area of dyes
- Urucum (*Bixa orellana*)
- Curcuma (*Curcuma longa*)
- Açai (*Euterpe oleracea*)
- Genipapo (*Genipa americana*)."[50]

Some of these natural products are still unknown to the international community. Nevertheless they are of interest because as a result of "a growing international demand for foods produced without agrotoxins, for medicinal plants and plant-based cosmetics, there is a strong trend toward substituting synthetic inputs for natural ones in industry. This is a reflex of the need for recycling in the industrialised countries, constituting a new market for fibres, oils, dyes, resins and latex."[51] POEMA carries out research on technological processes for natural products and aids local communities to diversify agroforestry production of industrial and edible forest resources, enabling them to have better access conditions to national and international markets. This generates more employment for the local communities and raises their income, as well as their interest to use the forest sustainably.

One of the partnerships that POEMA has initiated was with Mercedes Benz.[52] The partnership was for the period of 1993-96 between Praia Grande Community/POEMA and Daimler Benz/Mercedes Benz of Brazil.[53] Through this partnership, two pilot coconut fibre processing units were installed in Ponta de Pedras. The fibre processing units transform fibres into headrests for Mercedes Benz trucks. Nowadays, this experience is being expanded to transform the coconut fibre cords into new products and to involve new communities in the projects.

POEMA also carries out projects to set up foodstuffs-processing units by the communities themselves. It promotes studies and experimental research to evaluate and characterise the physical, physical-chemical and microbiological aspects of the products, as well as quality control of regional raw materials selected for foodstuffs processing. Small-scale foodstuffs-processing units are installed and rural producers are trained to enhance employment and income generation. The processing of the banana, for example, has been expanded to make liqueur, paste, caramelised banana with coconut, dried banana, banana flour and banana chips.

Traditional knowledge of local communities and indigenous populations in relation to the actual and potential source of the medicinal resources of Amazonian flora is also valued. The medicines used by the local communities and local populations are all found in the forest. POEMA foments the activities which research the pharmaceutical use of plants species, surveying and gathering information known by the communities and submitting it to ethnopharmaceutical methodology. The idea is to launch new pharmaceutical products in the market, by incorporating scientific knowledge and new technologies to traditional remedies. Community agents, while passing on traditional knowledge, are trained to manipulate the pharmaceutical inputs and research new techniques for using the medicinal plants of the region.

---

[50] Idem; at p. 51.
[51] Idem; at p. 11.
[52] Most of the information in this section on the biopartnership with Mercedes Benz and on POEMA projects was accessed through personal conversations with POEMA staff which attended the UNCTAD Biotrade Initiade, held in Lyon, 10-12 November 1998.
[53] Alamgir, Mohiuddin; "The Challenges of Sustainable Development and of Food Security"; POEMAtropic No. 1, January/July 1998; at p. 8.

3.3 - Conclusion

Apart from conserving the biodiversity of the region, POEMA's initiative to process forest resources activates research on the industrial use of plant products. Local communities enter into biopartnerships with national and multinational companies for the primary and industrial processing of natural products with technical and economic viability. The optimisation of the forest fibres, oils and dyes adds greater value to natural products, which increases their prices in local markets, as well as opening new markets at the local, national and international levels.

POEMA projects and activities add value to the biodiversity of the region. Through the quality control of raw materials and final products, the quality of the medicinal products utilised within the communities is also improved. Moreover, the technical and scientific knowledge applied to the traditional knowledge on medicinal plants contributes to the generation of employment and income to the local communities, thus helping to reduce poverty in the region.[54]

4 - BUILDING THE SCENERY OF TRADITIONAL KNOWLEDGE

4.1 - Introduction

Grassroot action in Brazil has been increasing to form biopartnerships among local communities as well as between local communities and companies interested in accessing traditional knowledge and wild species. Some of these people still hold the secret of how to use the natural resources without destroying the forest.[55] Furthermore, they have discovered many of the benefits that the region's biodiversity offers to humanity. Documentation of local and traditional knowledge is intensifying in Brazil.

One of the grassroot actions in formation is a system that originated in the Amazon region and is known as "Building the Scenery of Traditional Knowledge", (Scenery System). The Scenery System was invented by a teacher of the Federal University of Amazonas named Moacir Biondo.[56] For twenty years Moacir Biondo has been closely working with the local population in the state of Amazonas, in Brazil, recovering and documenting traditional knowledge, which in some cases had almost been forgotten. He himself possesses a wide and rich traditional knowledge about the medicinal uses of Amazonian plants.

---

[54] For more information on any of POEMA's projects send an e-mail to: poema@ufpa.br.

[55] For example, one of the characteristics of the forest is that in an area equivalent to 20 meters it is not easy to find three trees of the same family. Therefore, centres of rubber tree extractions are 100 or 200 metres apart from each other. Indigenous and local communities know that the mystery of this natural phenomena is to avoid the dispersion of pests, and thus, respect the natural ordre of the forest. This was not the case of Henry Ford, the pioneer in the construction of automobiles, who chopped down a vast area of forest during the 1930s to plant exclusively rubber trees. A pest attacked his plantation and completely destroyed it. See Alvarenga, T.; "A Destruiçao da Amazonia"; in the supplement Veja Especial Amazonica, 24 December 1997, of the Brazilian Magazine Veja Ano 30-No. 51; at p. 16.

[56] Moacir Biondo is also the technical director of the Permaculture Institute of Amazonia. All information regarding the Scenery System was provided by Moacir Biondo through personal e-mail contact. Anyone willing to expand his/her knowledge about the Scenery System should contact Moacir Biondo through the following e-mail address: biondo@netium.com.br.

Through the Scenery System the traditional knowledge is gathered, documented, and subsequently made available to all the local contributors of the system for the purpose of improving their life styles. By sharing their knowledge they aim to build the full scenery of all of the properties and functions of each Amazonian natural resource in the same way as one puts together a jigsaw puzzle to create the full picture once the puzzle is complete. By gaining understanding of the importance and value of each plant, and by entering into fair and equitable partnerships to commercialise products derived from Amazonian plants, local inhabitants feel encouraged to take responsibility to conserve and sustainably use the environment and its components.

The system consists of local people uniting their traditional knowledge in regard to fructiferous and medicinal plants that they commonly use.[57] One person, for example, revealed that he uses cinnamon to elevate low blood pressure while another local individual claimed he uses it to stop hair loss! The objectives of this system include the empowerment of the local people by uniting their knowledge. It shall be explained and analysed in this section.

4.2 - The Scenery System

The Scenery System involves local and indigenous communities, local universities and scientists. All of them are beneficiaries of the system and their knowledge has already started the construction of the scenery. The total construction of the picture will take many years to occur because the jigsaw puzzle will only be complete when all the properties of all the natural resources in the Amazon region have been identified. In this sense, the Scenery System is in harmony with the principle of global partnership as expressed in the Rio Declaration and in harmony with the CBD provisions.

The distribution of benefits and compensation is general because the traditional knowledge of each one of the contributors to the system increases when they unite their knowledge, giving them the possibility of improving their own health, diets, and life-styles through the use of natural resources in the forest. Through the act of sharing, the Scenery System provides the network to facilitate the exchange of plant and associated traditional knowledge.[58] According to Hahnel Robin, "Sharing information is undoubtedly the most efficient way to allocate productive resources."[59].

The Scenery System adopts permaculture as its action program. Permaculture is the development of agroecological ecosystems intended to be self-sustaining.[60] Through permaculture, medicinal plants are cultivated by the local people with the purpose of conserving their active medicinal principles while maintaining the balance

---

[57] Several plants have medicinal properties. The Brazilian oncologist Gilberto Schwartzmann, professor at the Federal University of Rio Grande do Sul in Brazil, stated: "Medicines are good, independent from where they come from. However, nature has substances that man is not able to make." Gullo, C. and Pereira, C.; "A Cura no Jardim"; in the Brazilian magazine Isto É, No. 1513; 30 September 1998, at p. 74.

[58] The act of sharing and exchanging traditional knowledge has been occurring for centuries. Records show that in the Bolivian Andes, hundreds of years before the arrival of the Spanish, highlanders in the Bolivian Andes received medicines from rainforest shamans. See Gray, Andrew; "Between the Spice of Life and the Melting Pot: Biodiversity Conservation and its Impact on Indigenous People"; IWGIA Document 70; Copenhagen; 1991; at p. 34.

[59] Hahnel, Robin; "Cooperación internacional, sí! NAFTA,no!"; *Z Magazine* 6(4), April 1993; at p. 47-52; Cited in Martin, Brian; "Against Intellectual Property"; located at: http://www.uow.edu.au/arts/sts.bmartin/pubs/95psa.html.

[60] According to Moacir Biondo, permaculture is a state of spirit. It is the cohesion of ethical and moral principles in the labour of cultivating lands and hearts.

of the ecosystems. The natural balance and qualities of the Amazon region are to be respected and preserved and projects that go against the nature of the region are to be avoided. The products derived from traditional knowledge, permaculture and the use of Amazonian plants may become objects of fair and equitable partnerships that the board of the Scenery System decides to undertake.

Local people in the Amazon region are used to exchanging among themselves their knowledge about the area's biodiversity. These good faith gestures have been easy victims of patent seekers. For the Scenery System to be effective it must provide sufficient protection against misappropriation of the gathered traditional knowledge to avoid having the adverse effect of making local resources and knowledge further accessible to biotechnology companies at the expense of local actors.[61]

The Scenery System creates the possibility of establishing "prior art" of orally transmitted traditional knowledge in regard to useful properties contained in genetic resources. The knowledge that is gathered is written and printed out in informative pamphlets. As such a single person would not be able to monopolise through patents the use of a medicinal plants commonly used by local communities because the Scenery System provides sufficient legal evidence to prove that the resource has long been known and used for certain purposes. It is worth clarifying that any sacred and spiritual traditional knowledge associated to natural species is not disrespected and its secrecy is preserved for religious purposes.

If the Scenery System were to be used as a *sui generis* system in compliance to TRIPs and in harmony to the CBD, Brazil should enact a law which recognises the rights of farmers, indigenous and local communities when they inspire and help the scientific field through the discoveries made through their traditional knowledge.[62] This law could help stop biopiracy and promote the equitable sharing of benefits between users and donors of germplasm. Michael Gollin's theory of "Discoverer's Right" can be further expanded and developed to be applicable to Scenery System to make it more effective.[63]

It is advisable for the Scenery System to work as a co-operative. There should be a board of management but the functioning of the whole system should be democratic. All the benefits that arise from the gathered traditional knowledge and biopartnerships should be devoted to the proper functioning of the system and to social projects. All of the system's members should vote on the social projects to be undertaken.

---

[61] Several NGOs and scientists have smuggled samples of plants and traditional knowledge out of Brazil. For instance, according to the Final Report of the Commission on Biopiracy in the Amazon, the NGO Associaçao Ecológica Alto Juruá, known as Selva Viva, of Ruedger von Reininghaus, an Austrian naturalised Brazilian, would sell medicinal plants and traditional knowledge to other countries. Under the pretext of offering health services to indigenous communities, Selva Viva gathered and sold to foreign countries medicinal plants and traditional knowledge of indigenous communities of the region of river Juruá, of those along the rivers Môa, Liberdade, Tarauacá and Morú, in the municipals of Tarauacá and Cruzeiro do Sul which were all associated to the NGO. See Final Report of the Commission on Biopiracy in the Amazon; Deputy Chamber of the Brazilian Congress; 18 November 1997; at p. 15.

[62] However, according to Darrel Posey "once TEK (Traditional Ecological Knowledge), or genetic materials leave the societies they are embedded, there is little national protection and virtually no international law to protect community 'knowledge, innovations and practices'". Posey, D.; "Culture and Nature - the Inextricable Link"; in Posey, D. (ed); Cultural and Spiritual Values of Biodiversity; Intermediate Technology Publications; London; 2000; at p. 11.

[63] See Gollin, Michael; "An Intellectual Property Rights Framework for Biodiversity Prospecting"; in World Resources Institute; Biodiversity Prospecting: Using Genetic Resources for Sustainable Development; World Resources Institute; USA; 1993; at p. 180.

A single fund dedicated to conservation of the environment, the creation of jobs, construction of hospitals and schools in local villages and so forth can solve the issue of sharing benefits with different communities that contribute knowledge to the Scenery System about a particular plant. In this sense, there would be recognition of the collective nature of the resources and knowledge. Collective resources and knowledge are in fact composed of contributions of many individuals throughout thousands of years. One generation transmits to the following generation traditional knowledge accumulated up to its time along with the improvements made on plant species through traditional breeding techniques. Both traditional knowledge and biodiversity are alive and constantly adapting to each other.

According to Biondo, there is already a project to develop a fund for the Scenery System, the Bio-Value Fund. The Bio-Value Fund is to be supported by part of the royalties derived from the commercialisation of products developed from Amazonian plants.[64] This fund will be administered by a council composed of representatives of non-governmental organisations that represent the interest of local and indigenous communities.

In this system, individuals work together towards a common goal, for the overall improvement in the quality of life and not mainly for the purpose of profit. The system focuses mainly on meeting the needs of the local and indigenous communities that work with it. However, it must be noted that the Brazilian Amazon forest is part of the State's national patrimony and thus it is logical that the State will want its share of benefits that arise from the use of forest's resources. The Brazilian government has a lot to gain from the "fruits" that will grow out of this system.

The government gains economic benefits with the entry of foreign currency into its economy once the Amazonian derived products are exported. As the benefits that arise from the Scenery System are to be used in social projects such as the construction of schools, hospitals, universities, laboratories and sanitary systems, the government saves the same quantity of money that it would have invested if it had undertaken these projects in compliance to its constitutional obligations.[65] Moreover, the government gains better and more competent citizens who are capable to conserve, sustainably use, manage and research natural resources.

It must be made clear that the State has sovereignty over its biological diversity but not over each person's traditional knowledge. Furthermore, owners of private land have the sovereignty over the resources on their own land. Therefore there is no legal duty on private land holders and indigenous communities, who have the original rights over the demarcated lands they traditionally occupy,[66] to share with the government the benefits that arise from their traditional knowledge and from

---

[64] Moacir Biondo stresses that there must be a greater distribution of benefits in the form of royalty payment to the local and indigenous people than a mere 3% as has been stipulated in other partnerships around the world.

[65] According to Article 208 of the Brazilian Constitution, the State has the duty to ensure compulsory and free elementary education, including those who did not have access to school at proper age. It is also a duty of the State to ensure the progressive extension of compulsory and free education to secondary school and the access to higher levels of education. Article 196 of the Brazilian Constitution mandates that health is a right of all and a duty of the State. It is the State's duty to provide the social and economic policies aimed at reducing the risks of illness and other hazards, as well as the universal and equal access to actions and services for its promotion, protection and recovery.

[66] Article 231 of the Brazilian Constitution states: "Indians shall have their social organisation, customs, languages, creeds and traditions recognised, as well as their original rights to the lands they traditionally occupy, it being incumbent upon the Union to demarcate them, protect and ensure respect for all their property."

biodiversity on their lands. Nevertheless, the State will always be benefited from the realisation and expansion of all social projects.

4.3 - Conclusion

Over and over it is repeated that the Amazon Forest is extraordinarily rich in natural resources. The Amazon forest houses more than 20 of each 100 plant and animal species existent in the world.[67] However, it is less commonly mentioned that this great natural wealth strongly contrasts with the poor and precarious survival conditions to which many of the inhabitants of that area, as well as an alarming part of the Brazilian population, are subject.

The payment of royalties, transfer of technology and the sharing of profits or research are issues that need to be regulated for the benefit of local and indigenous communities where biodiversity and associated knowledge were accessed. Amazon local and indigenous communities, who live in a biodiversity-rich region which they know better than anyone else, could be parties to contracts with institutions that wish to undertake research on Amazon resources. Private or public biodiversity prospectors may "use local knowledge by implementing royalty structures that place premiums on products derived from ethnobotanical knowledge."[68] This would only work in favour of poverty eradication in Brazil if the benefits derived from the local and indigenous traditional knowledge were in fact fairly and equitably shared with the local and indigenous communities. So far, this has not been the case. Few people have been enriched through the benefits derived from traditional knowledge while local and indigenous communities have been impoverished by giving it away freely.

The Scenery System provides local inhabitants with an assortment of traditional knowledge. It is the union of all traditional knowledge pursued by local and indigenous communities in the region. The first part of the Scenery System is the exchange of traditional information in regard to the properties of Amazon plants. The gathered traditional knowledge is shared among all those who contributed to its formation. The second part consists in uniting this knowledge in the same way as one joins the pieces of a jig-saw-puzzle. The final long-term result is complete jig-saw of all the functions and properties of all of the biodiversity in the Amazon. The efficiency of the third part of the Scenery System, the commercialisation of products derived from Amazonian plants, will depend on the adoption of national laws protecting traditional knowledge and compensating local and indigenous communities for their discoveries and innovations.

The Brazilian government preaches that the preservation of the Amazon region is a complex task due to its enormous size, social and economic factors and the limited administrative structure available.[69] However, instead of investing money in confronting these problems, it has opted for predatory projects to develop the region against its own natural capacity and qualities. From 1970 and 1985, the Brazilian government, with US$ 700 million fiscal incentives and subsidy credits for 950 projects, stimulated the occupation of the Amazon forest which resulted in huge areas of the forest being devastated to plant crops and to raise cows.[70] The Brazilian

---

[67] EMBRAPA; Atlas do Meio Ambiente do Brasil; Terra Viva; Brasilia, DF; 1994; at p. 82.
[68] Rubin, S. M. & Fish, S. C.; "Biodiversity Prospecting: Using Innovate Contractual Provisions to Foster Ethnobotanical Knowledge, Technology and Conservation"; 5 Colorado. Journal of International Environmental Law and Policy 1994; at p. 33.
[69] See Ministerio do Meio Ambiente, dos Recursos Hídricos e da Amazônia Legal; Primeiro Relatório Nacional para a Convençao sobre Diversidade Biológica: Brasil; 1998; at p. 22.
[70] Idem; at p. 42.

government should provide fiscal and other incentives towards projects like the Scenery System which can empower its own nationals by adequately and wisely using the Amazon region as an alliance to the country's sustainable development.

5 - GENERAL CONCLUSION

Brazil is a country rich in biological diversity, as well as cultural, ethnic and religious diversity which must be respected and duly protected in any biopartnership it undertakes. Brazil's biodiversity can and should be used in a sustainable manner to help eradicate poverty in the country. The natural or biotechnological use of biological resources can turn out to be, for example, a source for pharmaceuticals, agrochemicals or even cosmetics, all of which can generate high economic benefits. Through the legal mechanisms offered in the CBD, namely prior informed consent, mutually agreed contracts and fair and equitable share of benefits, Brazil has the possibility of conserving and sustainably using its biodiversity to create better social conditions, increase the country's revenues and its technological capacity.

However, Brazil must be aware that information contained in genetic resources can be exploited independently of the original raw material. Therefore, if there are not appropriate legal measures, Brazil could lose the sovereignty over genetic resources accessed by foreigners.

POEMA and the Scenery System genuinely work for the creation of biopartnerships to conserve and sustainably use biodiversity where all parties derive benefits from the their use. They promote the co-operation between local and indigenous communities and governments, NGOs and the private sector. The work is done in an integrated manner for the conservation, sustainable development and eradication of poverty in the Amazon region. In other words POEMA and the Scenery System have a multi-sectorial focus which unites social, economic and ecological concerns. The objective of this interdisciplinary work is to provide the opportunity for poor populations to sustainably use and manage the natural resources of the area in such a way that they can better meet their basic needs and strengthen their capacity for self-organisation.

POEMA and the Scenery System have been active with the local poor populations seeking their empowerment through integrated training programs which expand their capacity for organisation, as well as rescuing and recovering traditional knowledge in cases where it had almost been forgotten. Through such agencies and systems, local communities are given the opportunity to choose, decide and manage the projects in which they are involved. POEMA, for instance, acts as a conduit between the communities and different industries. Consequently, there has been a considerable increase of biopartnerships of POEMA involving local communities allowing them to face new socio-economic possibilities.

There is still, however, an increasing and urgent need for national and international co-operation to create new economic opportunities for local communities and indigenous peoples to effectuate the conservation and sustainable use of the Amazon region. Brazil will increase its capacity to enter into more productive and equitable biopartnerships if it creates a law and incentives to agroecological and permaculture productions. This would highlight its natural qualities and potentials giving it a long head start advantage.

CHAPTER TEN

FINAL CONCLUSION

The Convention on Biological Diversity established the sovereign rights of countries over their biological resources, as well as the conservation, sustainable use and equitable share of benefits arising from the utilisation of these resources. With the advent of the biotechnological era, those provisions became threats to the economic interests of developed countries and thus have been totally ignored. In many cases plants and traditional plant varieties of developing countries and traditional knowledge have been patented in developed countries. Furthermore, plant genetic material stored in international *ex situ* collections of plant genetic resources has been illegally patented or protected under plant variety protection systems. Hope Shand argues that the "real innovative genius behind recent drug developments has not come from the pharmaceutical industry but from indigenous knowledge."[1] Biotechnology firms have found through the indiscriminate use of patent laws a great new source of income and have no intention of equitably sharing it with source countries and those that contributed with their traditional knowledge.

It can be said that TRIPs was an attempt made by the biotechnological developed countries, especially the United States, to gain control over access and use of biological resources through the weaponry of patents. It seems a strategic tactic developed countries adopted to keep the world's economy, technology, plant varieties and genetic resources under their monopoly control. This is aggravated by the fact that patents in the United States are granted on wide sweeping monopoly claims that encompass not only the developed variety but its descendants and its genes as well. The pressure on countries to change their patent laws to allow the patenting of plant and animal varieties seems to be a trap to privatise biological diversity and traditional knowledge mainly found in developing countries.

Hurlbut notes a significant issue that proves the impossibility of having a global standardised IPR protection system. In his research, he discovered that intellectual property regimes differ naturally among countries due to their different historical and cultural way of viewing the ownership of ideas.[2] To harmonise all IPR protection systems of the world would mean to ignore part of each country's history and especially culture. Ironically, it would make history repeat itself too. Colonisation would return in the form of technologically rich countries ruling the lives of the technologically poor countries through the commercialisation of their patented products and processes.[3]

Article 27(2) of TRIPs allows Member States to exclude from patentability those inventions "the prevention within their territory of the commercial exploitation of which is necessary to protect ordre public or morality."[4] Furthermore, it specifies that this exclusion is justified and legal when it is necessary to avoid serious prejudice to the environment. The patenting of genetically engineered plants privatises those

---

[1] Shand, Hope; "No Cure for Patents. Biotech Patents Distort and Discourage Innovation and Increase Costs for Dubious Drugs"; RAFI Newsletter, 7 February 1997.
[2] Hurlbut, D.; "Fixing the Biodiversity Convention: Toward a Special Protocol for Related Intellectual Property"; 34 Nat. Resource. J. 1994; Spring; 379-409.
[3] Bhat refers to this type of colonialism as "intellectual colonialism". Bhat; "Trade-related intellectual property rights to biological resources: Socio-economic implications for developing countries"; 19 Ecological Economics, 1996; at p. 207.
[4] Article 27(2) of TRIPs.

resources and leads to monoculture cropping. A survey through US seed banks revealed that some non-commercial crop varieties, (i.e. chufas, martynia and rampion) have been lost entirely.[5] Therefore, following a logical reasoning, as patented crops increase, biological diversity decreases. This is probably the worst crime man can commit towards nature and towards himself because he stops evolution. As noted by Soule, "death is one thing; an end of birth is something else."[6]

If a breeder develops a plant variety that causes genetic erosion he should not receive any rights and rewards. On the contrary, he should be legally punished. In this sense, countries are advised to adopt a broad meaning for both public order and morality concepts. If patents on crops increase poverty in the country or if genetically altered patented crops cause an environmental catastrophe they ought to be cancelled because they go against public order, morality, environmental conservation and social welfare.

States are not obliged under TRIPs to allow patents on plant varieties. Compliance with Article 27(3)(b) of this agreement will vary from State to State. Several developing countries, such as Brazil, have adopted a *sui generis* system to protect plant varieties.[7] Others have been inclined to adopt an alternative form of protection which recognises farmers' rights and protects traditional knowledge. Developing countries with radical positions against IPR on living beings have developed *sui generis* systems, such as the Thammasat Resolution, that oppose the idea of living organisms being considered inventions in order to avoid legal monopolies on biological materials that could compromise the world's seed, food supply and health care systems.

Biodiversity-rich developing countries should protect their social and economic welfare by avoiding patents on plant and animal varieties and their parts as suggested by Correa. They can also use the *sui generis* option of protection to implement their standards, objectives and scope for plant variety protection, while at the same time duly recognise and compensate plant varieties developed through traditional knowledge as is the case of the CoFaB. Furthermore, their *sui generis* protection can adopt the objectives of the Convention on Biological Diversity and impose the conservation of biodiversity, sustainable use of its components and the equitable share of benefits that derive from their utilisation. This measure would place further safety rules on biotechnology, as well as promote the TRIPs objective of social and economic welfare in all sectors of society in their territory.

Trademarks and geographic indications can also inspire the creation of a *sui generis* system. For instance, Brazil, Malaysia and England form a biopartnership to create products derived from the traditional use of tropical forest biodiversity and adopt as a trademark the name BRAMAEN. England provides the technology and know-how to prepare inventories of each country's tropical forest. All products derived from this biopartnership will be labelled with a BRAMAEN sticker and an explanation to inform consumers that the product derives from the use of non-transgenic plants and associated traditional knowledge from tropical forests communities and that the biopartnership complies with the CBD provisions, including the equitable share of benefits with all stakeholders. BRAMAEN products would be sold competitively with its transgenic-free-traditional knowledge identification and consumers would have the liberty to decide what product to buy. In this way,

---
[5] Fowler, C. and Mooney, P; Shattering: Food, Politics and the Loss of Genetic Diversity; University of Arizona Press; 1990.
[6] Soule, M. E., Wilcox, B.A., (ed); Conservation Biology; Sunderland, MA; Sinaver Associates; 1980.
[7] See Chapter Eight of this book.

traditionally bred plant varieties and products derived from the use of traditional knowledge would be protected.

Brazil has a lot to learn from the biopartnerships presented in this book. The most imported lesson is for Brazil to keep its sovereignty over its genetic resources and this can only be accomplished by negotiating the golden eggs without selling the goose that laid them. This means that Brazil should form biopartnerships with NGOs, developed countries and foreign industries as long as they do not jeopardise its right of possession over its genetic diversity. Biopartnerships can be the motor for Brazil's sustainable development as long as certain requirements are met.

To start with, all biological material in Brazil should be collected by Brazilians who should be duly remunerated for their service. Such measure, as shown in the International Co-operative Biodiversity Group biopartnership in Suriname,[8] helps keep confidential the place where the plants were accessed, and thus prevents foreigners from illegally collecting Brazilian plants on their own. The second point is that Brazil should not sell its biodiversity as raw material because, despite all the medicinal value a plant might possess, as raw material it is worth very little. Brazil should follow the example of the Bioresources Development and Conservation Programme[9] and scientifically test and process its biological material to find its active components. In other words, it should add the maximum value it is capable of to its natural resources before selling licences allowing their use. In this way it negotiates the golden eggs and keeps the goose.

A third element to follow is that Brazilian citizens should form part of any research group that investigates any resource of Brazil's biodiversity for the purpose of developing medicines or any other product. This requirement not only trains and empowers Brazilians but also serves as a mechanism to control the action of foreigners in Brazilian territory.

Fourthly, Brazil should receive a percentage over the sales of products derived from its biodiversity. The amount should be negotiated when drafting each access contract. Fifth, if the traditional-knowledge-derived product, for instance a pharmaceutical, is to be patented, it should be a joint patent where the parties are the traditional healer or local person who discovered the medicinal properties of the plant and the scientist or industry which developed the whole process to make a medicine out of the medicinal plant.

A sixth requirement for the success of a biopartnership is the participation of local people. Ecooperation Foundation wisely noted that sustainable development cannot be achieved without the involvement of civil societies.[10] As a single leaf contains the entire genetic code of a plant, it is practically impossible to control the illegal exit of genetic resources without the assistance of local and indigenous communities. Thus, the biopartnerships Brazil undertakes must stimulate local people with professional opportunities, so that they will not easily facilitate the illegal exit of biological material in exchange for a bribe.

The seventh requisite of biopartnerships and one of the most important ones is the empowerment of Brazilians so that in the near future they can enter into more lucrative biopartnerships. For this to occur, Brazil should not only negotiate an up-front payment, a royalty percentage on the net sales of products derived from its

---

[8] See Chapter Seven, Section 4.5 of this book.
[9] See Chapter Seven, Section 4.4 of this book.
[10] See Chapter Seven, Section 4.3 of this book.

biodiversity, but also the transfer of technology and scientific and technological know-how and training programs. Brazil should use biopartnerships to prepare biodiversity inventories of its ecosystems following the example of INBio.[11] It should expand its botanical data-base to include information such as: medicinal traditional use, possible industrial application and so forth. All of these help Brazil increase its knowledge of what it has and how to use it.

The eighth requirement is to direct part of the benefits derived from products developed from the biopartnership to environmental conservation as biological diversity is the essence of such agreements. And finally, a ninth requisite of biopartnerships is that they be based on fairness, ethics, transparency, equitable share of benefits with all stakeholders, conservation of biodiversity and its sustainable use.

Brazil has the potential to be one of the world's great powers now that the world is recognising the value of biodiversity and traditional knowledge. It should wisely use this opportunity by undertaking biopartnerships which respect its sovereignty over its genetic resources and empowers Brazilians economically, scientifically and technologically in the short, medium and long-run.

Although some Brazilian governmental organs have started to biotechnologically create plant and animal varieties, underrating Brazil's potential of becoming the world's leading organic country, there are NGOs such as POEMA, and systems such as the Scenery System that value traditional knowledge and work closely with local and indigenous communities and with nature. POEMA's biopartnership with Mercedes Benz to create coconut fibre head-rests for the latter's trucks is a good example of how biopartnerships can intelligently use natural resources.

Thus, seeking inspiration from the Costa Rica, Bhutan, Benin and the Netherlands biopartnerships, Brazil should aim to form biopartnerships with organisations, the private sector and countries which are willing to sustainably use Brazil's biological diversity. Biopartnerships of this type not only "create new awareness"[12] but also create opportunities "to develop new products or programs"[13] where all parties mutually benefit and local people are empowered. The key to the success of biopartnerships is to use the differences between parties as complements to each other's social welfare and economic development.

The adoption of laws is a slow process. On the other hand, science and technology progress very quickly, widening the gap between laws and reality. Biopartnerships are thus a practical solution for the moment. However, they do not replace the necessity of adopting national and international laws to protect the rights of those that pursue traditional knowledge and recognise them as specialist in their one area. These laws will be an incentive to keep traditional knowledge alive and in continuous evolution as noted by the UNESCO Folklore Recommendations.[14]

Although the global partnership has still not been reached and patents on plant genetic resources and plant varieties work against it, the hope to see it accomplished still lives. This hope flourishes from the possibility of creating biopartnerships where parties mutually benefit from the equal distribution of rights and duties and with each

---

[11] See Chapter Seven, Section 4.2 of this book.
[12] The World Bank; "Strengthening Infrastructure for Social Development"; A Submission to the World Summit for Social Development Five Year Review; January 2000; at p. 12. This paper was produced by the staff oh Human Development Network under the stewardship of Mr. Eduardo Doryan, Vice President. Available on the internet in February 2000; located at http://www.un.org/esa/socdev/geneva2000/.
[13] Idem.
[14] See Chapter Five of this book.

other's contribution towards the biopartnership. Biopartnerships can thus serve as catalyst to the adoption of a right to protect traditional knowledge and all products derived from its use.

BIBLIOGRAPHY

BOOKS AND ARTICLES IN ENGLISH

- Acharya, Rohini; "Patenting of Biotechnology - GATT and the Erosion of the World's Biodiversity"; 25(6) Journal of World Trade 71, December 1991.
- Adelman, Martin J. and Baldi; "Prospects and limits of the Patent Provision in the TRIPs Agreement: The case of India"; 29(3) Vanderbilt Journal of Transnational Law, May 1996.
- Adler; "Can Patents Coexist with Breeders' Rights?"; 17(2) IIC 195, 1986.
- Alamgir, Mohiuddin; "The Challenges of Sustainable Development and of Food Security"; POEMAtropic No. 1, January/July 1998.
- Anne Bourjailly, Dale; "Market-Driven Instruments for a New era Adding Value to Bio-Resource Based Business"; paper presented at the conference "Bio-partnerships for Sustainable Development: commercialisation and the bio-industry challenge"; organised by UNCTAD; held 10-12 November 1998 in Lyon, France.
- Aubrey, J.M.; "A Justification of the Patent System"; in Phillips, Jeremy; Patents in Perspective, (ed); ESC Publishing Limited; Oxford; 1985.
- Barbier, E.; "The Concept of Sustainable Economic Development"; 14(2) Environmental Conservation, summer 1987.
- Bartelmus, P.; Environment and Development; Allen and Unwin; London; 1987.
- Barton, John; "Patent Scope in Biotechnology"; 26(5) IIC, 1995.
- Bate, Roger; "Organic Myths: The retreat from science"; 41 Biotechnology and Development Monitor, March 2000.
- Baumann, M., Bell, J., Koechlin, F., and Pimbert, M. (eds); The Life Industry: Biodiversity, People and Profits; Intermediate Technology Publications; London; 1996.
- BDCP; "ICBG Drug Development and Conservation of Biodiversity in Africa: A New Standard of Collaboration with Indigenous People"; in 1(1) Biological Resources, April 1996; located at BDCP website: http://www.bioresources.org.
- Bell, Janet; "Genetic engineering and biotechnology in industry"; in Baumann, M., Bell, J., Koechlin, F., Pimbert, M., (eds); The Life Industry: Biodiversity, People and Profits; Intermediate Technology Publications; London; 1996.
- Bell, Janet; Brazil's Transgenic Free Zone; Seedling; September 1999; located at: http://www.grain.org/publications/set99/set991.htm.
- Bennett, Philippe; "TRIPs - a Victory for US Industry"; Patent World, May 1994.
- Bennett, Virginia; "Plant Biotechnology"; in Sibley, Kenneth (ed); The Law and Strategy of Biotechnology Patents; Butterworth-Heinemann; London; 1994.
- Bhat, M. G.; "Trade-related intellectual property rights to biological resources: Socio-economic implications for developing countries"; 19 Ecological Economics 205, 1996.
- Birnie, P and Boyle, A.; International Law and the Environment; Clarendon Press; Oxford;1992.
- Boer, B.; "Institutionalising Ecologically Sustainable Development: the Roles of National, State, and Local Governments in Translating Grand Strategy into Action"; 31 Willamette Law Review, 1995; at p. 307-351.
- Bordwin, H.; "The Legal and Political Implications of the International Undertaking on Plant Genetic Resources"; 12 Ecology law Quarterly 1053, 1985.
- Brush, S. B.; "Farmer Conservation of New World Crops: the Case of Andean Potatoes"; 7 Diversity, 1991; pp. 75-79.
- Brush, S. B.; "Providing Farmers' Rights through *in Situ* Conservation of Crop Genetic Resources"; Commission on Plant Genetic Resources, First Extraordinary Session; 7-11 November 1994; Background Study Paper No. 3
- Brush, Steven; "The Issues of *In situ* Conservation of Crop Genetic Resources"; in Brush Steven; Genes in the Field; IPGRI; Rome; 1999.
- Burhenne-Guilmin, F. and Casey-Lefkowitz, S.; "The Convention on Biological Diversity: A Hard Won Global Achievement"; 3 YbIEL, 1992; pp. 43-59.

- Centre for International Environmental Law; "Comments on Improving Identification of Prior Art. Recommendations on Traditional Knowledge Relating to Biological Diversity"; Submitted to the United States Patent and Trademark Office; 2 August 1999; at p. 4. Located at http://ciel.org/ayahuascapatentcase.html.
- Christie, Andrew; "The Novelty Requirement in Plant Breeders' Rights Law"; 19(5) IIC 646.
- Cohen, J.;. Falconi, C.; Komen, J.; and Blakeney, M.; Proprietary Biotechnology Inputs and International Agricultural Research; Briefing Paper 39 of the International Service for National Agricultural Research; May 1998; located at http://www.cgiar.org/isnar/publications/briefing/bp39.htm.
- Cooter, R. and Ulen, T.; Law and Economics; Addison-Wesley; 2nd ed.; Reading, (Mass); 1997.
- Correa, Carlos; Intellectual Property Rights, the WTO and Developing Countries; Zed books Ltd.; London; 2000.
- Crespi, Stephen; "Patents and Plant Variety Rights: Is There an Interface Problem?"; 23(2) IIC 168, 1992.
- Cromwell, E.; "Local-level Seed Activities: opportunities ad challenges for regulatory frameworks"; in Tripp, Robert; New Seed and Old Laws (ed); Intermediate Technology Publications; London; 1997.
- Crouch, Martha; "How the Terminator Terminates"; located at http://www.bio.indiana.edu/people/terminator.html.
- Crucible Group; People, Plants and Patents; International Development Research Centre; Ottawa, Canada; 1994.
- Curry, Judith; The Patentability of Genetically Engineered Plants and Animals in the US and Europe; Intellectual Property Publishing Limited; London; 1987.
- Drahos, Peter; "Biotechnology Patents, Markets and Morality"; 21(9) European Intellectual Property Review 441, September 1999.
- Dreyfuss, R. C. & Zimmerman, D. L.; "Conveyors' Introduction: The Culture and Economics of Participation in an International Intellectual Property Regime"; 29 New York University Journal of International Law and Politics, Fall 1996 - Winter 1997.
- Dutfield, G.; Intellectual Property Rights, Trade and Biodiversity: Seeds and Plant Varieties; Earthscan; London; 2000.
- Dutfield, Graham; "Can the TRIPs Agreement Protect Biological and Cultural Diversity?"; ACTS Press; Nairobi, Kenya; 1997.
- Egziabher, Tewolde; "Patenting Life is Owning Life"; Available on http://:www.org.sg/souths/twn/focus.htm. Also available in Third World Resurgence No. 106; June 1999.
- Eisenberg, E.; "Genes, Patents, and Product Development"; 257 Science 903, 14 August 1992.
- Elias, Stephen; Patent, Copyright and Trademark; Nolo Press; Berkeley; 1997.
- Erdos, Jordan E.; "Current Legislative Efforts in Brazil to Regulate Access to Genetic Resources"; December 1999. Located at: http://www.sustain.org/biotech/library/admin/uploadedfiles/Current_Legislative_Efforts_in_Brazil_to_Regul.htm.
- Fernandes, Edesio; "Collective Interests in Brazilian Environmental Law"; in Dunkley, John (ed); Public Interest Perspectives in Environmental Law; Chancery Law Publishing Ltd; West Sussex, England; 1995.
- Fowler, C. and Mooney, P; "Shattering: Food, Politics and the Loss of Genetic Diversity"; University of Arizona Press; 1990.
- Frankel, O. H.; "Genetic Resources: Evolutionary and Social Responsibilities"; in Kloppenburg, Jack Jr. (ed); Seeds and Sovereignty - The Use and Control of Plant Genetic Resources; Duke University Press; London; 1988.
- Frankel, O. H.; "Genetic Resources: The founding years. II. The movement's constituent assembly"; 8 Diversity, 1985; pp 30-32.
- Frankel, O. H.; "Genetic Resources: The founding years. III. The long road to international board"; 9 Diversity, 1986; pp 30-33.
- Frankel, Otto; "Genetic Resources: The founding years. I. Early beginnings 1961-1966"; 7 Diversity, 1985; pp 26-29.

- Gaia Foundation and GRAIN; "Ten reasons not to join UPOV"; Global Trade in Conflict, No. 2; London/Barcelona; May 1998. Located at: http://www.grain.org/publications/gtbc/issue2.htm.
- Gana, Ruth; "Prospects for Developing Countries Under the TRIPs Agreement"; 29(4) Vanderbilt Journal of Transnational Law 735, October 1996.
- Ghijsen, Huib; "Plant Variety Protection in a Developing and Demanding World"; 36 Biotechnology and Development Monitor 2, September/December 1998.
- Glowka, L.; Burhenne-Guilmin, F.; Synge, H.; A Guide to the Convention on Biological Diversity; Environmental Policy and Law Paper No. 30; IUCN; Gland, Switzerland; 1994.
- Goldsmith, E. (ed); "Neem Tree Free!"; 30(4) The Ecologist, June 2000.
- Gollin, Michael; "An Intellectual Property Rights Framework for Biodiversity Prospecting"; in Reid, W., Laird, S.A.; Meyers, C.A; Gamez, R.; Sittenfeld, A.; Janzen, D.H.; Gollin, M.A; Juma, C.; (eds); Biodiversity Prospecting: Using Genetic Resources for Sustainable Development; World Resources Institute; Washington, D.C.; USA; 1993.
- GRAIN; "The Chickpea Scandal: Trust or Consequences?"; Seedling; March 1998; located at http://www.grain.org.
- GRAIN; "UPOV: Getting a Free Trips Ride?"; 13(6) Seedling, 1996. Located at: http://www.grain.org/publications/seedling.htm.
- Gray, Andrew; "Between the Spice of Life and the Melting Pot: Biodiversity Conservation and its Impact on Indigenous People"; IWGIA Document 70; Copenhagen; 1991.
- Greengrass, B.; "The 1991 Act of the UPOV Convention"; 13(12) EIPR, December 1991; pp. 466-472.
- Greengrass, Barry; "UPOV and the Protection of Plant Breeders - Past Developments, Future Perspectives"; 20(5) IIC, 1989; at pp. 622-636.
- Grossmann, R.; "Equalising the Flow: Institutional Restructuring of Germplasm Exchange"; in Kloppenburg Jr., Jack (ed); in Kloppenburg, Jack Jr. (ed); Seeds and Sovereignty - The Use and Control of Plant Genetic Resources; Duke University Press; London; 1988.
- Groves, Peter; Sourcebook on Intellectual Property Law; Cavendish Publishing Limited; London; 1997.
- Guérin-McManus, M., Famolare, L., Bowles, I., Malone, S., Mittermeier, R., Rosenfeld, A.; "Bioprospecting in Practice: A Case Study of the Suriname ICBG Project and Benefits Sharing under the Convention on Biological Diversity"; posted on CBD website in 1998: http://www.biodiv.org.
- Handl, G.; "Environmental Security and Global Change: The Challenge to International Law"; 1 Yb.I.E.L. 1990.
- Hart, Tina; Fazzani, Linda; Intellectual Property Law; Macmillan Press Ltd; London; 1997.
- Hassan, Sandro; "Ornamental Plant Variety Rights: A Recent Italian Judgement"; 18(2) IIC, 1987; pp. 219-222.
- Hitchcock, R. K.; "International Human Rights, the Environment, and Indigenous Peoples"; 5 Colorado Journal of International Environmental Law & Policy 1, 1994.
- Ho, Mae-Wan; "Special Safety Concerns of Transgenic Agriculture ad Related Issues"; paper presented at the International Seminar on the Right of Biodiversity held in Brasilia, Brazil; 11-14 May 1999. Located at:
http://www.cjf.gov.br/pages/SENbiodiversidade_textos_slides.htm; available in June 1999.
- Hosken, L. & Steranka, K.; A Tribute to Forest People, Gaia Foundation; London; 1990.
- Hurlbut, David; "Fixing the Biodiversity Convention: Toward a Special Protocol for Related Intellectual Property"; 34 Natural Resource Journal 379, 1994.
- INBio; "INBio-Merck Research Agreement Renewal/Questions and Answers". Sent as electronic mail attachment by Priscilla Hurtado, askinbio@inbio.ac.cr; 1999.
- International Federation of Organic Agriculture Movements; "Background Paper of the Neem Challenge"; located at http://www.ifoam.org/press/neem_back.html.
- Iwu, Maurice and Laird, Sarah; "The International Co-operative Biodiversity Group Drug Development and Biodiversity Conservation in Africa: Case Study of a Benefit-Sharing Plan"; February 1998; case-study submitted in response to the Call for Benefit Sharing Case Studies by the Secretariat of the Convention on Biological Diversity; posted on CBD website in 1998: http://www.biodiv.org.

- Iwu; Maurice; "Development of Medicinal Plants Through Strategic Business Alliances: Case Study from West Africa", presented by Maurice Iwu at the conference "Bio-partnerships for Sustainable Development: commercialisation and the bio-industry challenge"; organised by UNCTAD; held 10-12 November 1998 in Lyon, France.
- Jackson, J.; The World Trade Organisation; Royal Institute of International Affairs; London; 1998
- Jeremy Carew-Reid et al., Strategies for National Sustainable Development: A Handbook for Their Planning and Implementation; IUCN, IIED, Earthscan; 1994.
- Johnston, S.; "Conservation Role of Botanical Gardens and Gene Banks"; 2 RECIEL, 1993.
- Johnston, Sam; "Sustainability, Biodiversity and International Law" in Redgwell and Bowman (eds); International Law and the Conservation of Biological Diversity; Kluwer Law International; Great Britain; 1995.
- Juma, C.; The Gene Hunters: Biotechnology and the Scramble for Seeds; 1989; London; Zed Books.
- Kadidal, S.; "Subject-matter imperialism? Biodiversity, foreign prior art and the neem patent controversy"; 37(2) Idea: The Journal of Law and Technology, 1997; at pp.371-403.
- Kerry ten Kate and Amanda Collis; "The Genetic Resources Recognition Fund of the University of California, Davis" case-study was prepared by Kerry ten Kate and Amanda Collis on behalf of the Royal Botanic Gardens, Kew in London, and submitted to the Executive Secretary of the Convention on Biological Diversity. Copy accessed through personal contact with Kerry ten Kate of the Royal Botanic Gardens, Kew.
- Kloppenburg, Jack Jr. and Kleinman, Daniel; "Plant Genetic Resources: The Common Bowl"; in Kloppenburg, Jack Jr. (ed); Seeds and Sovereignty - The Use and Control of Plant Genetic Resources; Duke University Press; London; 1988.
- Kloppenburg, Jack; "Changes in the Genetic Supply Industry"; in Baumann, M., Bell, J., Koechlin, F., Pimbert, M., (eds); The Life Industry. Biodiversity, people and Profits; Intermediate Technology Publications; London; 1996.
- Kocken, J., Roozendaal, G. Van; "The Neem Tree Debate"; 30 Biotechnology and Development Monitor, March 1997; at pp. 8-11.
- Kothari, A. & Anuradha, R. V.; "Biodiversity, Intellectual Property Rights, and the GATT Agreement: How to Address the Conflicts?"; 2 Biopolicy, Paper 4, PY97004, 1997.
- Kothari, A. & Bhatia, S.; "Access to Biological Resources: Some Proposed Actions by Countries and COP2"; Indian Institute of Public Administration; 1995. This article can be ordered through the following e-mail: akothari@unv.ernet.in.
- LaClavière; "The Convention of Paris of December 2, 1961, for the Protection of New varieties of Plants and the International Union for the Protection of New Varieties of Plants"; 4 Ind. Prop., 1965; at pp. 227-228.
- Lama, Abraham; "Ills of Unregulated Medicinal Plant Exports"; IPS News Wires; February 2000; located at http://www.ips.org.
- Lawrence, E., Jackson, A., Jackson, J.; Longman Dictionary of Environmental Science; Longman; Essex; England; 1998.
- Lehmann, Volker; "Patents on Seed Sterility Threatens Seed Saving"; 35 Biotechnology and Development Monitor, June 1998.
- Leskien, D. & Flitner, M.; "The TRIPs Agreement and Intellectual Property Rights for Plant Varieties"; in GRAIN; Signposts to *Sui Generis* Rights; February 1998. Located at: http://www.grain.org/publications/signposts.htm.
- Marett, Paul; Intellectual Property Law; Sweet & Maxwell; London; 1996.
- Martin, Brian; "Against Intellectual Property"; located at: http://www.uow.edu.au/arts/sts.bmartin/pubs/95psa.html.
- McNally, Ruth and Wheale, Peter; "Biotechnology and Biodiversity - Comparative Advantages in the New Global Order"; 26(5) The Ecologist, September/October 1996.
- Meibom, Wolfgang von and Pitz, Johann; "Broad Biotech Claims"; Patent World; August 1996.
- Miranda, Santos and Lewontin; "Genetics, plant breeding and patents: conceptual contradictions and practical problems in protecting biological innovations"; Plant Genetic Resources Newsletter, No. 112, 1997; International Plant Genetic Resources Institute (IPGRI); Rome.

- Mitschein, Thomas, Miranda, Pedro; POEMA: A Proposal of Sustainable Development in Amazonia, Belem-Para-Brazil; Federal University of Para; Para, Brazil; 1996.
- Mooney, Pat; "The Parts of Life. Agricultural Biodiversity, Indigenous Knowledge, and the Role of the Third System"; Development Dialogue, Special Issue; 1998; at pp. 152-154.
- Moufang, Rainer; "Protection for Plant Breeding and Plant Varieties - A Frontier of Patent Law"; Nordiskt Immateriellt Rattsskydd; 1992; pp 330-348.
- Mulvany, Patrick; "TRIPS, Biodiversity and Commonwealth Countries: capacity building priorities for the 1999 review of TRIPS article 27.3(b)"; Commonwealth Secretariat; London; 1998.
- Myers, Norman; "Draining the Gene Pool: The Causes, Course and Consequences of Genetic Erosion"; in Kloppenburg, Jr. (ed); Seeds and Sovereignty; Duke University Press; London; 1988.
- Nijar, Gurdial Singh; "In Defence of Indigenous Knowledge and Biodiversity"; Third World Network; Malaysia; 1995. Copies can be ordered by the following e-mail: twn@igc.apc.org.
- Noiville, C.; "Patenting Life - trends in the US and Europe"; in Baumann et al (eds); The Life Industry; Intermediate Technology Publications; London; 1996.
- Nott, Robin; "Plants and animals: Why they should be protected by patents and variety rights"; Patent World 45, July/August 1993.
- O'Brien, D. P.; "Patents: An Economist's View"; in Phillips, Jeremy; Patents in Perspective, (ed); ESC Publishing Limited; Oxford; 1985.
- O'Shaughnessy, Brian; "Patentable Subject Matter"; in Sibley, Kenneth (ed); The Law and Strategy of Biotechnology Patents; Butterworth-Heinemann; London; 1994.
- Peters, P. & Schrijver, N. & Waart, P.; "Responsibility of States I Respect of the Exercise of Permanent Sovereignty Over Natural Resources"; 36 Netherlands International Law Review; 1989.
- POEMA, Alliances in Defence of Life; Universidade Federal do Para, Nucleo de Meio Ambiente; copies my asked from poema@ufpa.br.
- Posey, D, & Dutfield, G.; Beyond Intellectual Property; International Development Research Centre; Ottawa, Canada; 1996.
- Posey, D. (ed); Cultural and Spiritual Values of Biodiversity; Intermediate Technology Publications; London; 2000.
- Prakash, S.; "Country Study: India"; 1998; located at World Bank/ WTO Trade and Development Centre website http://www.itd.org/issues/india6.htm.
- Price, S.; "Public and Private Plant Breeding"; 17 Nature Biotechnology, October 1999. Located at: http://biotech.nature.com/.
- Primo Braga, C., Fink, C., Sepulveda, C.; "Intellectual Property Rights and Economic Development"; Background Paper to the World Development Report 1998.
- RAFI News Release; "Plant Breeders' Wrongs Righted in Australia"; 11 November 1998; http://www.rafi.org.
- RAFI, "Recent Australian Claims to Indian and Iranian Chickpeas Countered by NGOs and ICRISAT"; News Release 1/6/98; http://www.rafi.org.
- RAFI; "1996 Biopiracy Update: US Patent Claim Exclusive Monopoly Control of Food Crop, Medicinal Plants, Soil Microbes and Traditional Knowledge from the South"; RAFI Communique; December 1996; http://www.rafi.org.
- RAFI; "Aussies 'pirate' others genius?"; Press release, 1 February 1998; http://www.rafi.org.
- RAFI; "Australia's Unresolved Plant Piracy Problems"; RAFI News 4/12/99; http://www.rafi.org.
- RAFI; "CGIAR Urges Halt to Granting of Intellectual Property Rights for Designated Plant Germplasm"; posted on Web 11 February 1998; http://www.rafi.org.
- RAFI; "Doing Well by Doing Little or Nothing? A partial list of varieties under RAFI investigation"; 1998; http://www.rafi.org.
- RAFI; "International Research Centre (ICARDA) Breaks Trust"; News Release 2/2/98; http://www.rafi.org.
- RAFI; "No Cure for Patents. Biotech Patents Distort and Discourage Innovation and Increase Costs for Dubious Drugs"; RAFI Newsletter, 2.7.97; http://www.rafi.org.

- RAFI; "RAFI Genotype on Recent Terminator Developments"; 2 July 1999; http://www.rafi.org.
- RAFI; "Terminator 2 Years Later: Suicide Seeds on the Fast Track"; RAFI Communique February/March 2000; http://www.rafi.org.
- RAFI; "The Australian PBR scandal: UPOV meets a scandal 'down under' by burying its head in the sand"; RAFI Communique January-February 1998; http://www.rafi.org.
- RAFI; "The Terminator Technology"; RAFI Communique March-April 1998; http://www.rafi.org.
- RAFI; "US Patent on New Genetic Technology Will Prevent Farmers from Saving Seed"; 11 March 1998; http://www.rafi.org.
- Rana, R. S.; "Access to Genetic Resources and Equitable Benefit Sharing: The Indian Experience"; 1(2) RIS Biotechnology an Development Review; April 1998.
- Rappert, Brian; "The US Extension of Plant Variety Protection: a critical evaluation"; 22(2) Science and Policy, April 1995.
- Reid, W., Laird, S., Gámez, R., Sittenfeld, A., Janzen, D., Gollin, M., Juma, C.; "A New Lease on Life"; in Reid, W., Laird, S., Meyer, C., Gámez, R., Sittenfeld, A., Janzen, D., Gollin, M., Juma, C.; Biodiversity Prospecting: Using Genetic Resources for Sustainable Development; World Resources Institute; USA; 1993.
- Reid, W.V.; "Genetic Resources and Sustainable Agriculture: Creating Incentives for Local Innovation and Adaptation"; Biopolicy International No. 2; African Centre for Technology Studies; Nairobi & Maastricht, 1992.
- Rissler, Jane and Mellon, Margaret; The Ecological Risks of Engineered Crops; Massachusetts Institute of Technology; Massachusetts; 1996.
- Roberts, Tim; "Patenting Plants Around the World"; 10 EIPR 531, 1996.
- Roht-Arriaza, Naomi; "Of Seeds and Shamans: the Appropriation of the Scientific and Technological Knowledge of Indigenous and Local Communities"; 17 Michigan Journal of International Law, 1996.
- Rose, G.; "International Regimes for the Conservation and Control of Plant Genetic Resources"; in Bowman, Michael and Redgwell, Catherine (eds); International Law and the Conservation of Biological Diversity; Kluwer Law International; London; 1996.
- Rosecrance, R. et al.; "Whither Interdependence"; 31(3) International Organisation; at 425; 1977.
- Roth, Bernhard; "Current Problems in the Protection of Inventions in the Field of Plant Biotechnology – A Position Paper"; 18(1) IIC 41, 1987.
- Rubin, S. M. & Fish, S. C.; "Biodiversity Prospecting: Using Innovate Contractual Provisions to Foster Ethnobotanical Knowledge, Technology and Conservation"; 5 Colorado. Journal of International Environmental Law and Policy 1994.
- Sahai, Suman; Gene Campaign; "Protection of New Plant Varieties: a Developing Country Alternative"; XXXIV Economic and Political Weekly, Nos. 10 & 11; March 1999.
- Sahai; Suman; "An Alternative to UPOC called CoFaB"; 7 March 1999. Available at http://ds.dial.pipex.com/ukfg/UKabc/cofab.htm.
- Salas, Maria; "'The technicians only believe in science and cannot read the sky': the cultural dimension of the knowledge conflict in the Andes"; in Scoones and Thompson, Beyond Farmer First; Intermediate Technology Publications; London; 2000.
- Sawnson, T.; "The Reliance of Northern Economies on Southern Biodiversity: Biodiversity as Information"; 17 Ecological Economics, 1996; pp. 1-8.
- Scalise, David and Nugent, Daniel; "International Intellectual Property Protections for Living Matter: Biotechnology, Multinational Conventions and the Exception for Agriculture"; 27 Case W. Res. J. Int'l L. 83, 1995.
- School of International and Public Affairs Columbia University; "Access to Genetic Resources: An Evaluation of the Development and Implementation of Recent Regulation and Access Agreements"; Columbia University; Environmental Policy Studies Working Paper No. 4, Prepared for the Biodiversity Action Network; June 1999.
- Schrell, Andreas; "Are Plants (Still) Patentable"; 4 EIPR, 1996.
- Sedjo, Roger A.; "Property Rights and the Protection of Plant Genetic Resources"; in Kloppenburg, Jr. (ed); Seeds and Sovereignty; Duke University Press; London; 1988.
- Shand, Hope; "No Cure for Patents. Biotech Patents Distort and Discourage Innovation and Increase Costs for Dubious Drugs"; RAFI Newsletter, 7 February 1997.

- Sharma, Devinder; "Biotechnology and Food Security in Third World"; 1(2) Biotechnology and Development Review, April 1998; Research and Information System for the Non-Aligned and Other Developing Countries; New Delhi.
- Shiva, V.; "The Losers' Perspective"; Baumann, M., Bell, J., Koechlin, F., Pimbert, M., (eds); The Life Industry. Biodiversity, people and Profits; Intermediate Technology Publications; London; 1996.
- Shiva, Vandana and Holla-Bhar, Radha; "Intellectual Piracy and the Neem Tree"; 23(6) The Ecologist 223, November/December 1993.
- Sibley, Kenneth; "Patent Claims"; in Sibley, Kenneth (ed); The Law and Strategy of Biotechnology Patents; Butterworth-Heinemann; London; 1994.
- Soule, M. E., Wilcox, B.A., (ed); Conservation Biology; Sunderland, MA; Sinaver Associates; 1980.
- Spruce, Richard; "On some remarkable narcotics of the Amazon Valley and Orinoco, Ocean highways"; 1(55) The Geographic Review, 1873; pp. 184-193.
- Sterckx, Sigrid; Biotechnology, Patents and Morality; Ashgate; Hants, England; 1997.
- Straus, Joseph; "Protection of Inventions in Plants"; 20(5) IIC, 1989; at p. 619.
- Straus, Joseph; "The Relationship Between Plant Variety Protection and Patent Protection for Biotechnological Inventions from an International Viewpoint"; 18(6) IIC 723, 1987.
- Straus; "Industrial Property Protection: Biotechnological Invention, Analysis of Certain Basic Issues"; World Intellectual Property Organisation BIG/281.
- Swaminathan, M. S.; "South and Southeast Asia Regional Workshop on Access to Genetic Resources and Traditional Knowledge"; Chennai (Madras), India; 22-25 February 1998; in I(2) Biotechnology and Development Review, 1998; New Delhi.
- Swanson, Timothy and Goeschl, Timo; "Optimal Genetic Resource Conservation: *in situ* and *ex situ*"; in Brush, Stephen (ed); Genes in the Field; IPGRI; Rome, Italy; 1999.
- Tansey, G.; "Trade, Intellectual Property, Food and Biodiversity"; Quaker United Nations Office; Geneva. Located at http://www.quaker.org.com.
- UPOV; "About UPOV"; located at: http://www.upov.int/eng/content.htm.
- UPOV; "Modern Biotechnology"; located at: http://www.upov.int/eng/content.htm.
- UPOV; "The Breeding of Plant Varieties"; located at: http://www.upov.int/eng/content.htm.
- UPOV; "The Need for Legal Protection for New Plant Varieties"; located at: http://www.upov.int/eng/content.htm.
- UPOV; "The Need for New Plant Varieties"; located at http://www.upov.int/eng/content.htm.
- Vellve, R.; "The Decline of diversity in European Agriculture"; 23(2) The Ecologist, March/April 1993.
- Verma, S. K.; "TRIPs and Plant Variety Protection in Developing Countries"; 6 EIPR 281, 1995.
- Weiss, Edith; Environmental Change and International Law; United Nations University Press; Tokyo, Japan; 1992.
- Wiser, Glen; "PTO Rejection of the 'Ayahuasca' Patent Claim"; November 1999; located at http://ciel.org/ayahuascapatentcase.html.
- Woodliffe, John; "Biodiversity and Indigenous Peoples"; in Bowman, Michael and Redgwell, Catherine (eds); International Law and the Conservation of Biological Diversity; Kluwer Law International; London; 1996.
- Zerner, C. and Kennedy, K.; "Equity Issues in Bioprospecting"; in Baumann M., Bell, J., Koechlin, F., Pimbert, M., (eds); The Life Industry. Biodiversity, people and Profits; Intermediate Technology Publications; London; 1996.
- Zysman, J., Tyson, L., Dosi, G., & Cohen, S.; "Trade Technology and National Competition"; in Technology and Investment: Crucial Issues for the 1990s.

BOOKS AND ARTICLES IN FOREIGN LANGUAGE

- Adeodato, Sérgio; "O Vigor do Campo"; in the Brazilian magazine Época No. 102, 1 May 2000.
- Alvarenga, T.; "A Destruiçao da Amazonia"; in the supplement Veja Especial Amazonica, 24 December 1997, of the Brazilian Magazine Veja Ano 30-No. 51.
- Alvarenga, T.; "A Destruiçao da Amazonia"; in the supplement Veja Especial Amazonica, 24 December 1997, of the Brazilian Magazine Veja Ano 30-No. 51.
- Alvim; Código do Consumidor Comentado; 2 edition; RT; Sao Paulo; 1995.
- Andrade E. N., Brito, Andrade E. O., Neves, Cavalcante, Oberlander, Cardoso, Okimura, Callaway, Mckenna, Grob et al.; "Farmacologia Humana da Hoasca, Chá Obtido de Plantas Alucinógenas Usado em Contexto Ritual no Brasil: parte clínica"; Copy obtained through personal contact with the Centro de Estudos Médicos-UDV, Brasil.
- Araujo, Rosalina Correa de; Direitos da Natureza no Brasil; Liber Juris; Rio de Janeiro, Brazil; 1992.
- Arcanjo, Francisco Eugênio M.; "Convenção sobre Diversidade Biológica e Projeto de Lei do Senado N° 306/95: Soberania, Propriedade e Acesso aos Recursos Genéticos"; in Benjamin, Antonio H. V. (ed) 5 Anos após a ECO-92; proceedings of the 1997 International Conference on Environmental Law held by the Lawyers for a Green Planet Institute; São Paulo, Brazil; 1997.
- Brazilian newspaper Estadao; "Soja Alterada da Monsanto Não Resiste a Clima Quente"; 22 November 1999.
- Brazilian newspaper Jornal da Tarde; "Madeira: R$ 10 mil em Multas"; in, 20 August 1999; at p. 18A.
- Campos, Otavio & Brito, Glacus; "Ayahuasca (Hoasca): Historico, Botanica, Fitoquimica, Farmacologia, Efeitos Clinicos e Neuropsicologicos"; provided by the Centro de Estudos Médicos - UDV; Sao Paulo, Brazil.
- Cardenas, M., Correa , H., & Baron, M. (eds); Derecho Territoriales Indígenas y Ecología del America; Bogota; CEREC and Gaia Foundation; London; 1991.
- Centro Espírita Benificente Uniao do Vegetal; Uniao do Vegetal: Hoasca, Fundamentos e Objetivos; Sede Geral; 1989.
- Correa, Carlos; "Derechos Soberanos y de Propiedad sobre los Recursos Fitogenéticos"; prepared at the request of the Secretariat of the FAO Commission on Plant Genetic Resources; First Extraordinary meeting of the Commission on Plant Genetic Resources; Rome; 7-11 November 1994.
- EMBRAPA; Atlas do Meio Ambiente do Brasil; Terra Viva; Brasilia, DF; 1994.
- Fabiano, Ruy; "Chá Hoasca É Inofensivo À Saúde"; in the Brazilian newspaper Correio Braziliense; 10 July 1996.
- Freitas, Vladimir Passos and Freitas, Gilberto Passos; Crimes Contra a Natureza; Editora Revista dos Tribunais Ltda.; Sao Paulo, Brazil; 1992.
- Furtado, Lucas Rocha; Sistema de Propriedade Industrial no Direito Brasileiro; Brasilia Juridica; Brasilia; 1996.
- García, César; "Manual de Derecho Romano"; Editorial Tecnos, S.A.; second edition; Madrid; 1996.
- Gomes, Orlando; "Condicoes Gerais dos Contratos"; De. Revista dos Tribunais; Sao Paulo, Brazil; 1972.
- Grob, McKenna, Callaway, Brito, Neves, Oberlander, Saide, Labigalint, Tacla, Miranda, Strassman, Boone; "Farmacologia Humana da Hoasca, Planta Alucinógena Usada em Context Ritual no Brasil: Efeitos Psicológicos"; 15(2) Informaçao Psiquiatrica, 1996; at pp. 39-45.
- Gullo, C. and Pereira, C.; "A Cura no Jardim"; in the Brazilian magazine Isto É, No. 1513; 30 September 1998.
- Iglesias, Juan; Derecho Romano; Editorial Ariel; sixth edition; Barcelona; 1972.
- Lerrer, Débora; As Portas de Uma Outra Dimensao; Revista Planeta; 23 April 2000. Located at http://www.terra.com.br/planetanaweb/transcendendo/mente/outra_dimensao.htm.
- Luna, L. E.; "Appendices"; 46(1) America Indigena, 1986; pp. 247-251.

- Luna, L. E.; "Vegitalismo: Shamanism Among the Mestizo Population of the Peruvian Amazon"; Almquist and Weiskell International; Stockholm; 1986.
- Machado, Paulo Affonso Leme; Direito Ambiental Brasileiro; Malheiros Editores Ltda.; Sao Paulo, Brazil; 1992.
- Magalhaes, Juraci; A Ocupaçao Desordenada da Amazonia e Seus Efeitos Economicos Socias e Ecologicos; Gráfica e Editora Competa Ltda.; Brasilia, Brazil; 1990.
- Mateo, Nader, Tamayo; "Utilización de la biodiversidad con Fines Económicos"; Prospección de Biodiversidad; INBio; Costa Rica; Received by e-mail by Carolina Roldan (croldan@inbio.ac.cr).
- POEMA; Desenvolvimento e Conservaçao na Amazonia Brazileira: Inventario e Analise de Projetos"; For a copy of this publication send and e-mail to: poema@ufpa.br.
- Savini, Marcos; "Florestas Tropicais Fora dos Eixos"; Correio Braziliense; Brasilia; 5 December 1999; Mundo.
- Silva, Jose Afonso da; Direito Ambiental Constitucional; Malheiros Editores Ltda.; Sao Paulo; 1994.
- Tachinardi, Maria Helena; A Guerra das Patentes; Paz e Terra; Sao Paulo, Brazil; 1993.
- Varella, Flavia; "Calderao da Vida"; in the supplement Veja Especial Amazonica, 24 December 1997, of the Brazilian Magazine Veja Ano 30-No. 51.
- Varella, M., Fontes, E., Rocha, F.; "Biossegurança e Biodiversidade: Contexto Científico e Regulamentar"; Del Rey Editors; Belo Horizonte, Brazil; 1999.
- Veiga Rios, A. V.; "Biossegurança - Aspectos Jurídicos e Políticos"; paper presented at the International Congress on the Right of Biodiversity held in Brasilia, Brazil; 11-14 May 1999.

INTERNATIONAL AND REGIONAL CONVENTIONS, LAWS AND DOCUMENTS

- African Convention on the Conservation of Nature and Natural Resources, text in 1001 UNTS 3 and in A. Kiss, ed., 1 Selected Multilateral Treaties in the Field of the Environment, UNEP, 1983, at 207.
- Agenda 21; UN Doc. A/CONF. 151/26/REV. 1, Vols. I-III; 1992.
- Agreement on Trade-Related Aspects of Intellectual Property Rights, Including Trade in Counterfeit Goods; Annex 1C, Uruguay Round, 1994, WTA/GATT. TRIPs entered into force on 1 January 1996. 33 I.L.M. 1125, 1994.
- ASEAN Agreement on the Conservation of Nature and Natural Resources, Kuala Lumpur, 1985, text in I. Rummel-Bulska & S. Osafo, eds., 2 Selected Multilateral Treaties in the Field of the Environment 343, UNEP, 1991, at 343.
- CGRFA; Eighth Regular Session of the CGRFA; Revision of the International Undertaking on Plant Genetic Resources: Legal and Institutional Options; Rome 19-23 April 1999.
- Conference of the Parties - Decision 11/15 of the Second Session of the Conference of the Parties to the Convention on Biological Diversity, Jakarta, Indonesia, 6-17 November 1995.
- Convention Concerning the Protection of the World Cultural and Natural Heritage, text in 11 ILM 1358, 1972.
- Convention on Biological Diversity; text in 31 ILM 822, 1992 and 3 YbIEL 663 et seq., 1992.
- Convention on International Trade in Endangered Species of Wild Fauna and Flora, (known as CITES), unamended text in 12 ILM 1055, 1973.
- Convention on Migratory Species of Wild Animals, text in 19 ILM 15, 1980.
- Convention on Nature and Wildlife Preservation in the Western Hemisphere, 1940; text in 161 UNTS 193.
- Convention on the Conservation of European Wildlife and Natural Habitats (Berne, 1979), text in ETS 104, UKTS 56, 1982, Cmnd. 8738, and in A. Kiss, ed., 1 Selected Multilateral Treaties in the Field of the Environment, UNEP, 1983, at 509.

- Convention on Wetlands of International Importance, (known as Ramsar Convention), text in 11 ILM 963, 1972.
- Council of the European Union; Council Regulation No. 40/94 of 20 December 1993 on the Community Trademark.
- Electronic versions of the 1961, 1978, and 1991 UPOV Conventions can be found at http://www.upov.int/eng/convntns/; accessed in 2000. The texts of these conventions are available in printed form on application to the Office of UPOV: 34, Chemin des Colombettes, CH-1211, Geneva 20, Switzerland.
- European Biotechnology Patent Directive; Directive 98/44/EC of the European Parliament and of the Council of 6 July 1998 on the legal protection of biotechnological inventions; 1998 O.J. L 213; at 0013–0021.
- European Patent Convention; Munich, 5 October 1973. It entered into force on 7 October 1977. Text found Christie, Andrew and Gare, Stephen; Blackstone's Statutes on Intellectual Property; Blackstone Press Limited; London; 4th edition; 1998; pp. 423-432.
- FAO Conference Resolution 4/89; Adopted 29 November 1989; 25 Session of the FAO Conference; FAO, Rome.
- FAO Conference Resolution 5/89; Adopted 29 November 1989; 25 Session of the FAO Conference; Rome.
- FAO Resolution 3/91; Adopted 25 November 1991. Report of the Conference of FAO, C91/REP, 26 Session, Rome, 9-27 November 1991.
- FAO Resolution 7/93; Adopted in 27th Session of the FAO Conference in November 1993. The report on the implementation of Resolution 7/93 is found in document C 95/INF/19-Sup. 1
- FAO; Background Documentation for the International Technical Conference on Plant Genetic Resources; Leipzig, Germany; 17-23 June 1996.
- FAO; Fourth International Technical Conference on Plant Genetic Resources; Leipzig, Germany; 17-23 June 1996.
- FAO; International Code of Conduct for Plant Germplasm Collecting and Transfer; FAO Conference Resolution 8/93. Adopted by the 27th session of the FAO Conference, November 1993.
- FAO; Progress Report on the Global System for the Conservation and Utilisation of Plant Genetic Resources for Food and Agriculture; Document C 95/INF/19 of the Conference of the FAO, 28th Session, 20 October-2 November 1995.
- FAO; Report of the International Technical Conference on Plant Genetic Resources; FAO ITCPGR/96/ REP; Leipzig, Germany; 17-23 June 1996.
- FAO; Report on the State of the World's Plant Genetic Resources for Food and Agriculture; prepared for the International Technical Conference on Plant Genetic Resources; Leipzig, Germany; 17-23 June 1996.
- Ficsor, Mihaly; "Attempts to Provide International Protection for Folklore by Intellectual Property Rights"; in the codification of the texts of speeches and papers presented at the UNESCO-WIPO World Forum on the Protection of Folklore, held in Phuket, Thailand; 8-10 April 1997; at p. 213.UNESCO Publication No. CLT/CIC/98/1; WIPO Publication No. 758(E/F/S).
- Final Act Embodying the Results of the Uruguay Round of Multilateral Trade Negotiations. Marrakech, 15 April 1994. Reprinted in The Results of the Uruguay Round of Multilateral Trade Negotiations - The Legal Texts 2-3; GATT Secretariat (ed); 1994. 33 I.L.M. 1125, 1994.
- General Agreement on Tariffs and Trade; 30 October 1947; 61 Stat. A-11, T.I.A.S. 1700, 55 U.N.T.S. 194.
- ILO Convention 169; ILO International Labour Conference, 7th Session; Geneva; 27 June 1989. Reprinted in 28 ILM 1384 et seq, 1989.
- IPGRI: APO Newsletter - Regional No. 27, December 1998. Located at IPGRI website; http://www.ipgri.cgiar.org.
- IPGRI; "The Agreement on Trade-Related Aspects of Intellectual Property Rights (TRIPs) – A Decision Check List"; Rome; 1999; Located at: http://www.cgiar.org/ipgri.
- OAU Draft Model Legislation on Community Rights and on Access To Biological Resources; Accepted as Doc.CM/2075 (LXVIII) ADD.1; Attached to OAU Resolution on the Draft Law and Convention on Community Rights and on Access to Biological Resources; Ougadougou, June 1998; Doc. CM/2075 (LXVIII).

- OAU/STRC/DEPA/KIPO; Workshop on Medicinal Plants and Herbal Medicine in Africa: Policy Issues on Ownership, Access and Conservation; held in Nairobi, Kenya, on 14-17 April 1997.
- Paris Convention; 20 March 1883. In 1891 the Paris Convention for the Protection of Industrial Property was completed by an Interpretative Protocol in Madrid. It was then revised at Brussels in 1900, at Washington in 1911, at the Hague in 1925, at London in 1934, at Lisbon in 1958 and at Stockholm in 1967, and it was amended in 1979. U.N.T.S. No. 11851, vol. 828, pp.305-388.
- Patent Co-operation Treaty, 19 June 1970. It was amended 2 October 1979 and 3 February 1984 and is in force since January 1985. Available at World Intellectual Property Organisation website: www.wipo.org/eng/main.htm.
- PCT International Search Guidelines, PCT Gazette, Chapter VI, paragraph 1.2; Special Issue No. 06/1998, 8 October 1998. Available at www.wipo.org/eng/main.htm.
- Report of the 27th Session of FAO Conference; Appendix F; 6-24 November 1993; Rome.
- Rio Declaration; General Assembly Resolution 47/190; 1992. Reprinted in 31 I.L.M. 874, 1992.
- Stockholm Declaration on the Human Environment; U.N. Doc. A/CONF.48/14 Corr., at 3. Reprinted in 11 I.L.M. 1416, 1972.
- Third Business Forum of the Americas; Working Group VII: Technology and Intellectual Property Rights; Belo Horizonte, Brazil; May 1997.
- Third Session of Commission on Sustainable Development; UN E/CN.17/1995/14; 11-28 April 1995.
- UN Draft Declaration on Indigenous Rights as agreed upon by the members of the Working Group at its Eleventh Session; Published by the United Nations, 23 August 1993; See also UN E/CN.4/1995/2. E/CN.4/Sub.2/1994/56; 26 August 1994.
- UNCTAD; The TRIPS Agreement and Developing Countries; UNCTAD/ITE/1; United Nations; Geneva; 1996.
- UNDP; 1999 Human Development Report. The 1999 Human Development Report can be found on the UNDP website, at http://www.undp.org/hdro; accessed in September 2000.
- UNESCO Recommendation on the Safeguarding of Traditional Culture and Folklore, adopted by the General Conference at its twenty-fifth session; Paris; 15 November 1989.
- UNESCO/WIPO; Model Provisions for National Laws on the Protection of Expressions of Folklore against Illicit Exploitation and Other Prejudicial Actions; UNESCO/WIPO; Geneva, Switzerland; 1985.
- UPOV Press Release, No. 32, 28 September 1998; UPOV, Geneva. Available at http://www.upov.int/eng/prssrlss/32.htm.
- WIPO; Madrid Agreement concerning the International Registration of Marks; 1891, revised in 1967 and amended in 1979.
- World Bank; "Knowledge for Development – World Development Report"; 1998/99 OUP; 1998.
- World Bank; "Strengthening Infrastructure for Social Development"; Paper submitted by the by the World Bank in January 2000 to the World Summit for Social Development Five Year Review, in Geneva; June 2000. This paper was produced by the staff oh Human Development Network under the stewardship of Mr. Eduardo Doryan, Vice President. Located at: http://www.un.org/esa/socdev/geneva2000/docs/wbinfra.pdf.
- World Charter for Nature, G.A. RES: 37/7, U.N. GAOR, 37th Session, U.N. Doc. A/Res/37/7, Supp. No. 51, at 17, 1982, reprinted in 22 I.L.M. 455, 1983.

CASES

- Action brought in October 1998 by Kingdom of the Netherlands against the European Parliament and Council of the European Union; Case C-377/98, O.J. C 378, Dec. 5, 1998.
- Brazil; Interlocutory injunction no. 98.34.00027681-8; IDEC v. Federal Union.
- Brazil; Public civil action no. 97.00036170-4; Greenpeace v. President of CTNBio. Public civil action no.98.00.027682-0; IDEC v. Federal Union.
- Ciba-Geigy case; (1979-85) EPOR Volume c 758. Board of Appeal Decision T49/83, Ciba-Geigy, Official Journal EPO 1984, at p. 112.

- Dennis v Pitner, 106 F. 2d 142, (7th Cir. 1939) (Sparks, J. Concurring), cert. denied, 308 US 606/1939.
- Diamond v Chakrabarty, 447 US 303, at 309, 100 S.Ct. 2204; 206 USPQ 193 (1980).
- EPO Decision T 356/93 - Plant Genetics Systems, Official Journal EPO, 1995; at 545.
- Ex parte Allen; 2 USPQ 2d 1425, Bd. Pat. App. 1987, aff'd, 846 F. 2d 77 (Fed. Circuit, 1988).
- Ex parte Hibberd 227 USPQ 443 Bd. Pat. App. 1985.
- Funk Bros. Seed Co. v Kalo Inoculant Co., 333 US 127, (1948).
- Le Roy v Tatham, 55 US (14 How.) 156, (1852).
- Lubrizol case; T320/87 Lubrizol/Hybrid plants (1990); EPOR, 173.

LAWS AND DOCUMENTS OF DIFFERENT STATES

- Benin, Bhutan, Costa Rica and the Netherlands Joint Report on Biological Diversity; Report presented to the Conference of the Parties to the Convention on Biological Diversity in Bratislava, Slowakia, 1998. Provided by Ecooperation Foundation, Netherlands, through personal contact by the following e-mail: Ecooperation@antenna.nl.
- Biodiversity Action Plan for Bhutan; December 1997; at p. 29. - Located at http://www.biodiv.org/natrep/Bhutan/Bhutan.pdf.
- Brazil, Regulates the CTNBio; Decree No. 1.752 of 20 December 1995.
- Brazil; Final Report of the Commission on Biopiracy in the Amazon; Deputy Chamber of the Brazilian Congress; 18 November 1997.
- Brazil; Bill of Law no. 306/95; numbered as Bill of Law no. 4.842/98 when sent to the Chamber of Deputies for revision in November 1998.
- Brazil; Biosafety Law No. 8.974/95; adopted 5 January 1995; D.O.U. of 6 January 1995, section I, p. 337. The Biosafety Law can also be found at the following site: http://www.mct.gov.br/ctnbiotec/lei8974.htm.
- Brazil; CONFEN Resolution , published 24 August 1992 in the Diario Oficial da Uniao, section 1, p. 11.467.
- Brazil; CONFEN Resolution, published on 9 May 1995, in the Diario Oficial da Uniao, section 1, p. 6.533.
- Brazil; Constitution of the Federal Republic of Brazil; 1988; English version printed in. Constitution of the Federative Republic of Brazil; Central Graphic of Brazil's Federal Senate; Brasilia; 1990.
- Brazil; Cultivar Law; Law no. 9.456/97; April 1997; Diario Oficial da Uniao; 28 April 1997.
- Brazil; Deputy Bill of Law no. 4.579/98 as approved by the Chamber of Deputies in June 1998.
- Brazil; Execute Bill; Bill of Law 4.751/98; August 1998.
- Brazil; IBAMA; Administrative Ruling, No. 44N, published 17 August 1998, in section 1 of the Diario Oficial da Uniao.
- Brazil; Industrial Property Law; Law no.: 9.279/96; enacted on 14 May 1996.
- Brazil; Ministerio do Meio Ambiente, dos Recursos Hídricos e da Amazônia Legal; Primeiro Relatório Nacional para a Convençao sobre Diversidade Biológica: Brasil; Brasilia, Brazil, 1998.
- Brazil; Publi Civil Actions; Law no. 7.347, 1985.
- Brazil; Supplements the Cultivar Law; Decree No. 2.366 of 5 November 1997.
- Brazil; Technical Ruling on Labelling of Genetically Modified Foods and Ingredients prepared by the Consumer Defence and Protection Department of the Economic Law Secretary of the Justice Ministry in Brazil; 1999. Located at: http://www.mct.gov.br/ctnbiotec/consultapublica2.htm.
- Convention of Farmers and Breeders (CoFaB); Gene Campaign; New Delhi, India; 1999. available on request to Dr Suman Sahai (drsahai@nde.vsnl.net.in) or in the following website: http://ds.dial.pipex.com/ukfg/UKabc/cofab.htm.
- Costa Rica Biodiversity Law; Ley de Biodiversidad, No.: 7788; April 1998.
- England; Treasure Act 1996; 32(s) Halbury's Statute (4th edn.); Open Spaces.
- Spanish Civil Code; Editorial Tecnos, S.A.; seventh edition; Madrid; 1988.

- Sustainable Development Treaties between the Netherlands, Costa Rica, Bhutan and Benin. For information about the Sustainable Development Treaties contact Mr. Lammers from Ecooperation Foundation at Ecooperation@antenna.nl.
- The Thammasat Resolution - Building and strengthening our sui generis rights. Final declaration of the meeting held by the Thai Network on Community Rights and Biodiversity (BIOTHAI) and Genetic Resource action International (GRAIN), in Bangkok, Thailand, from 1 to 6 December 1997.
- US Plant Patent Act; 35 USC, Paragraphs 161-164.
- US Plant Variety Protection Act; (1970); 84 Statute 1542, 7 USC. Paragraph 2321 *et seq..*

INDEX

bt-toxins, 96

A

Access Bills, vi, 167, 168, 170, 172, 175
access contract, 84, 159, 160, 161, 162, 172, 187
Advance Informed Agreement Procedure, 97
Africa, 48, 53, 54, 77, 78, 81, 102, 124, 126, 127, 128, 190, 192, 193, 200
Agenda 21, 58, 93, 100, 198
Amazon, viii, 3, 51, 71, 99, 102, 129, 137, 138, 139, 147, 163, 165, 167, 168, 169, 170, 171, 173, 175, 176, 177, 179, 180, 181, 182, 183, 184, 196, 198, 201
Amazon Biodiversity Permanent Fund, 163
Andean Pact, 107
APBRO, viii, 41
Australia, viii, 2, 40, 41, 42, 194
Ayahuasca, 167, 168, 169, 170, 171, 172, 173, 174, 196, 197

B

Banco Axial, 163
Banisteriopsis caapi, 168, 171
Basmati, 43, 63, 72, 85, 144
BDCP, viii, 126, 127, 128, 190. *See Bioresources Development and Conservation Programme*
Benin, v, 121, 123, 124, 125, 188, 201, 202
Bhutan, v, 121, 123, 124, 125, 188, 201, 202
Bill 306/95, vi, 155, 156, 157, 158, 159, 160, 161, 162, 164, 165, 167, 170, 171, 172, 173, 174
BIOAMAZÔNIA, 163
Biondo, 3, 179, 180, 182
biopartnership, vii, 1, 2, 3, 114, 117, 118, 119, 120, 121, 123, 124, 125, 131, 133, 134, 135, 165, 166, 167, 179, 181, 184, 187, 188
bioprospecting, 108, 119, 121, 122, 133, 134, 167, 173
bio-prospecting, 88, 105
Bioresources Development and Conservation Programme, viii, 126, 187
Biosafety Law, vi, 149, 151, 201
Biosafety Protocol, 97, 98
biotechnology, 1, 3, 25, 43, 48, 50, 57, 61, 64, 65, 92, 93, 95, 97, 102, 106, 108, 117, 118, 130, 132, 133, 135, 147, 148, 149, 153, 163, 175, 181, 186, 190
BIOTHAI, viii, 81, 202
BIOTRADE Initiative, 125, 163
Brazil, ii, vi, vii, viii, ix, x, 1, 2, 3, 16, 17, 34, 37, 45, 51, 59, 64, 89, 92, 105, 107, 113, 136, 137, 138, 139, 140, 141, 142, 143, 144, 145, 146, 147, 148, 149, 150, 151, 152, 153, 154, 155, 156, 157, 158, 159, 160, 163, 164, 165, 166, 167, 168, 169, 170, 172, 174, 175, 177, 178, 179, 180, 181, 183, 184, 186, 187, 188, 190, 191, 192, 194, 197, 198, 200, 201

C

cat's claw, 102, 103
CBD, viii, 31, 56, 57, 58, 59, 61, 66, 68, 71, 72, 73, 77, 78, 82, 85, 88, 91, 92, 93, 94, 95, 96, 97, 98, 99, 101, 102, 103, 104, 105, 106, 107, 108, 109, 110, 111, 112, 113, 114, 115, 116, 118, 119, 120, 121, 127, 129, 132, 133, 134, 135, 137, 139, 144, 156, 158, 160, 164, 165, 166, 167, 180, 181, 184, 186, 192. *See Convention on Biological Diversity*
CGIAR, viii, 40, 41, 42, 44, 45, 48, 72, 85, 101, 132, 194
Chacrona, vi, 168, 170, 172, 173, 174, 175
Chakrabarty, 5, 8, 9, 10, 23, 28, 147, 201
Ciba-Geigy, 12, 13, 200
Code of Conduct, iv, 45, 46, 58, 59, 60, 199
CoFaB, viii, 85, 86, 87, 88, 89, 186, 195, 201
collective knowledge, 110
common concern, 54, 95
common heritage of mankind, 49, 54
compulsory licences, 27, 39
CONFEN, viii, 169, 172, 201
contracts, 73, 84, 85, 108, 109, 112, 114, 118, 119, 134, 158, 160, 161, 162, 163, 165, 172, 173, 183, 184
Convention on Biological Diversity, viii, 1, 2, 45, 54, 56, 58, 59, 79, 92, 93, 95, 119, 124, 127, 129, 131, 185, 186, 190, 192, 193, 198, 201
Costa Rica, v, ix, x, 109, 110, 111, 112, 113, 121, 122, 123, 124, 125, 163, 188, 198, 201, 202
Costa Rica Biodiversity Law, 110, 111, 112, 201
country of origin, 42, 56, 71, 96, 102, 106, 133, 156
CTNBio, viii, 149, 150, 151, 152, 153, 200, 201
cultivar certificates, 145, 146
Cultivar Law, 145, 146, 147, 148, 165, 201

D

Darjeeling, 70
Dennis v Pitner, 6, 7, 8, 201
Deputy Bill, 155, 156, 157, 160, 161, 162, 164, 165, 167, 170, 171, 172, 173, 174, 201
disclosure requirement, 21, 25, 39
discoverer's right, 82, 84
discoverers, 40, 84, 88, 102, 103

E

Eco, 125. *See Ecooperation Foundation*
economic development, 21, 79, 90, 101, 105, 111, 129, 131, 137, 139, 188

Ecooperation Foundation, viii, 124, 125, 187, 201, 202
EMBRAPA, ix, 95, 137, 147, 183, 197
empowerment of poor people, 93, 115, 120
EPC, 12, 13, 14, 23, 28. *See European Patent Convention*
equitable share of benefits, 1, 2, 59, 60, 61, 66, 71, 72, 78, 83, 84, 88, 90, 93, 94, 101, 102, 103, 104, 105, 106, 107, 109, 111, 112, 113, 126, 130, 133, 134, 135, 140, 144, 157, 159, 163, 165, 170, 184, 185, 186, 188
essentially derived, 36, 38, 42, 145, 146
European Patent Convention, 1, 11, 13, 17, 22, 23, 28, 63, 199
Ex parte Hibberd, 9, 10, 201
ex situ conservation, 55, 56, 61, 65, 92, 97
Executive Bill, 156, 157, 158, 159, 161, 162, 163, 164, 167, 170, 172, 173, 174, 175

F

Farmers' privilege, 6, 36
folklore, 74, 75, 76, 77, 80, 107
Funk Bros. Seed Co. v Kalo Inoculant Co, 8

G

gene banks, 40, 46, 47, 48, 54, 56, 57, 65, 71, 105
genetically uniform, 1, 31, 45, 51, 52, 56, 61, 87, 89, 95, 152
geographical indications, 4, 16, 71, 72
germplasm, 2, 38, 40, 42, 44, 45, 46, 49, 53, 56, 58, 59, 60, 65, 66, 72, 85, 87, 101, 105, 132, 142, 181
Global Environmental Facility, 105
global partnership, 1, 2, 3, 60, 93, 115, 116, 117, 136, 180, 188
Global System, 44, 45, 46, 48, 58, 60, 199
Gollin, 82, 83, 84, 118, 181, 192, 195
GRAIN, ix, 35, 41, 43, 68, 81, 82, 192, 193, 202
Great Famine, 52

H

Hoasca, 167, 168, 169, 170, 172, 173, 174, 175, 197
HSCA, ix, 41
hybrids, 23, 64, 95, 147

I

IARCs, 48
ICRISAT, ix, 41, 194
IDEC, ix, 150, 151, 152, 153, 154, 155, 200
in situ conservation, 55, 56, 58, 95, 96
India, viii, 11, 26, 53, 62, 63, 70, 72, 85, 86, 89, 90, 123, 131, 132, 144, 190, 194, 196, 201
indigenous peoples, 1, 43, 57, 62, 64, 68, 71, 74, 76, 77, 78, 81, 84, 99, 102, 103, 107, 108, 110, 111, 118, 157, 168, 171, 184
industrial application, 20, 25, 26, 39, 69, 128, 141, 142, 143, 188
INPI, ix, 142, 143, 147
intergenerational equity, 3, 66, 99, 115

International Undertaking, iv, x, 45, 46, 47, 48, 50, 51, 53, 57, 58, 60, 61, 66, 78, 91, 133, 134, 137, 190, 198
intragenerational equity, 2, 57, 65, 99, 115
inventive step, 19, 20, 26, 39, 62, 69, 142, 143
inventories, 122, 126, 186, 188
IU, x, 45, 46, 47, 48, 49, 54, 57, 58, 61. *See International Undertaking*
Iwu, 126, 127, 128, 192, 193

K

Kayapo, 177

L

labelling, 70, 149, 151, 152, 153, 155
Law 9.279/96, 140, 141, 142, 143, 144, 147, 148
Le Roy v Tatham, 6, 201
LMOs, 97
local communities, 43, 58, 59, 60, 68, 71, 74, 77, 78, 79, 81, 82, 84, 85, 88, 93, 99, 101, 103, 105, 109, 110, 111, 116, 117, 119, 120, 123, 127, 133, 135, 140, 141, 158, 160, 162, 165, 167, 173, 174, 176, 178, 179, 181, 184
Lubrizol, 13, 201

M

Mae-Wan Ho, 51, 153
Marina Silva, 140, 155, 156
Mariri, vi, 168, 170, 171, 172, 173, 174, 175
medicinal plant, 73, 102, 108, 120, 143, 187
medicinal plants, 73, 77, 84, 113, 124, 126, 130, 143, 145, 170, 173, 178, 179, 180, 181
Mercedes Benz, 178, 188
Merck-INBio, v, 121, 122, 123, 125, 133, 134, 163
Mexico, 56, 103, 107, 118, 169
micoorganisms, 27
Model Law, 77, 78, 79, 80
Monsanto, x, 45, 63, 64, 148, 150, 151, 152, 153, 155, 159, 197
morality, 12, 13, 21, 22, 142, 143, 170, 171, 185, 186

N

national sovereignty, 49
Neem, iv, 43, 62, 63, 192, 193, 196
Netherlands, v, viii, 14, 29, 54, 103, 121, 123, 124, 125, 126, 188, 194, 200, 201, 202
Nigeria, 77, 126, 128
Non-monetary benefits, 120
novelty, 11, 20, 26, 39, 63, 141, 142, 143, 144, 171

O

OAU, x, 77, 79, 108, 199, 200. *See Organisation of African Unity*
ordre public, 21, 185. *See public order*
organic food, 3, 148, 153
Organisation of African Unity, iv, x, 77, 108

P

Paris Convention, iii, 15, 16, 17, 18, 19, 26, 29, 38, 141, 200
Patent Co-operation Treaty, iii, x, 15, 17, 64, 200
patents, vii, 1, 2, 4, 9, 10, 11, 12, 14, 15, 16, 18, 19, 20, 21, 22, 23, 24, 25, 26, 27, 29, 33, 36, 37, 38, 39, 40, 41, 42, 43, 45, 53, 58, 61, 62, 63, 64, 65, 66, 69, 70, 73, 74, 80, 81, 83, 88, 89, 93, 94, 95, 96, 103, 113, 116, 126, 131, 140, 141, 142, 143, 145, 147, 164, 171, 181, 185, 186, 188, 193, 194
  broad claims, 20
  most-favoured nation, 26, 79
  national treatment, 16, 19, 26, 30, 68, 79, 159
  plant patents, 5
  right of priority, 16
PBRs, iii, x, 29, 30, 32, 33, 34, 35, 36, 37, 38, 39, 40, 41, 42. *See plant breeders' rights*
PCT, x, 17, 18, 200. *See Patent Co-operation Treaty*
peace, 13, 22, 98, 100, 135
permaculture, 147, 180, 184
Peru, 51, 103, 137, 168
pharmaceuticals, 27, 55, 79, 135, 140, 163, 164, 176, 184
plant breeders' rights, 1, 2, 29, 49, 50, 53, 61, 66, 80, 94, 113
plant genetic resources, 1, 2, 4, 5, 13, 14, 28, 41, 44, 45, 46, 48, 49, 51, 53, 54, 55, 57, 59, 60, 61, 65, 113, 133, 134, 167, 185, 188
Plant Genetics Systems, 13, 201
Plant Patent Act. *See PPA*
Plant Variety Protection Act. *See PVPA*
POEMA, vi, x, 3, 167, 175, 176, 177, 178, 179, 184, 188, 194, 198
Pope's Weromba Cardinal, 42. *See Telopea speciosissima*
poverty eradication, 100, 101, 104, 117, 135, 183
PPA, x, 5
prior informed consent, 74, 77, 84, 85, 93, 106, 107, 109, 112, 113, 127, 144, 158, 160, 173, 174, 184
prior user, 143, 144
PROBEM, x, 163
Psychotria viridis, 168
public order, 21, 186
PVPA, x, 5, 6

R

RAFI, x, 40, 41, 42, 61, 62, 63, 64, 66, 103, 185, 194, 195
religious communities, 167, 168, 170, 171, 172, 174, 175
research exemption, 6, 32, 33, 42
Resolution 3/91, iv, 48, 53, 54, 55, 57, 199
Resolution 4/89, iv, 48, 49, 50, 199
Resolution 5/89, iv, 48, 50, 51, 53, 199
right of priority, 30
rights and duties, vii, 1, 66, 69, 112, 113, 155, 156, 157, 160, 166, 188
Rio Declaration, 60, 93, 98, 99, 100, 101, 115, 116, 120, 135, 156, 180, 200
Roundup Ready, x, 150
royalties, 79, 105, 122, 127, 128, 129, 130, 131, 182, 183
RR soya, x, 150, 151, 152, 155. *See Roundup Ready*

S

sacred plants, 169, 170, 171, 172, 174, 175
sacred tea, 168, 169, 170
Scenery System, vi, 179, 180, 181, 182, 183, 184, 188
SDT, x, 124, 125, 134
Shiva, 62, 134, 135, 196
social welfare, 117, 186, 188
soybean, x, 64, 147, 148, 150, 151, 152, 155
spiritual communities, 174
spiritual value, 167, 170, 171, 175
sui generis system, vii, 2, 22, 23, 27, 28, 43, 46, 66, 68, 69, 70, 71, 72, 77, 79, 80, 88, 90, 91, 157, 181, 186
Suriname, v, viii, 121, 129, 130, 131, 187, 192
sustainable development, vii, 1, 93, 95, 98, 99, 100, 101, 103, 104, 115, 123, 125, 126, 135, 136, 154, 164, 166, 167, 184, 187
sustainable use, 1, 2, 41, 56, 58, 78, 92, 93, 97, 98, 99, 101, 103, 104, 106, 107, 108, 109, 111, 113, 115, 116, 117, 118, 119, 133, 134, 135, 156, 157, 167, 169, 174, 184, 185, 186, 188

T

Telopea speciosissima, 41
terminator technology, 63, 64
Thailand, viii, 74, 81, 199, 202
Thammasat Resolution, iv, 81, 82, 88, 186, 202
The Bioresources Development and Conservation Program, v, 121, 126
trade secrets, 4, 16, 73, 74, 79
trademark, 16, 69, 70, 79, 186
traditional farmers, 1, 27, 43, 45, 50, 58, 60, 61, 68, 82, 85, 99, 102, 133, 134, 148
traditional knowledge, vii, 1, 2, 3, 11, 17, 20, 36, 40, 60, 61, 62, 63, 64, 65, 66, 71, 73, 74, 75, 76, 77, 78, 79, 80, 81, 82, 84, 85, 88, 90, 93, 95, 102, 105, 106, 107, 108, 110, 111, 112, 113, 117, 118, 120, 121, 126, 129, 131, 133, 134, 135, 141, 143, 144, 156, 157, 158, 159, 161, 162, 164, 165, 167, 170, 173, 178, 179, 180, 181, 182, 183, 184, 185, 186, 188, 189
  pirating, 89, 103
Training, 127
transfer of technology, 24, 104, 107, 108, 109, 112, 134, 172, 183, 188
transgenic crops, 51, 64, 106, 135, 147, 151, 152, 153, 154
transgenic micro-organisms, 8, 142, 143
treasure, 48, 52, 83, 84, 85
Treasure Act, 83, 84, 201
TRIPs, iii, x, 1, 4, 10, 16, 18, 19, 20, 21, 22, 23, 24, 25, 26, 27, 28, 39, 43, 45, 46, 64, 66, 68, 69, 70, 71, 72, 73, 79, 80, 81, 82, 85, 86, 88, 89, 90, 91, 104, 113, 137, 140, 141, 143, 144, 165, 167, 181, 185, 186, 190, 191, 192, 193, 196, 198, 199

U

UN Draft Declaration on Indigenous Rights, 76, 200
Uncaria tomentosa, 102. *see cat's claw*
UNCED, xi, 92, 100, 136
UNCTAD, xi, 20, 24, 69, 70, 71, 73, 74, 79, 90, 118, 125, 144, 163, 178, 190, 193, 200
UNEP, xi, 92, 94, 97, 122, 198
UNESCO, iv, xi, 74, 75, 76, 80, 188, 199, 200
University of California, v, xi, 121, 131, 132, 169, 193
UPOV, iii, xi, 2, 6, 29, 30, 31, 32, 33, 34, 35, 36, 37, 38, 39, 40, 42, 43, 45, 48, 49, 50, 51, 56, 60, 66, 68, 85, 86, 104, 137, 145, 148, 158, 192, 195, 196, 199, 200

V

Vegetal, 168, 172, 197
Victoria blight, 52

W

Weiss, 54, 99, 115, 196
WIPO, iv, xi, 16, 17, 18, 33, 71, 74, 199, 200
World Charter for Nature, 94, 200
World Scientists' Statement, 96, 103